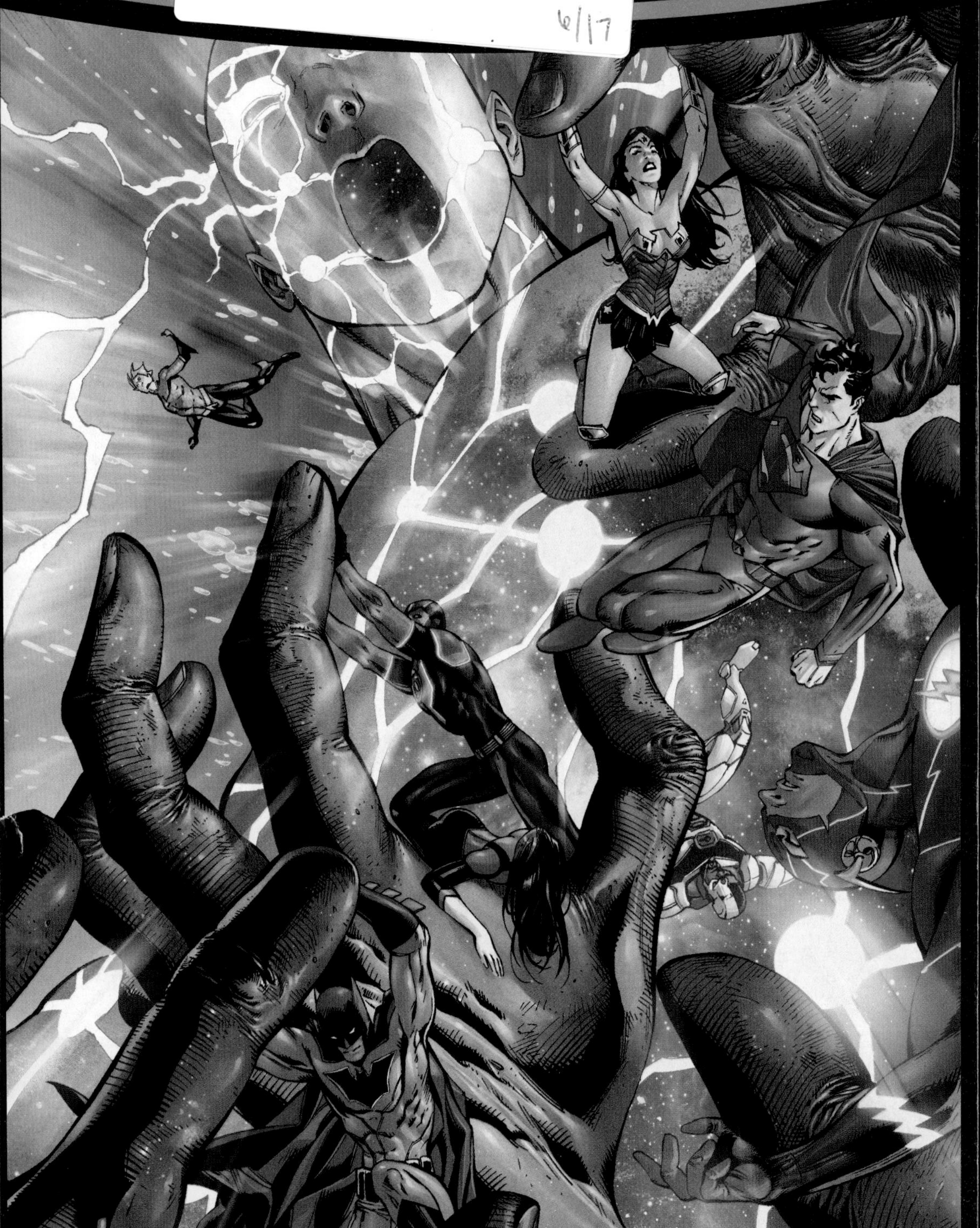

# JUSTICE LEAGUE

## VOL.1 THE EXTINCTION MACHINES

# JUSTICE LEAGUE
## VOL.1 THE EXTINCTION MACHINES

**BRYAN HITCH**
writer

**TONY S. DANIEL**
BRYAN HITCH * JESUS MERINO
pencillers

**SANDU FLOREA**
DANIEL HENRIQUES * SCOTT HANNA
ANDY OWENS * JESUS MERINO
inkers

**TOMEU MOREY**
ALEX SINCLAIR
colorists

**RICHARD STARKINGS & COMICRAFT**
letterers

**TONY S. DANIEL & TOMEU MOREY**
collection cover artists

**SUPERMAN** created by **JERRY SIEGEL** and **JOE SHUSTER**
By special arrangement with the Jerry Siegel family

**BRIAN CUNNINGHAM** Editor - Original Series ✳ **AMEDEO TURTURRO  DIEGO LOPEZ** Assistant Editors - Original Series
**JEB WOODARD** Group Editor - Collected Editions ✳ **ROBIN WILDMAN** Editor - Collected Edition
**STEVE COOK** Design Director - Books

**BOB HARRAS** Senior VP - Editor-in-Chief, DC Comics

**DIANE NELSON** President ✳ **DAN DiDIO** Publisher ✳ **JIM LEE** Publisher ✳ **GEOFF JOHNS** President & Chief Creative Officer
**AMIT DESAI** Executive VP - Business & Marketing Strategy, Direct to Consumer & Global Franchise Management
**SAM ADES** Senior VP - Direct to Consumer ✳ **BOBBIE CHASE** VP - Talent Development
**MARK CHIARELLO** Senior VP - Art, Design & Collected Editions ✳ **JOHN CUNNINGHAM** Senior VP - Sales & Trade Marketing
**ANNE DePIES** Senior VP - Business Strategy, Finance & Administration ✳ **DON FALLETTI** VP - Manufacturing Operations
**LAWRENCE GANEM** VP - Editorial Administration & Talent Relations ✳ **ALISON GILL** Senior VP - Manufacturing & Operations
**HANK KANALZ** Senior VP - Editorial Strategy & Administration ✳ **JAY KOGAN** VP - Legal Affairs
**THOMAS LOFTUS** VP - Business Affairs ✳ **JACK MAHAN** VP - Business Affairs
**NICK J. NAPOLITANO** VP - Manufacturing Administration ✳ **EDDIE SCANNELL** VP - Consumer Marketing
**COURTNEY SIMMONS** Senior VP - Publicity & Communications
**JIM (SKI) SOKOLOWSKI** VP - Comic Book Specialty Sales & Trade Marketing
**NANCY SPEARS** VP - Mass, Book, Digital Sales & Trade Marketing

**JUSTICE LEAGUE VOLUME 1: THE EXTINCTION MACHINES**

DC Comics, 2900 West Alameda Ave., Burbank, CA 91505
Printed by LSC Communications, Owensville, MO, USA. 12/12/16. First Printing.
ISBN: 978-1-4012-6779-7

Library of Congress Cataloging-in-Publication Data is available.

PEFC Certified

Printed on paper from
sustainably managed
forests, controlled
sources

PEFC/29-31-337    www.pefc.org

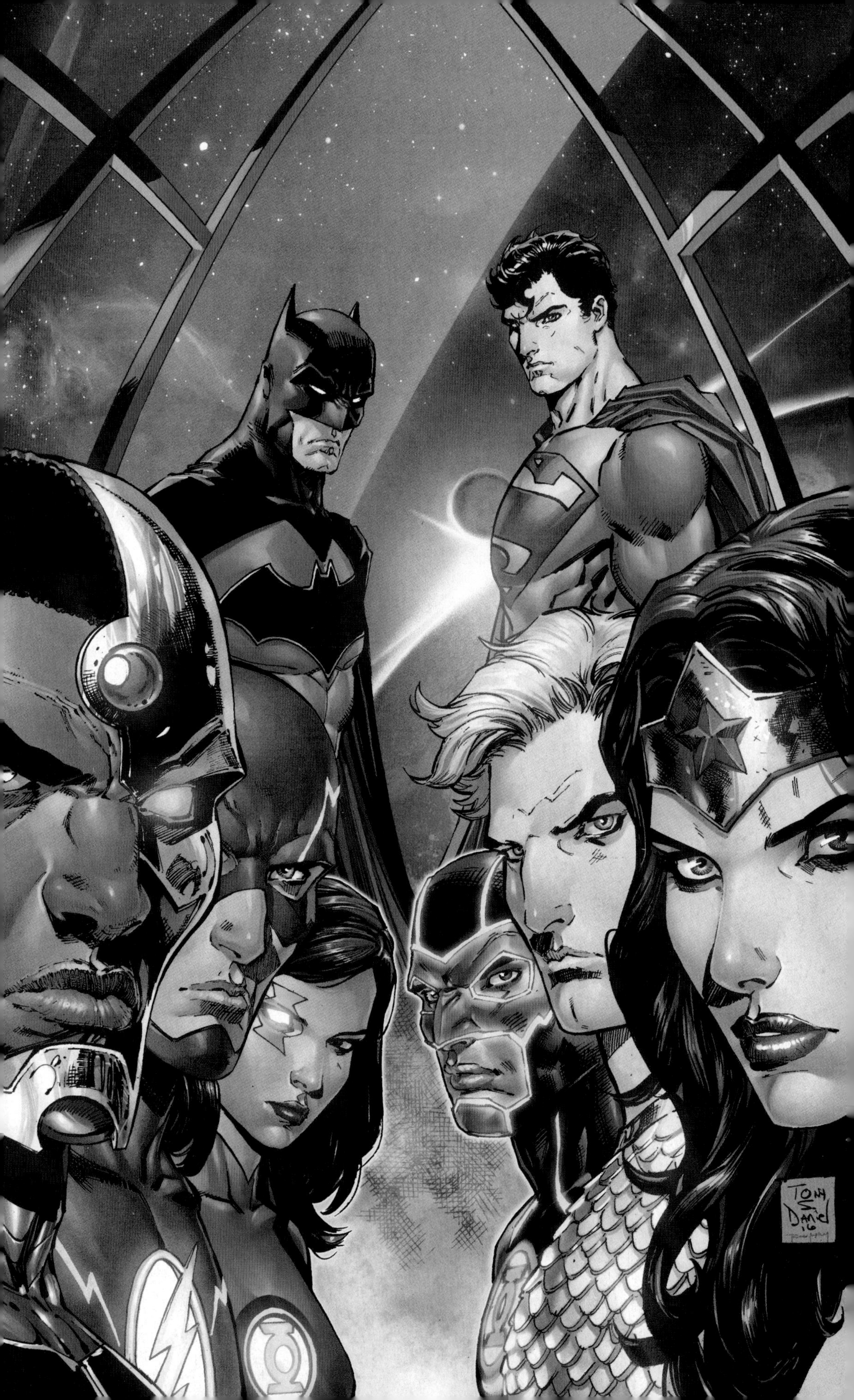
TONY S. DANIEL 16

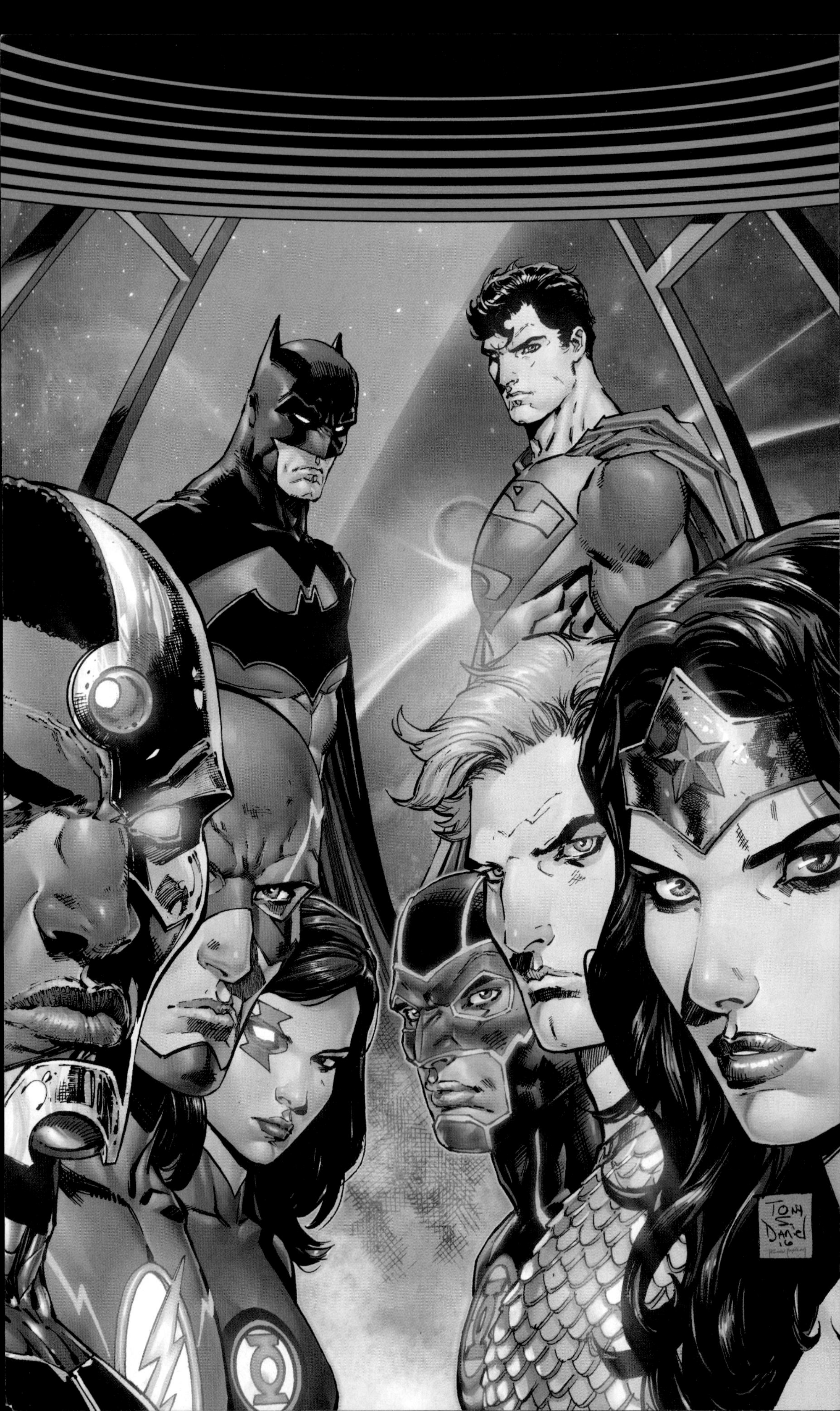

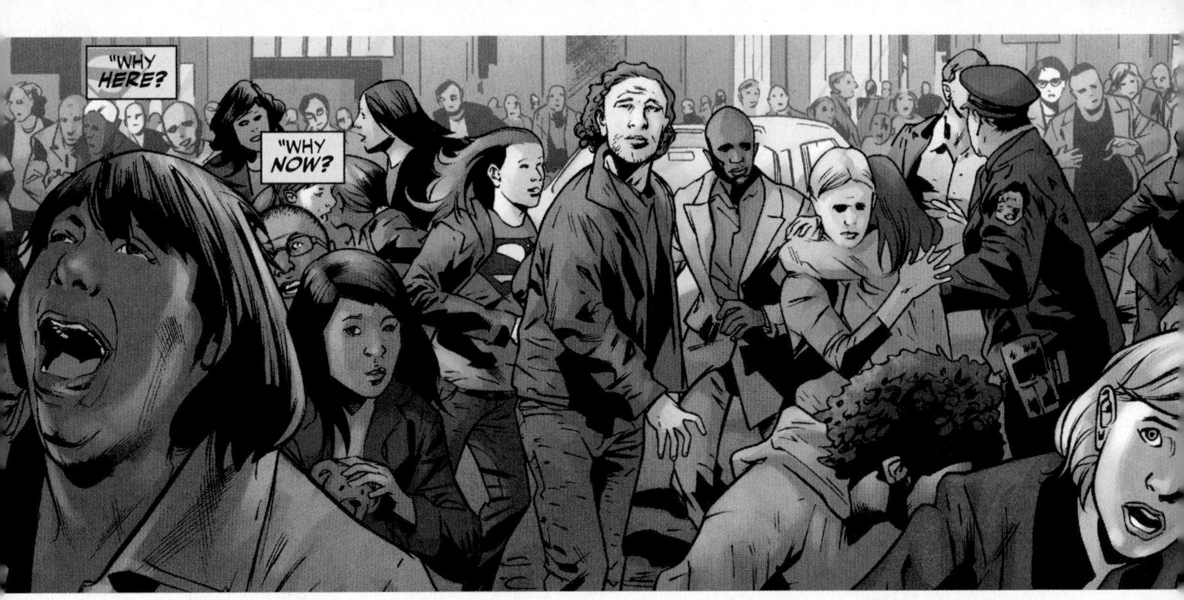
"WHY HERE?
"WHY NOW?

# FEAR THE REAPER

By **BRYAN HITCH**

Inks by **DANIEL HENRIQUES** with **SCOTT HANNA**

COLORED by **ALEX SINCLAIR**

LETTERED by **RICHARD STARKINGS & COMICRAFT**

COVER by **TONY S. DANIEL & TOMEU MOREY**

VARIANT COVER by **JOE MADUREIRA & ALEX SINCLAIR**

ASSISTS by **AMEDEO TURTURRO**

EDITS by **BRIA CUNNINGHA**

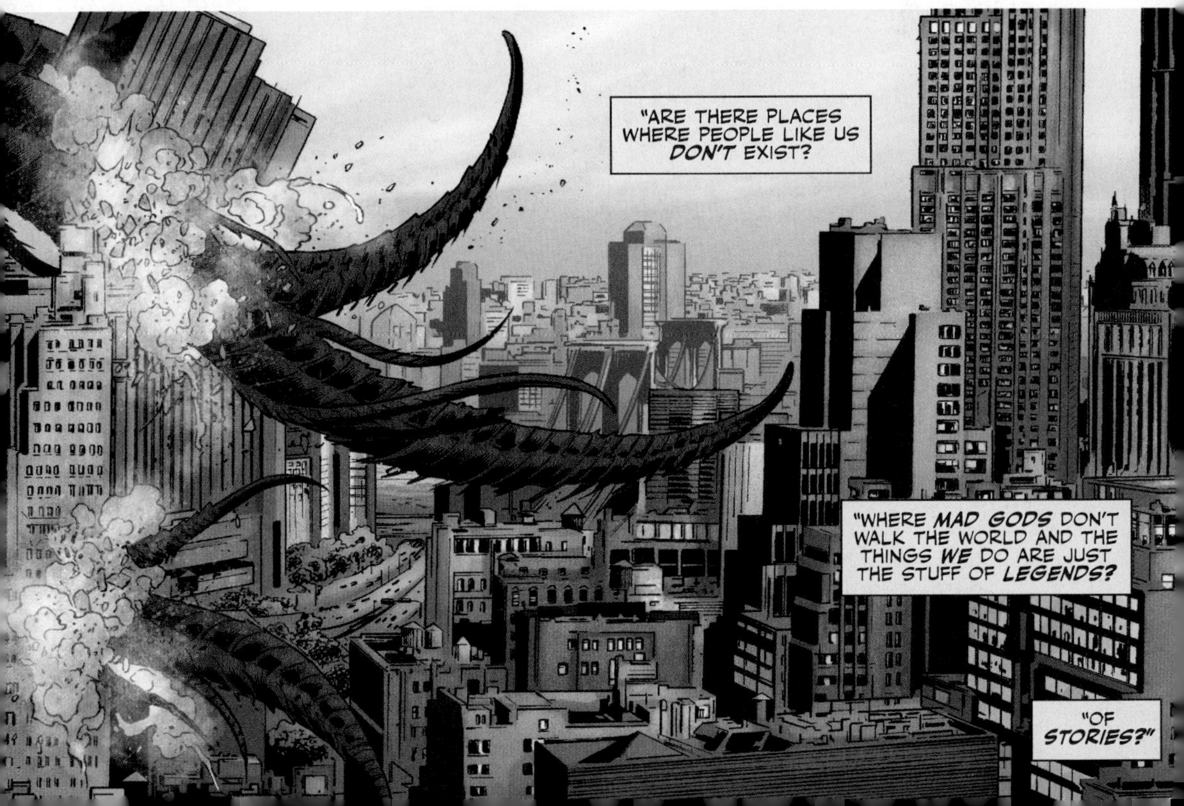
"ARE THERE PLACES WHERE PEOPLE LIKE US *DON'T* EXIST?
"WHERE *MAD GODS* DON'T WALK THE WORLD AND THE THINGS *WE* DO ARE JUST THE STUFF OF *LEGENDS?*
"OF *STORIES?"*

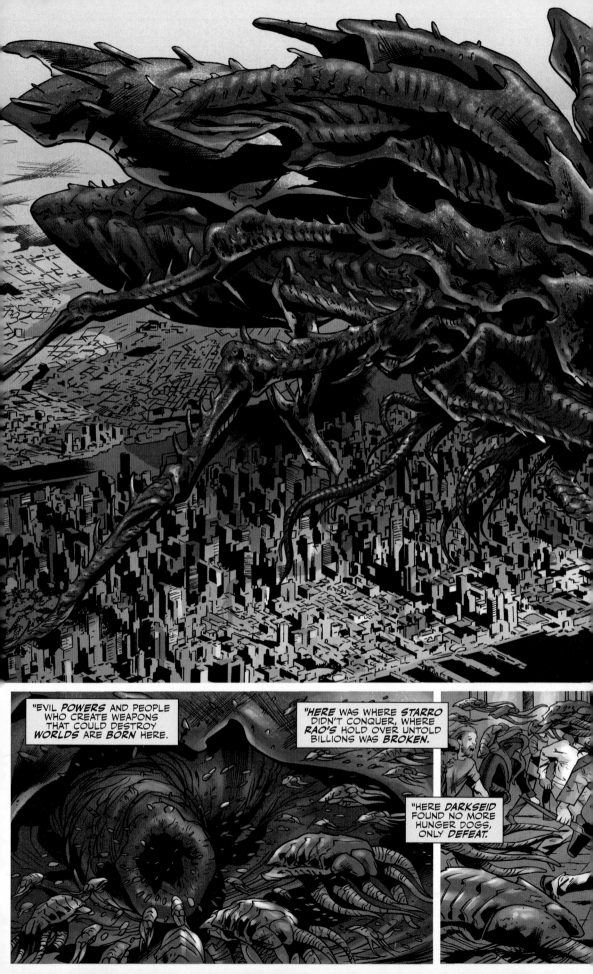

"EVIL **POWERS** AND PEOPLE WHO CREATE WEAPONS THAT COULD DESTROY **WORLDS** ARE **BORN** HERE.

"**HERE** WAS WHERE **STARRO** DIDN'T CONQUER, WHERE **RAO'S** HOLD OVER UNTOLD BILLIONS WAS **BROKEN**.

"HERE **DARKSEID** FOUND NO MORE HUNGER DOGS, ONLY **DEFEAT**.

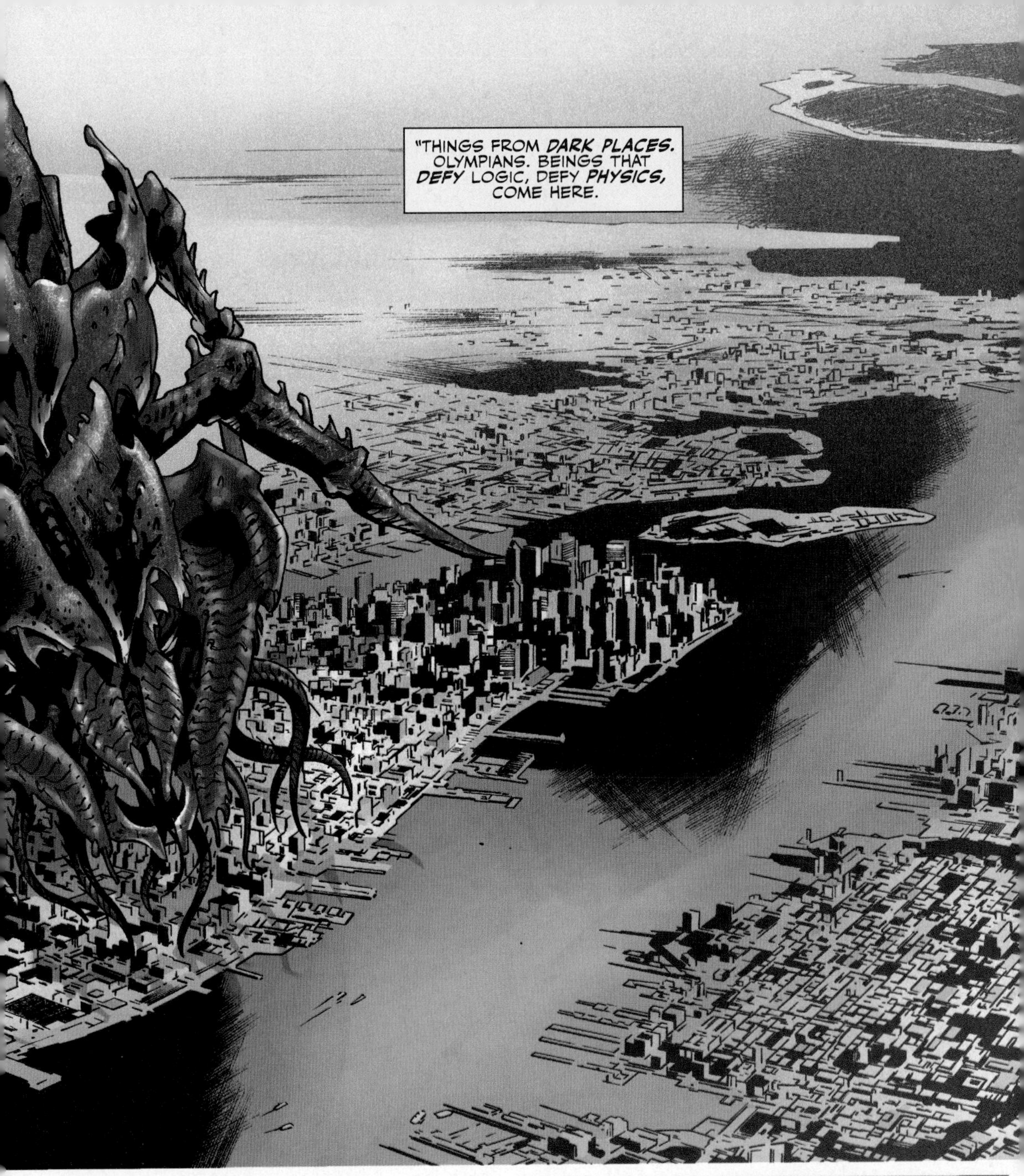
"THINGS FROM DARK PLACES.
OLYMPIANS. BEINGS THAT DEFY LOGIC, DEFY PHYSICS, COME HERE.

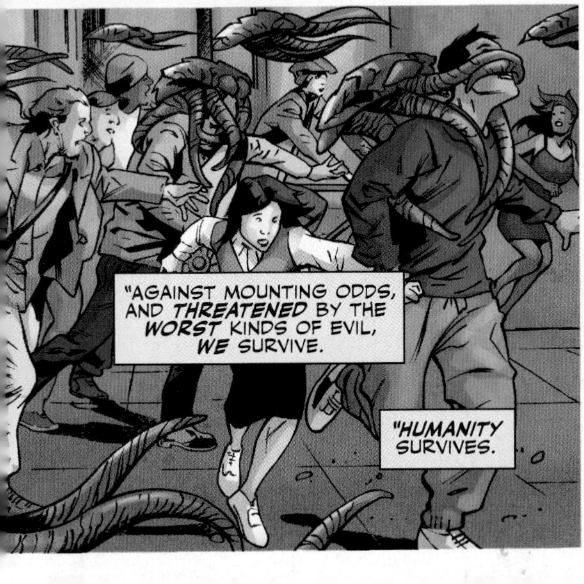
"AGAINST MOUNTING ODDS, AND THREATENED BY THE WORST KINDS OF EVIL, WE SURVIVE.
"HUMANITY SURVIVES.

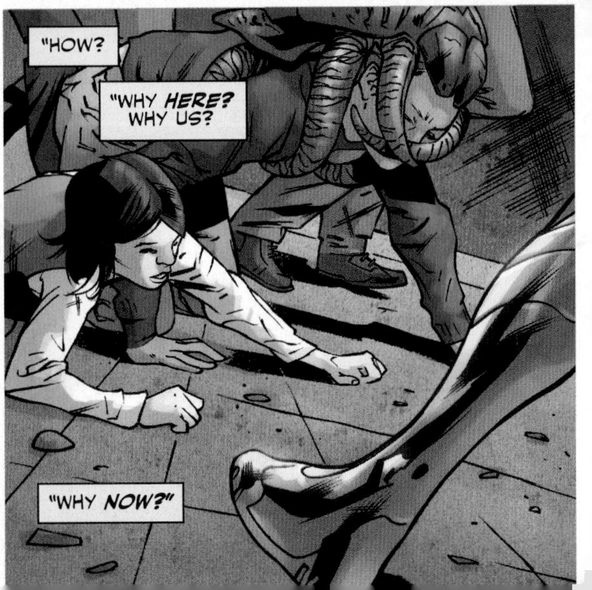
"HOW?
"WHY HERE? WHY US?
"WHY NOW?"

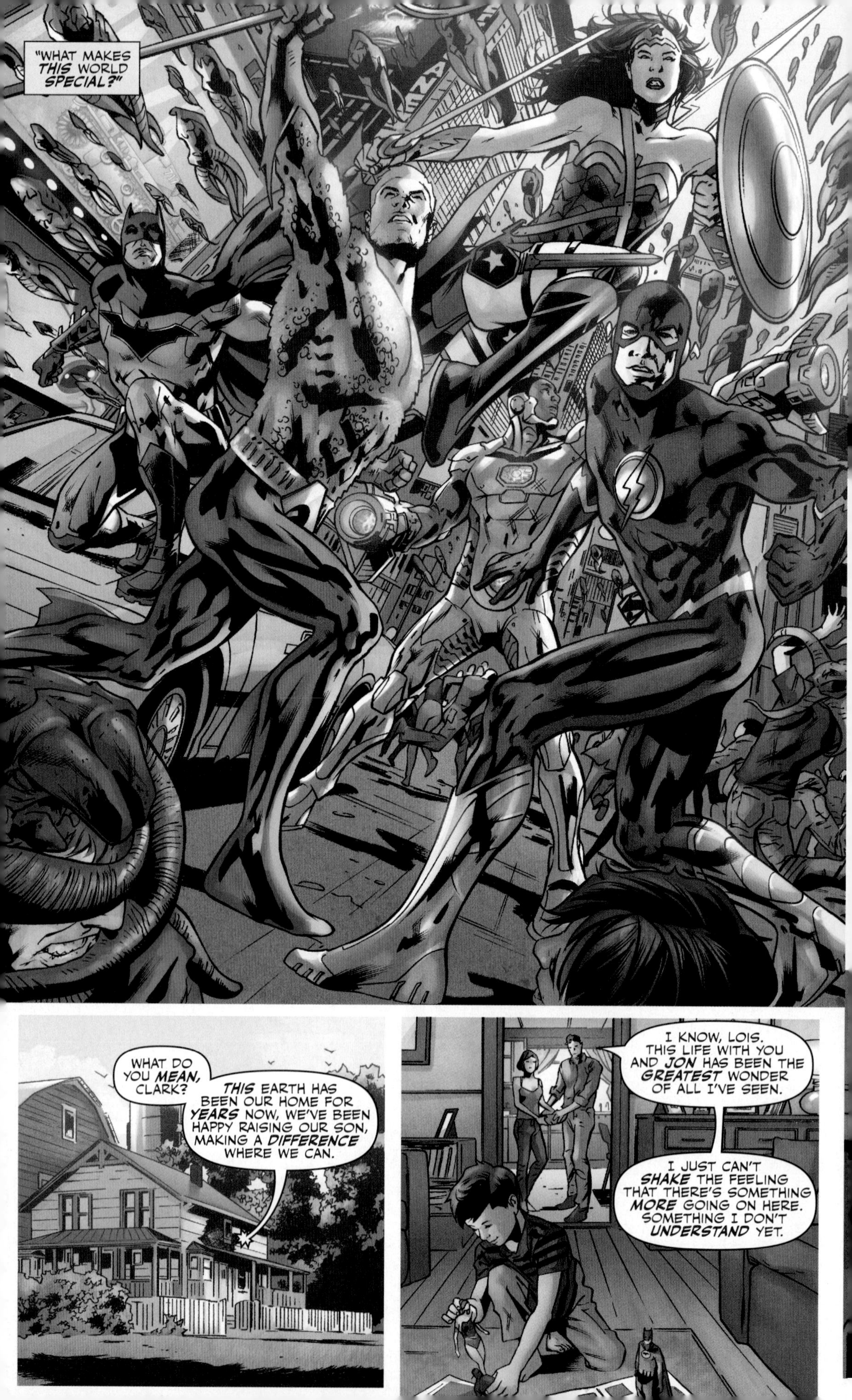
"WHAT MAKES THIS WORLD SPECIAL?"
WHAT DO YOU MEAN, CLARK?
THIS EARTH HAS BEEN OUR HOME FOR YEARS NOW, WE'VE BEEN HAPPY RAISING OUR SON, MAKING A DIFFERENCE WHERE WE CAN.
I KNOW, LOIS. THIS LIFE WITH YOU AND JON HAS BEEN THE GREATEST WONDER OF ALL I'VE SEEN.
I JUST CAN'T SHAKE THE FEELING THAT THERE'S SOMETHING MORE GOING ON HERE. SOMETHING I DON'T UNDERSTAND YET.

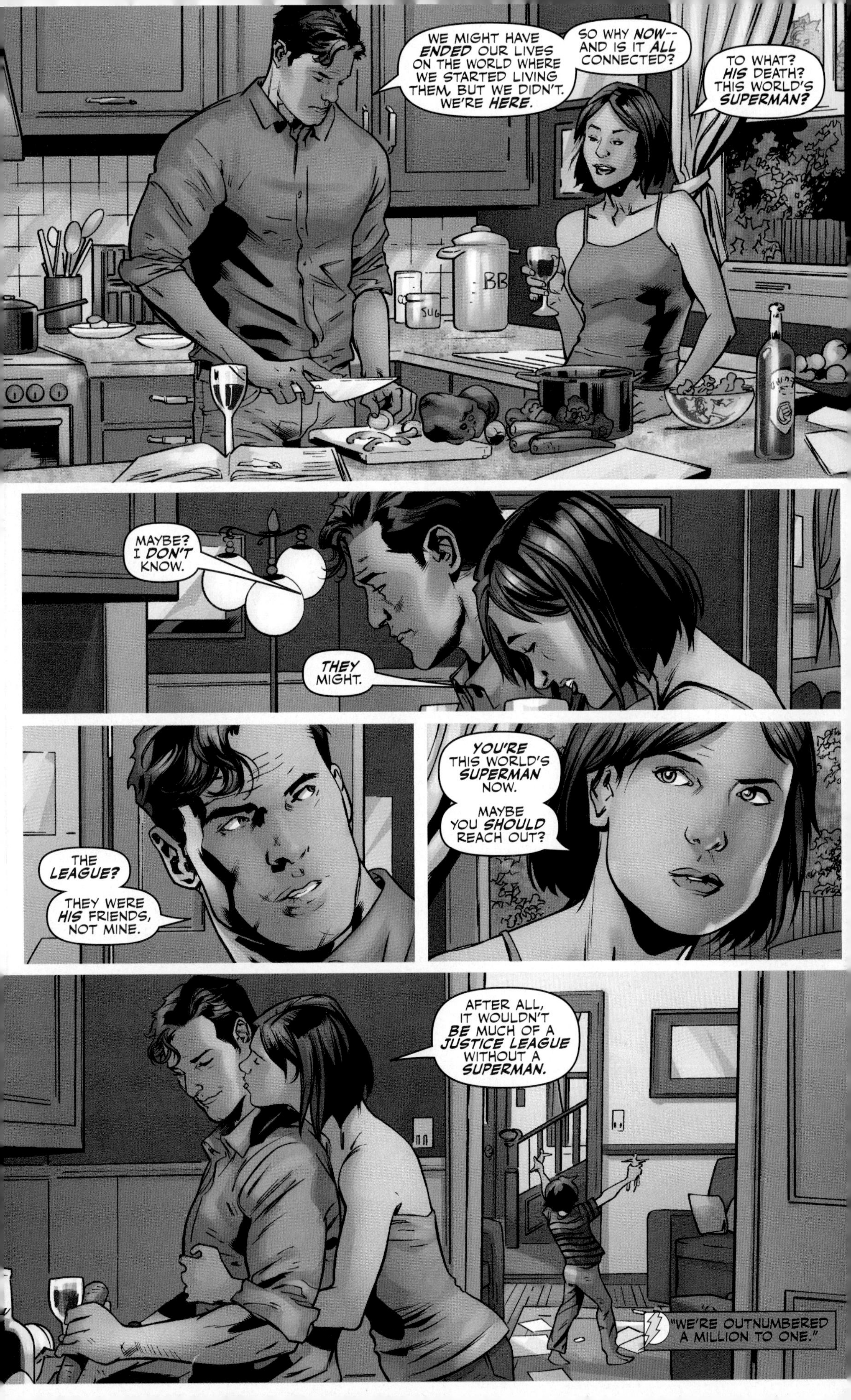
WE MIGHT HAVE ENDED OUR LIVES ON THE WORLD WHERE WE STARTED LIVING THEM, BUT WE DIDN'T. WE'RE HERE.
SO WHY NOW-- AND IS IT ALL CONNECTED?
TO WHAT? HIS DEATH? THIS WORLD'S SUPERMAN?
BB
SUG
MAYBE? I DON'T KNOW.
THEY MIGHT.
THE LEAGUE?
THEY WERE HIS FRIENDS, NOT MINE.
YOU'RE THIS WORLD'S SUPERMAN NOW.
MAYBE YOU SHOULD REACH OUT?
AFTER ALL, IT WOULDN'T BE MUCH OF A JUSTICE LEAGUE WITHOUT A SUPERMAN.
"WE'RE OUTNUMBERED A MILLION TO ONE."

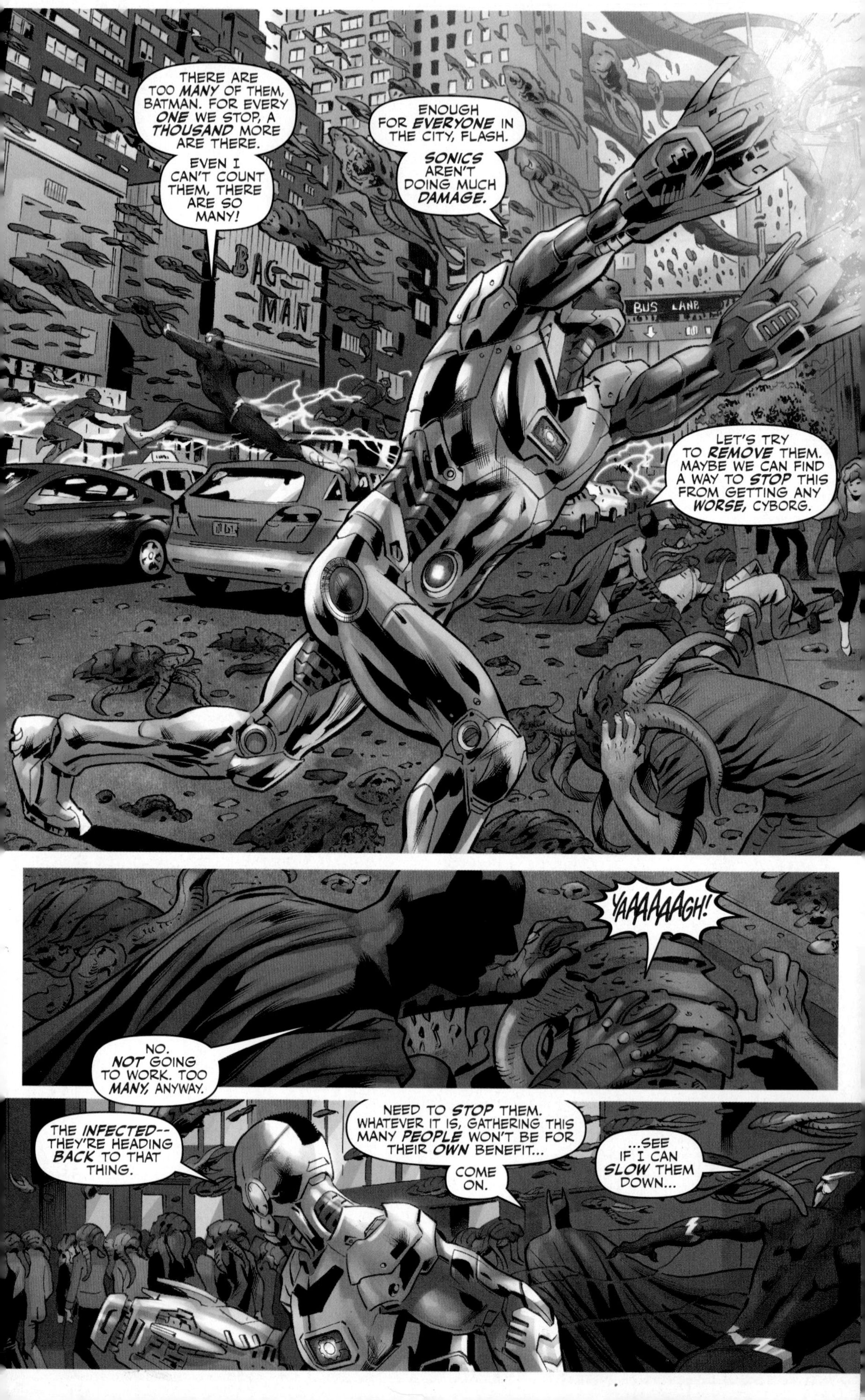
THERE ARE TOO *MANY* OF THEM, BATMAN. FOR EVERY *ONE* WE STOP, A *THOUSAND* MORE ARE THERE.
EVEN I CAN'T COUNT THEM, THERE ARE SO MANY!
ENOUGH FOR *EVERYONE* IN THE CITY, FLASH.
*SONICS* AREN'T DOING MUCH *DAMAGE.*
BAG MAN
LET'S TRY TO *REMOVE* THEM. MAYBE WE CAN FIND A WAY TO *STOP* THIS FROM GETTING ANY *WORSE,* CYBORG.
YAAAAAAGH!
NO. *NOT* GOING TO WORK. TOO *MANY,* ANYWAY.
THE *INFECTED*-- THEY'RE HEADING *BACK* TO THAT THING.
NEED TO *STOP* THEM. WHATEVER IT IS, GATHERING THIS MANY *PEOPLE* WON'T BE FOR THEIR *OWN* BENEFIT...
COME ON.
...SEE IF I CAN *SLOW* THEM DOWN...

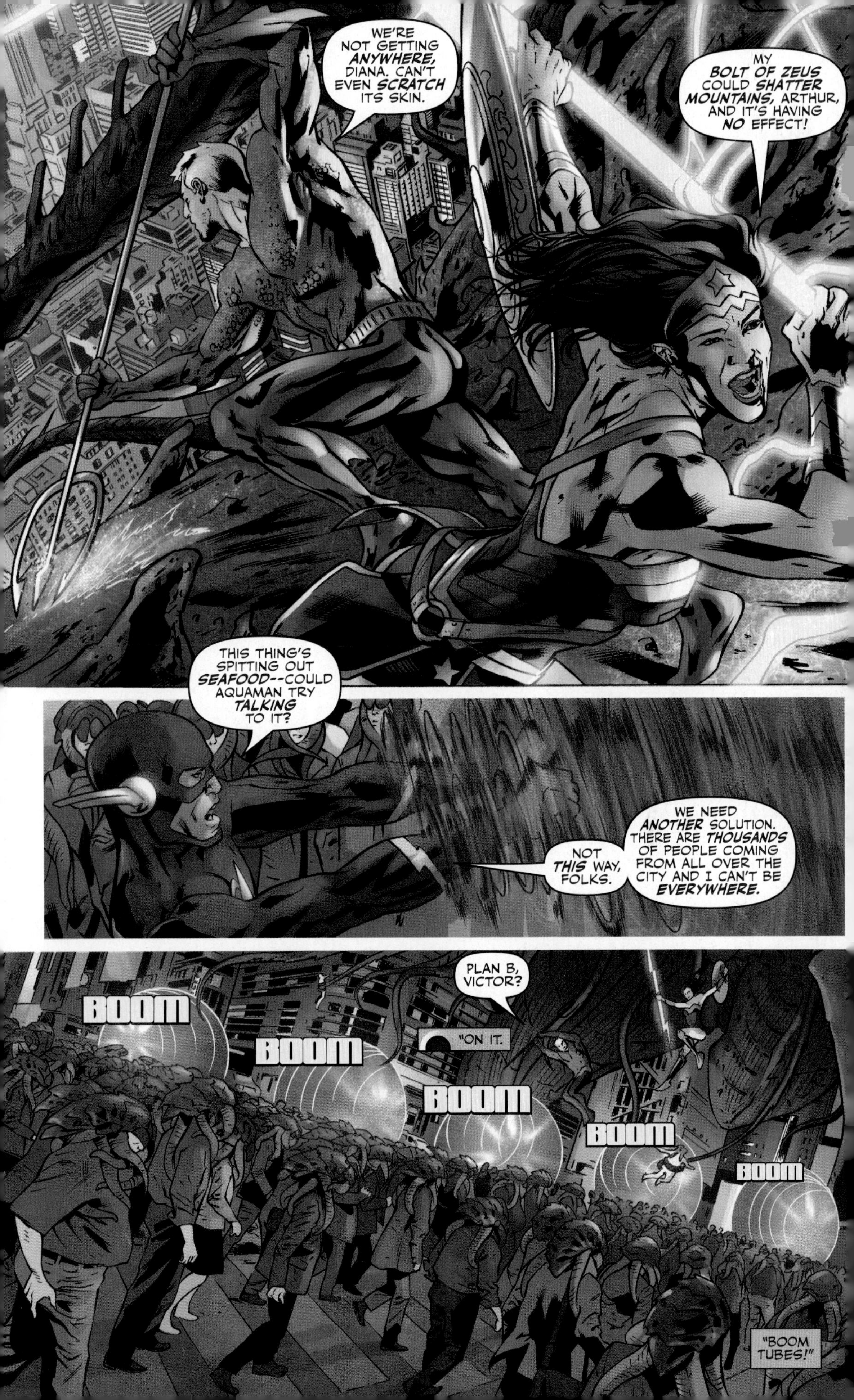
WE'RE NOT GETTING ANYWHERE, DIANA. CAN'T EVEN SCRATCH ITS SKIN.
MY BOLT OF ZEUS COULD SHATTER MOUNTAINS, ARTHUR, AND IT'S HAVING NO EFFECT!
THIS THING'S SPITTING OUT SEAFOOD--COULD AQUAMAN TRY TALKING TO IT?
NOT THIS WAY, FOLKS.
WE NEED ANOTHER SOLUTION. THERE ARE THOUSANDS OF PEOPLE COMING FROM ALL OVER THE CITY AND I CAN'T BE EVERYWHERE.
PLAN B, VICTOR?
"ON IT.
BOOM
BOOM
BOOM
BOOM
BOOM
"BOOM TUBES!"

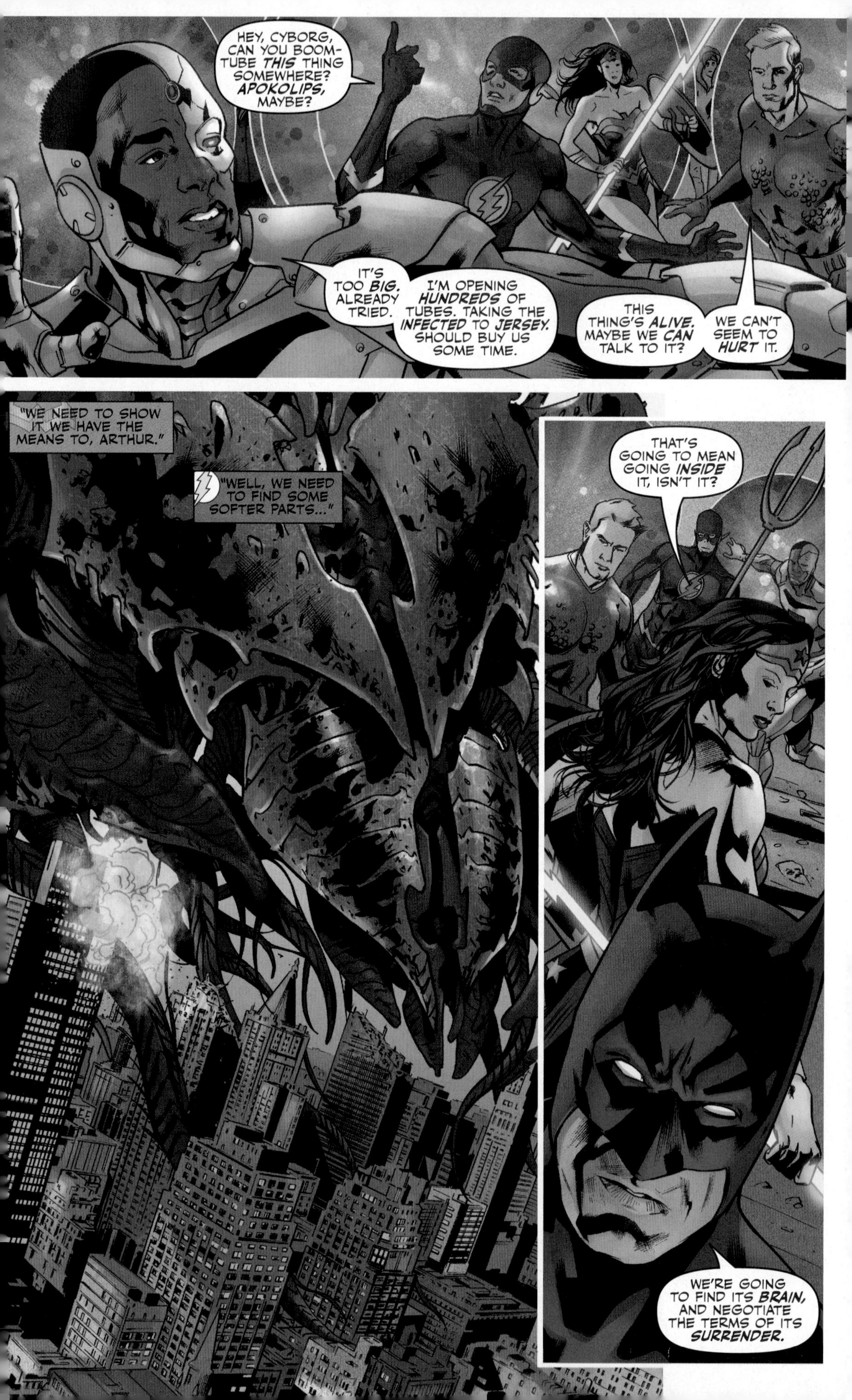
HEY, CYBORG, CAN YOU BOOM-TUBE *THIS* THING SOMEWHERE? *APOKOLIPS,* MAYBE?
IT'S TOO *BIG.* ALREADY TRIED.
I'M OPENING *HUNDREDS* OF TUBES. TAKING THE *INFECTED* TO *JERSEY.* SHOULD BUY US SOME TIME.
THIS THING'S *ALIVE.* MAYBE WE *CAN* TALK TO IT?
WE CAN'T SEEM TO *HURT* IT.
"WE NEED TO SHOW IT WE HAVE THE MEANS TO, ARTHUR."
"WELL, WE NEED TO FIND SOME SOFTER PARTS..."
THAT'S GOING TO MEAN GOING *INSIDE* IT, ISN'T IT?
WE'RE GOING TO FIND ITS *BRAIN,* AND NEGOTIATE THE TERMS OF ITS *SURRENDER.*

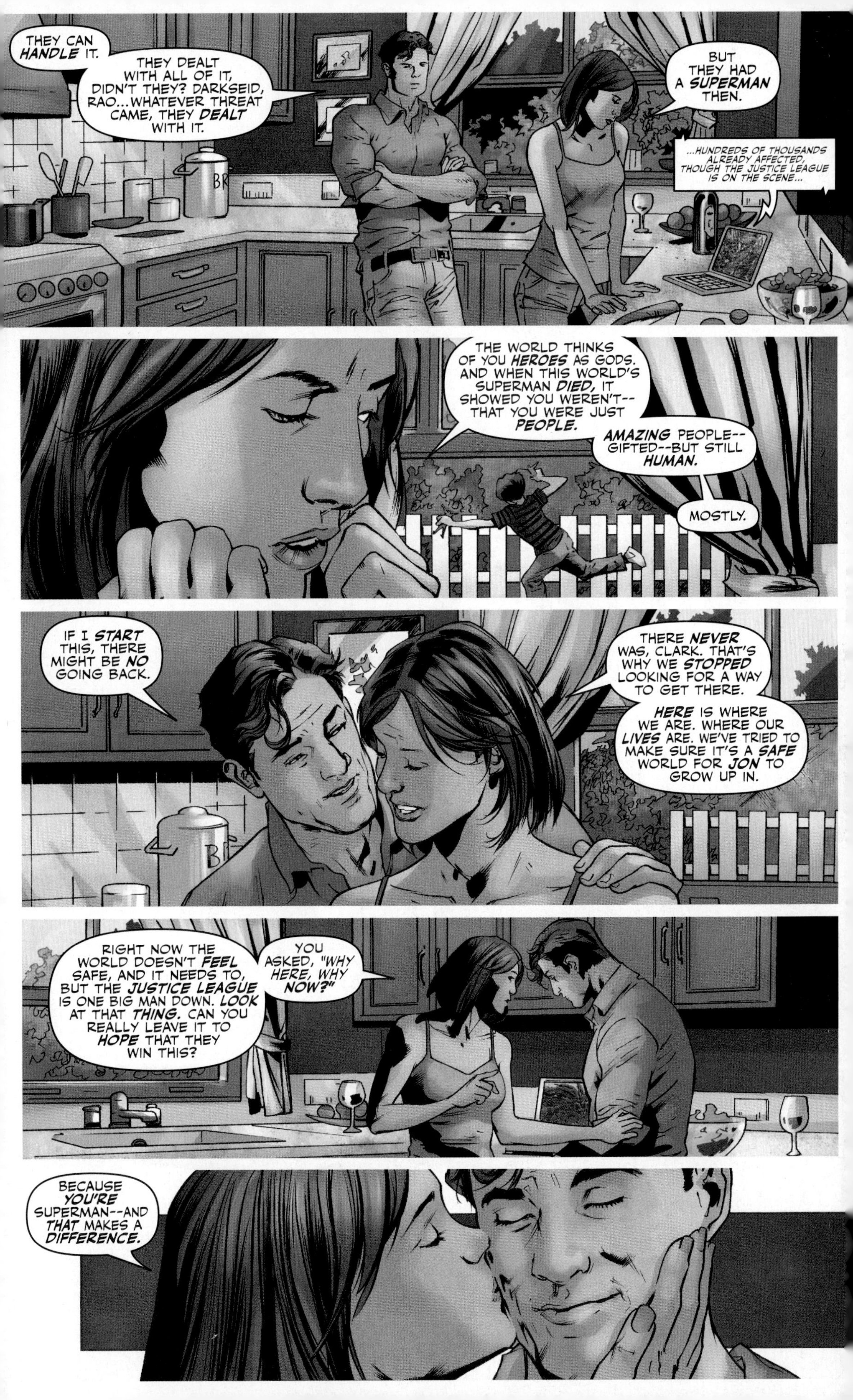
THEY CAN HANDLE IT.
THEY DEALT WITH ALL OF IT, DIDN'T THEY? DARKSEID, RAO...WHATEVER THREAT CAME, THEY DEALT WITH IT.
BUT THEY HAD A SUPERMAN THEN.
...HUNDREDS OF THOUSANDS ALREADY AFFECTED, THOUGH THE JUSTICE LEAGUE IS ON THE SCENE...
THE WORLD THINKS OF YOU HEROES AS GODS. AND WHEN THIS WORLD'S SUPERMAN DIED, IT SHOWED YOU WEREN'T--THAT YOU WERE JUST PEOPLE.
AMAZING PEOPLE--GIFTED--BUT STILL HUMAN.
MOSTLY.
IF I START THIS, THERE MIGHT BE NO GOING BACK.
THERE NEVER WAS, CLARK. THAT'S WHY WE STOPPED LOOKING FOR A WAY TO GET THERE.
HERE IS WHERE WE ARE. WHERE OUR LIVES ARE. WE'VE TRIED TO MAKE SURE IT'S A SAFE WORLD FOR JON TO GROW UP IN.
RIGHT NOW THE WORLD DOESN'T FEEL SAFE, AND IT NEEDS TO, BUT THE JUSTICE LEAGUE IS ONE BIG MAN DOWN. LOOK AT THAT THING. CAN YOU REALLY LEAVE IT TO HOPE THAT THEY WIN THIS?
YOU ASKED, "WHY HERE, WHY NOW?"
BECAUSE YOU'RE SUPERMAN--AND THAT MAKES A DIFFERENCE.

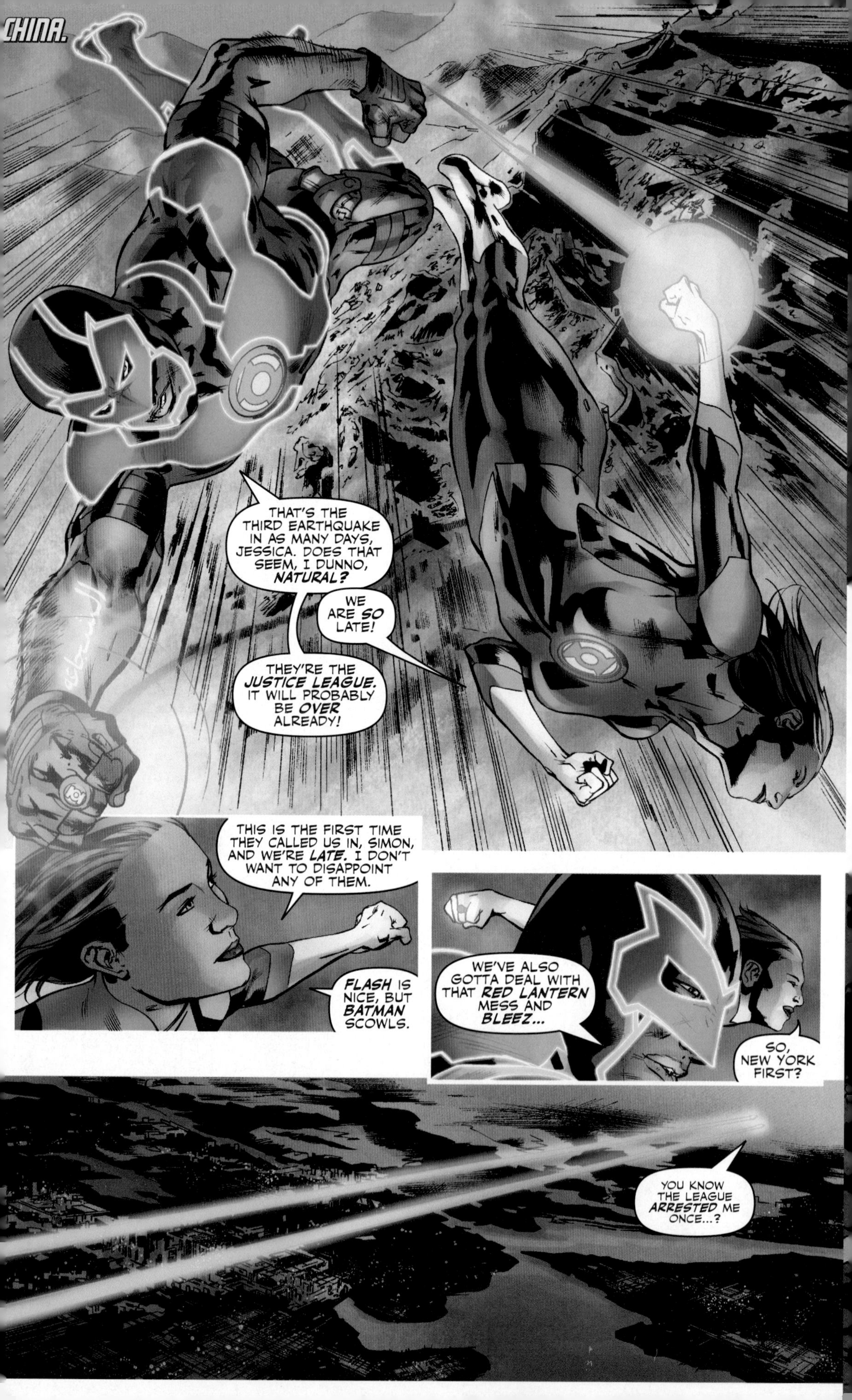
CHINA.
THAT'S THE THIRD EARTHQUAKE IN AS MANY DAYS, JESSICA. DOES THAT SEEM, I DUNNO, NATURAL?
WE ARE SO LATE!
THEY'RE THE JUSTICE LEAGUE. IT WILL PROBABLY BE OVER ALREADY!
THIS IS THE FIRST TIME THEY CALLED US IN, SIMON, AND WE'RE LATE. I DON'T WANT TO DISAPPOINT ANY OF THEM.
FLASH IS NICE, BUT BATMAN SCOWLS.
WE'VE ALSO GOTTA DEAL WITH THAT RED LANTERN MESS AND BLEEZ...
SO, NEW YORK FIRST?
YOU KNOW THE LEAGUE ARRESTED ME ONCE...?

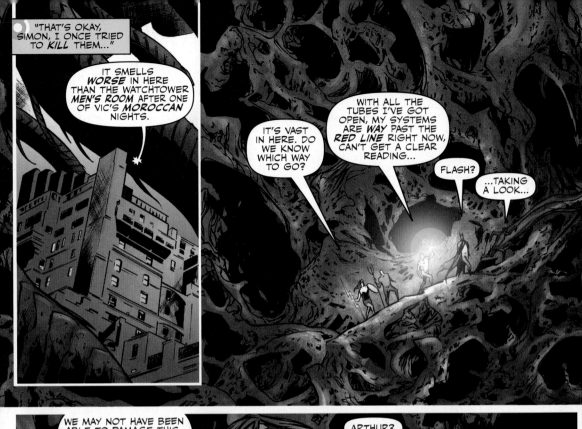

"THAT'S OKAY, SIMON, I ONCE TRIED TO *KILL* THEM..."

IT SMELLS *WORSE* IN HERE THAN THE WATCHTOWER *MEN'S ROOM* AFTER ONE OF VIC'S *MOROCCAN* NIGHTS.

IT'S VAST IN HERE. DO WE KNOW WHICH WAY TO GO?

WITH ALL THE TUBES I'VE GOT OPEN, MY SYSTEMS ARE *WAY* PAST THE *RED LINE* RIGHT NOW, CAN'T GET A CLEAR READING...

FLASH?

...TAKING A LOOK...

WE MAY NOT HAVE BEEN ABLE TO DAMAGE THIS CREATURE'S *EXTERIOR*, BUT WE COULD INFLICT SOME DAMAGE FROM *INSIDE* WHATEVER THIS IS.

ARTHUR?

≥NNG≤ HEADACHE.

DOES NO ONE ELSE HEAR THAT *BUZZING?* LIKE A BILLION *BEES?*

SCOUTED. THIS WAY.

DEFINITELY *BIGGER* THAN *NEW YORK* IN HERE.

SMELLS EVEN *WORSE.*

I'M GETTING *SONAR IMAGES* BACK. FUZZY, THOUGH.

THERE'S A *MASSIVE* CHAMBER ABOUT THE SIZE OF *CENTRAL PARK* WITH SOME HUGE *STRUCTURE* IN THE MIDDLE. LOOKS LIKE IT'S *CONNECTED* TO EVERY OTHER PART OF THIS THING.

CONNECTED...

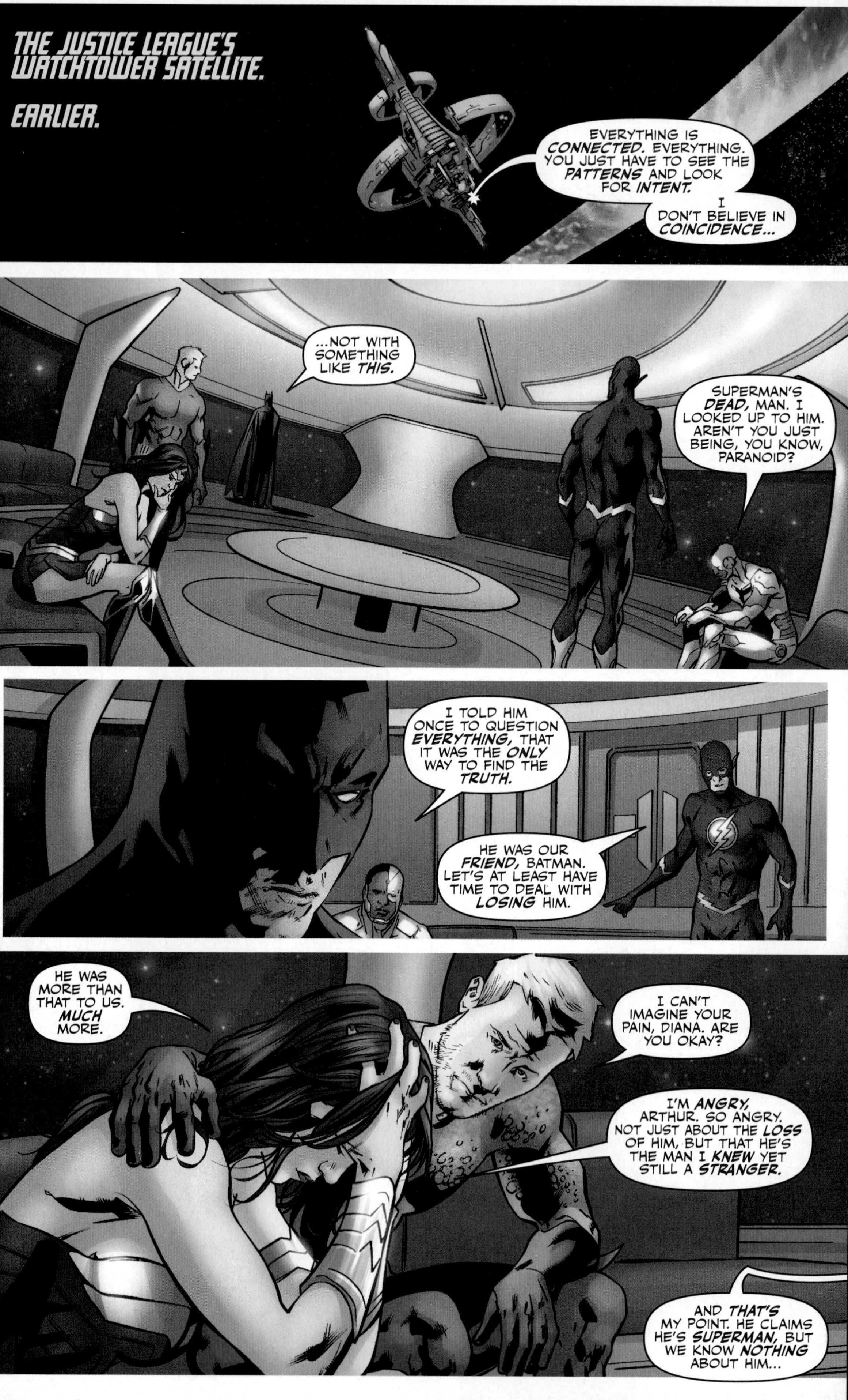
THE JUSTICE LEAGUE'S WATCHTOWER SATELLITE.
EARLIER.
EVERYTHING IS CONNECTED. EVERYTHING. YOU JUST HAVE TO SEE THE PATTERNS AND LOOK FOR INTENT.
I DON'T BELIEVE IN COINCIDENCE...
...NOT WITH SOMETHING LIKE THIS.
SUPERMAN'S DEAD, MAN. I LOOKED UP TO HIM. AREN'T YOU JUST BEING, YOU KNOW, PARANOID?
I TOLD HIM ONCE TO QUESTION EVERYTHING, THAT IT WAS THE ONLY WAY TO FIND THE TRUTH.
HE WAS OUR FRIEND, BATMAN. LET'S AT LEAST HAVE TIME TO DEAL WITH LOSING HIM.
HE WAS MORE THAN THAT TO US. MUCH MORE.
I CAN'T IMAGINE YOUR PAIN, DIANA. ARE YOU OKAY?
I'M ANGRY, ARTHUR. SO ANGRY. NOT JUST ABOUT THE LOSS OF HIM, BUT THAT HE'S THE MAN I KNEW YET STILL A STRANGER.
AND THAT'S MY POINT. HE CLAIMS HE'S SUPERMAN, BUT WE KNOW NOTHING ABOUT HIM...

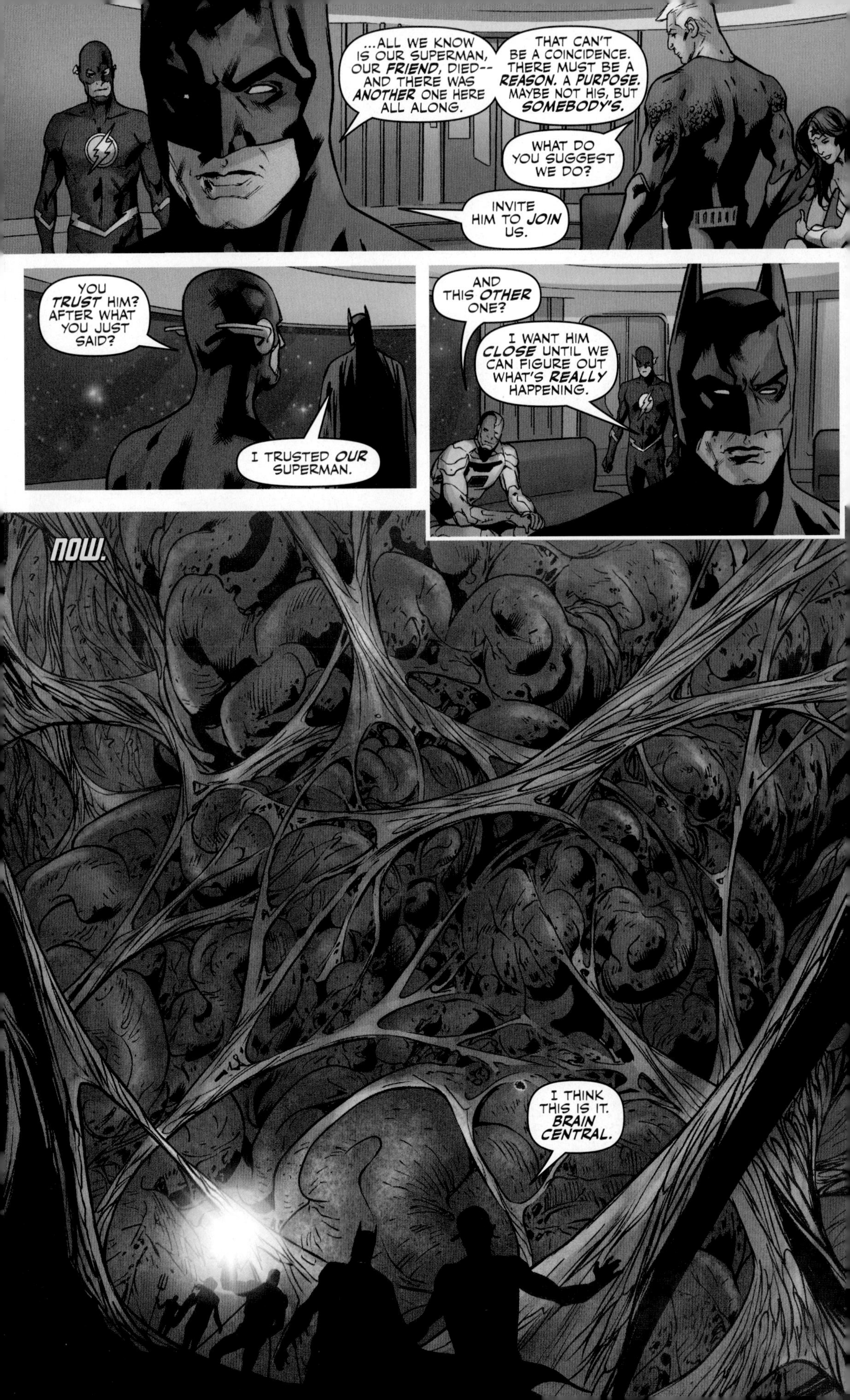
...ALL WE KNOW IS OUR SUPERMAN, OUR FRIEND, DIED-- AND THERE WAS ANOTHER ONE HERE ALL ALONG.
THAT CAN'T BE A COINCIDENCE. THERE MUST BE A REASON. A PURPOSE. MAYBE NOT HIS, BUT SOMEBODY'S.
WHAT DO YOU SUGGEST WE DO?
INVITE HIM TO JOIN US.
YOU TRUST HIM? AFTER WHAT YOU JUST SAID?
I TRUSTED OUR SUPERMAN.
AND THIS OTHER ONE?
I WANT HIM CLOSE UNTIL WE CAN FIGURE OUT WHAT'S REALLY HAPPENING.
NOW.
I THINK THIS IS IT. BRAIN CENTRAL.

GAAH!

ARTHUR, WHAT IS IT?

I CAN *HEAR* IT.

I CAN HEAR IT *THINKING*. IT'S CALLED A *REAPER*-- AND I THINK IT'S HERE TO *HARVEST* HUMANITY.

*HARVEST?* WHAT FOR?

I CAN'T MAKE IT *ALL* OUT, JUST THAT IT'S OUR *TIME* TO BE *HARVESTED.*

THIS IS JUST THE *FIRST.* THERE ARE *OTHERS* COMING, *LOTS* OF OTHERS. MORE *REAPERS.*

ENOUGH FOR THE *WHOLE* WORLD.

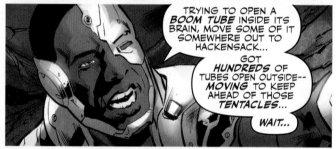

TRYING TO OPEN A *BOOM TUBE* INSIDE ITS BRAIN, MOVE SOME OF IT SOMEWHERE OUT TO HACKENSACK...

GOT *HUNDREDS* OF TUBES OPEN OUTSIDE-- *MOVING* TO KEEP AHEAD OF THOSE *TENTACLES*...

*WAIT...*

*GAH!* TOO MUCH. OVERLOADING--

ACTION SCENE, PEOPLE!

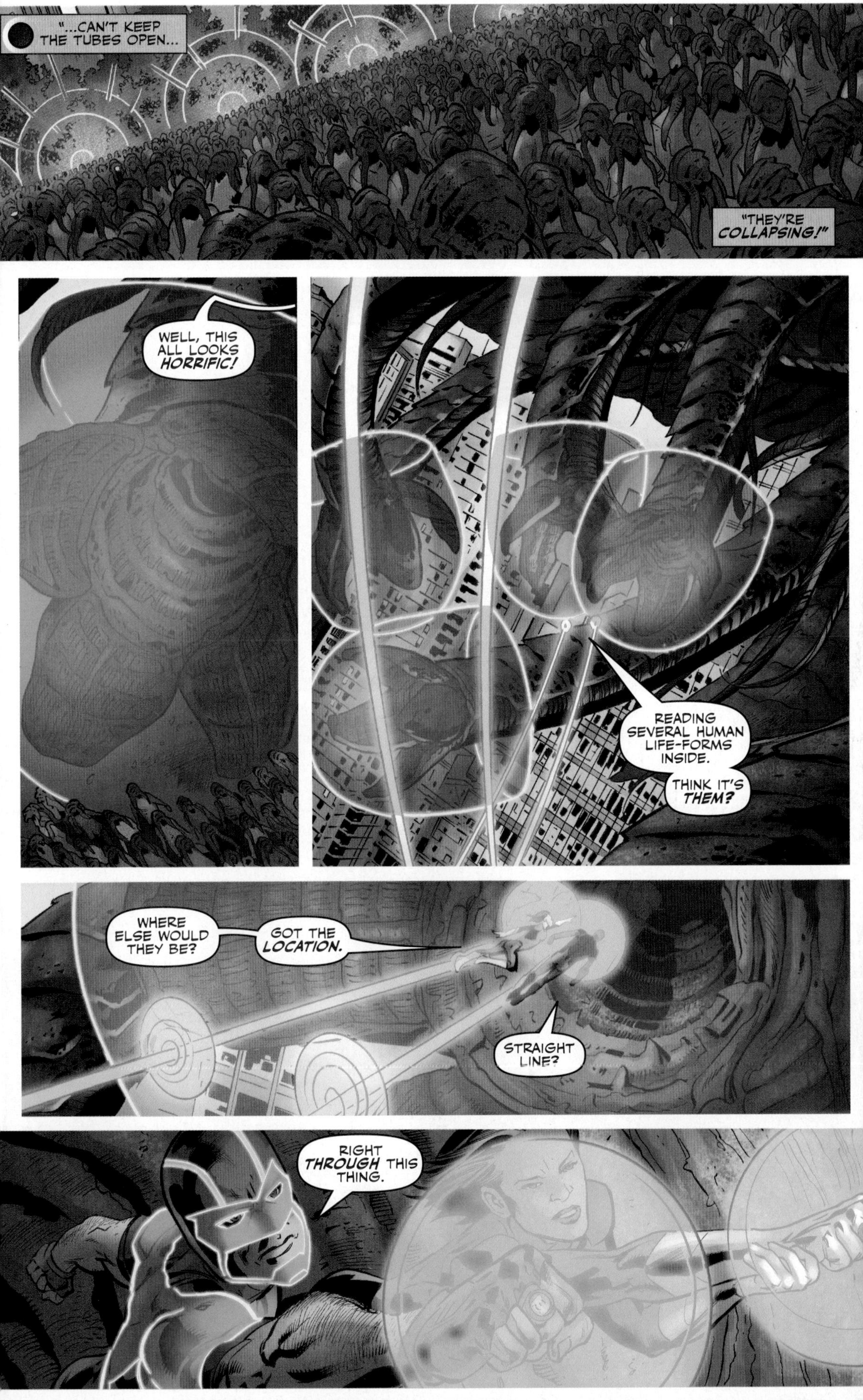
"...CAN'T KEEP THE TUBES OPEN...
"THEY'RE COLLAPSING!"
WELL, THIS ALL LOOKS HORRIFIC!
READING SEVERAL HUMAN LIFE-FORMS INSIDE.
THINK IT'S THEM?
WHERE ELSE WOULD THEY BE?
GOT THE LOCATION.
STRAIGHT LINE?
RIGHT THROUGH THIS THING.

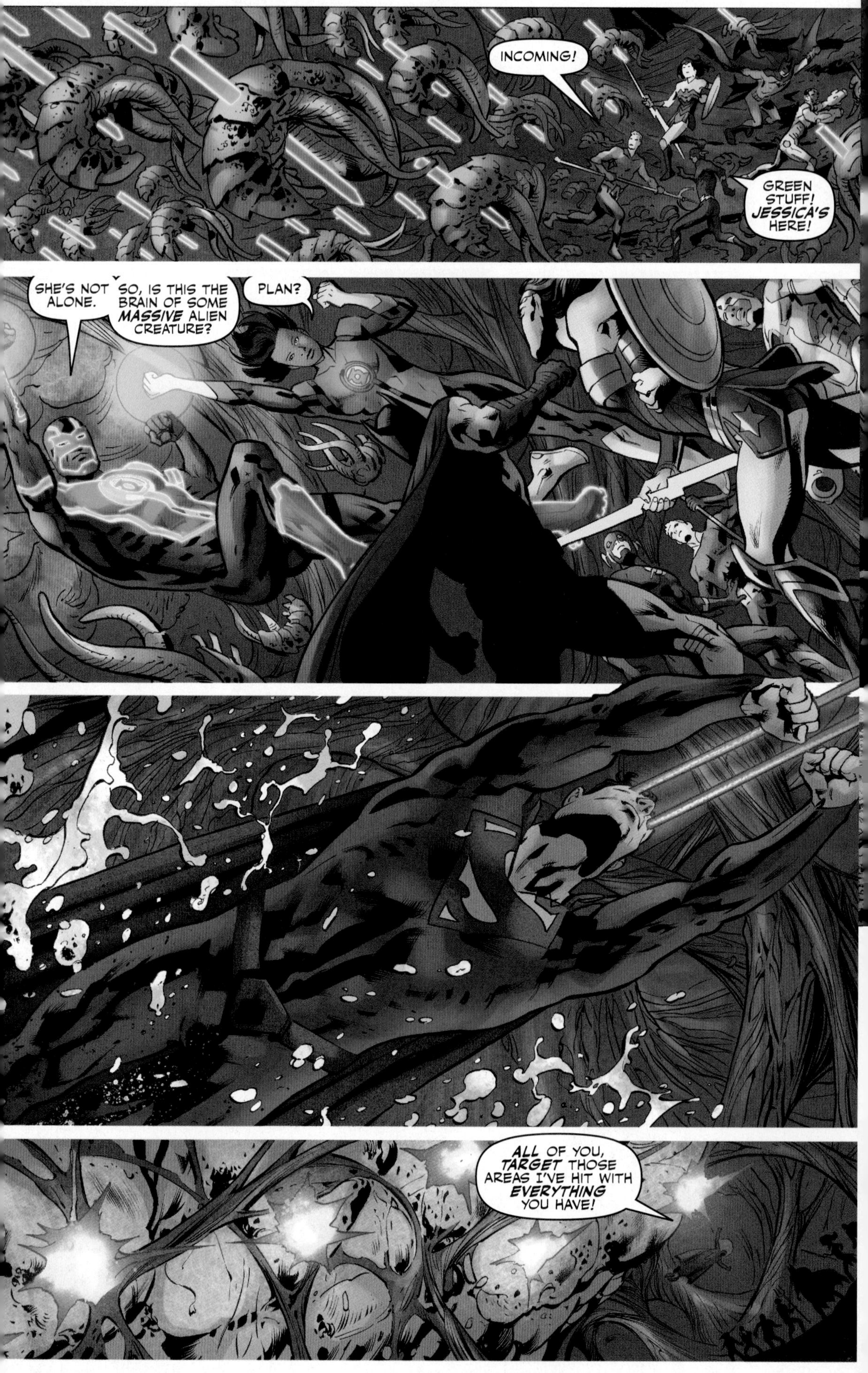
INCOMING!
GREEN STUFF! JESSICA'S HERE!
SHE'S NOT ALONE.
SO, IS THIS THE BRAIN OF SOME MASSIVE ALIEN CREATURE?
PLAN?
ALL OF YOU, TARGET THOSE AREAS I'VE HIT WITH EVERYTHING YOU HAVE!

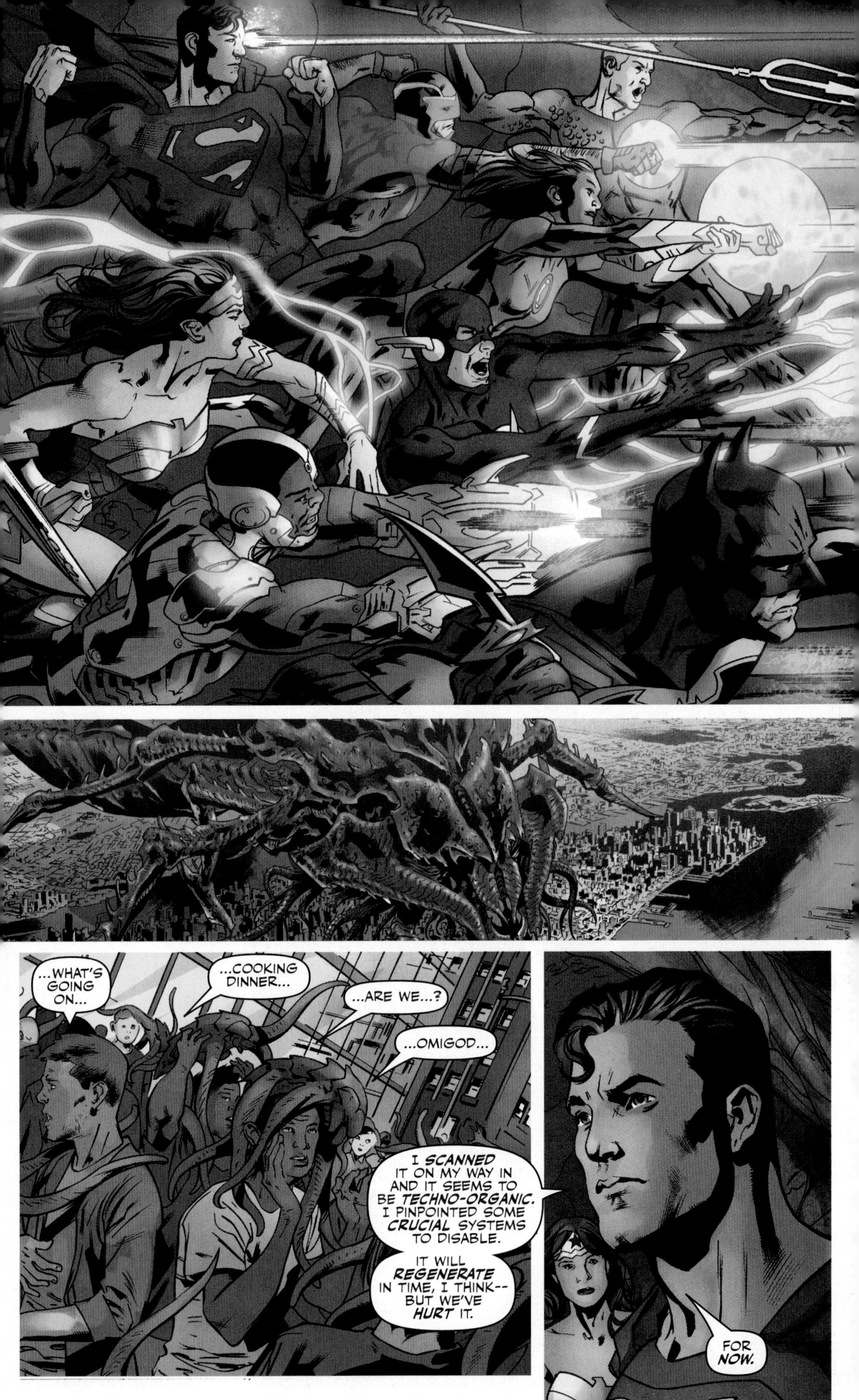
...WHAT'S GOING ON...
...COOKING DINNER...
...ARE WE...?
...OMIGOD...
I SCANNED IT ON MY WAY IN AND IT SEEMS TO BE TECHNO-ORGANIC. I PINPOINTED SOME CRUCIAL SYSTEMS TO DISABLE.
IT WILL REGENERATE IN TIME, I THINK-- BUT WE'VE HURT IT.
FOR NOW.

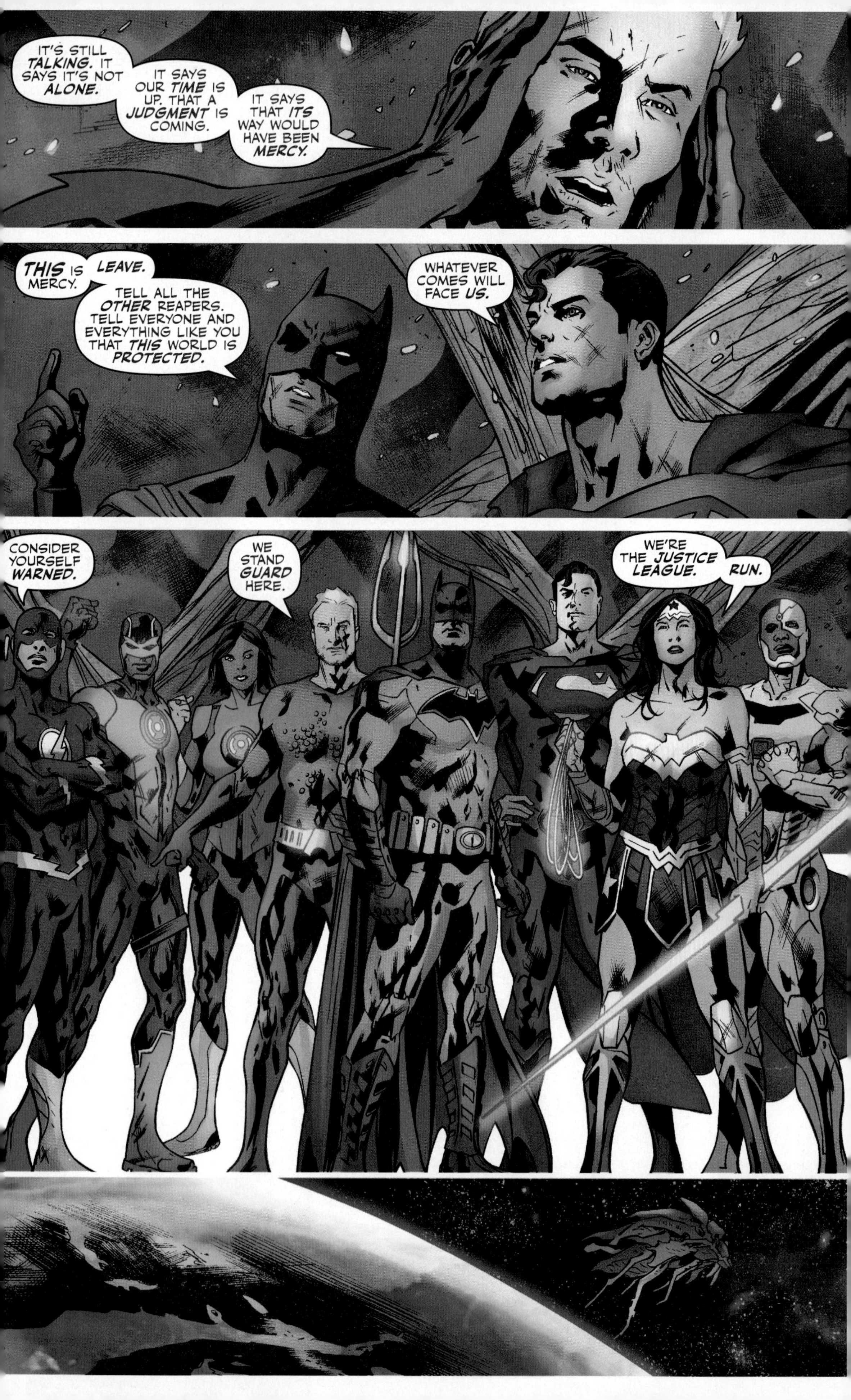
IT'S STILL TALKING. IT SAYS IT'S NOT ALONE.
IT SAYS OUR TIME IS UP. THAT A JUDGMENT IS COMING.
IT SAYS THAT ITS WAY WOULD HAVE BEEN MERCY.
THIS IS MERCY.
LEAVE.
TELL ALL THE OTHER REAPERS. TELL EVERYONE AND EVERYTHING LIKE YOU THAT THIS WORLD IS PROTECTED.
WHATEVER COMES WILL FACE US.
CONSIDER YOURSELF WARNED.
WE STAND GUARD HERE.
WE'RE THE JUSTICE LEAGUE.
RUN.

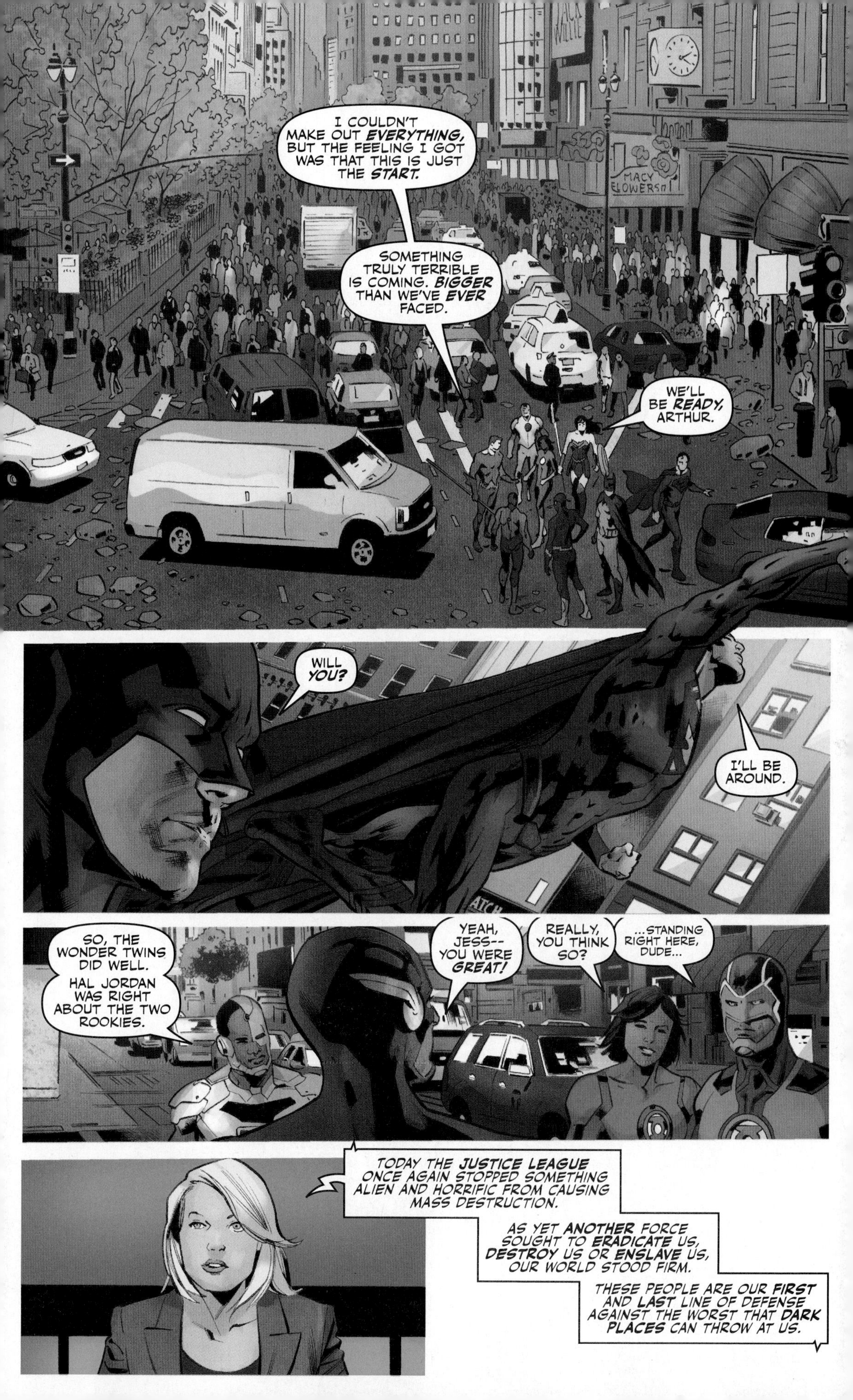
I COULDN'T MAKE OUT EVERYTHING, BUT THE FEELING I GOT WAS THAT THIS IS JUST THE START.
SOMETHING TRULY TERRIBLE IS COMING. BIGGER THAN WE'VE EVER FACED.
WE'LL BE READY, ARTHUR.
MACY FLOWERS
WILL YOU?
I'LL BE AROUND.
SO, THE WONDER TWINS DID WELL.
HAL JORDAN WAS RIGHT ABOUT THE TWO ROOKIES.
YEAH, JESS-- YOU WERE GREAT!
REALLY, YOU THINK SO?
...STANDING RIGHT HERE, DUDE...
TODAY THE JUSTICE LEAGUE ONCE AGAIN STOPPED SOMETHING ALIEN AND HORRIFIC FROM CAUSING MASS DESTRUCTION.
AS YET ANOTHER FORCE SOUGHT TO ERADICATE US, DESTROY US OR ENSLAVE US, OUR WORLD STOOD FIRM.
THESE PEOPLE ARE OUR FIRST AND LAST LINE OF DEFENSE AGAINST THE WORST THAT DARK PLACES CAN THROW AT US.

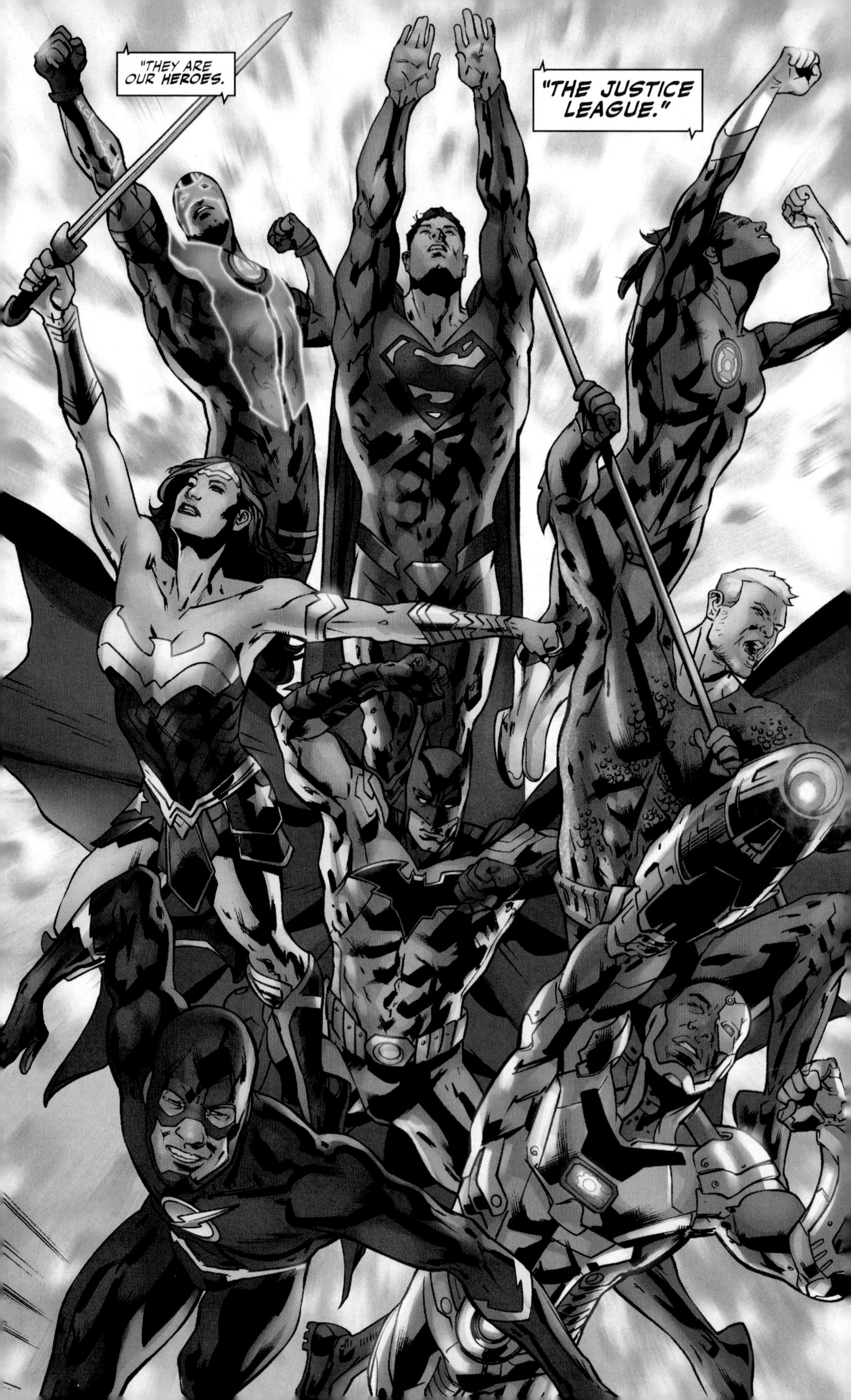
"THEY ARE OUR HEROES.
"THE JUSTICE LEAGUE."

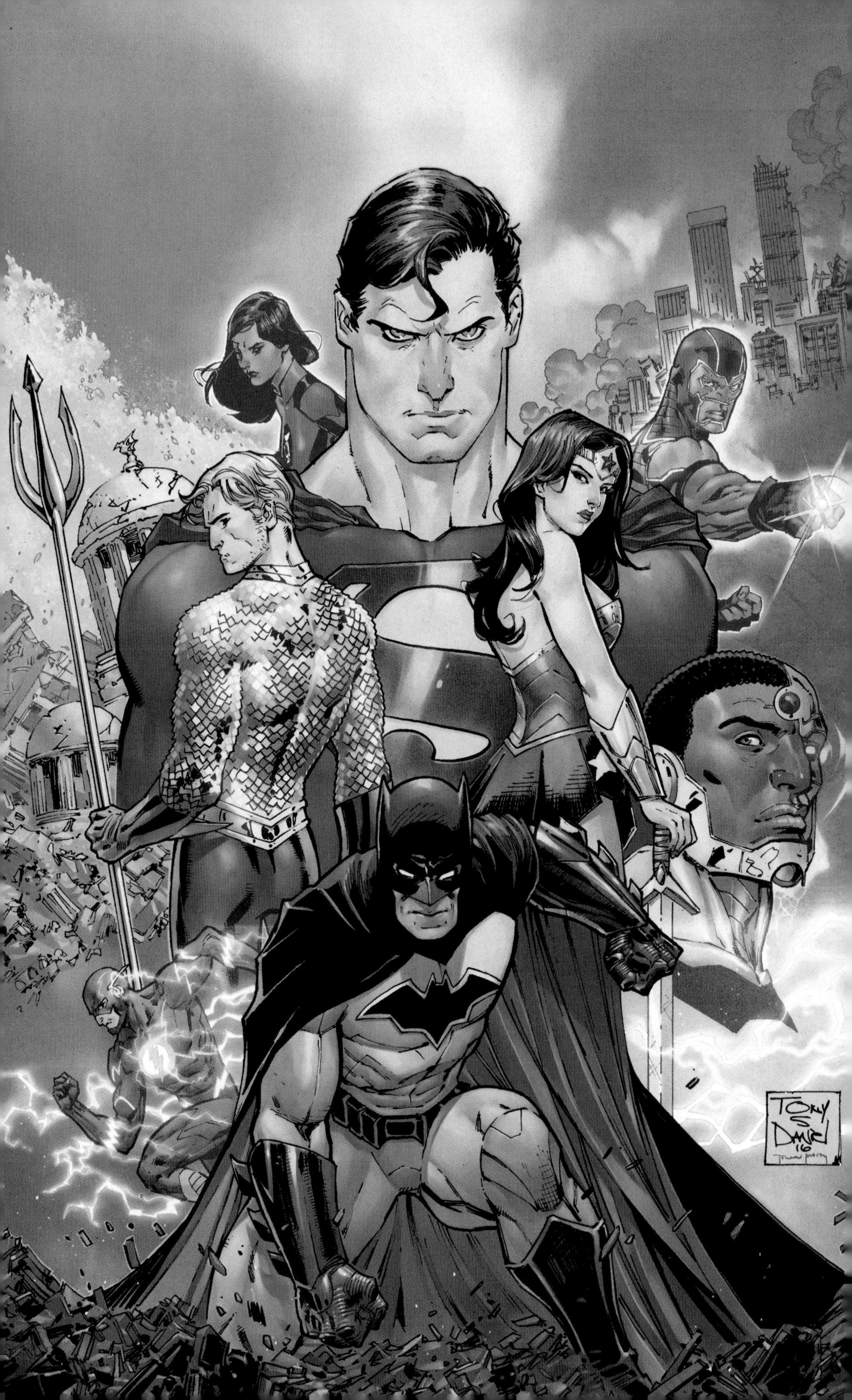

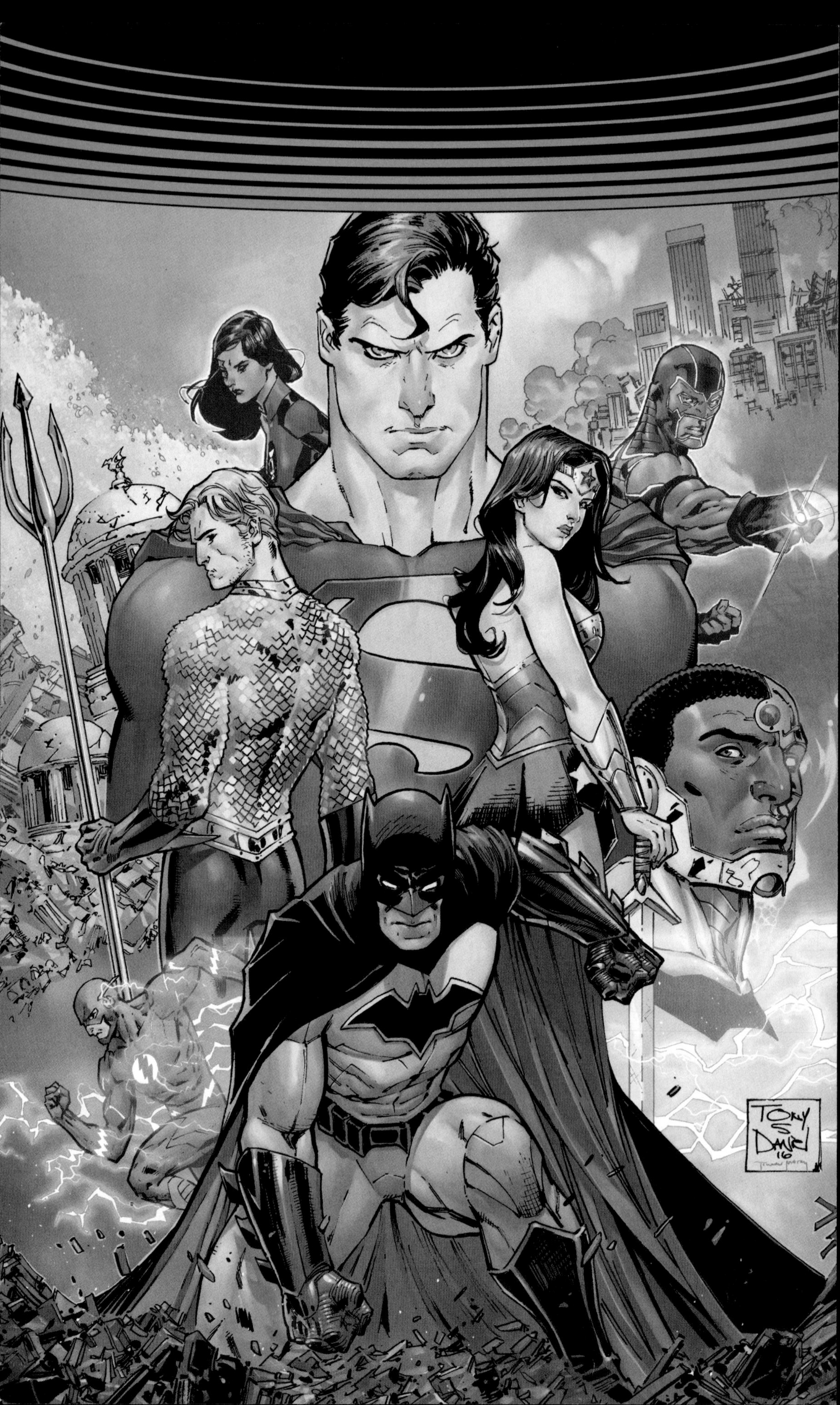

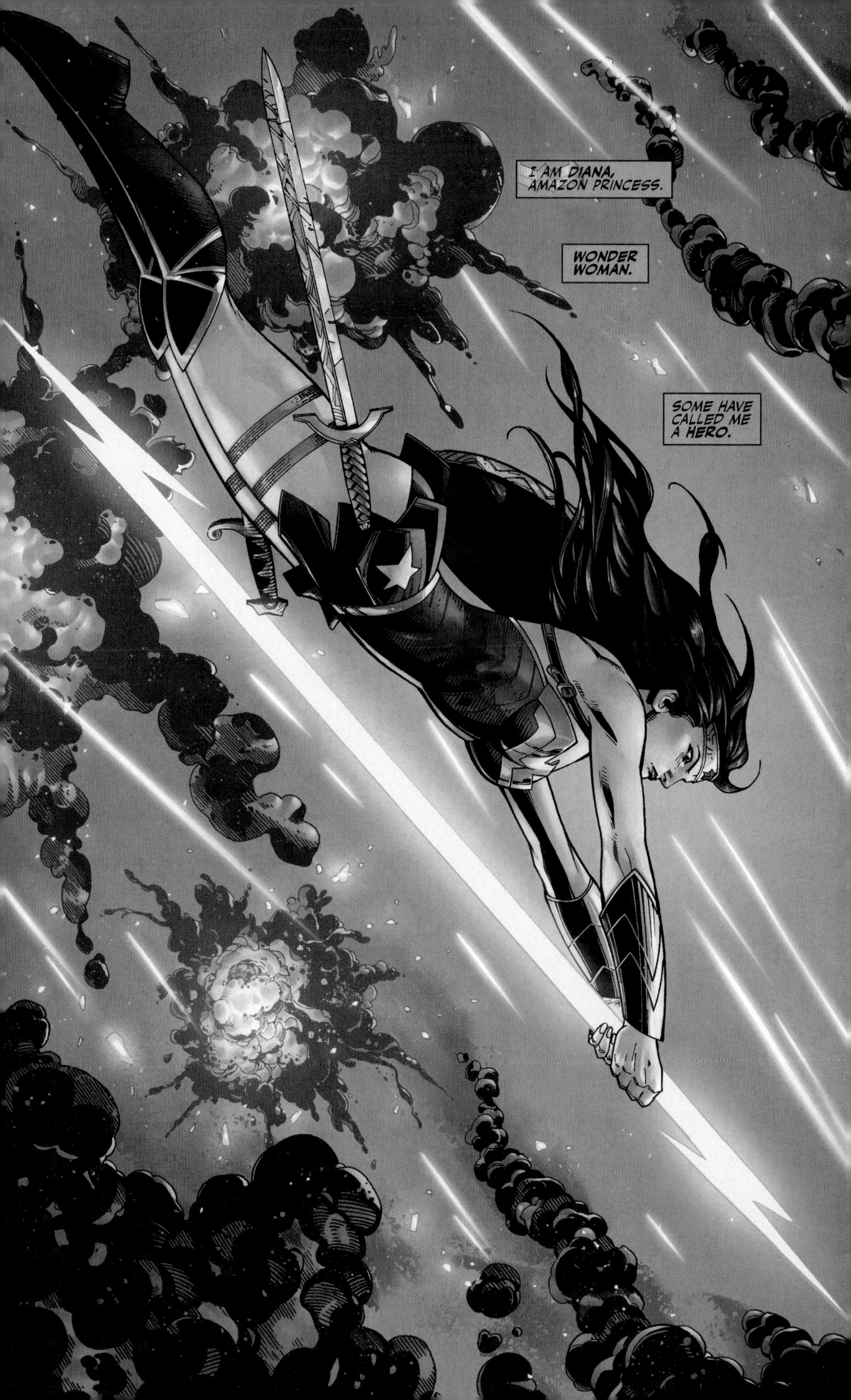
I AM DIANA, AMAZON PRINCESS.
WONDER WOMAN.
SOME HAVE CALLED ME A HERO.

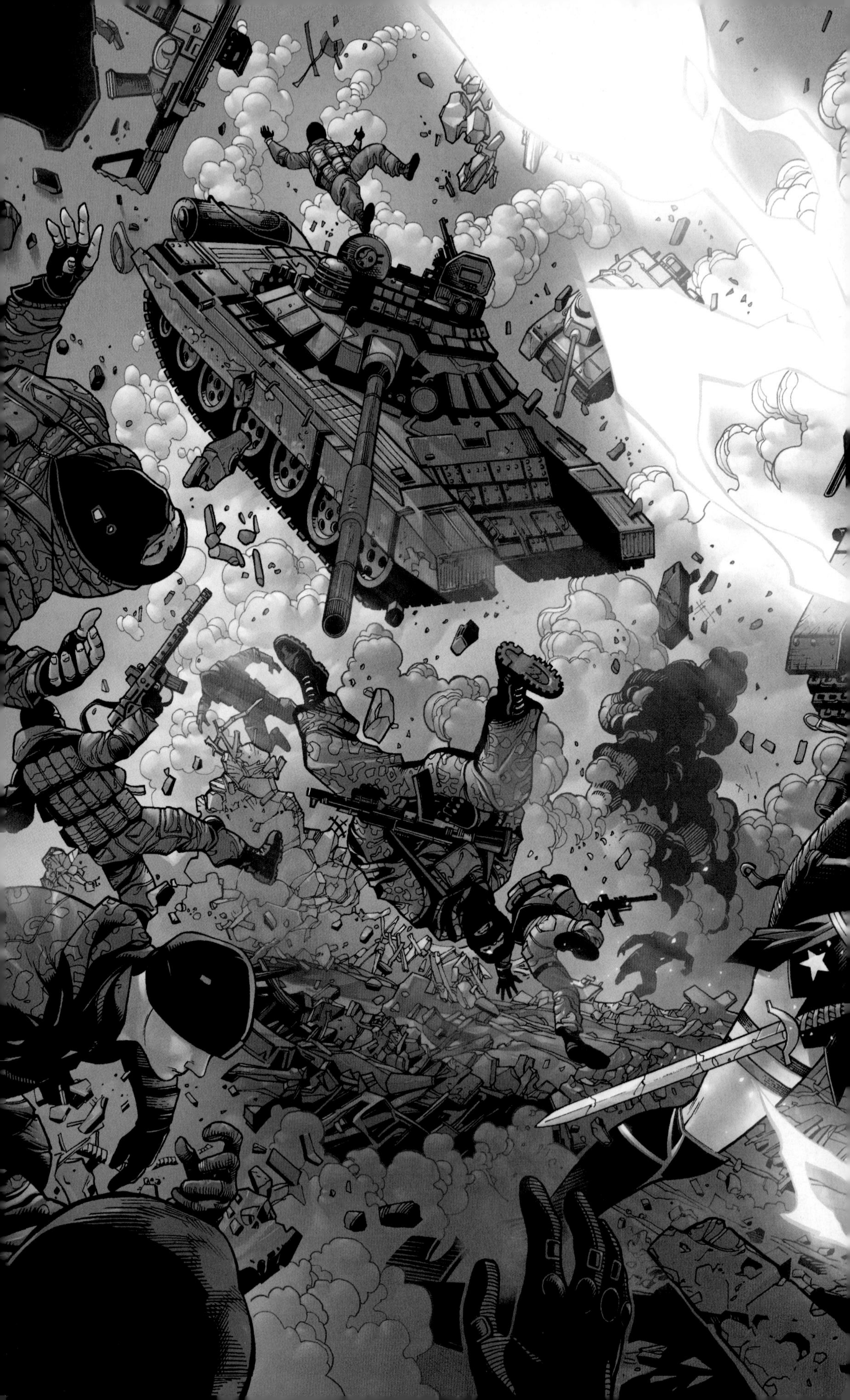

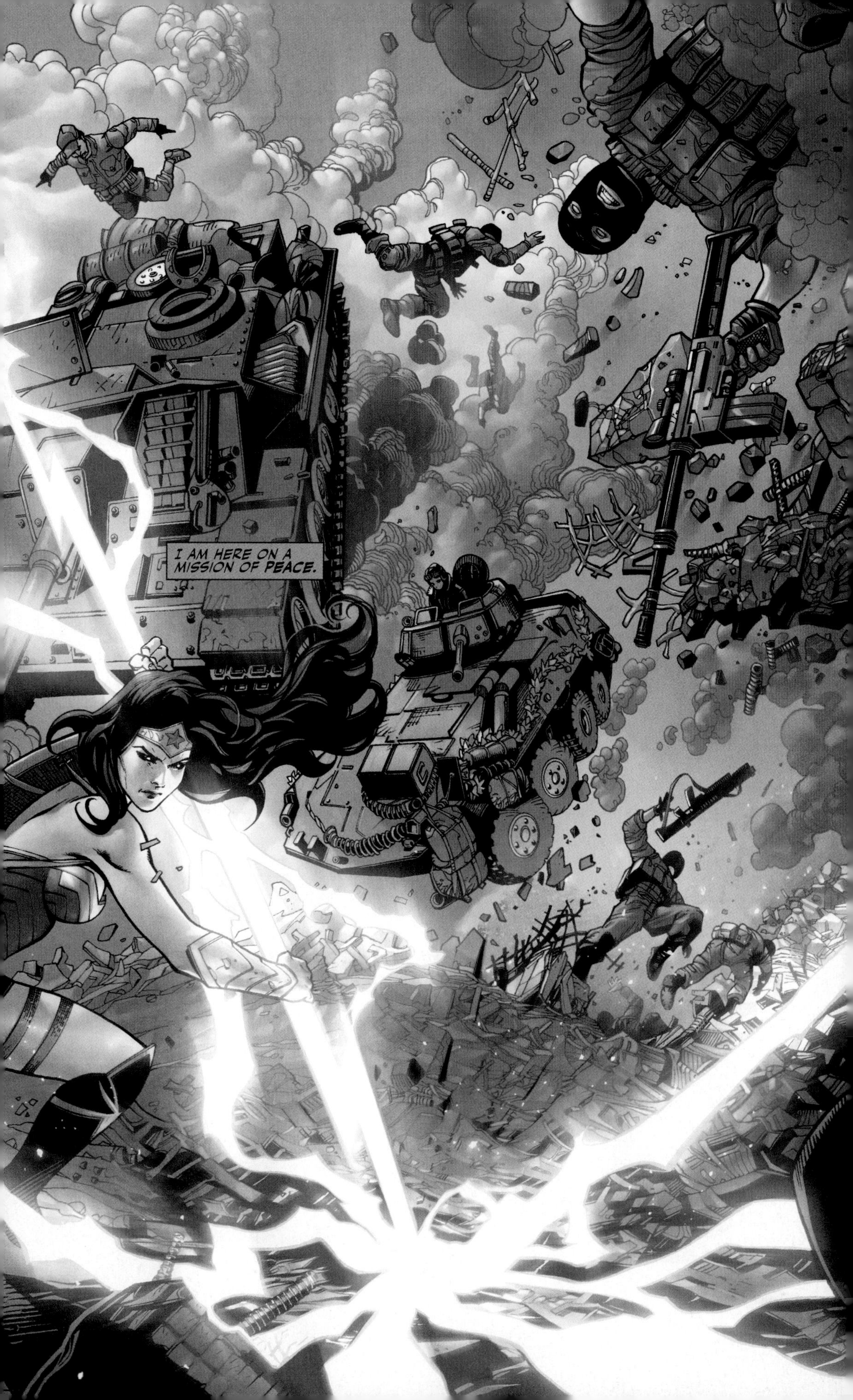
I AM HERE ON A MISSION OF PEACE.

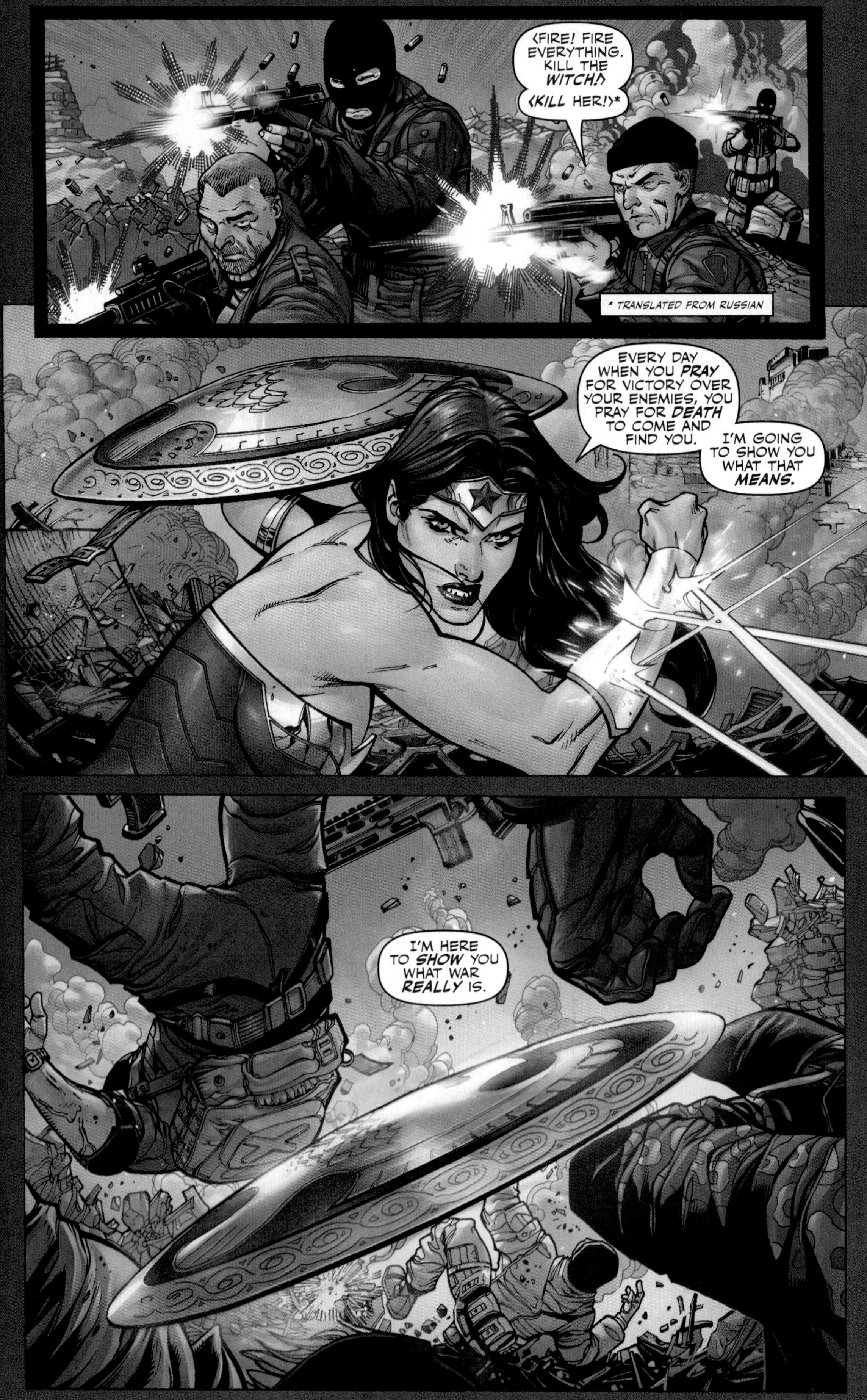
‹FIRE! FIRE EVERYTHING. KILL THE WITCH!›
‹KILL HER!›*
* TRANSLATED FROM RUSSIAN
EVERY DAY WHEN YOU PRAY FOR VICTORY OVER YOUR ENEMIES, YOU PRAY FOR DEATH TO COME AND FIND YOU.
I'M GOING TO SHOW YOU WHAT THAT MEANS.
I'M HERE TO SHOW YOU WHAT WAR REALLY IS.

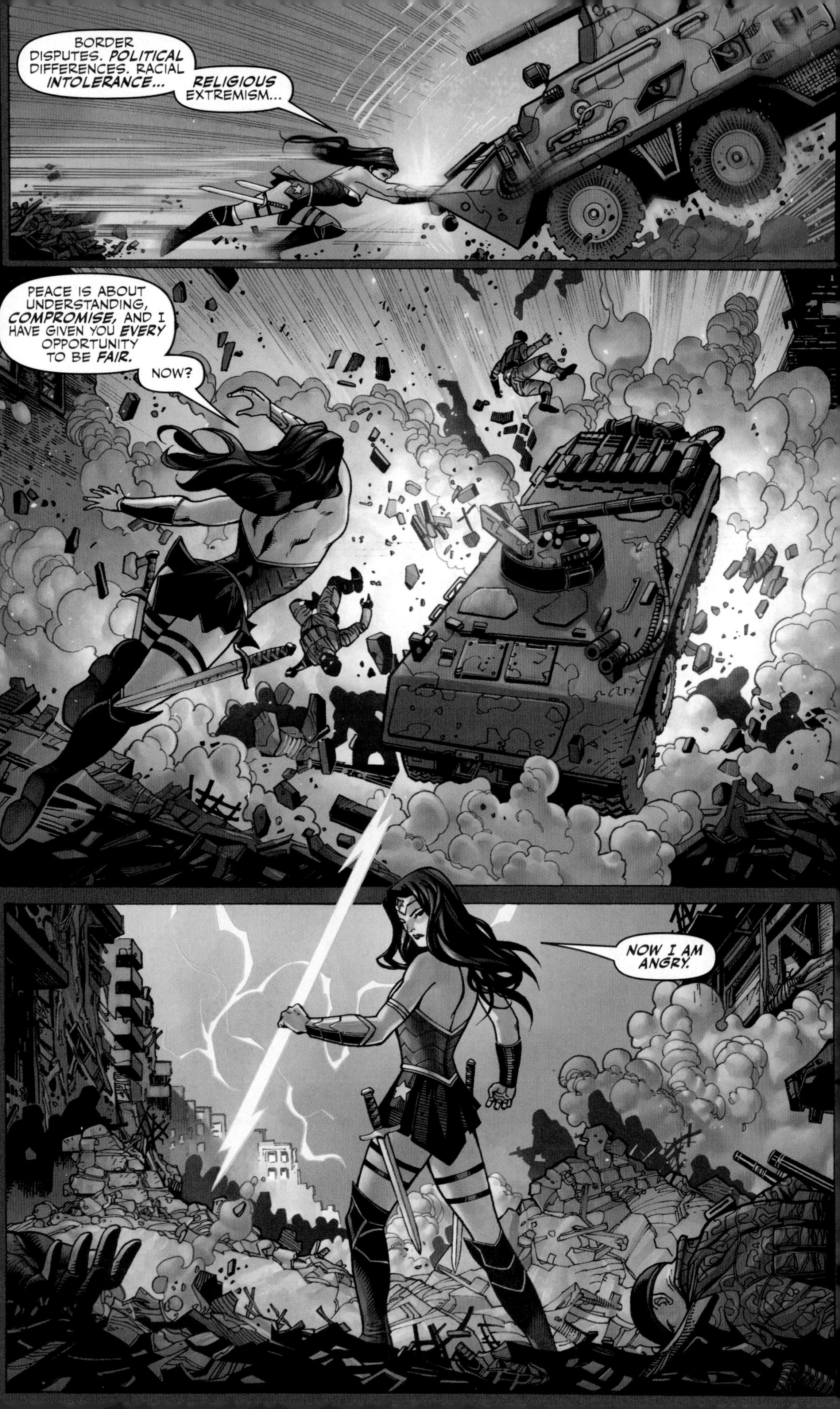
BORDER DISPUTES. POLITICAL DIFFERENCES. RACIAL INTOLERANCE...
RELIGIOUS EXTREMISM...
PEACE IS ABOUT UNDERSTANDING, COMPROMISE, AND I HAVE GIVEN YOU EVERY OPPORTUNITY TO BE FAIR.
NOW?
NOW I AM ANGRY.

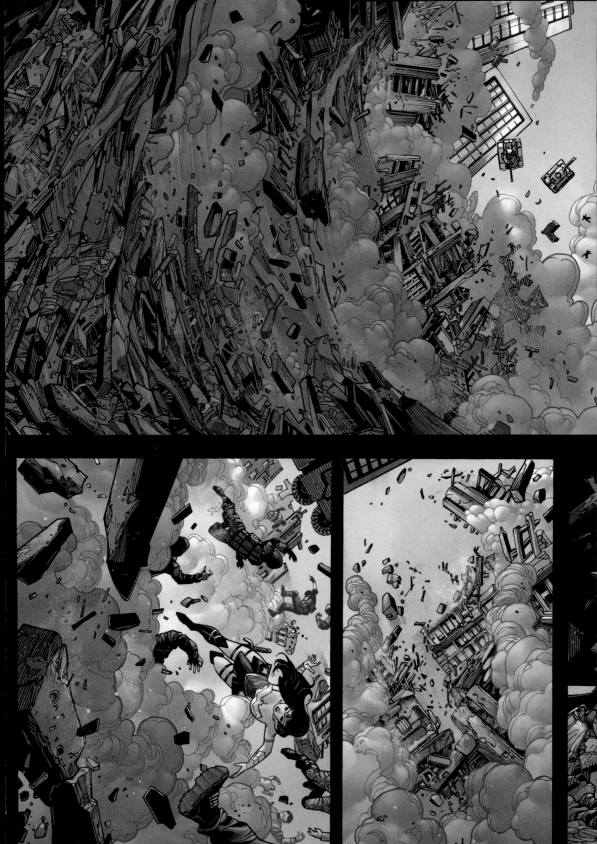

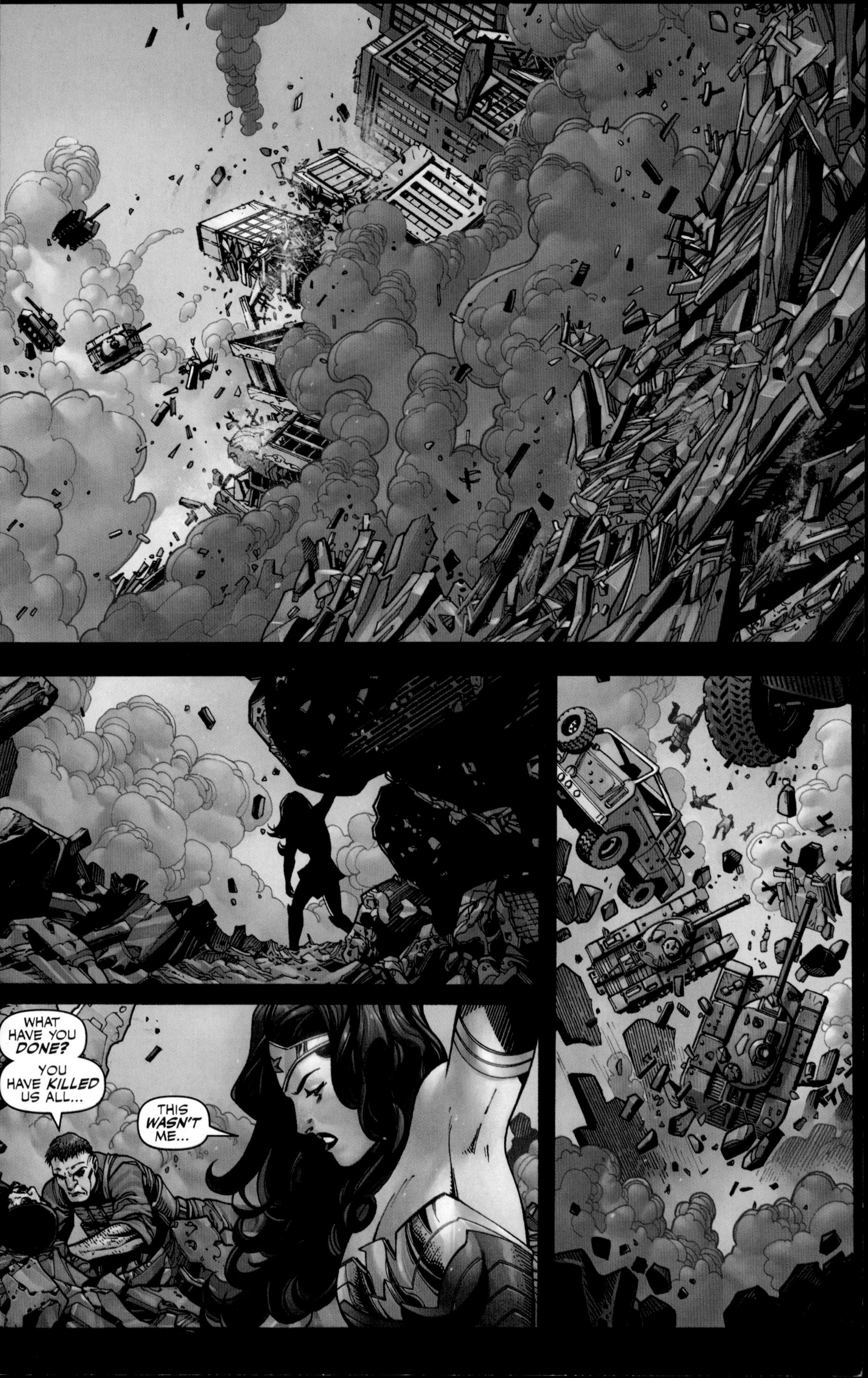
WHAT HAVE YOU DONE? YOU HAVE KILLED US ALL...
THIS WASN'T ME...

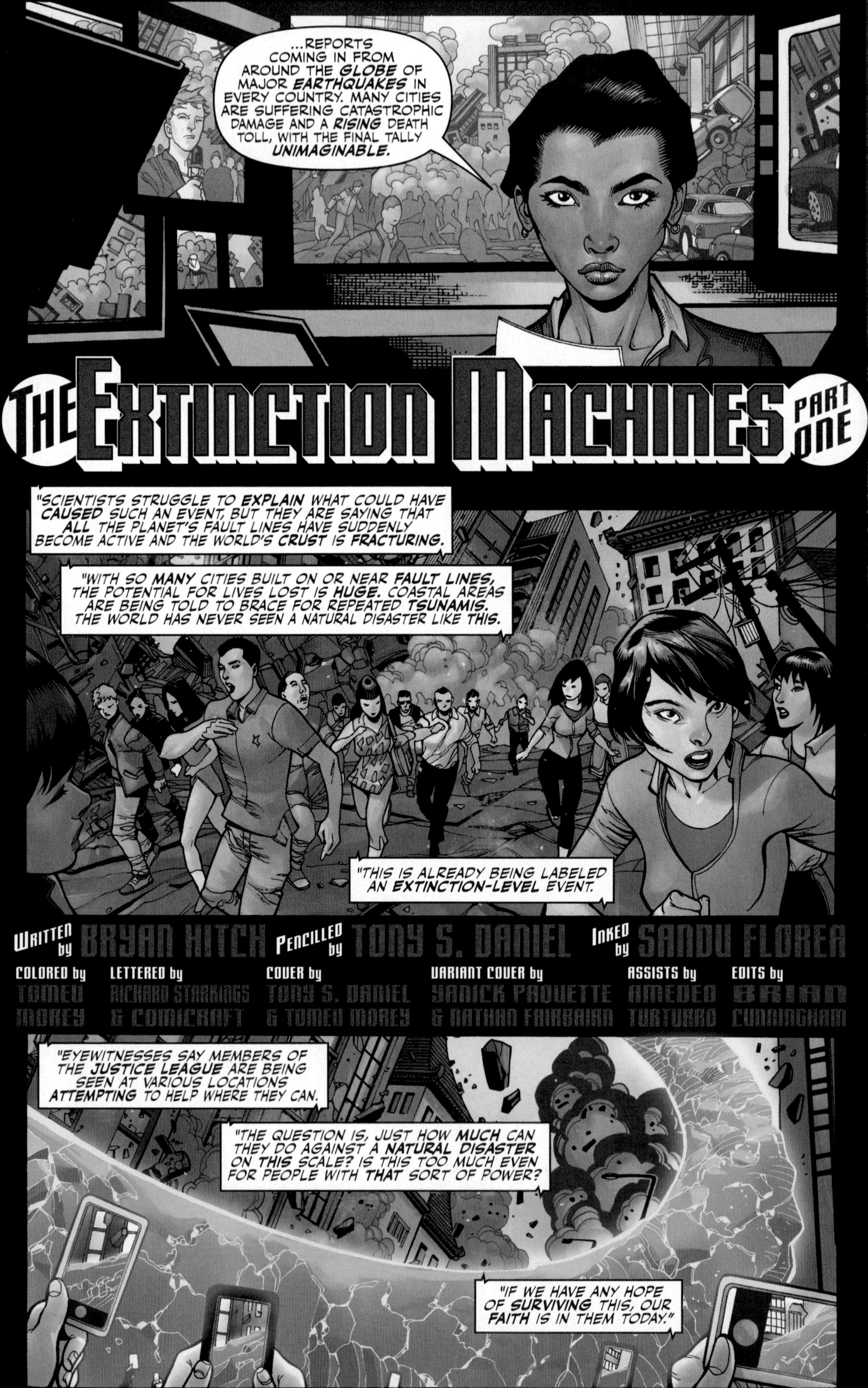
...REPORTS COMING IN FROM AROUND THE GLOBE OF MAJOR EARTHQUAKES IN EVERY COUNTRY. MANY CITIES ARE SUFFERING CATASTROPHIC DAMAGE AND A RISING DEATH TOLL, WITH THE FINAL TALLY UNIMAGINABLE.
THE EXTINCTION MACHINES PART ONE
"SCIENTISTS STRUGGLE TO EXPLAIN WHAT COULD HAVE CAUSED SUCH AN EVENT, BUT THEY ARE SAYING THAT ALL THE PLANET'S FAULT LINES HAVE SUDDENLY BECOME ACTIVE AND THE WORLD'S CRUST IS FRACTURING.
"WITH SO MANY CITIES BUILT ON OR NEAR FAULT LINES, THE POTENTIAL FOR LIVES LOST IS HUGE. COASTAL AREAS ARE BEING TOLD TO BRACE FOR REPEATED TSUNAMIS. THE WORLD HAS NEVER SEEN A NATURAL DISASTER LIKE THIS.
"THIS IS ALREADY BEING LABELED AN EXTINCTION-LEVEL EVENT.
WRITTEN by BRYAN HITCH PENCILLED by TONY S. DANIEL INKED by SANDU FLOREA
COLORED by TOMEU MOREY
LETTERED by RICHARD STARKINGS & COMICRAFT
COVER by TONY S. DANIEL & TOMEU MOREY
VARIANT COVER by YANICK PAQUETTE & NATHAN FAIRBAIRN
ASSISTS by AMEDEO TURTURRO
EDITS by BRIAN CUNNINGHAM
"EYEWITNESSES SAY MEMBERS OF THE JUSTICE LEAGUE ARE BEING SEEN AT VARIOUS LOCATIONS ATTEMPTING TO HELP WHERE THEY CAN.
"THE QUESTION IS, JUST HOW MUCH CAN THEY DO AGAINST A NATURAL DISASTER ON THIS SCALE? IS THIS TOO MUCH EVEN FOR PEOPLE WITH THAT SORT OF POWER?
"IF WE HAVE ANY HOPE OF SURVIVING THIS, OUR FAITH IS IN THEM TODAY."

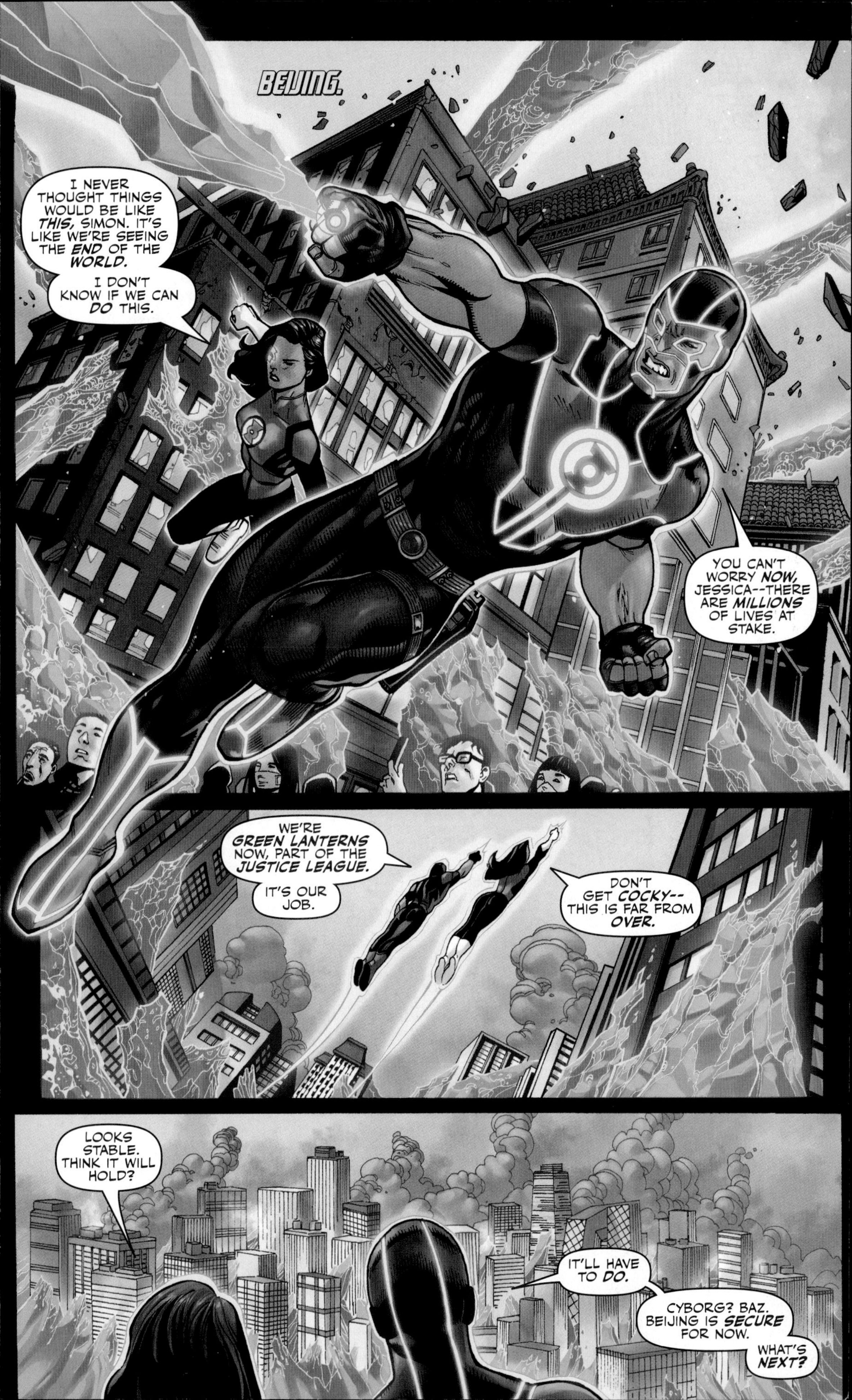
BEIJING.
I NEVER THOUGHT THINGS WOULD BE LIKE THIS, SIMON. IT'S LIKE WE'RE SEEING THE END OF THE WORLD.
I DON'T KNOW IF WE CAN DO THIS.
YOU CAN'T WORRY NOW, JESSICA--THERE ARE MILLIONS OF LIVES AT STAKE.
WE'RE GREEN LANTERNS NOW, PART OF THE JUSTICE LEAGUE.
IT'S OUR JOB.
DON'T GET COCKY-- THIS IS FAR FROM OVER.
LOOKS STABLE. THINK IT WILL HOLD?
IT'LL HAVE TO DO.
CYBORG? BAZ. BEIJING IS SECURE FOR NOW.
WHAT'S NEXT?

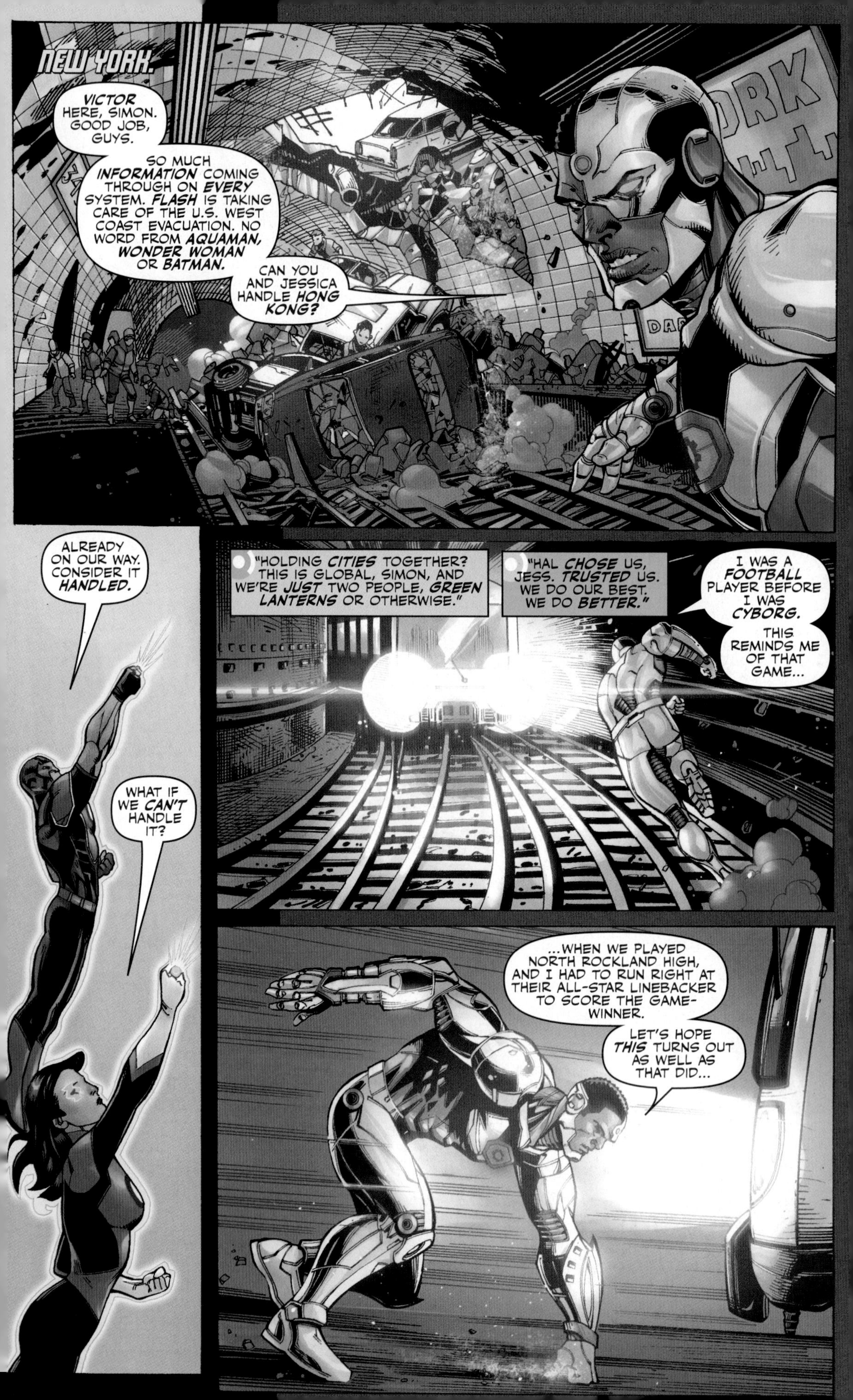
NEW YORK.
VICTOR HERE, SIMON. GOOD JOB, GUYS.
SO MUCH INFORMATION COMING THROUGH ON EVERY SYSTEM. FLASH IS TAKING CARE OF THE U.S. WEST COAST EVACUATION. NO WORD FROM AQUAMAN, WONDER WOMAN OR BATMAN.
CAN YOU AND JESSICA HANDLE HONG KONG?
ALREADY ON OUR WAY. CONSIDER IT HANDLED.
WHAT IF WE CAN'T HANDLE IT?
"HOLDING CITIES TOGETHER? THIS IS GLOBAL, SIMON, AND WE'RE JUST TWO PEOPLE, GREEN LANTERNS OR OTHERWISE."
"HAL CHOSE US, JESS. TRUSTED US. WE DO OUR BEST. WE DO BETTER."
I WAS A FOOTBALL PLAYER BEFORE I WAS CYBORG.
THIS REMINDS ME OF THAT GAME...
...WHEN WE PLAYED NORTH ROCKLAND HIGH, AND I HAD TO RUN RIGHT AT THEIR ALL-STAR LINEBACKER TO SCORE THE GAME-WINNER.
LET'S HOPE THIS TURNS OUT AS WELL AS THAT DID...

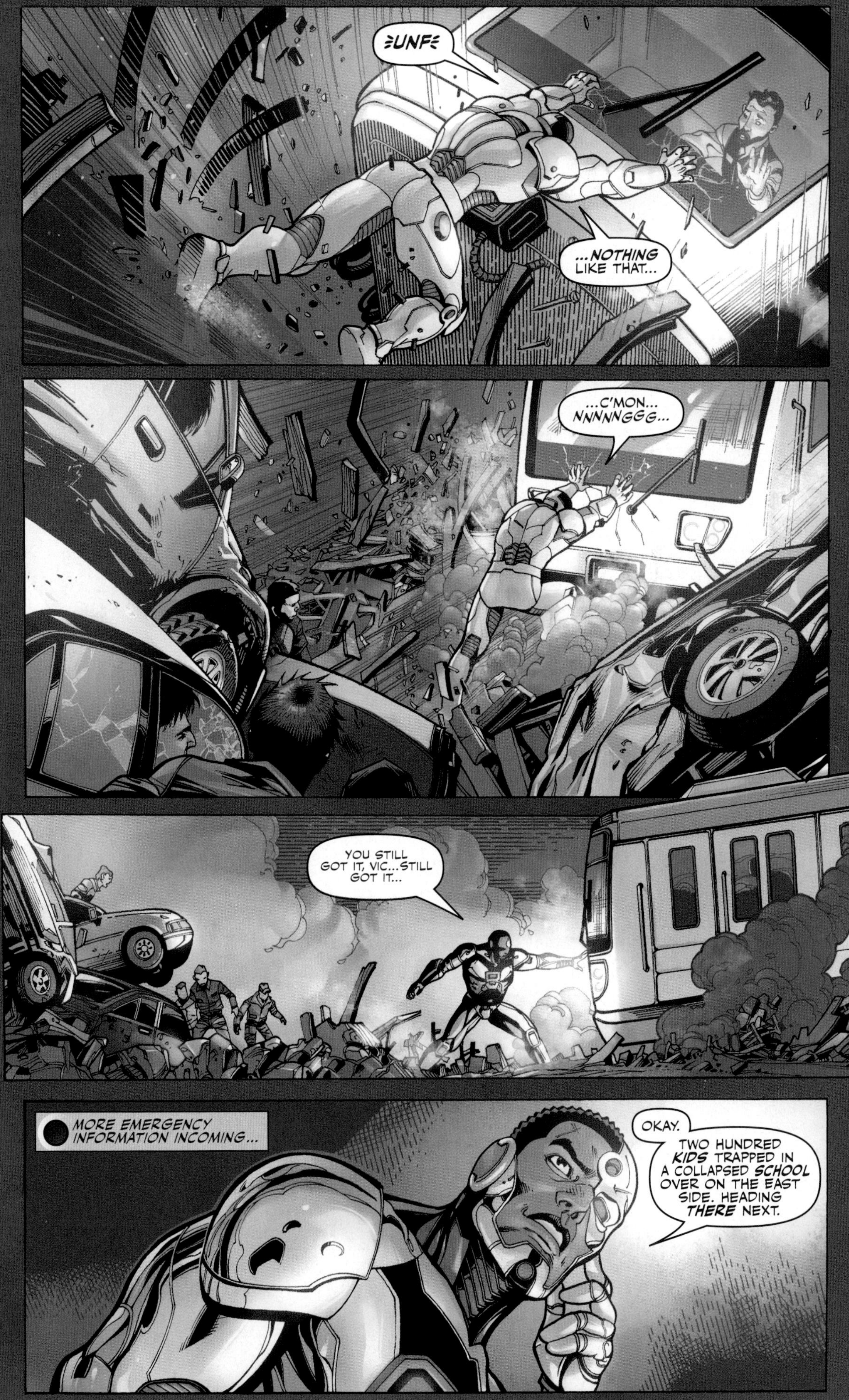
UNF
...NOTHING LIKE THAT...
...C'MON... NNNNNGGG...
YOU STILL GOT IT, VIC...STILL GOT IT...
MORE EMERGENCY INFORMATION INCOMING...
OKAY.
TWO HUNDRED KIDS TRAPPED IN A COLLAPSED SCHOOL OVER ON THE EAST SIDE. HEADING THERE NEXT.

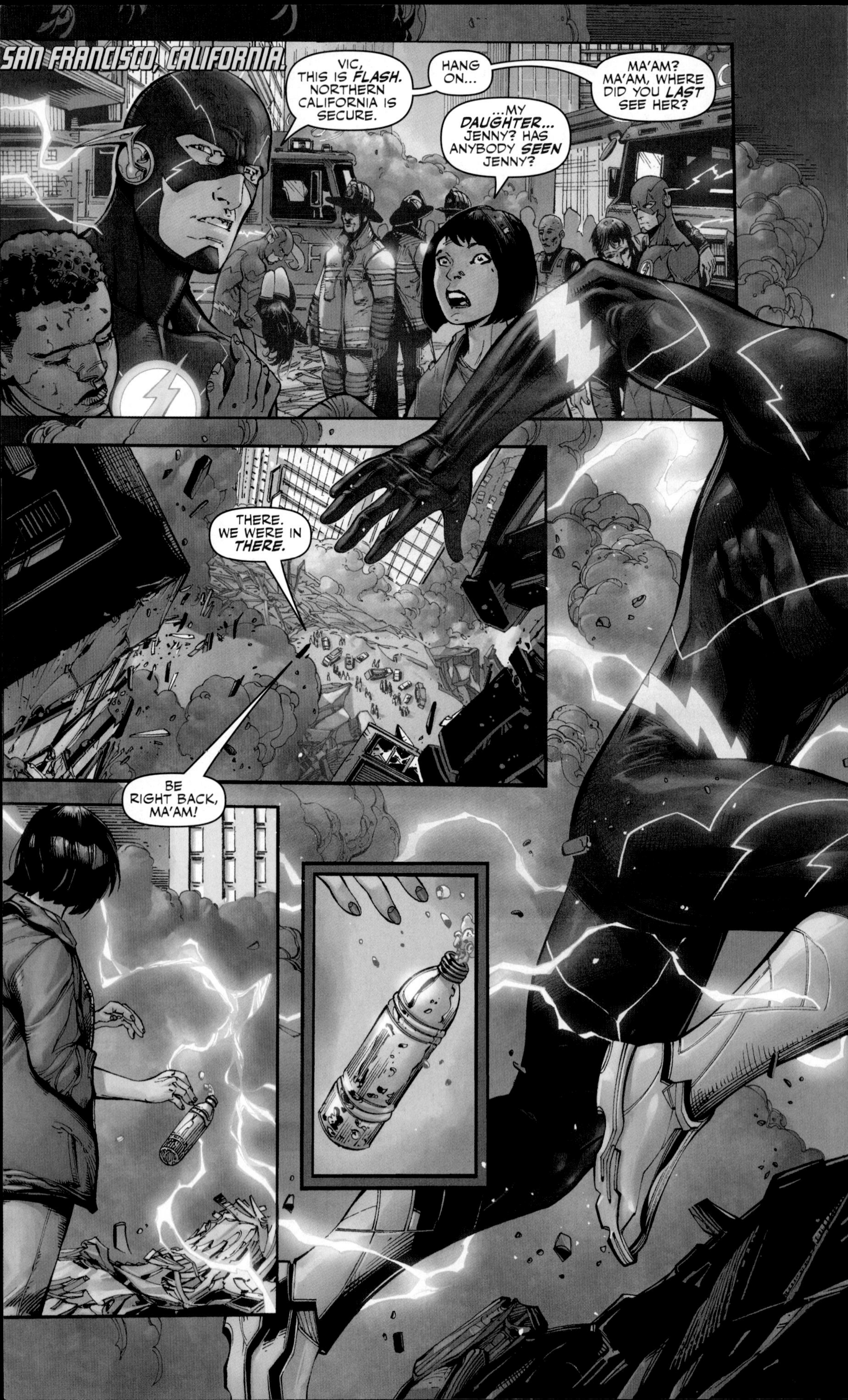
SAN FRANCISCO, CALIFORNIA.
VIC, THIS IS FLASH. NORTHERN CALIFORNIA IS SECURE.
HANG ON...
...MY DAUGHTER... JENNY? HAS ANYBODY SEEN JENNY?
MA'AM? MA'AM, WHERE DID YOU LAST SEE HER?
THERE. WE WERE IN THERE.
BE RIGHT BACK, MA'AM!

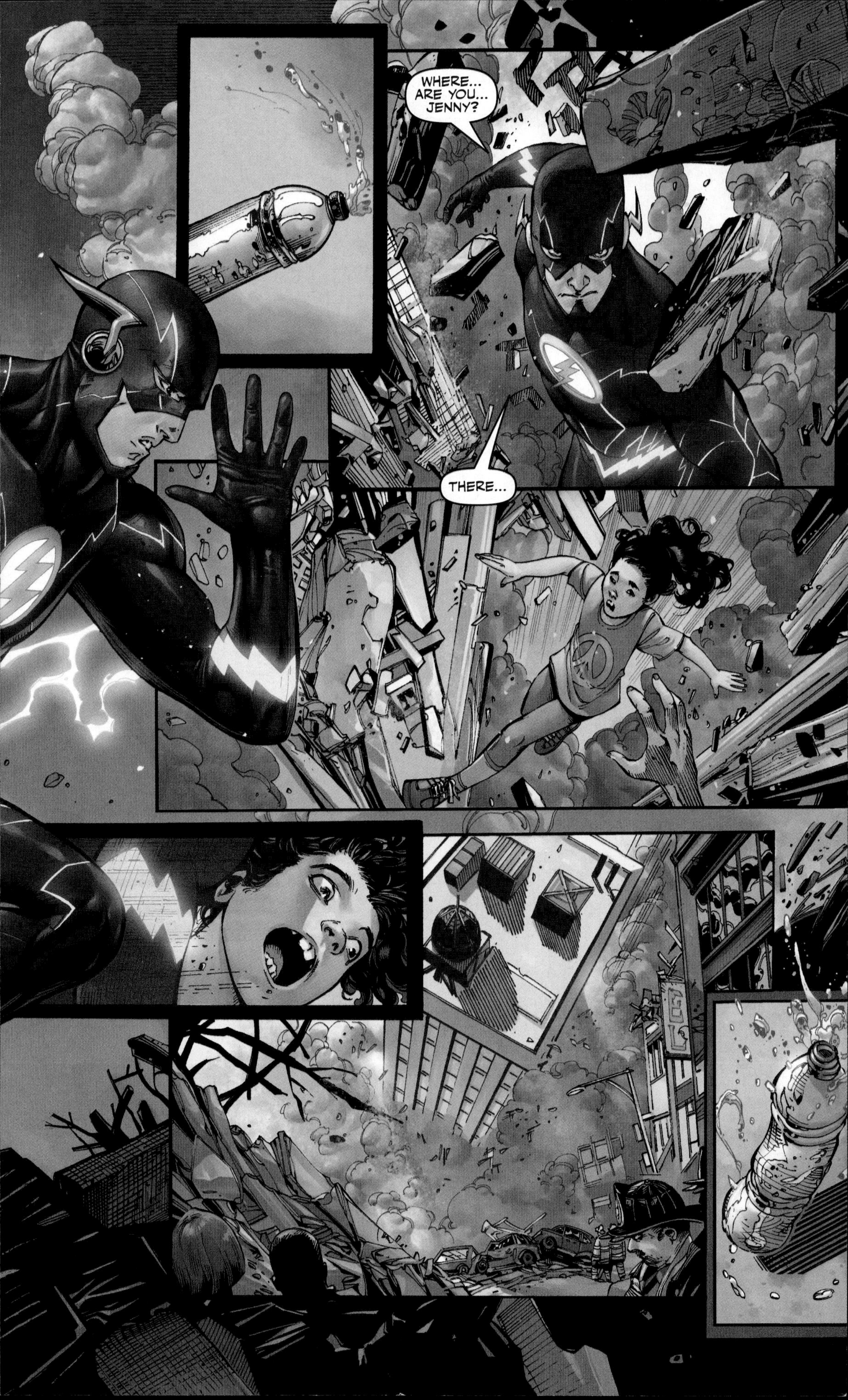
WHERE... ARE YOU... JENNY?
THERE...

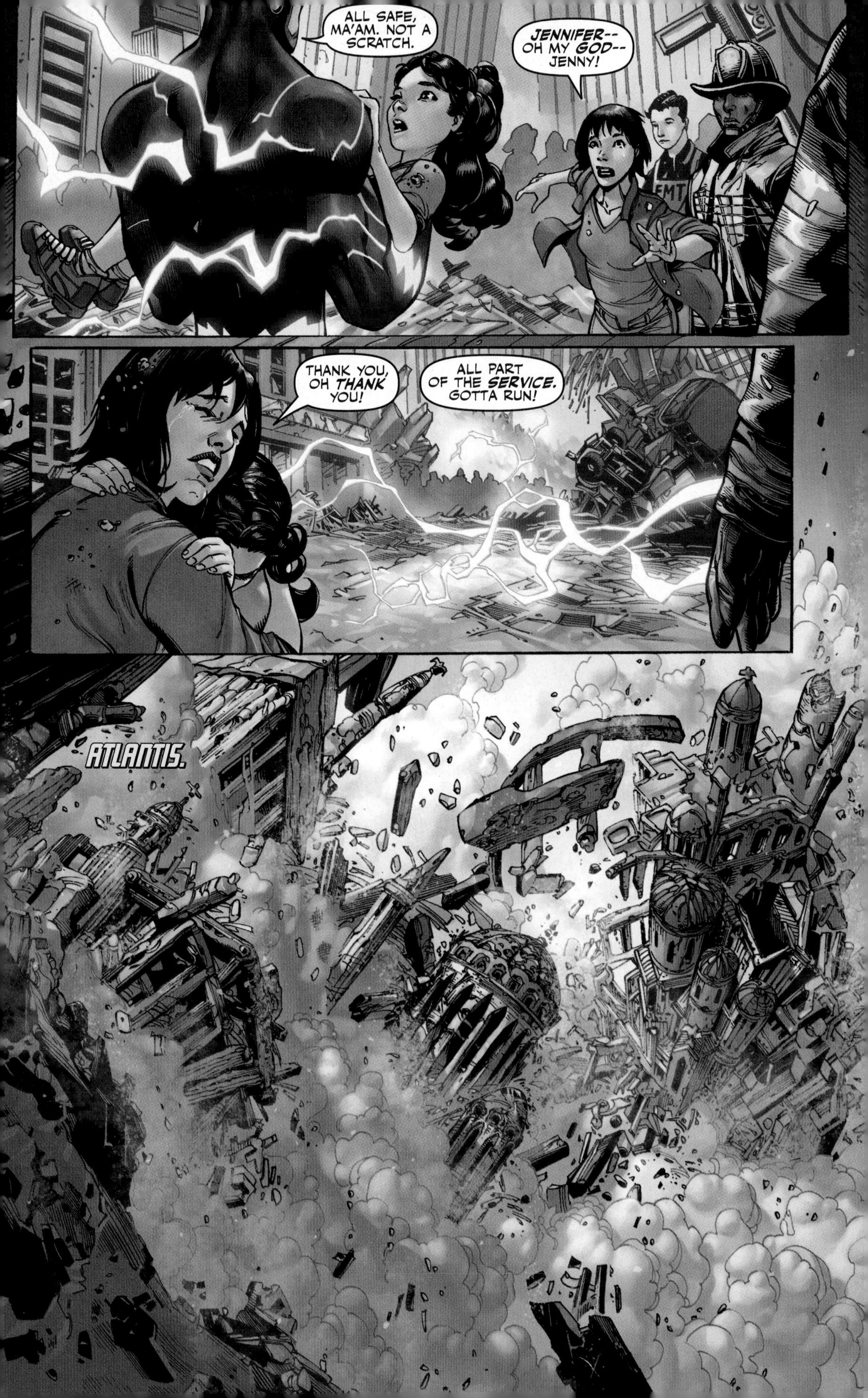
ALL SAFE, MA'AM. NOT A SCRATCH.
JENNIFER-- OH MY GOD-- JENNY!
EMT
THANK YOU, OH THANK YOU!
ALL PART OF THE SERVICE. GOTTA RUN!
ATLANTIS.

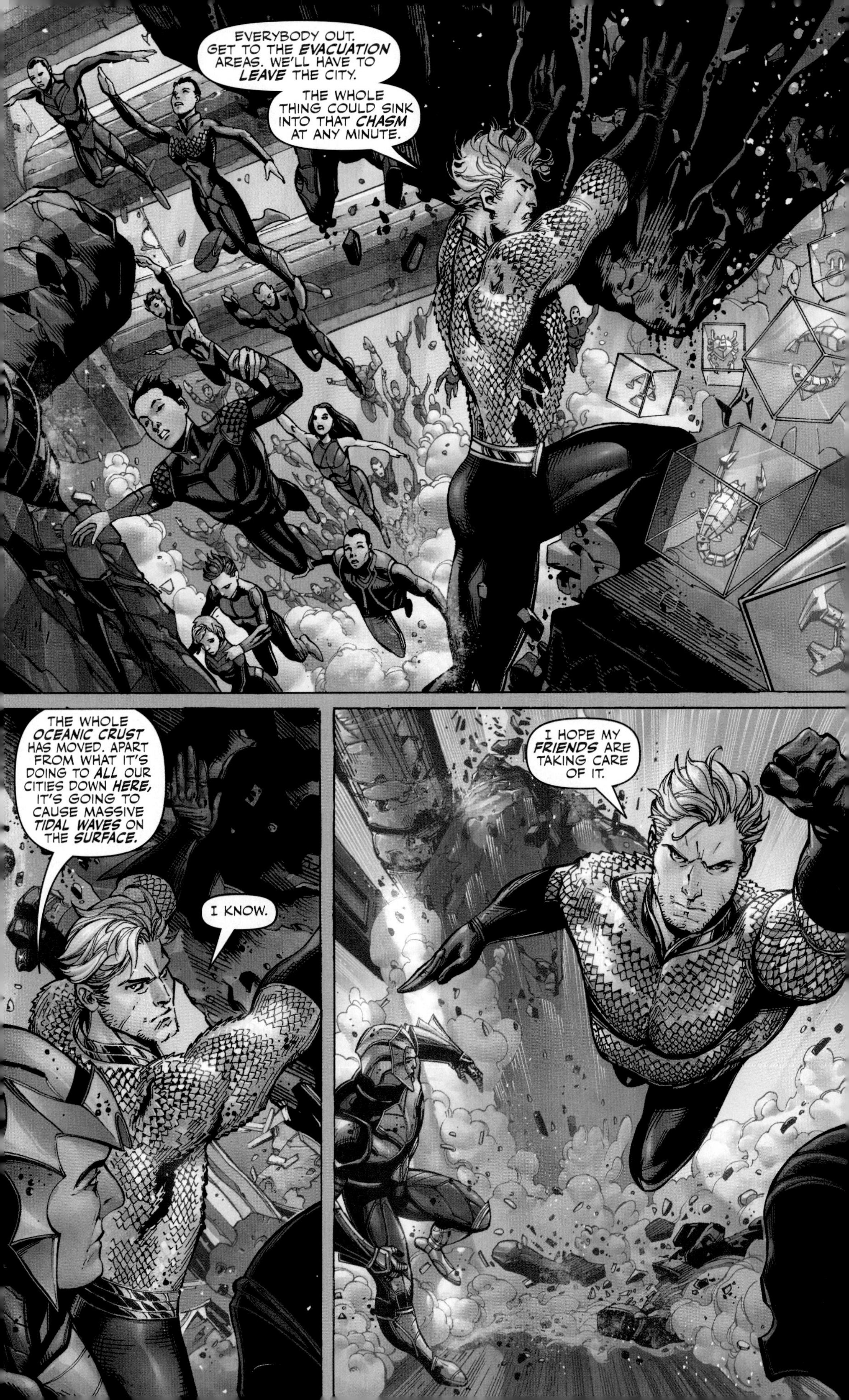
EVERYBODY OUT. GET TO THE EVACUATION AREAS. WE'LL HAVE TO LEAVE THE CITY.
THE WHOLE THING COULD SINK INTO THAT CHASM AT ANY MINUTE.
THE WHOLE OCEANIC CRUST HAS MOVED. APART FROM WHAT IT'S DOING TO ALL OUR CITIES DOWN HERE, IT'S GOING TO CAUSE MASSIVE TIDAL WAVES ON THE SURFACE.
I KNOW.
I HOPE MY FRIENDS ARE TAKING CARE OF IT.

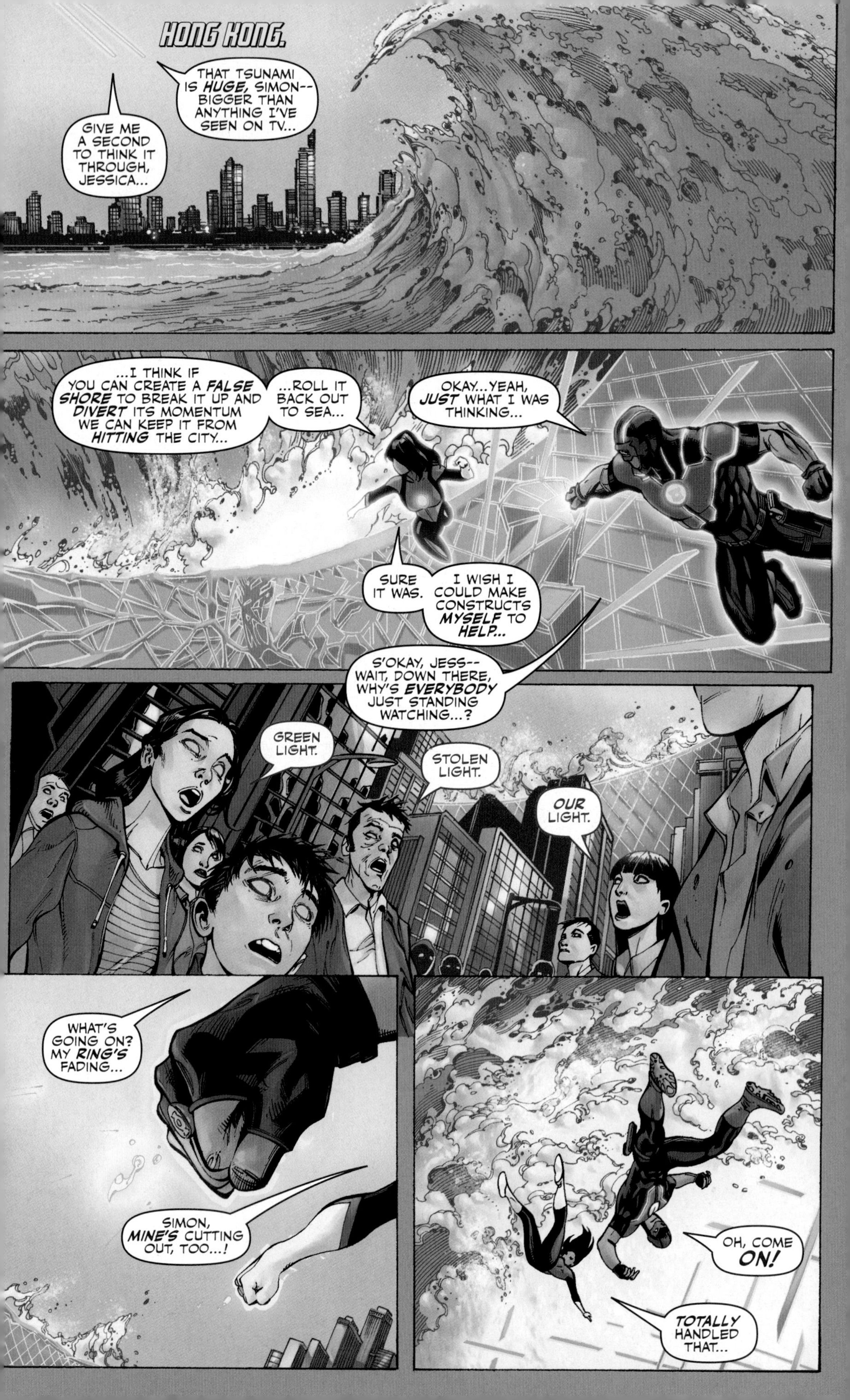
HONG KONG.
THAT TSUNAMI IS HUGE, SIMON-- BIGGER THAN ANYTHING I'VE SEEN ON TV...
GIVE ME A SECOND TO THINK IT THROUGH, JESSICA...
...I THINK IF YOU CAN CREATE A FALSE SHORE TO BREAK IT UP AND DIVERT ITS MOMENTUM WE CAN KEEP IT FROM HITTING THE CITY...
...ROLL IT BACK OUT TO SEA...
OKAY...YEAH, JUST WHAT I WAS THINKING...
SURE IT WAS.
I WISH I COULD MAKE CONSTRUCTS MYSELF TO HELP...
S'OKAY, JESS-- WAIT, DOWN THERE, WHY'S EVERYBODY JUST STANDING WATCHING...?
GREEN LIGHT.
STOLEN LIGHT.
OUR LIGHT.
WHAT'S GOING ON? MY RING'S FADING...
SIMON, MINE'S CUTTING OUT, TOO...!
OH, COME ON!
TOTALLY HANDLED THAT...

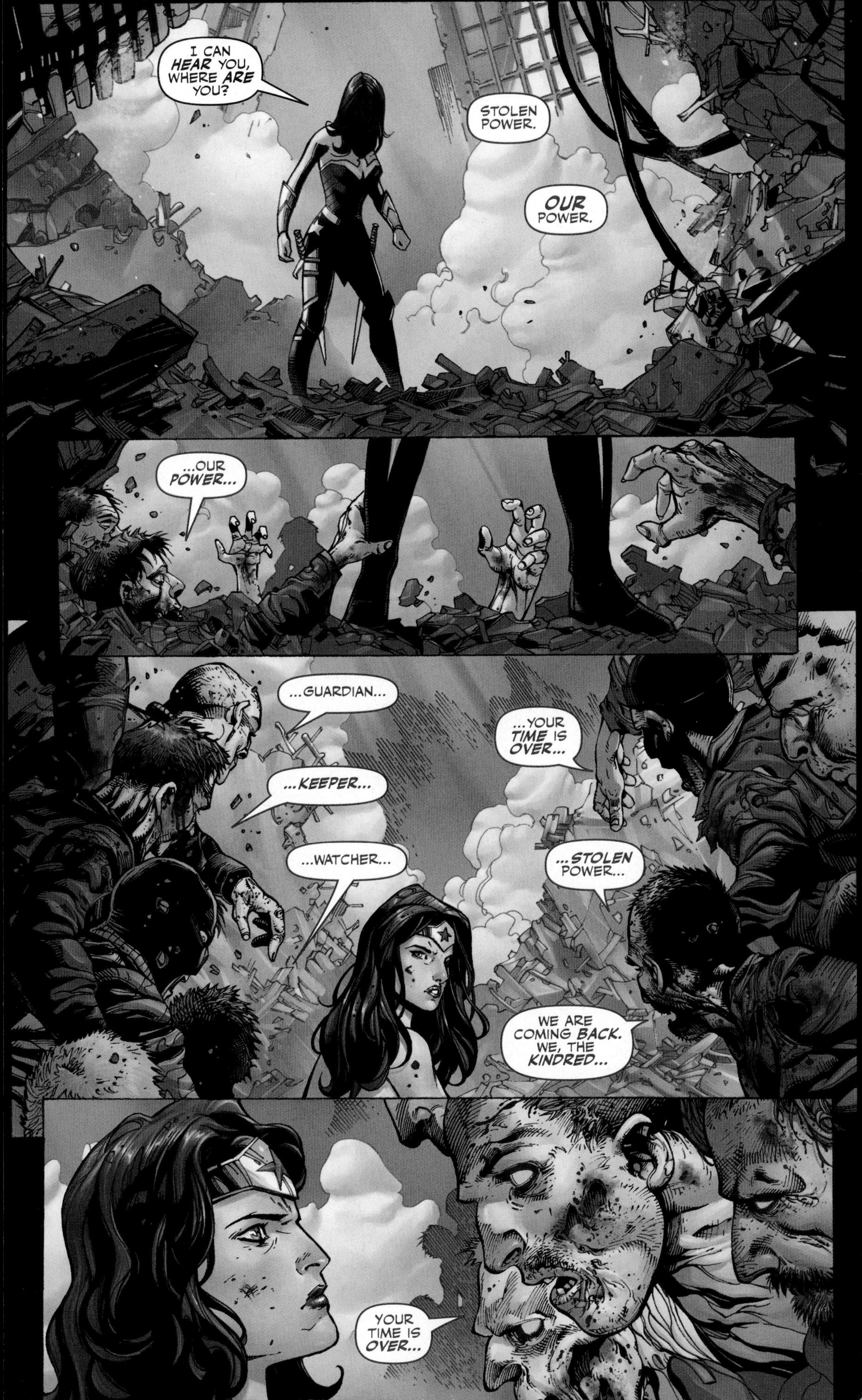
I CAN HEAR YOU, WHERE ARE YOU?
STOLEN POWER.
OUR POWER.
...OUR POWER...
...GUARDIAN...
...KEEPER...
...WATCHER...
...YOUR TIME IS OVER...
...STOLEN POWER...
WE ARE COMING BACK. WE, THE KINDRED...
YOUR TIME IS OVER...

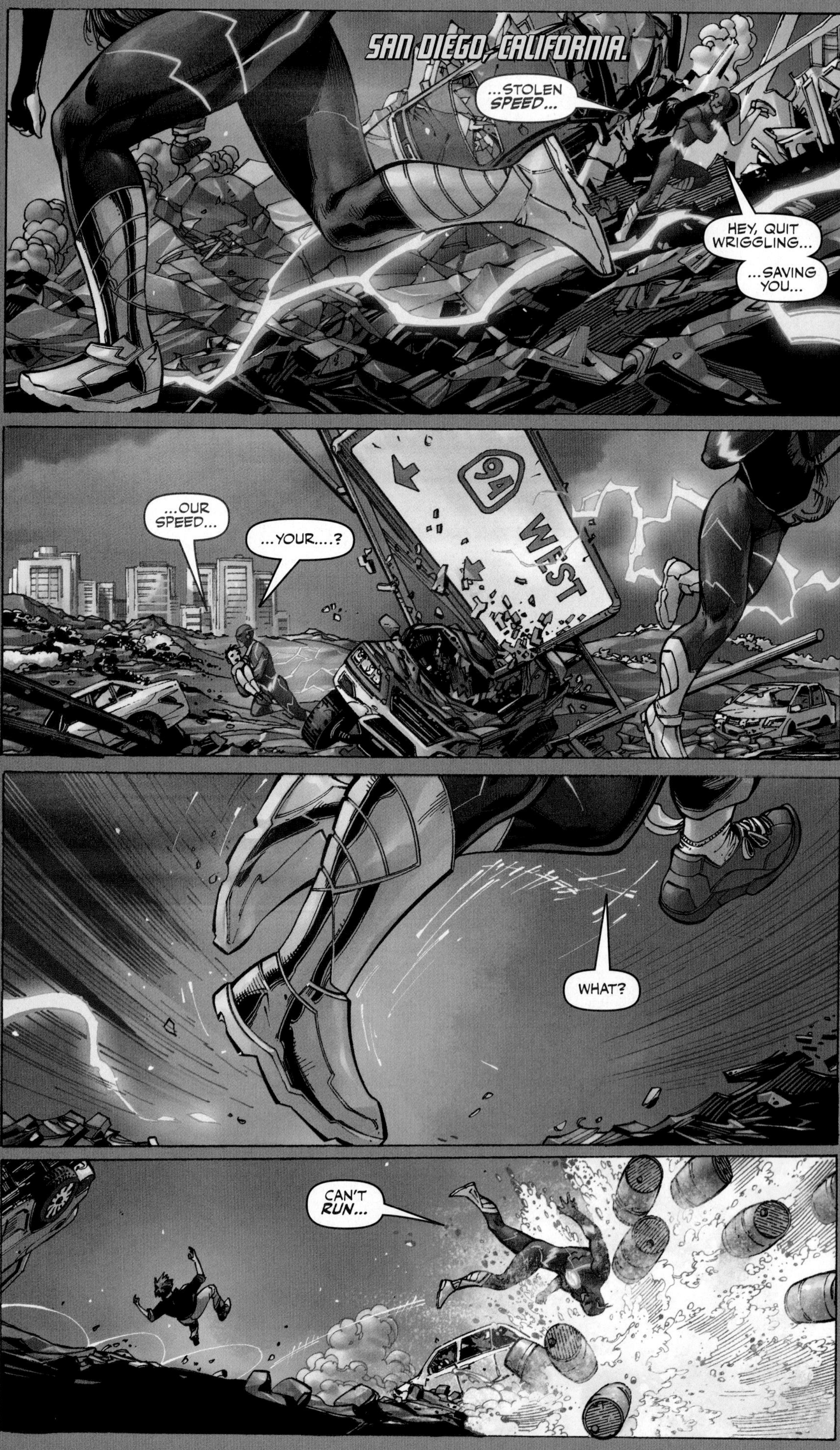
SAN DIEGO, CALIFORNIA.
...STOLEN SPEED...
HEY, QUIT WRIGGLING...
...SAVING YOU...
...OUR SPEED...
...YOUR....?
94
WEST
WHAT?
CAN'T RUN...

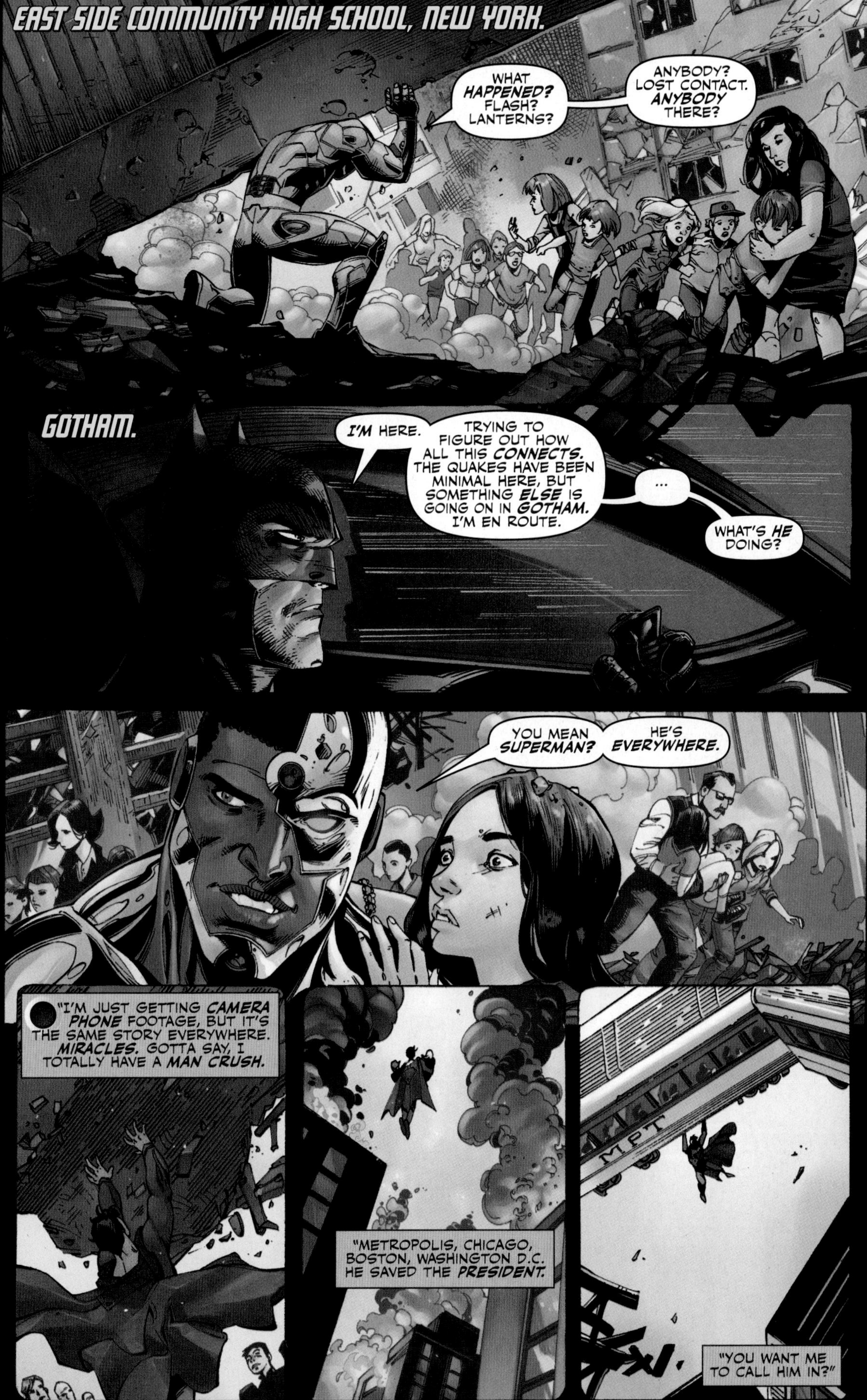
EAST SIDE COMMUNITY HIGH SCHOOL, NEW YORK.
WHAT HAPPENED? FLASH? LANTERNS?
ANYBODY? LOST CONTACT. ANYBODY THERE?
GOTHAM.
I'M HERE.
TRYING TO FIGURE OUT HOW ALL THIS CONNECTS. THE QUAKES HAVE BEEN MINIMAL HERE, BUT SOMETHING ELSE IS GOING ON IN GOTHAM. I'M EN ROUTE.
...
WHAT'S HE DOING?
YOU MEAN SUPERMAN?
HE'S EVERYWHERE.
"I'M JUST GETTING CAMERA PHONE FOOTAGE, BUT IT'S THE SAME STORY EVERYWHERE. MIRACLES. GOTTA SAY, I TOTALLY HAVE A MAN CRUSH.
MPT
"METROPOLIS, CHICAGO, BOSTON, WASHINGTON D.C. HE SAVED THE PRESIDENT.
"YOU WANT ME TO CALL HIM IN?"

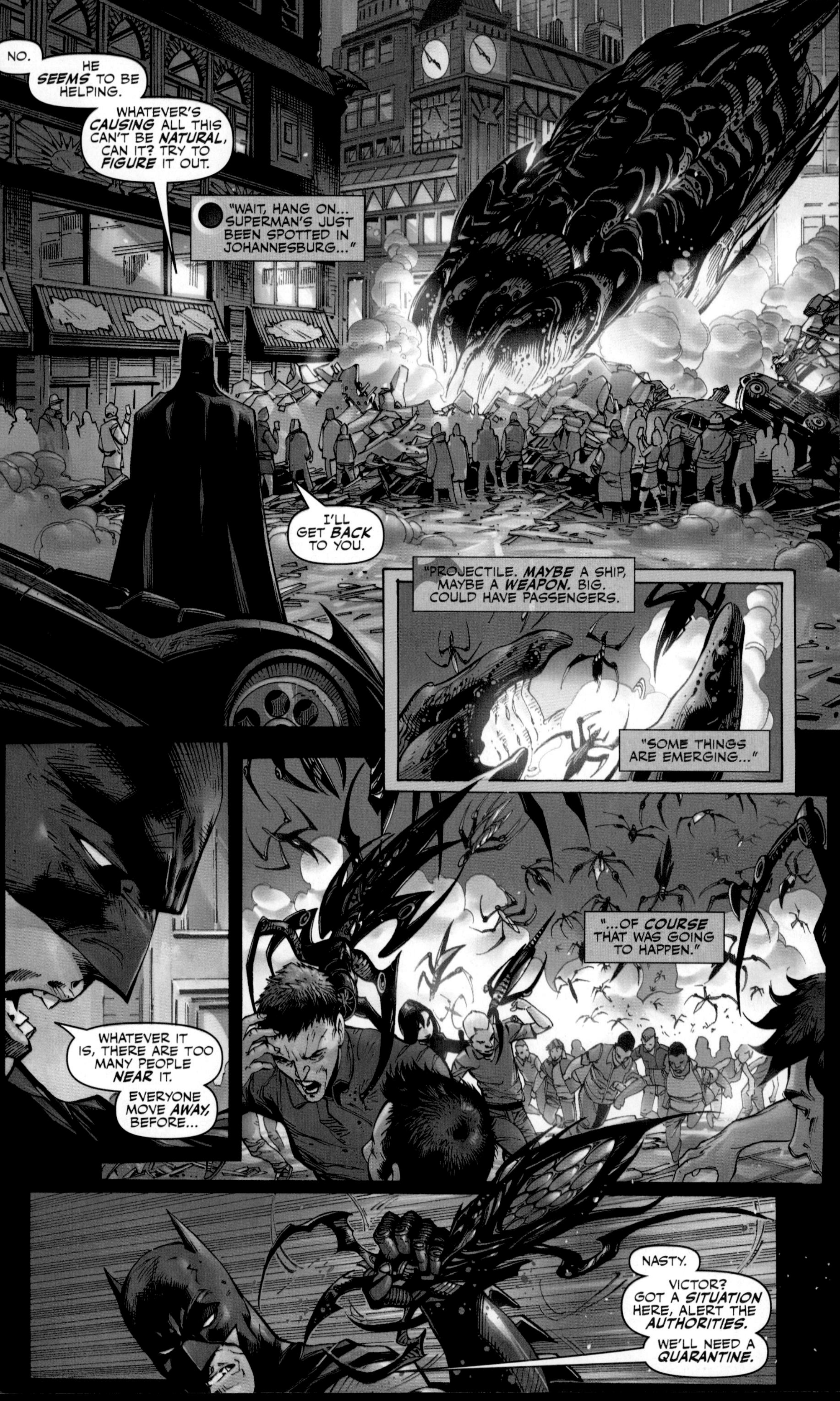
NO.
HE SEEMS TO BE HELPING.
WHATEVER'S CAUSING ALL THIS CAN'T BE NATURAL, CAN IT? TRY TO FIGURE IT OUT.
"WAIT, HANG ON... SUPERMAN'S JUST BEEN SPOTTED IN JOHANNESBURG..."
I'LL GET BACK TO YOU.
"PROJECTILE. MAYBE A SHIP, MAYBE A WEAPON. BIG. COULD HAVE PASSENGERS.
"SOME THINGS ARE EMERGING..."
WHATEVER IT IS, THERE ARE TOO MANY PEOPLE NEAR IT.
EVERYONE MOVE AWAY, BEFORE...
"...OF COURSE THAT WAS GOING TO HAPPEN."
NASTY.
VICTOR? GOT A SITUATION HERE, ALERT THE AUTHORITIES.
WE'LL NEED A QUARANTINE.

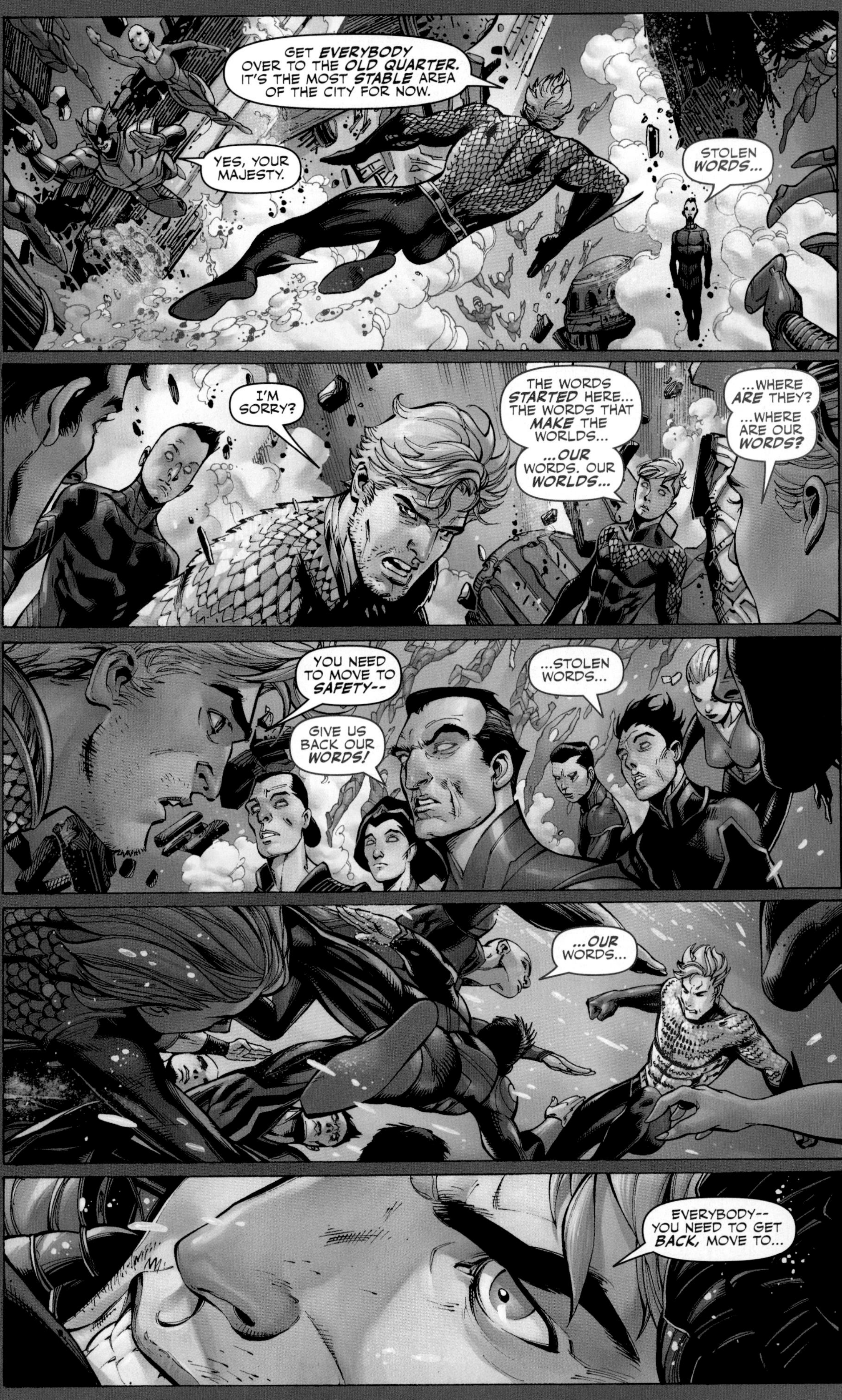
GET EVERYBODY OVER TO THE OLD QUARTER. IT'S THE MOST STABLE AREA OF THE CITY FOR NOW.
YES, YOUR MAJESTY.
STOLEN WORDS...
I'M SORRY?
THE WORDS STARTED HERE... THE WORDS THAT MAKE THE WORLDS...
...OUR WORDS. OUR WORLDS...
...WHERE ARE THEY?
...WHERE ARE OUR WORDS?
YOU NEED TO MOVE TO SAFETY--
GIVE US BACK OUR WORDS!
...STOLEN WORDS...
...OUR WORDS...
EVERYBODY-- YOU NEED TO GET BACK, MOVE TO...

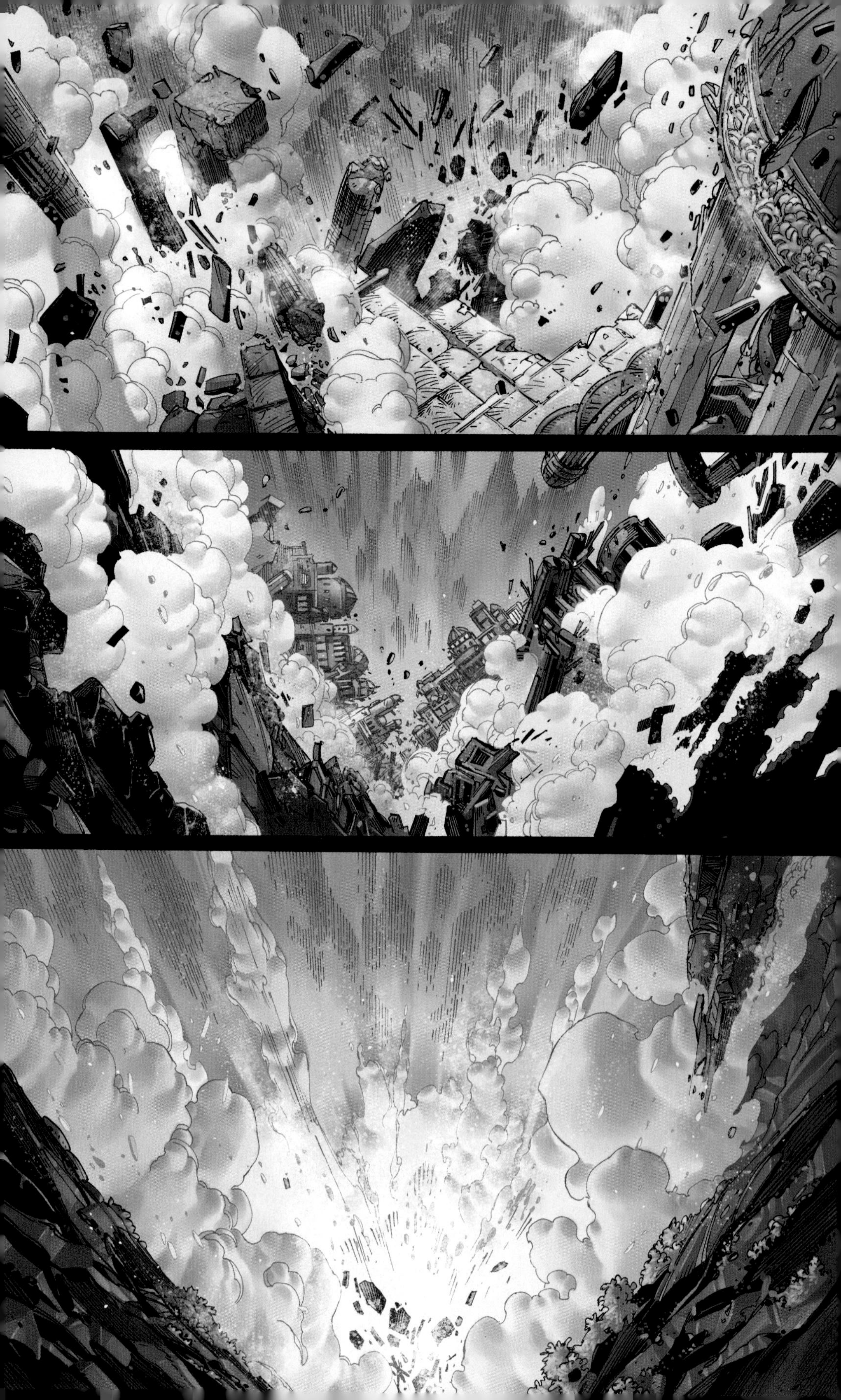

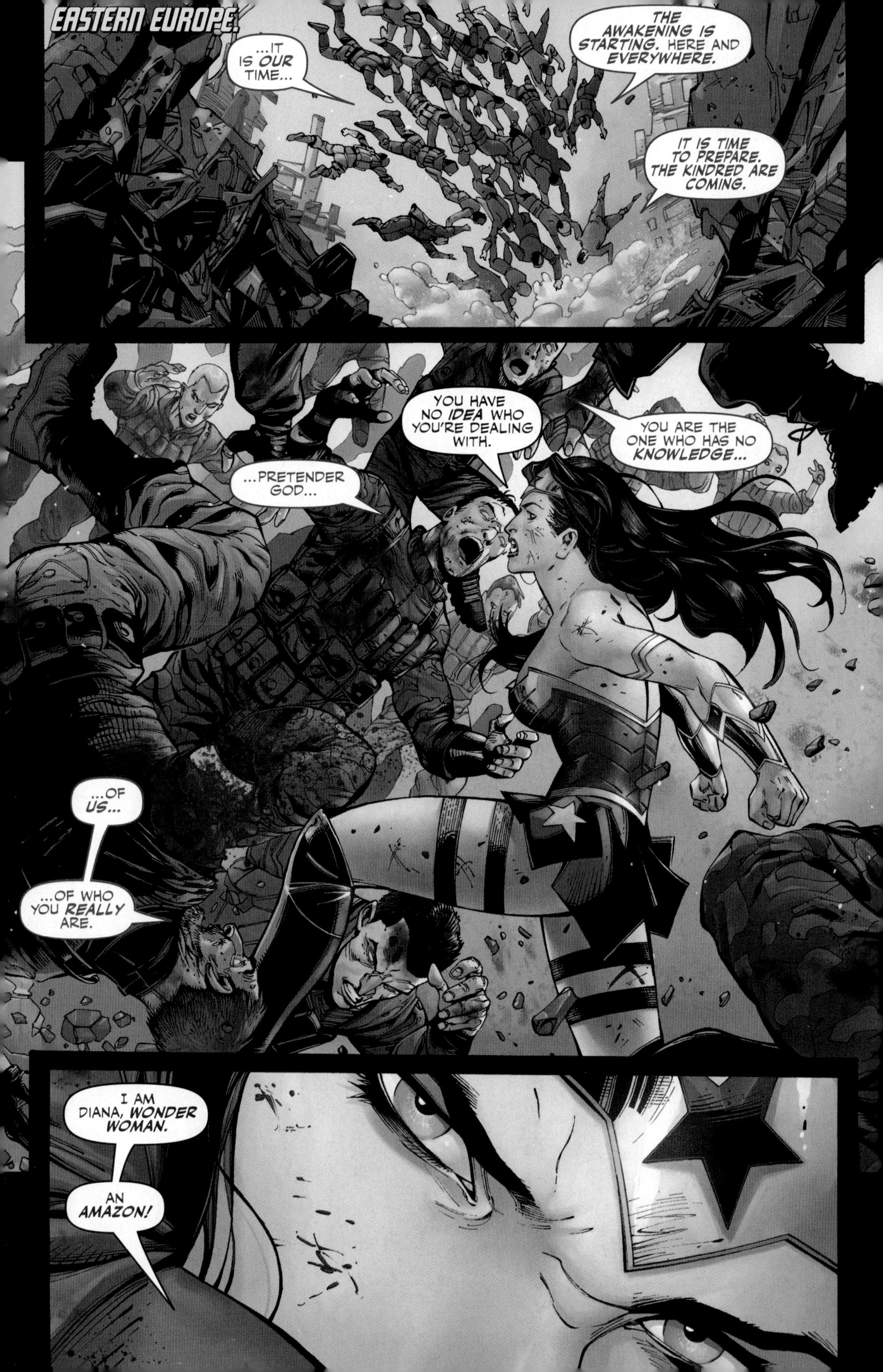
EASTERN EUROPE.
...IT IS OUR TIME...
THE AWAKENING IS STARTING. HERE AND EVERYWHERE.
IT IS TIME TO PREPARE. THE KINDRED ARE COMING.
...PRETENDER GOD...
YOU HAVE NO IDEA WHO YOU'RE DEALING WITH.
YOU ARE THE ONE WHO HAS NO KNOWLEDGE...
...OF US...
...OF WHO YOU REALLY ARE.
I AM DIANA, WONDER WOMAN.
AN AMAZON!

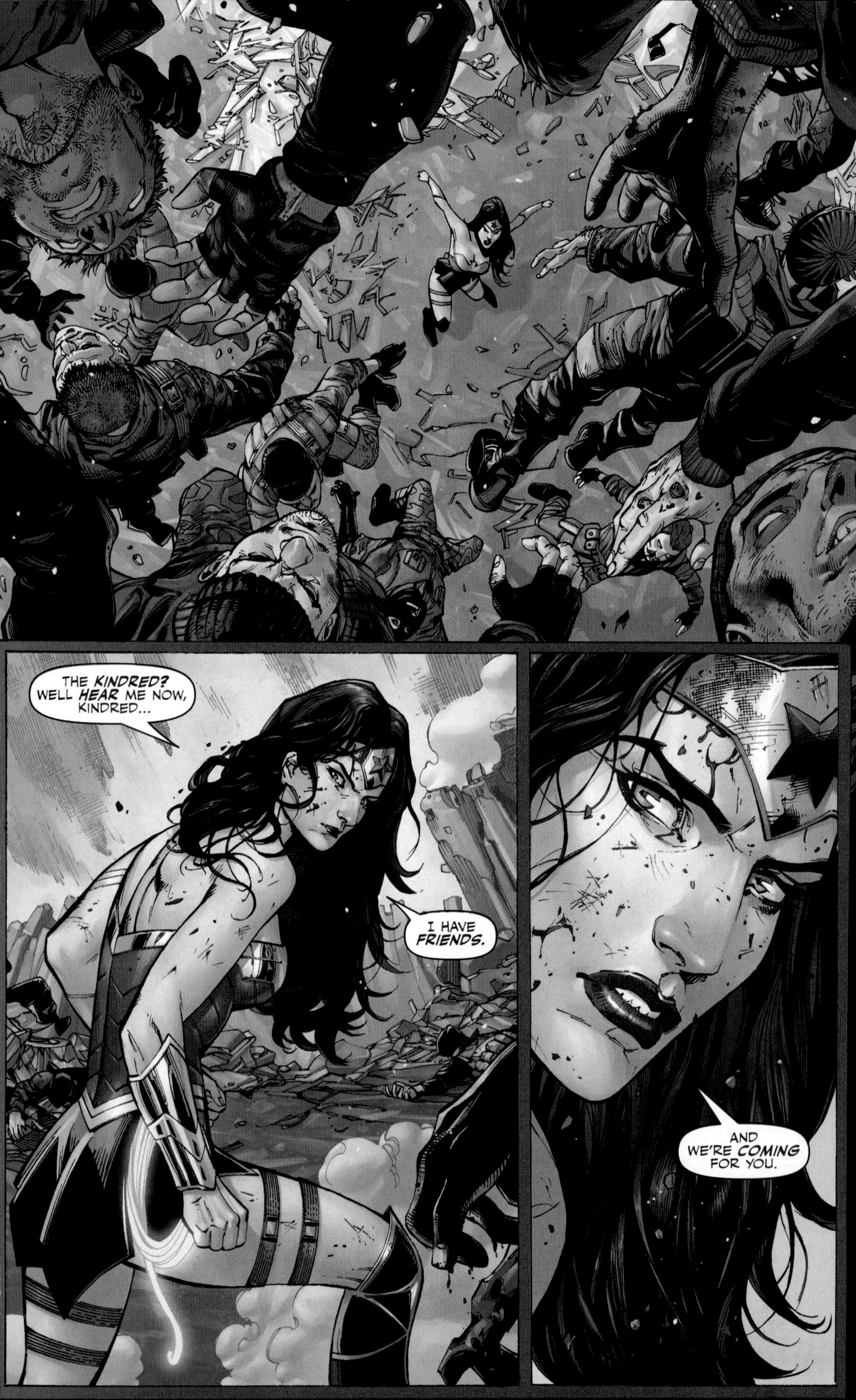
THE KINDRED? WELL HEAR ME NOW, KINDRED...
I HAVE FRIENDS.
AND WE'RE COMING FOR YOU.

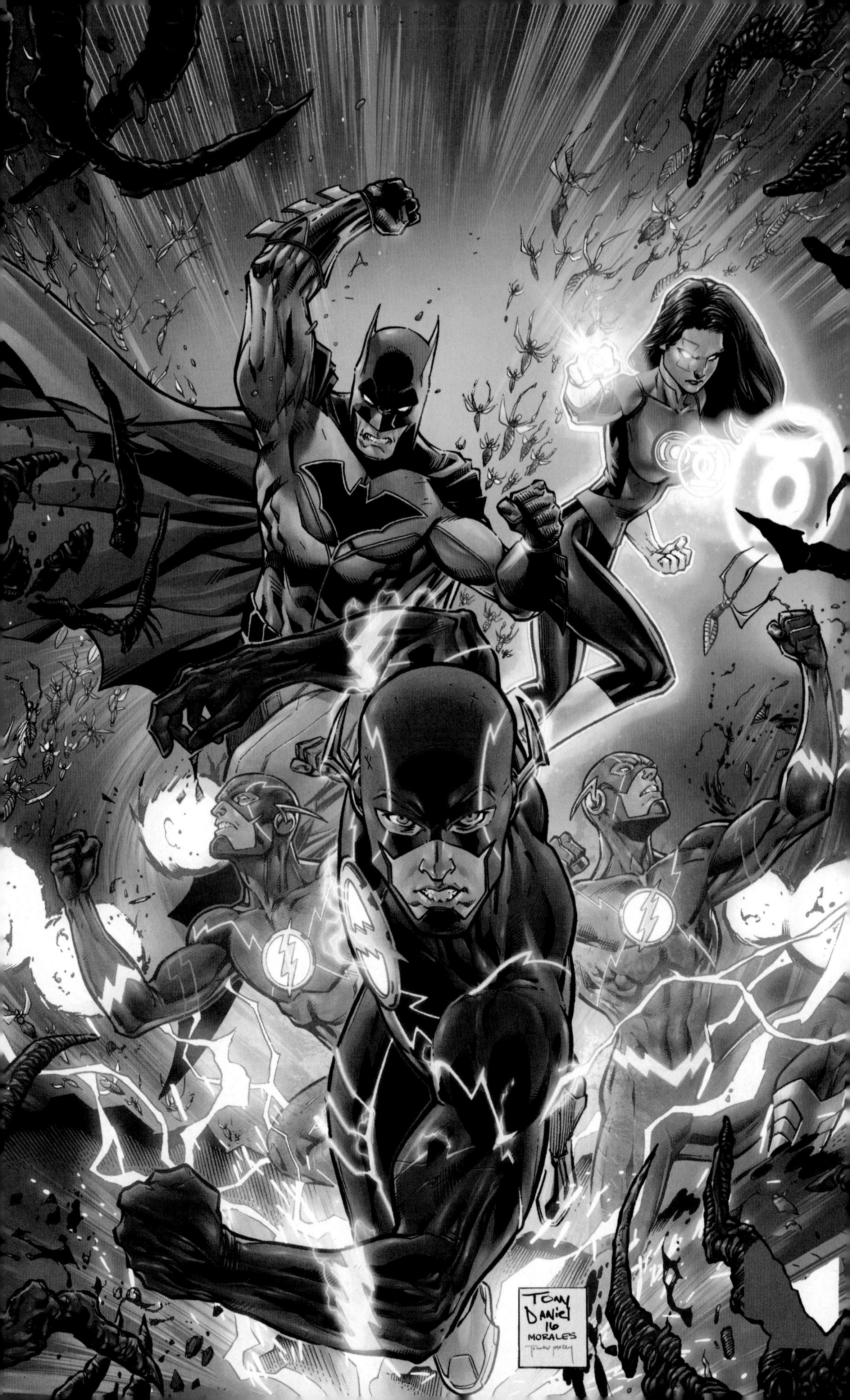

TONY DANIEL 16
MORALES

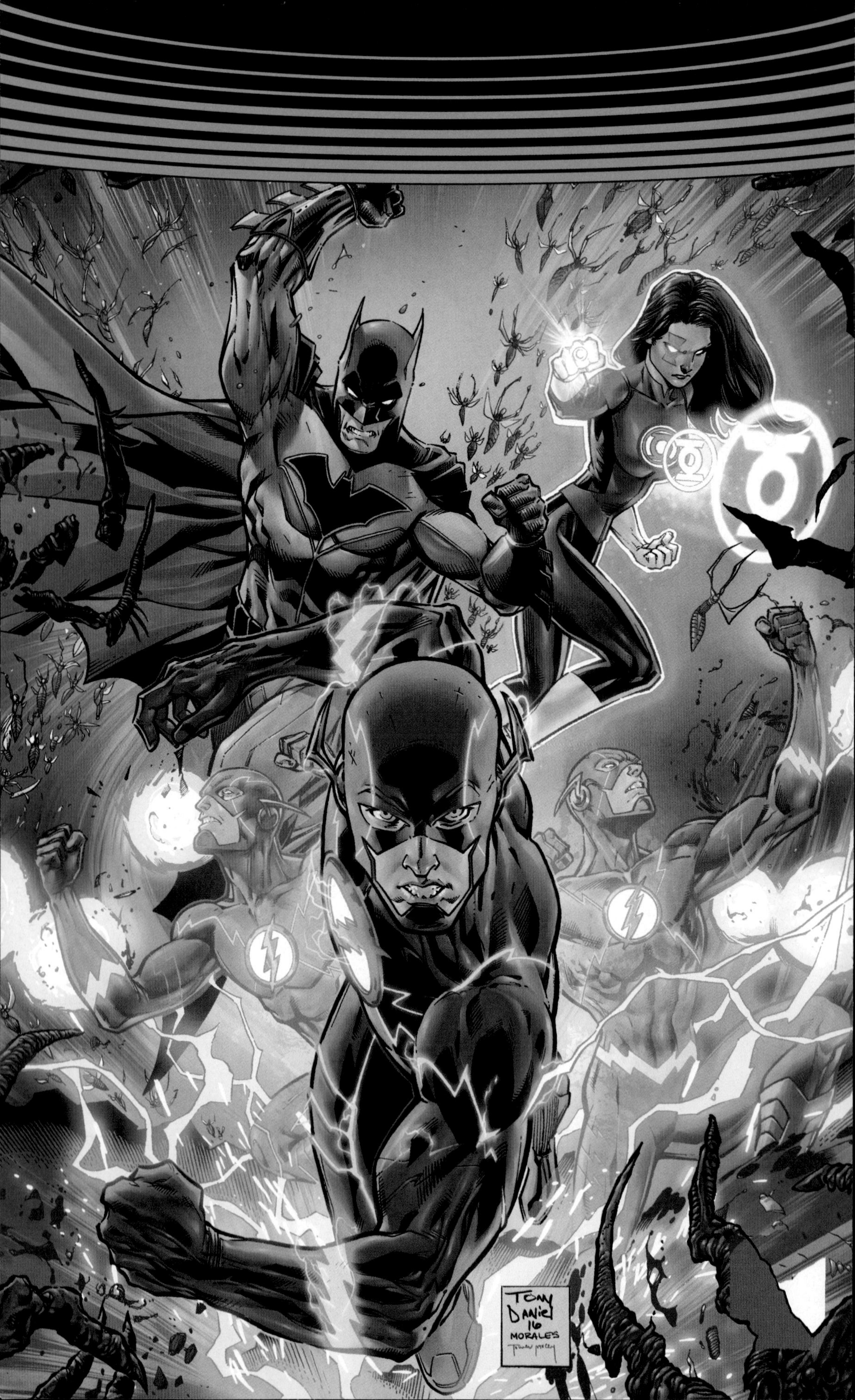
TONY DANIEL 16
MORALES

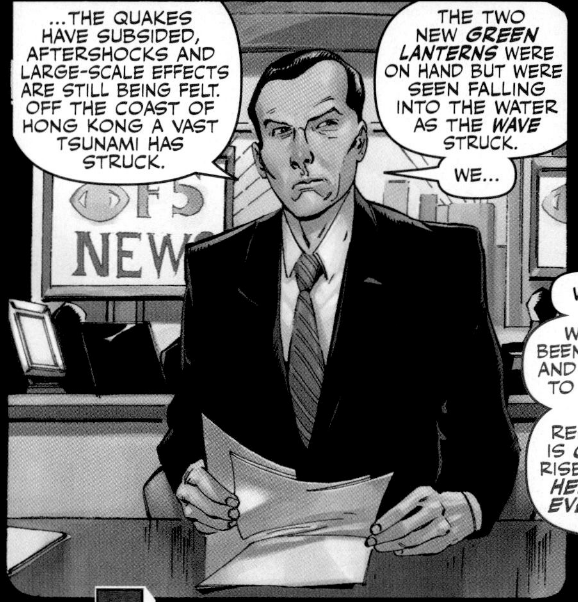
...THE QUAKES HAVE SUBSIDED, AFTERSHOCKS AND LARGE-SCALE EFFECTS ARE STILL BEING FELT. OFF THE COAST OF HONG KONG A VAST TSUNAMI HAS STRUCK.
THE TWO NEW GREEN LANTERNS WERE ON HAND BUT WERE SEEN FALLING INTO THE WATER AS THE WAVE STRUCK.
WE...
FS NEWS

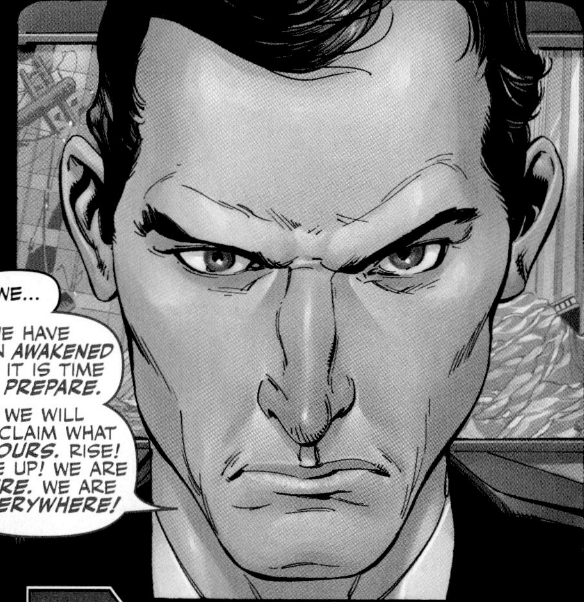
WE...
WE HAVE BEEN AWAKENED AND IT IS TIME TO PREPARE.
WE WILL RECLAIM WHAT IS OURS. RISE! RISE UP! WE ARE HERE. WE ARE EVERYWHERE!

# THE EXTINCTION MACHINES PART TWO

WRITTEN by BRYAN HITCH PENCILLED by TONY S. DANIEL INKED by SANDU FLOREA

COLORED by TOMEU MOREY
LETTERED by RICHARD STARKINGS & COMICRAFT
COVER by TONY S. DANIEL, MARK MORALES & TOMEU MOREY
VARIANT COVER by YANICK PAQUETTE & NATHAN FAIRBAIRN
ASSISTS by AMEDEO TURTURRO
EDITS by CUNNINGHAM

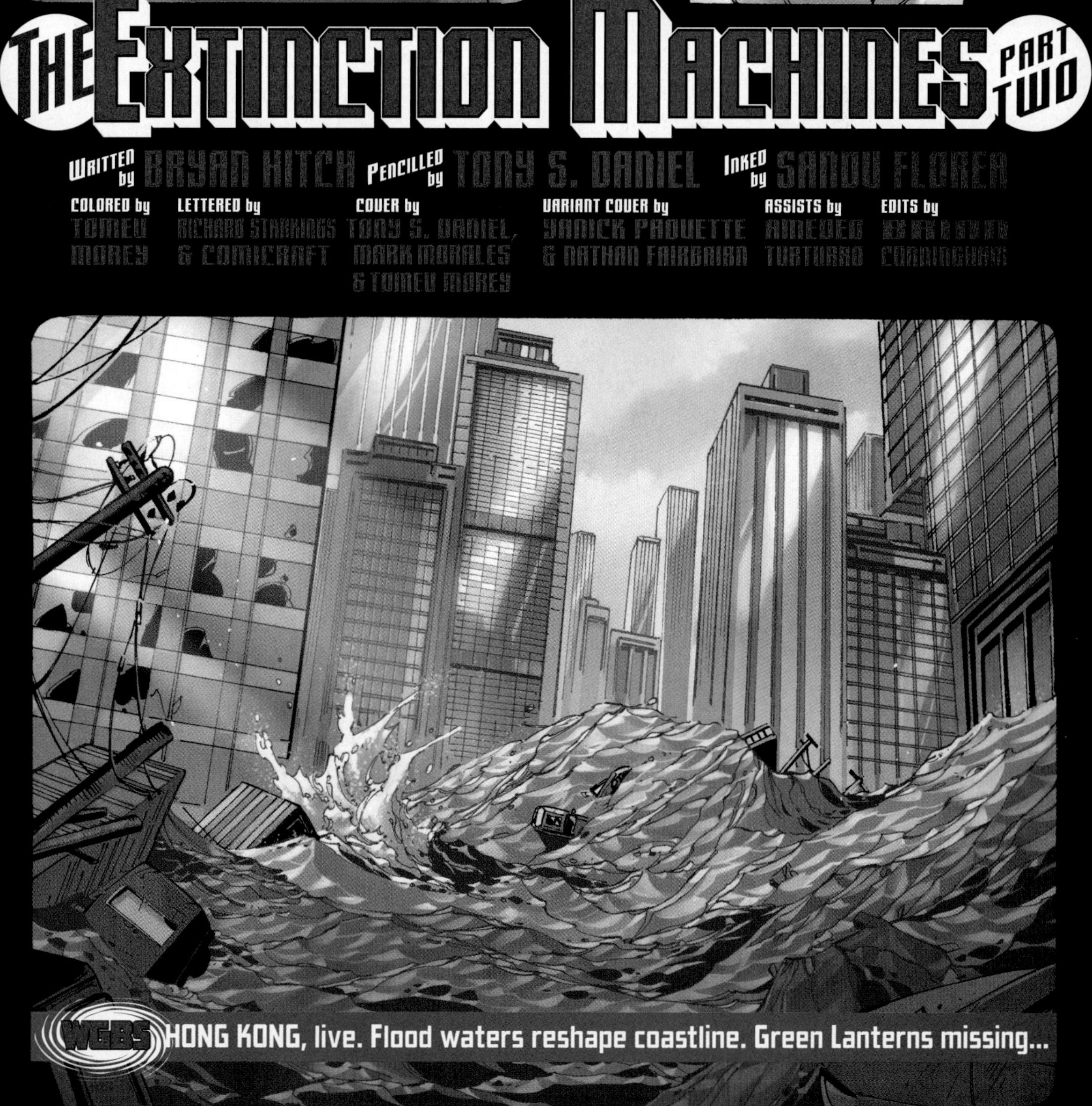
WGBS HONG KONG, live. Flood waters reshape coastline. Green Lanterns missing...

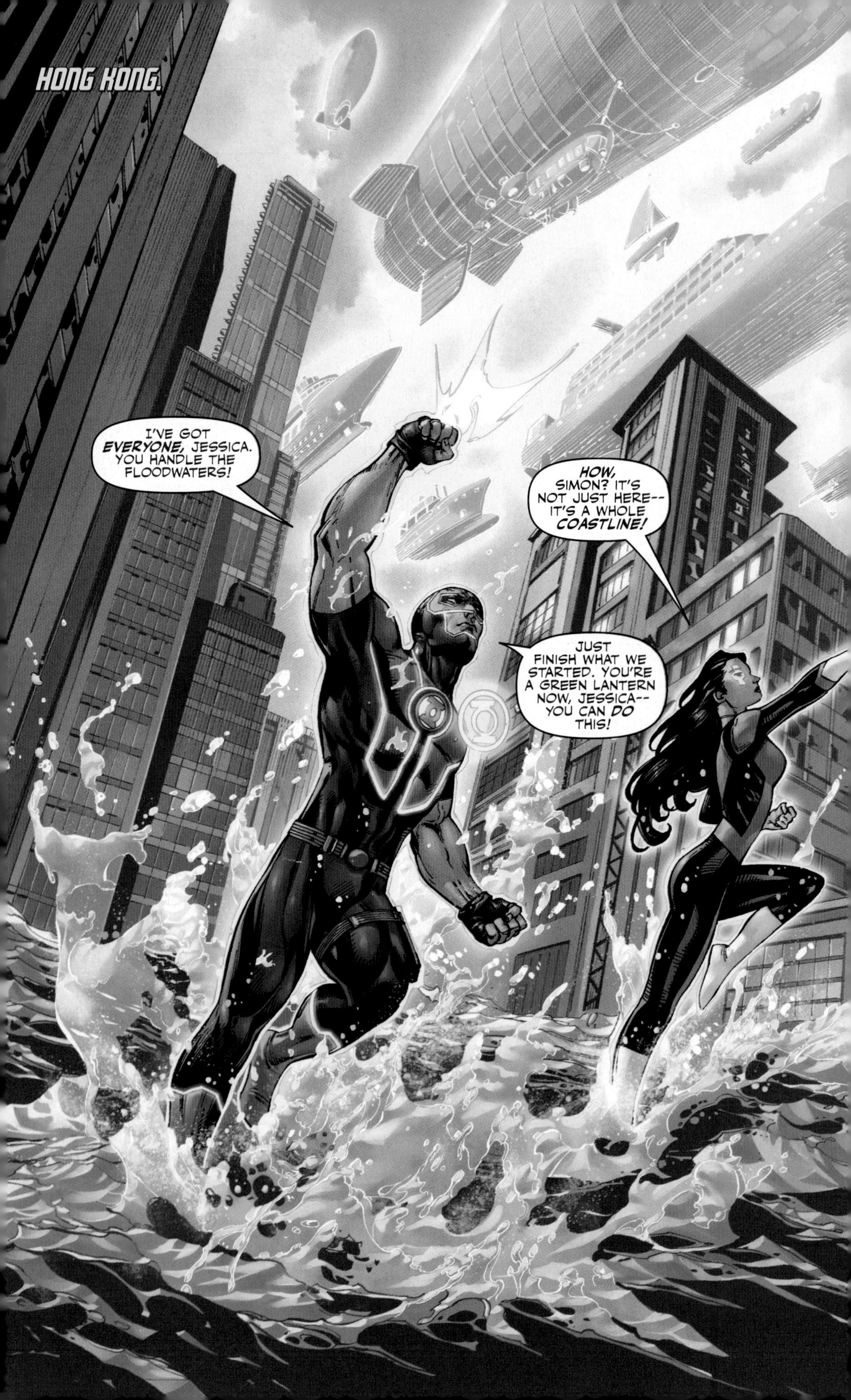
HONG KONG.
I'VE GOT EVERYONE, JESSICA. YOU HANDLE THE FLOODWATERS!
HOW, SIMON? IT'S NOT JUST HERE-- IT'S A WHOLE COASTLINE!
JUST FINISH WHAT WE STARTED. YOU'RE A GREEN LANTERN NOW, JESSICA-- YOU CAN DO THIS!

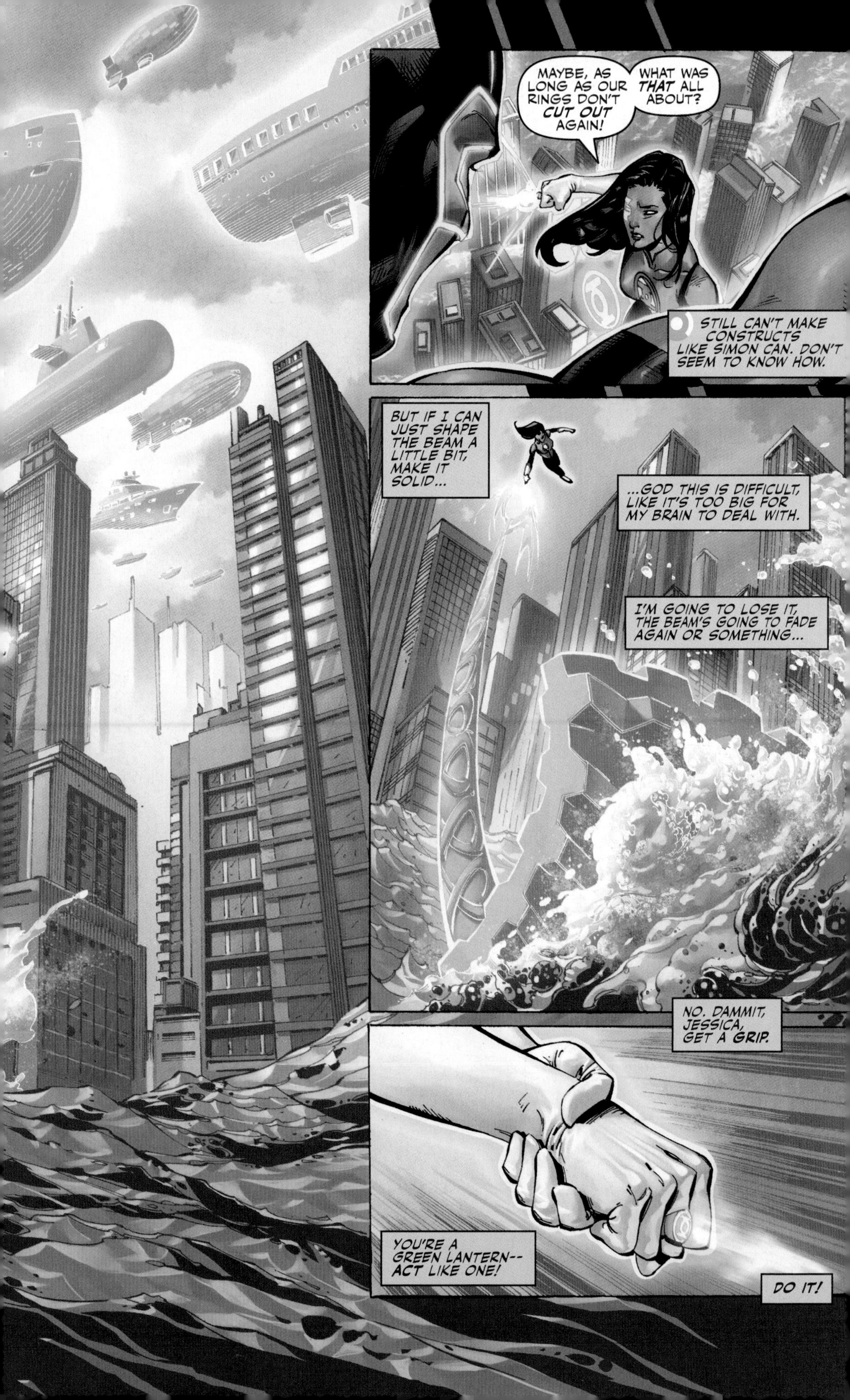
MAYBE, AS LONG AS OUR RINGS DON'T CUT OUT AGAIN!
WHAT WAS THAT ALL ABOUT?
STILL CAN'T MAKE CONSTRUCTS LIKE SIMON CAN. DON'T SEEM TO KNOW HOW.
BUT IF I CAN JUST SHAPE THE BEAM A LITTLE BIT, MAKE IT SOLID...
...GOD THIS IS DIFFICULT, LIKE IT'S TOO BIG FOR MY BRAIN TO DEAL WITH.
I'M GOING TO LOSE IT, THE BEAM'S GOING TO FADE AGAIN OR SOMETHING...
NO. DAMMIT, JESSICA, GET A GRIP.
YOU'RE A GREEN LANTERN-- ACT LIKE ONE!
DO IT!

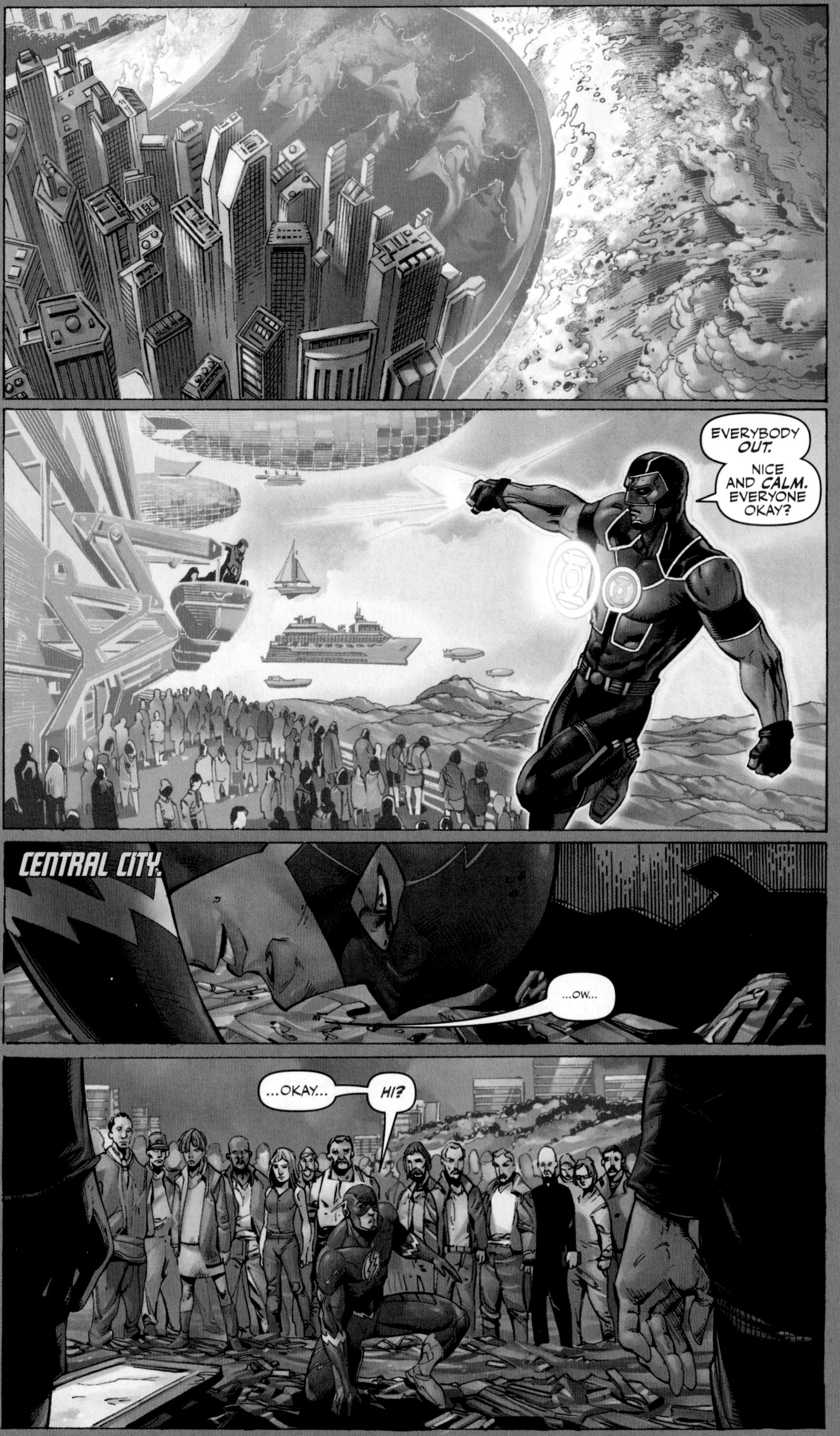
EVERYBODY OUT.
NICE AND CALM. EVERYONE OKAY?
CENTRAL CITY.
...OW...
...OKAY...
HI?

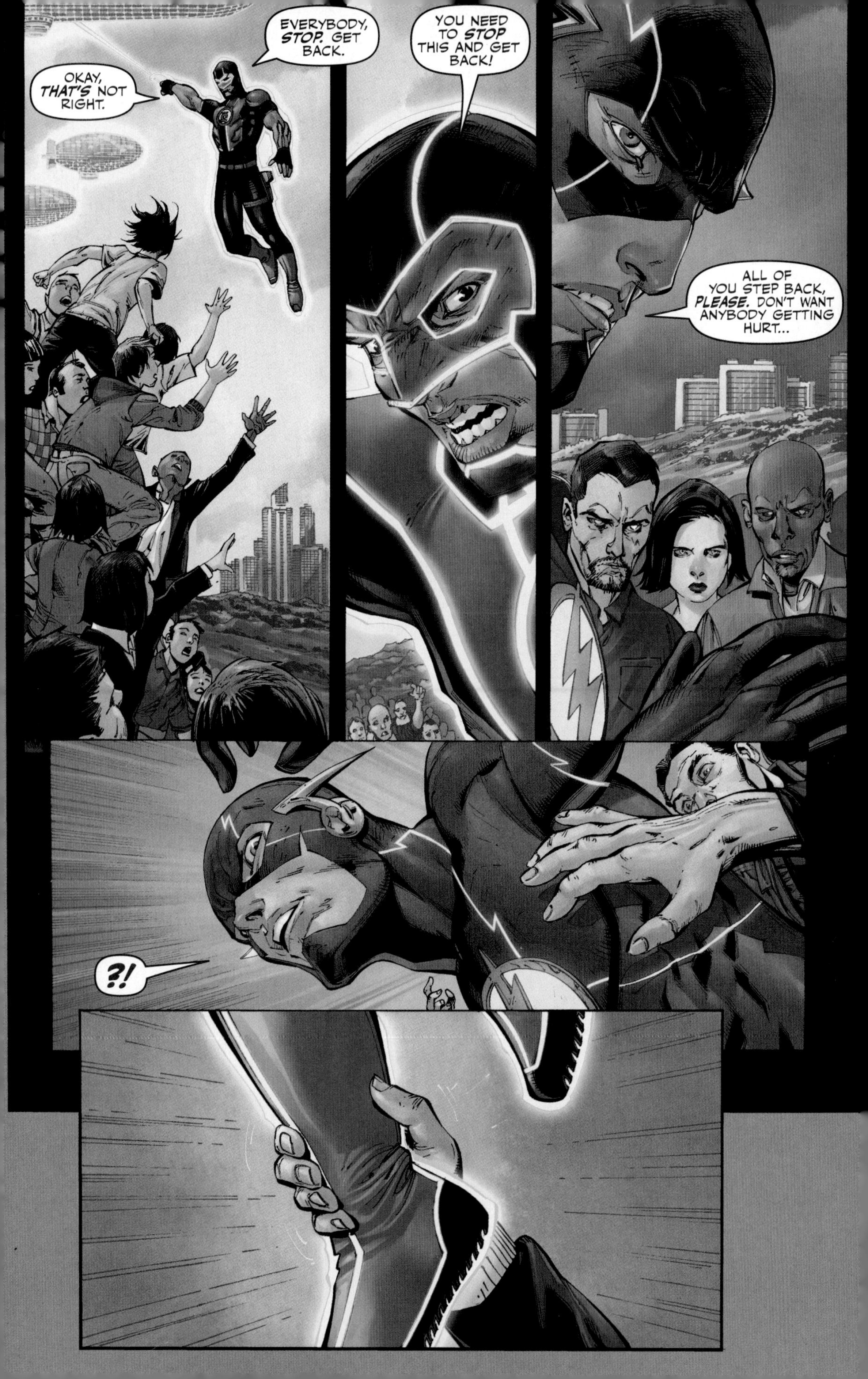
OKAY, THAT'S NOT RIGHT.
EVERYBODY, STOP. GET BACK.
YOU NEED TO STOP THIS AND GET BACK!
ALL OF YOU STEP BACK, PLEASE. DON'T WANT ANYBODY GETTING HURT...
?!

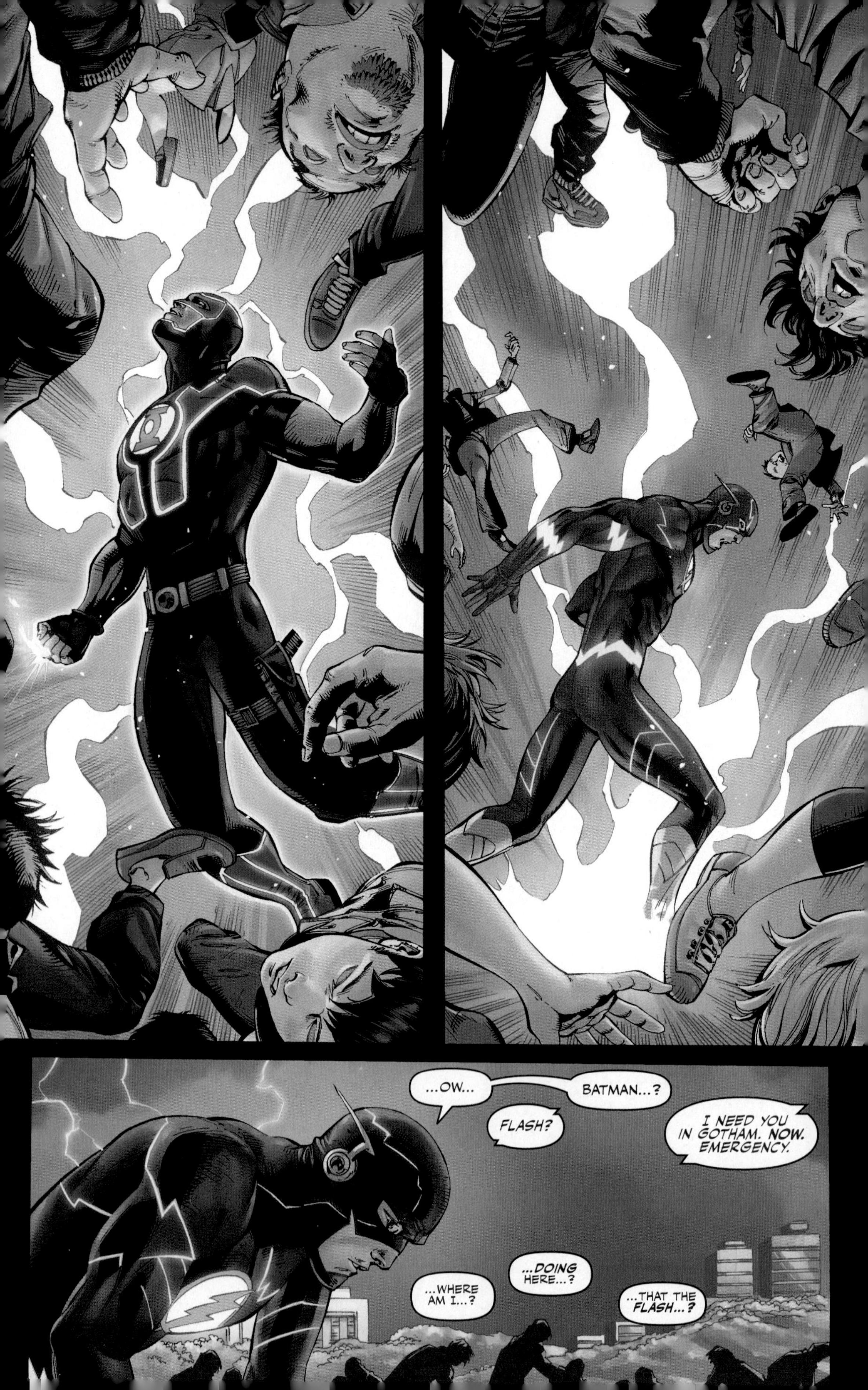
...OW...
BATMAN...?
FLASH?
I NEED YOU IN GOTHAM. NOW. EMERGENCY.
...WHERE AM I...?
...DOING HERE...?
...THAT THE FLASH...?

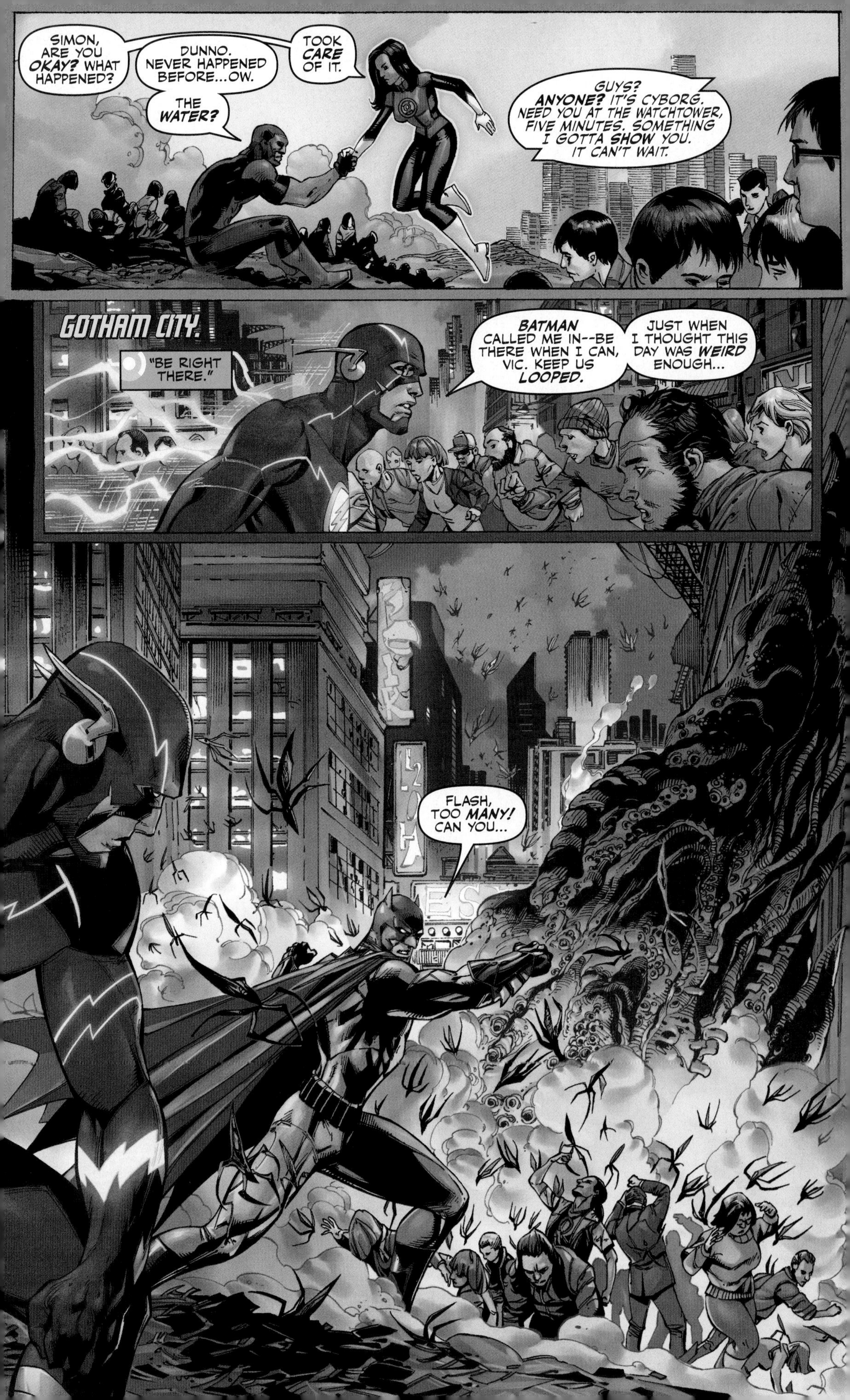
SIMON, ARE YOU OKAY? WHAT HAPPENED?
DUNNO. NEVER HAPPENED BEFORE...OW.
TOOK CARE OF IT.
THE WATER?
GUYS? ANYONE? IT'S CYBORG. NEED YOU AT THE WATCHTOWER, FIVE MINUTES. SOMETHING I GOTTA SHOW YOU. IT CAN'T WAIT.
GOTHAM CITY.
"BE RIGHT THERE."
BATMAN CALLED ME IN--BE THERE WHEN I CAN, VIC. KEEP US LOOPED.
JUST WHEN I THOUGHT THIS DAY WAS WEIRD ENOUGH...
FLASH, TOO MANY! CAN YOU...

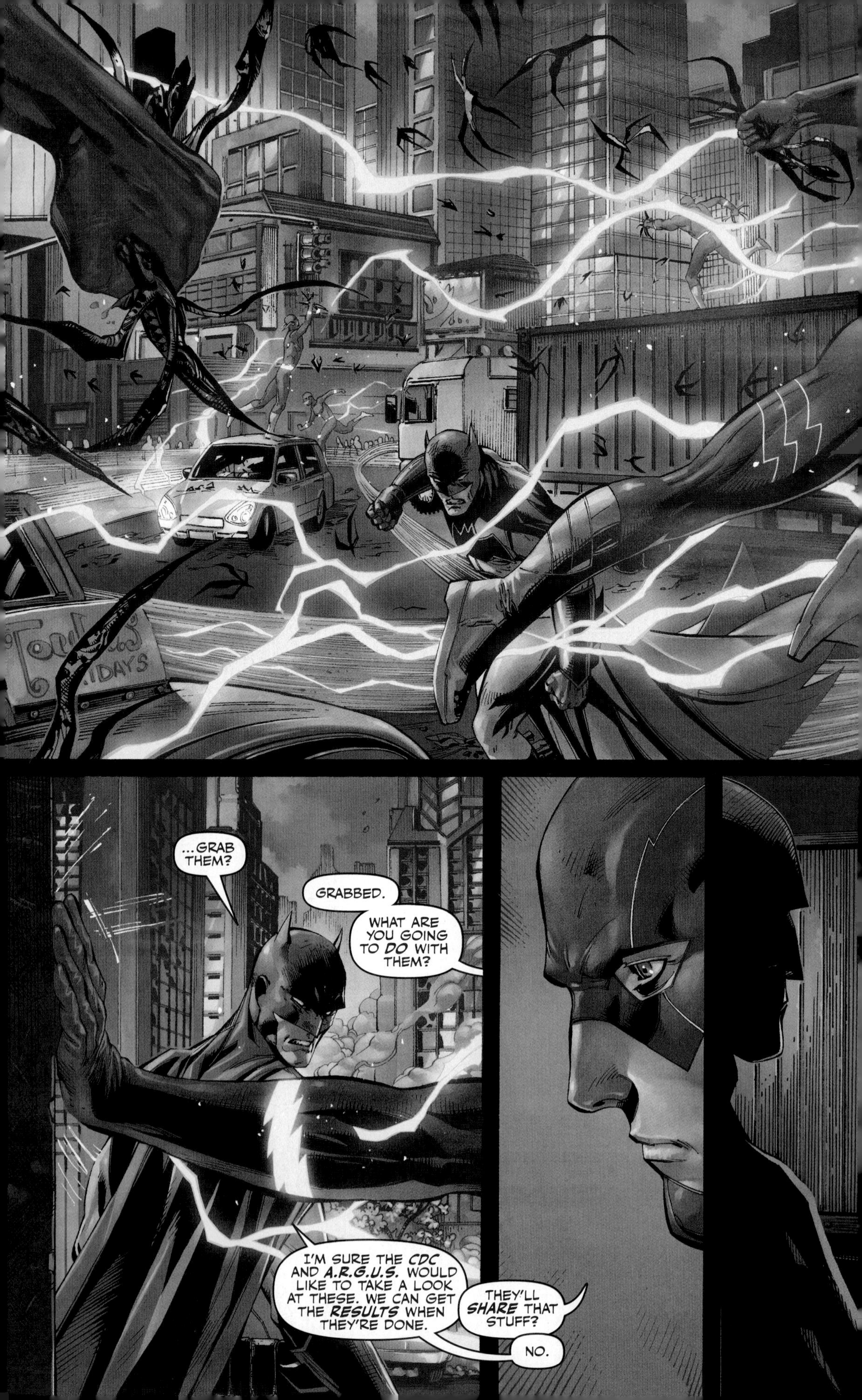
...GRAB THEM?
GRABBED.
WHAT ARE YOU GOING TO DO WITH THEM?
I'M SURE THE CDC AND A.R.G.U.S. WOULD LIKE TO TAKE A LOOK AT THESE. WE CAN GET THE RESULTS WHEN THEY'RE DONE.
THEY'LL SHARE THAT STUFF?
NO.

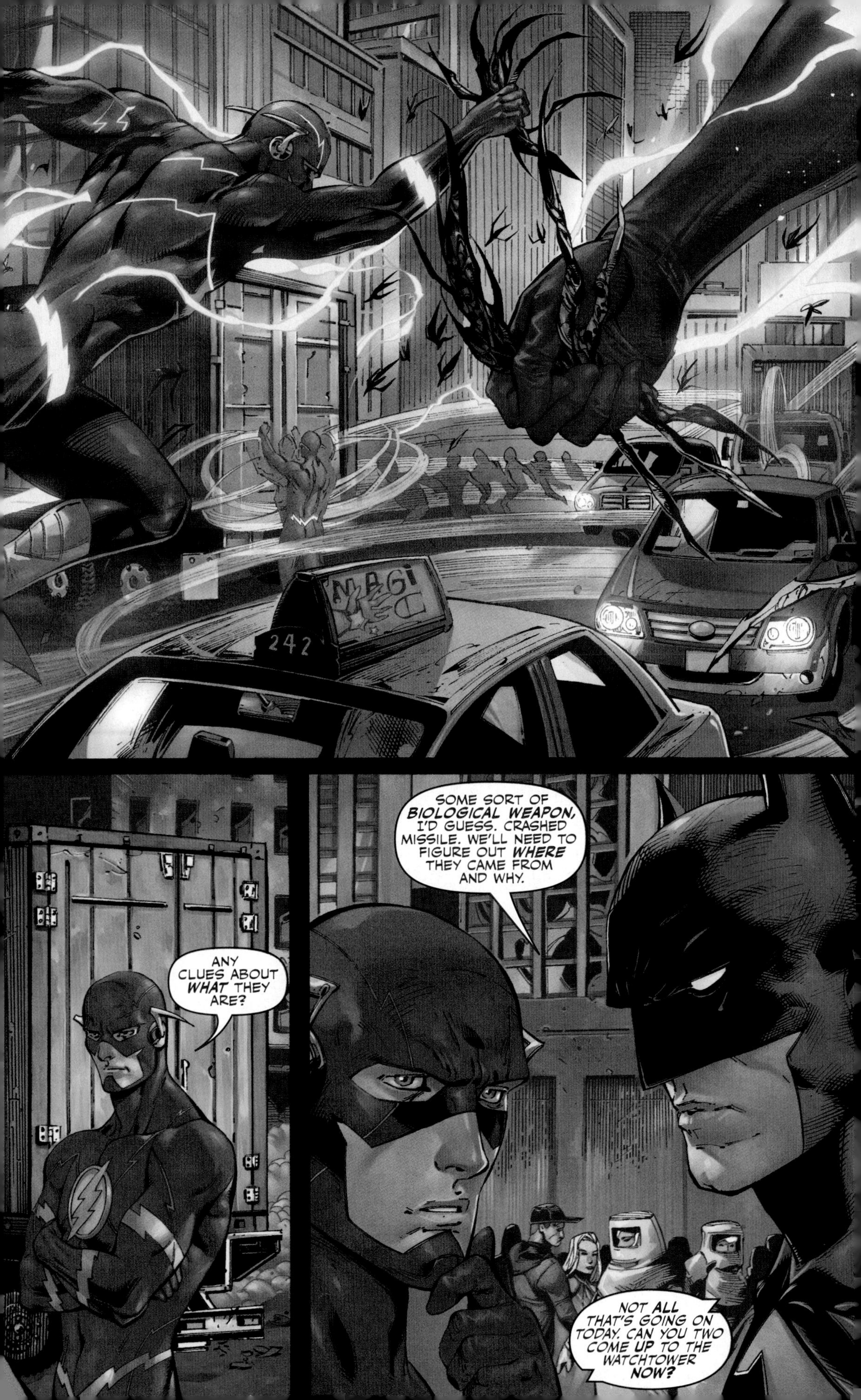
SOME SORT OF BIOLOGICAL WEAPON, I'D GUESS. CRASHED MISSILE. WE'LL NEED TO FIGURE OUT WHERE THEY CAME FROM AND WHY.
ANY CLUES ABOUT WHAT THEY ARE?
NOT ALL THAT'S GOING ON TODAY. CAN YOU TWO COME UP TO THE WATCHTOWER NOW?

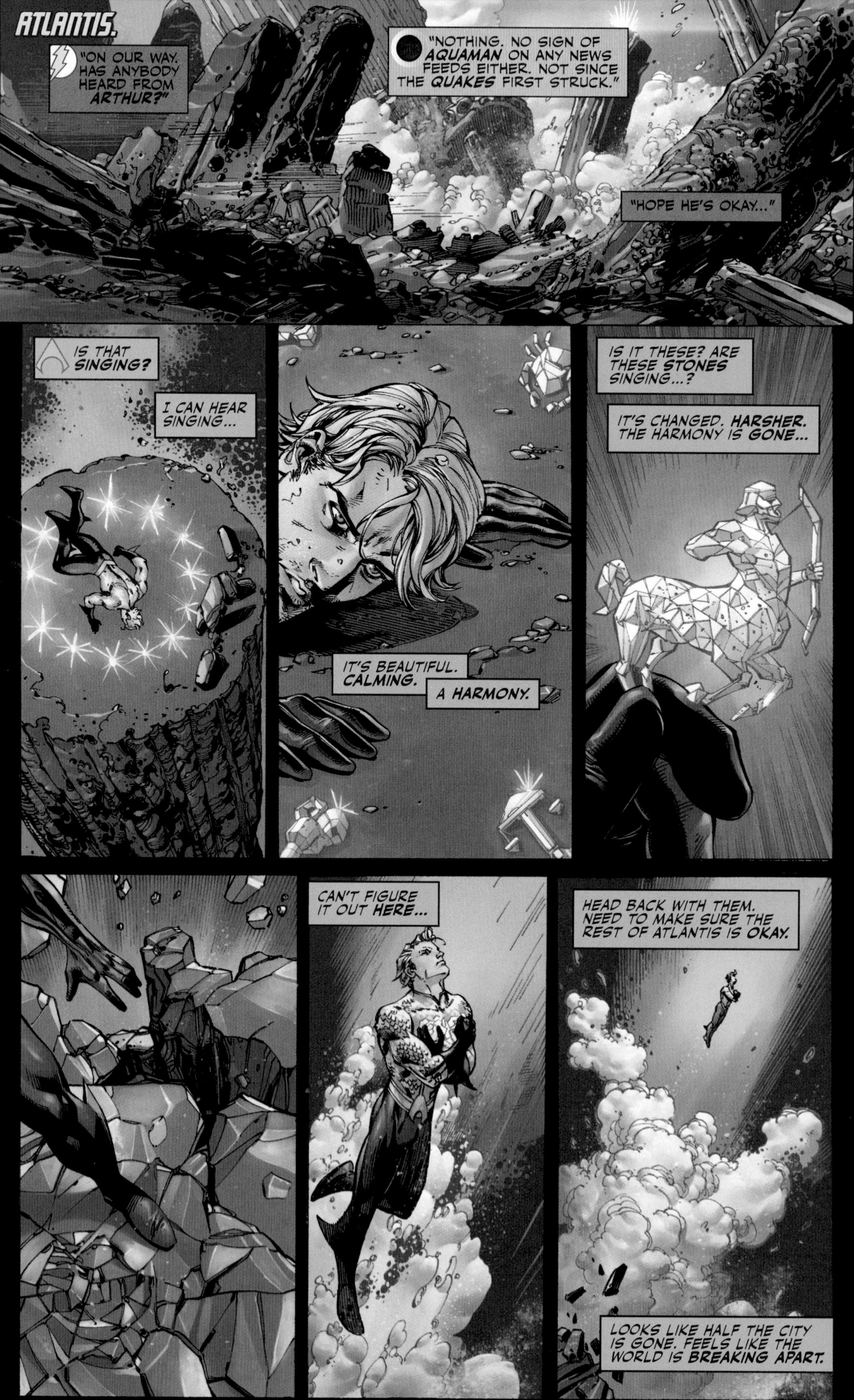
ATLANTIS.
"ON OUR WAY. HAS ANYBODY HEARD FROM ARTHUR?"
"NOTHING. NO SIGN OF AQUAMAN ON ANY NEWS FEEDS EITHER. NOT SINCE THE QUAKES FIRST STRUCK."
"HOPE HE'S OKAY..."
IS THAT SINGING?
I CAN HEAR SINGING...
IT'S BEAUTIFUL. CALMING.
A HARMONY.
IS IT THESE? ARE THESE STONES SINGING...?
IT'S CHANGED. HARSHER. THE HARMONY IS GONE...
CAN'T FIGURE IT OUT HERE...
HEAD BACK WITH THEM. NEED TO MAKE SURE THE REST OF ATLANTIS IS OKAY.
LOOKS LIKE HALF THE CITY IS GONE. FEELS LIKE THE WORLD IS BREAKING APART.

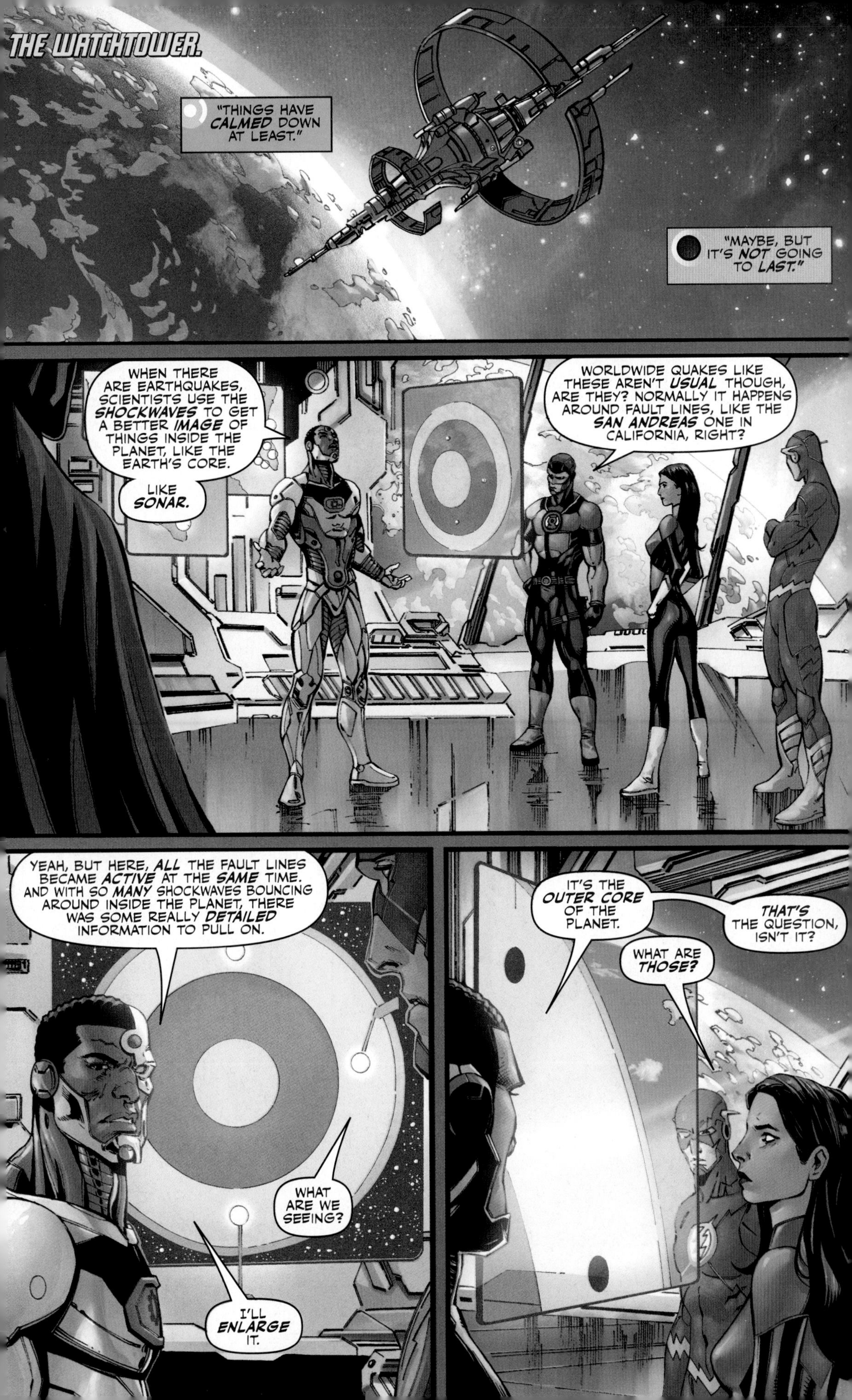
THE WATCHTOWER.
"THINGS HAVE CALMED DOWN AT LEAST."
"MAYBE, BUT IT'S NOT GOING TO LAST."
WHEN THERE ARE EARTHQUAKES, SCIENTISTS USE THE SHOCKWAVES TO GET A BETTER IMAGE OF THINGS INSIDE THE PLANET, LIKE THE EARTH'S CORE.
LIKE SONAR.
WORLDWIDE QUAKES LIKE THESE AREN'T USUAL THOUGH, ARE THEY? NORMALLY IT HAPPENS AROUND FAULT LINES, LIKE THE SAN ANDREAS ONE IN CALIFORNIA, RIGHT?
YEAH, BUT HERE, ALL THE FAULT LINES BECAME ACTIVE AT THE SAME TIME. AND WITH SO MANY SHOCKWAVES BOUNCING AROUND INSIDE THE PLANET, THERE WAS SOME REALLY DETAILED INFORMATION TO PULL ON.
WHAT ARE WE SEEING?
I'LL ENLARGE IT.
IT'S THE OUTER CORE OF THE PLANET.
WHAT ARE THOSE?
THAT'S THE QUESTION, ISN'T IT?

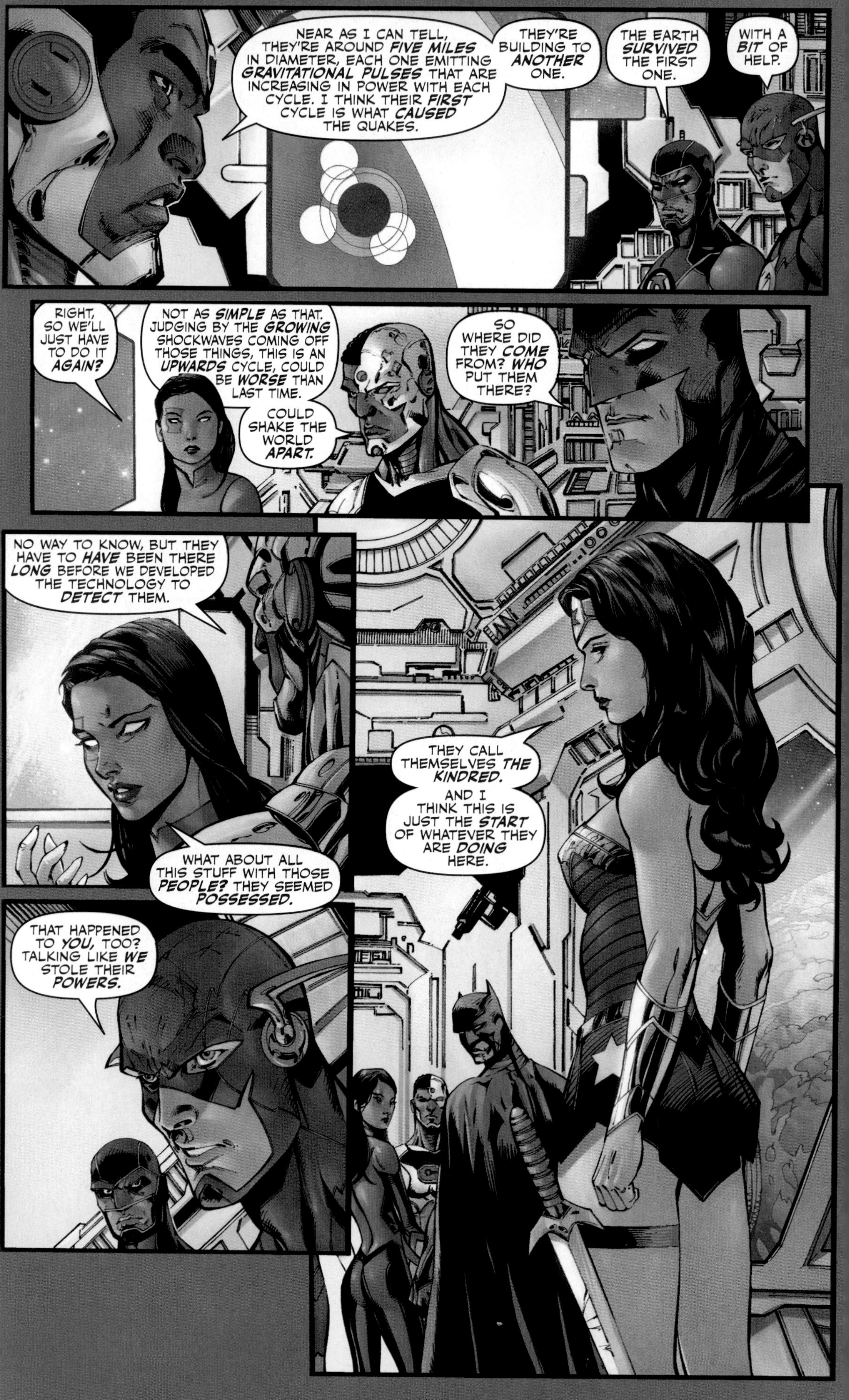
NEAR AS I CAN TELL, THEY'RE AROUND FIVE MILES IN DIAMETER, EACH ONE EMITTING GRAVITATIONAL PULSES THAT ARE INCREASING IN POWER WITH EACH CYCLE. I THINK THEIR FIRST CYCLE IS WHAT CAUSED THE QUAKES.
THEY'RE BUILDING TO ANOTHER ONE.
THE EARTH SURVIVED THE FIRST ONE.
WITH A BIT OF HELP.
RIGHT, SO WE'LL JUST HAVE TO DO IT AGAIN?
NOT AS SIMPLE AS THAT. JUDGING BY THE GROWING SHOCKWAVES COMING OFF THOSE THINGS, THIS IS AN UPWARDS CYCLE, COULD BE WORSE THAN LAST TIME.
COULD SHAKE THE WORLD APART.
SO WHERE DID THEY COME FROM? WHO PUT THEM THERE?
NO WAY TO KNOW, BUT THEY HAVE TO HAVE BEEN THERE LONG BEFORE WE DEVELOPED THE TECHNOLOGY TO DETECT THEM.
WHAT ABOUT ALL THIS STUFF WITH THOSE PEOPLE? THEY SEEMED POSSESSED.
THAT HAPPENED TO YOU, TOO? TALKING LIKE WE STOLE THEIR POWERS.
THEY CALL THEMSELVES THE KINDRED.
AND I THINK THIS IS JUST THE START OF WHATEVER THEY ARE DOING HERE.

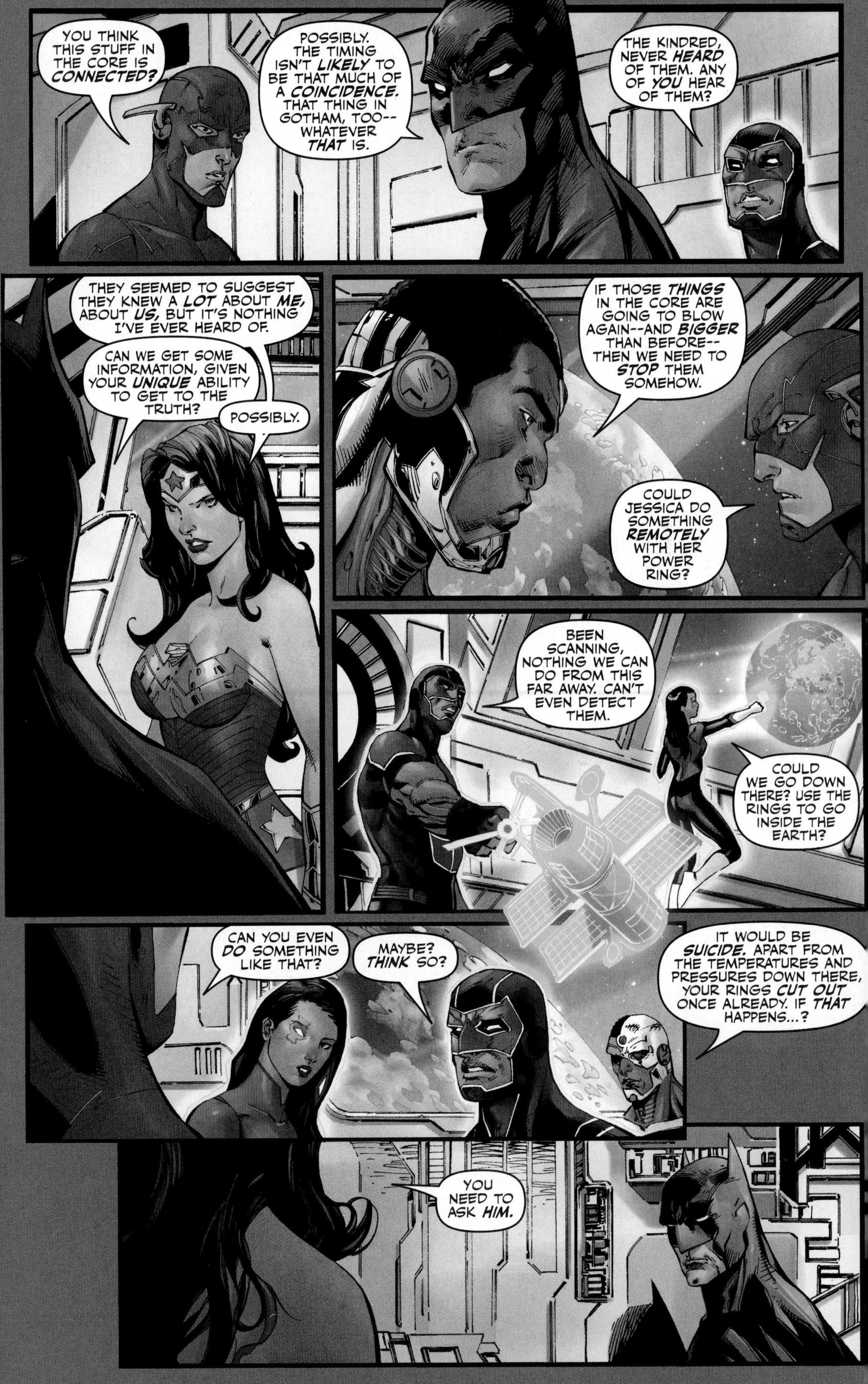
YOU THINK THIS STUFF IN THE CORE IS CONNECTED?
POSSIBLY. THE TIMING ISN'T LIKELY TO BE THAT MUCH OF A COINCIDENCE. THAT THING IN GOTHAM, TOO-- WHATEVER THAT IS.
THE KINDRED, NEVER HEARD OF THEM. ANY OF YOU HEAR OF THEM?
THEY SEEMED TO SUGGEST THEY KNEW A LOT ABOUT ME, ABOUT US, BUT IT'S NOTHING I'VE EVER HEARD OF.
CAN WE GET SOME INFORMATION, GIVEN YOUR UNIQUE ABILITY TO GET TO THE TRUTH?
POSSIBLY.
IF THOSE THINGS IN THE CORE ARE GOING TO BLOW AGAIN--AND BIGGER THAN BEFORE-- THEN WE NEED TO STOP THEM SOMEHOW.
COULD JESSICA DO SOMETHING REMOTELY WITH HER POWER RING?
BEEN SCANNING, NOTHING WE CAN DO FROM THIS FAR AWAY. CAN'T EVEN DETECT THEM.
COULD WE GO DOWN THERE? USE THE RINGS TO GO INSIDE THE EARTH?
CAN YOU EVEN DO SOMETHING LIKE THAT?
MAYBE? THINK SO?
IT WOULD BE SUICIDE. APART FROM THE TEMPERATURES AND PRESSURES DOWN THERE, YOUR RINGS CUT OUT ONCE ALREADY. IF THAT HAPPENS...?
YOU NEED TO ASK HIM.

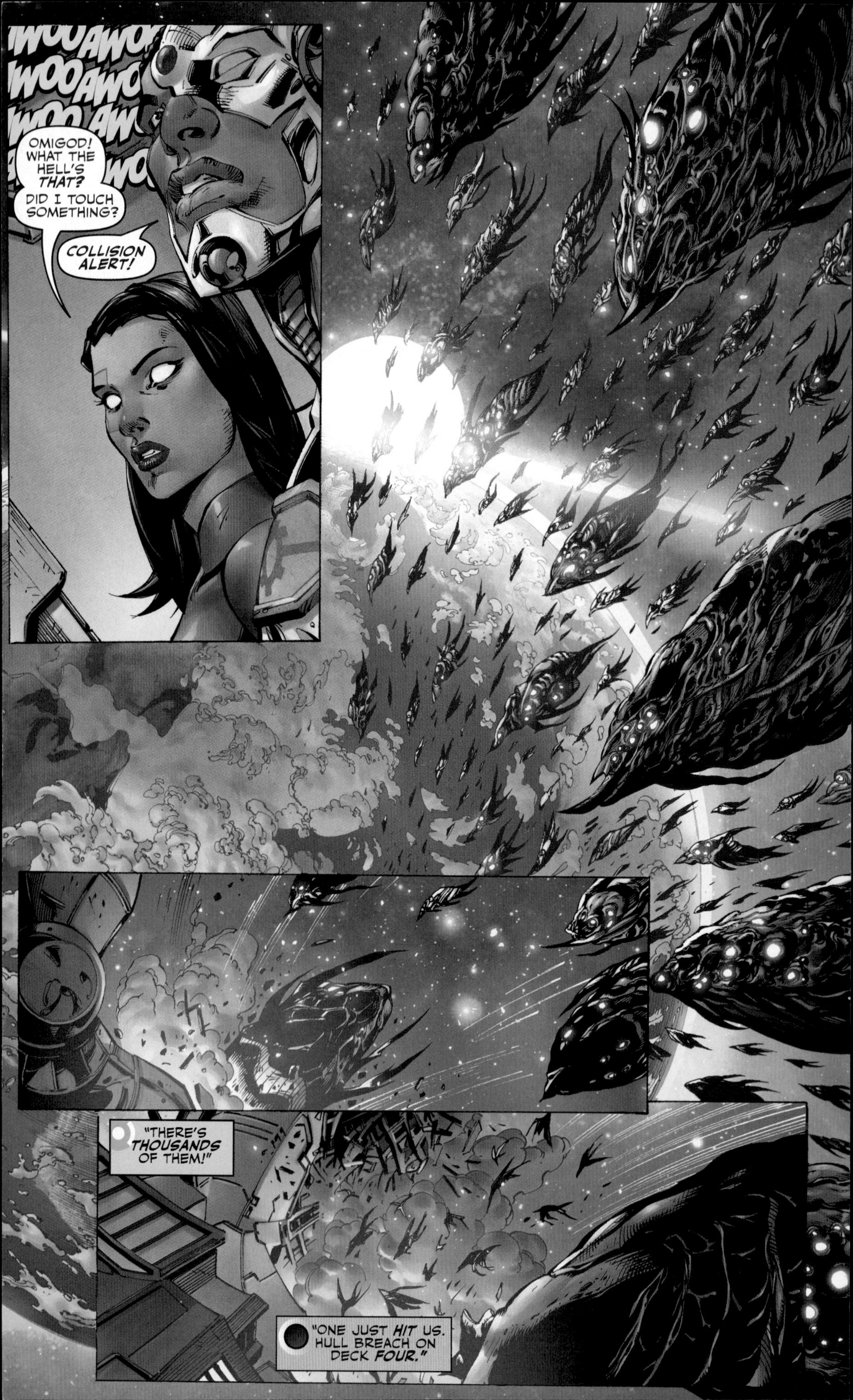
WOOAWOO
WOOAWOO
WOOAWOO
OMIGOD! WHAT THE HELL'S THAT? DID I TOUCH SOMETHING?
COLLISION ALERT!
"THERE'S THOUSANDS OF THEM!"
"ONE JUST HIT US. HULL BREACH ON DECK FOUR."

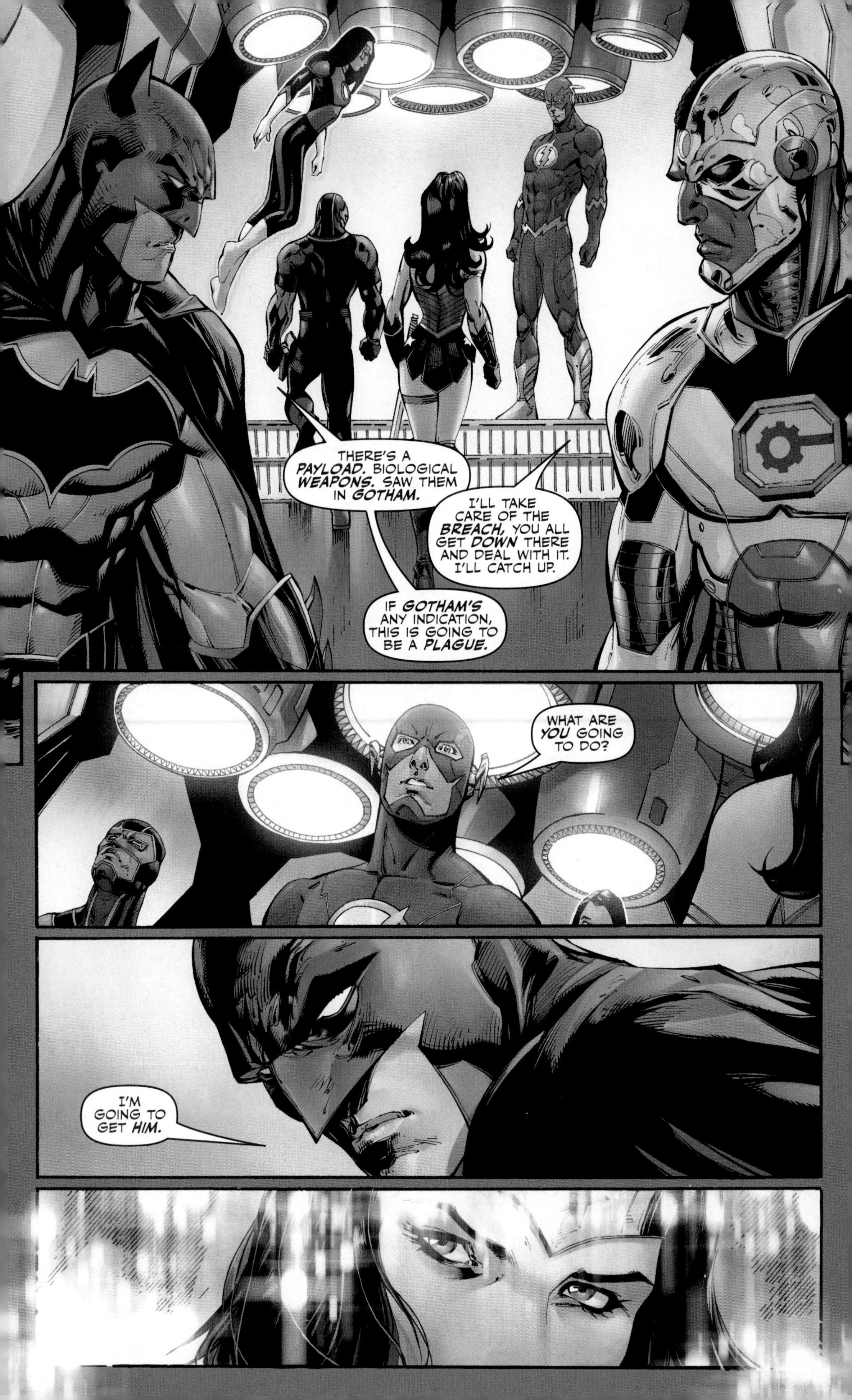
THERE'S A PAYLOAD. BIOLOGICAL WEAPONS. SAW THEM IN GOTHAM.
I'LL TAKE CARE OF THE BREACH, YOU ALL GET DOWN THERE AND DEAL WITH IT. I'LL CATCH UP.
IF GOTHAM'S ANY INDICATION, THIS IS GOING TO BE A PLAGUE.
WHAT ARE YOU GOING TO DO?
I'M GOING TO GET HIM.

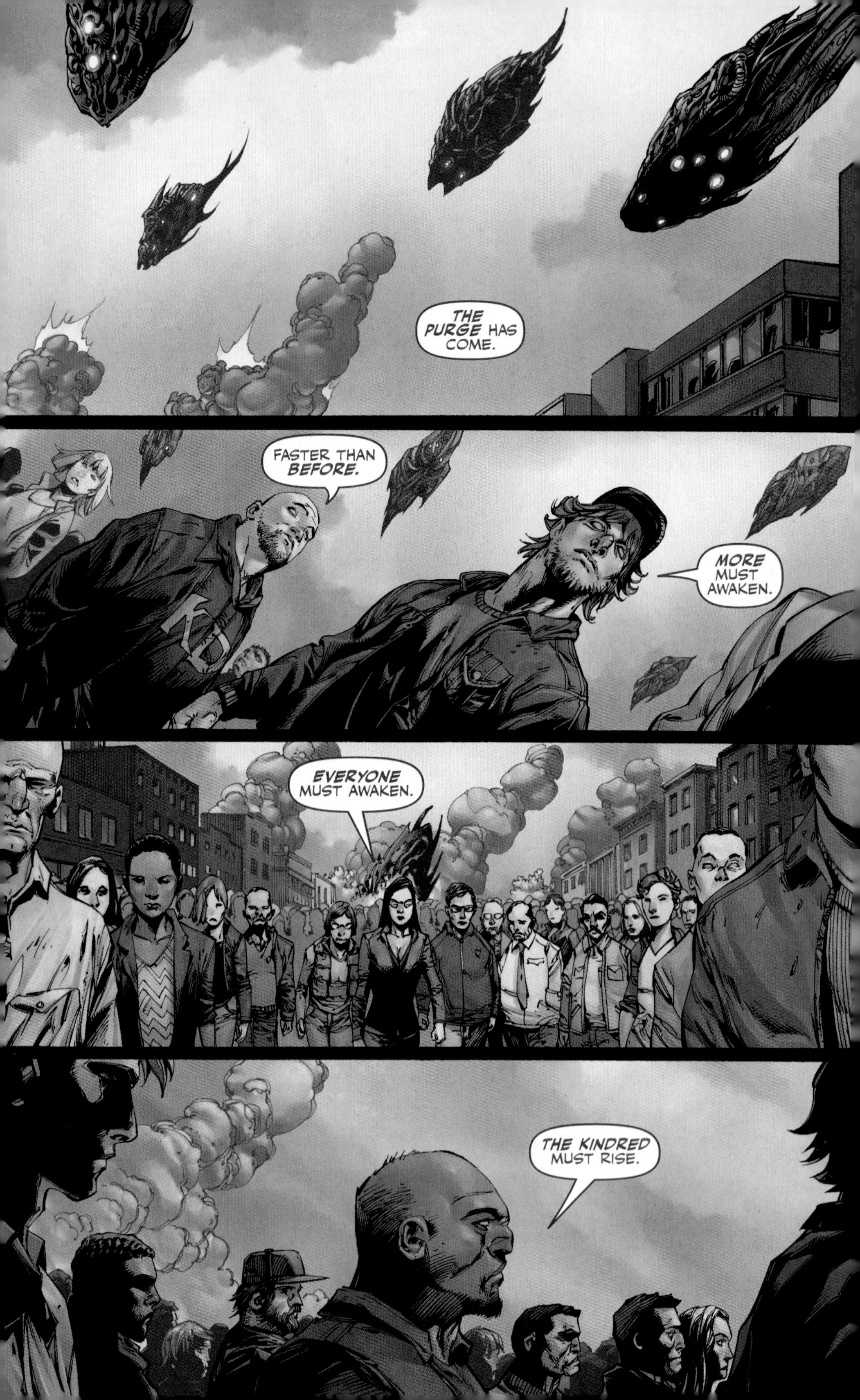
THE PURGE HAS COME.
FASTER THAN BEFORE.
MORE MUST AWAKEN.
EVERYONE MUST AWAKEN.
THE KINDRED MUST RISE.

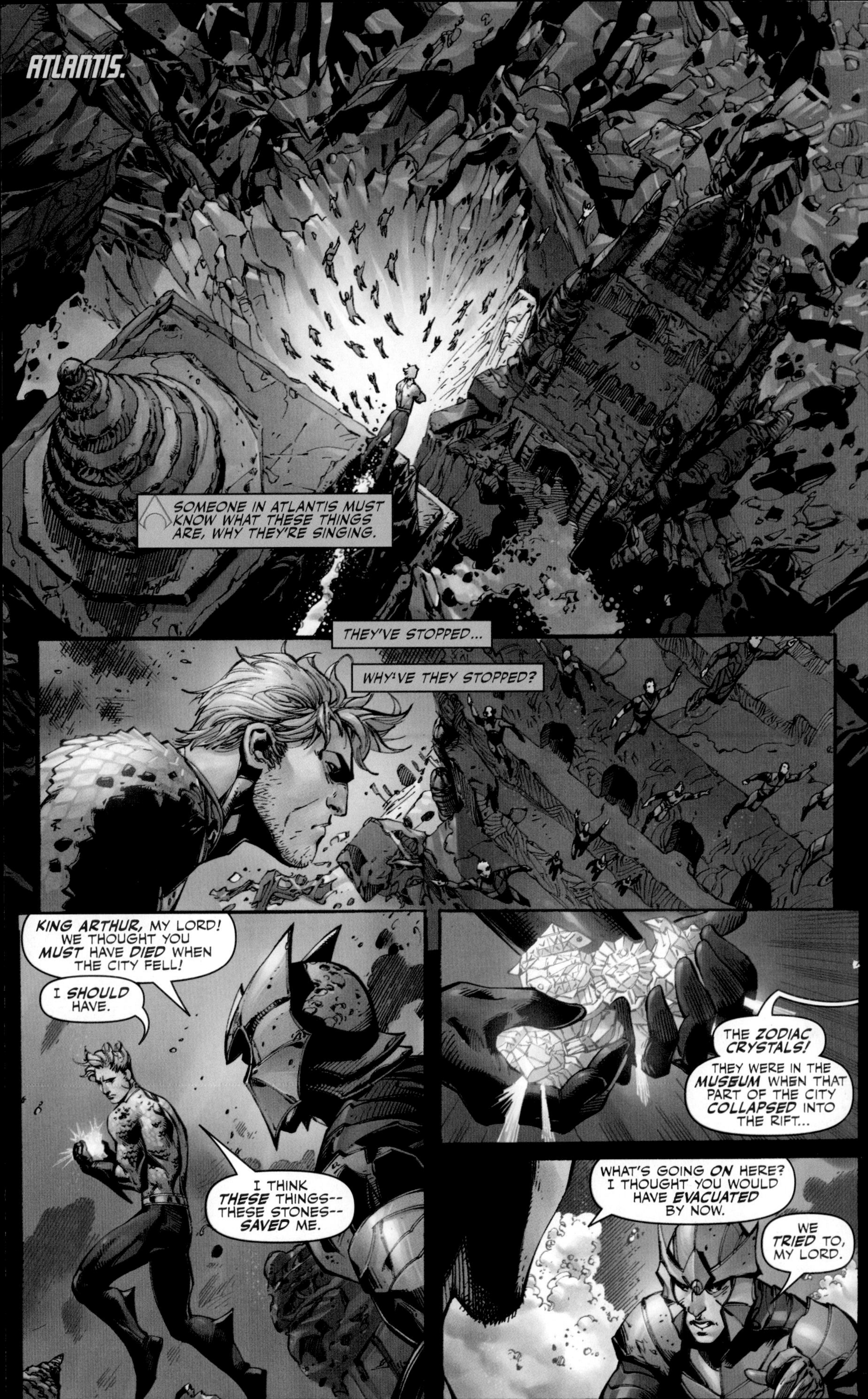
ATLANTIS.
SOMEONE IN ATLANTIS MUST KNOW WHAT THESE THINGS ARE, WHY THEY'RE SINGING.
THEY'VE STOPPED...
WHY'VE THEY STOPPED?
KING ARTHUR, MY LORD! WE THOUGHT YOU MUST HAVE DIED WHEN THE CITY FELL!
I SHOULD HAVE.
I THINK THESE THINGS-- THESE STONES-- SAVED ME.
THE ZODIAC CRYSTALS!
THEY WERE IN THE MUSEUM WHEN THAT PART OF THE CITY COLLAPSED INTO THE RIFT...
WHAT'S GOING ON HERE? I THOUGHT YOU WOULD HAVE EVACUATED BY NOW.
WE TRIED TO, MY LORD.

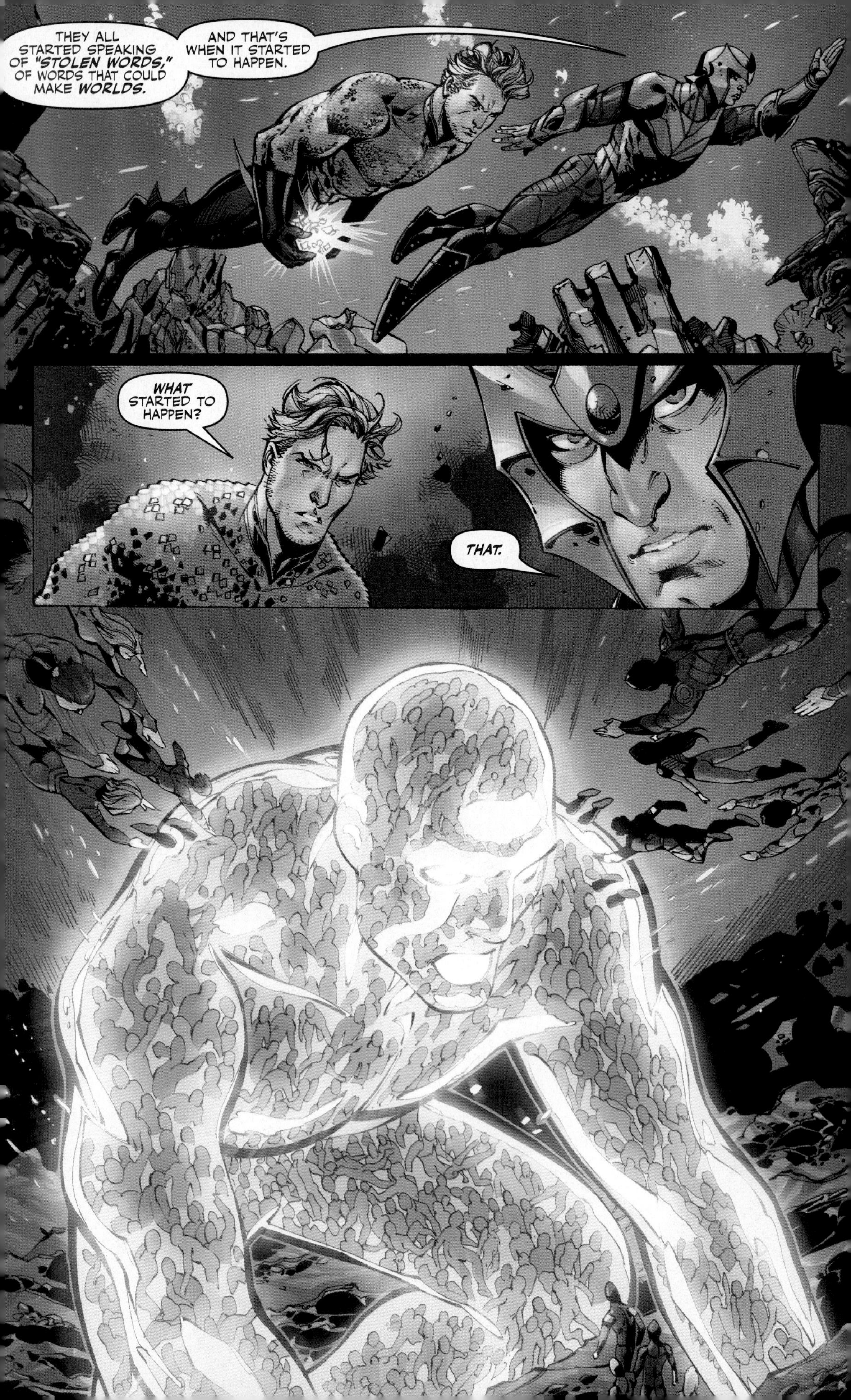
THEY ALL STARTED SPEAKING OF "STOLEN WORDS," OF WORDS THAT COULD MAKE WORLDS.
AND THAT'S WHEN IT STARTED TO HAPPEN.
WHAT STARTED TO HAPPEN?
THAT.

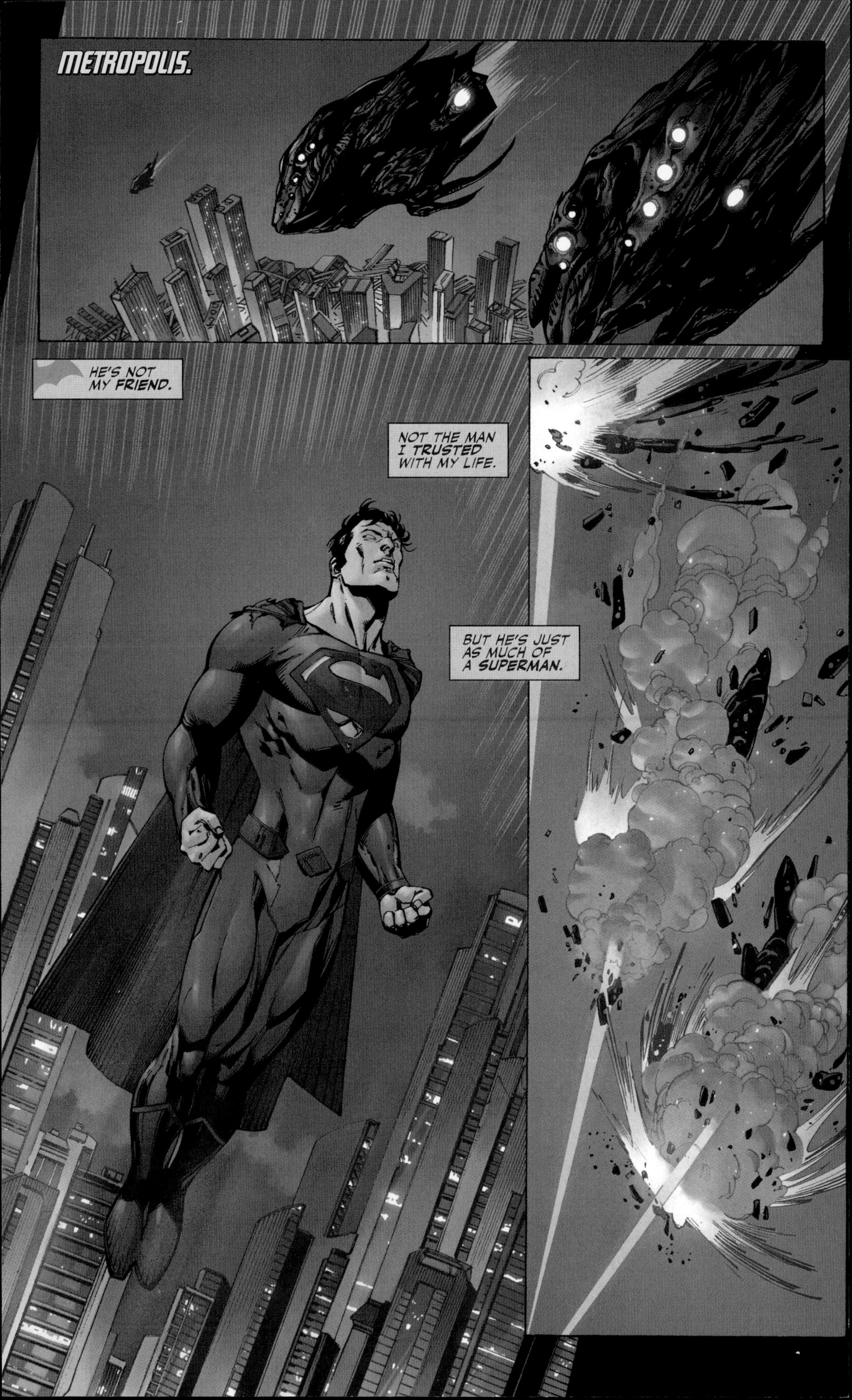

METROPOLIS.
HE'S NOT MY FRIEND.
NOT THE MAN I TRUSTED WITH MY LIFE.
BUT HE'S JUST AS MUCH OF A SUPERMAN.

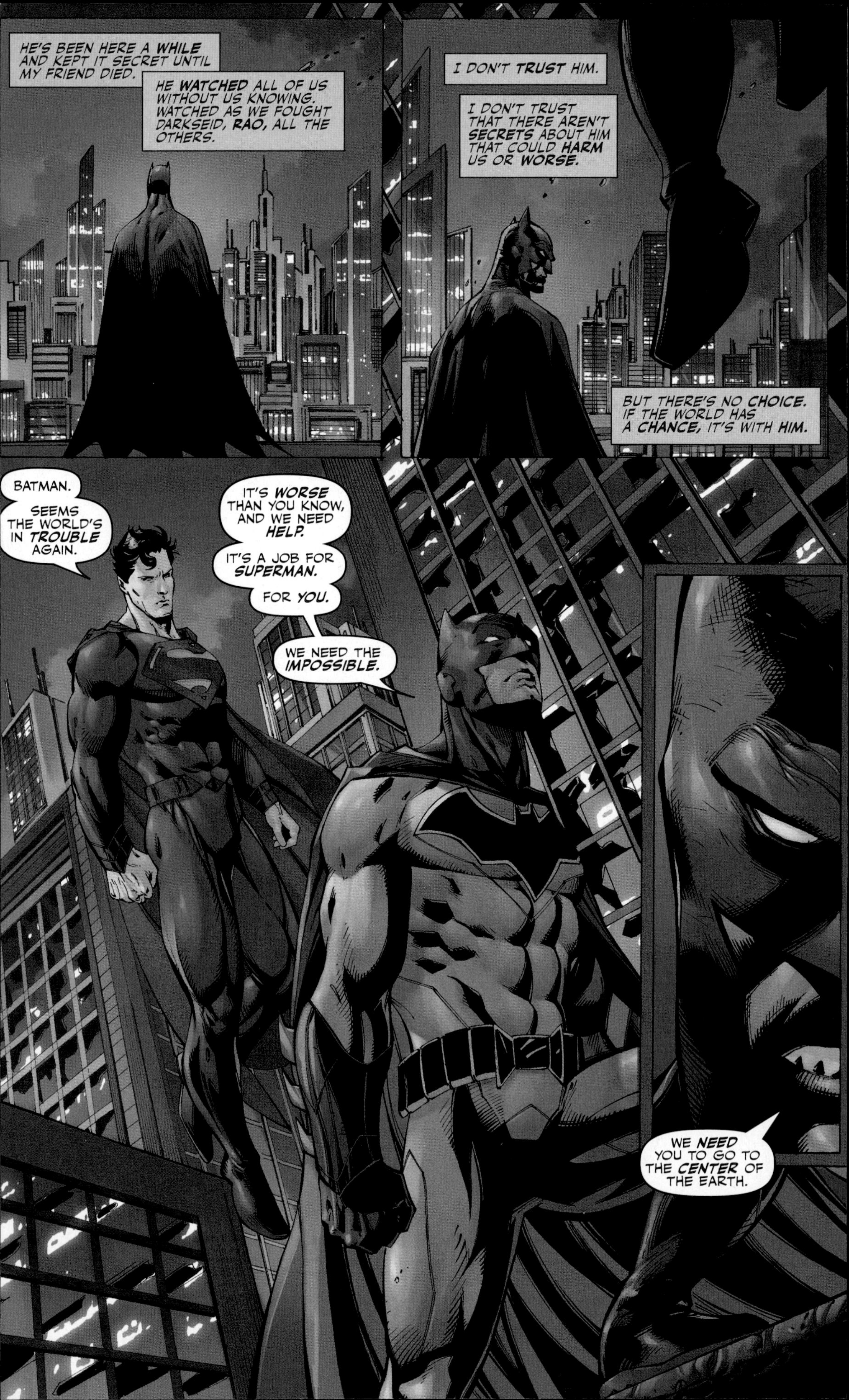
HE'S BEEN HERE A WHILE AND KEPT IT SECRET UNTIL MY FRIEND DIED.
HE WATCHED ALL OF US WITHOUT US KNOWING. WATCHED AS WE FOUGHT DARKSEID, RAO, ALL THE OTHERS.
I DON'T TRUST HIM.
I DON'T TRUST THAT THERE AREN'T SECRETS ABOUT HIM THAT COULD HARM US OR WORSE.
BUT THERE'S NO CHOICE. IF THE WORLD HAS A CHANCE, IT'S WITH HIM.
BATMAN.
SEEMS THE WORLD'S IN TROUBLE AGAIN.
IT'S WORSE THAN YOU KNOW, AND WE NEED HELP.
IT'S A JOB FOR SUPERMAN.
FOR YOU.
WE NEED THE IMPOSSIBLE.
WE NEED YOU TO GO TO THE CENTER OF THE EARTH.

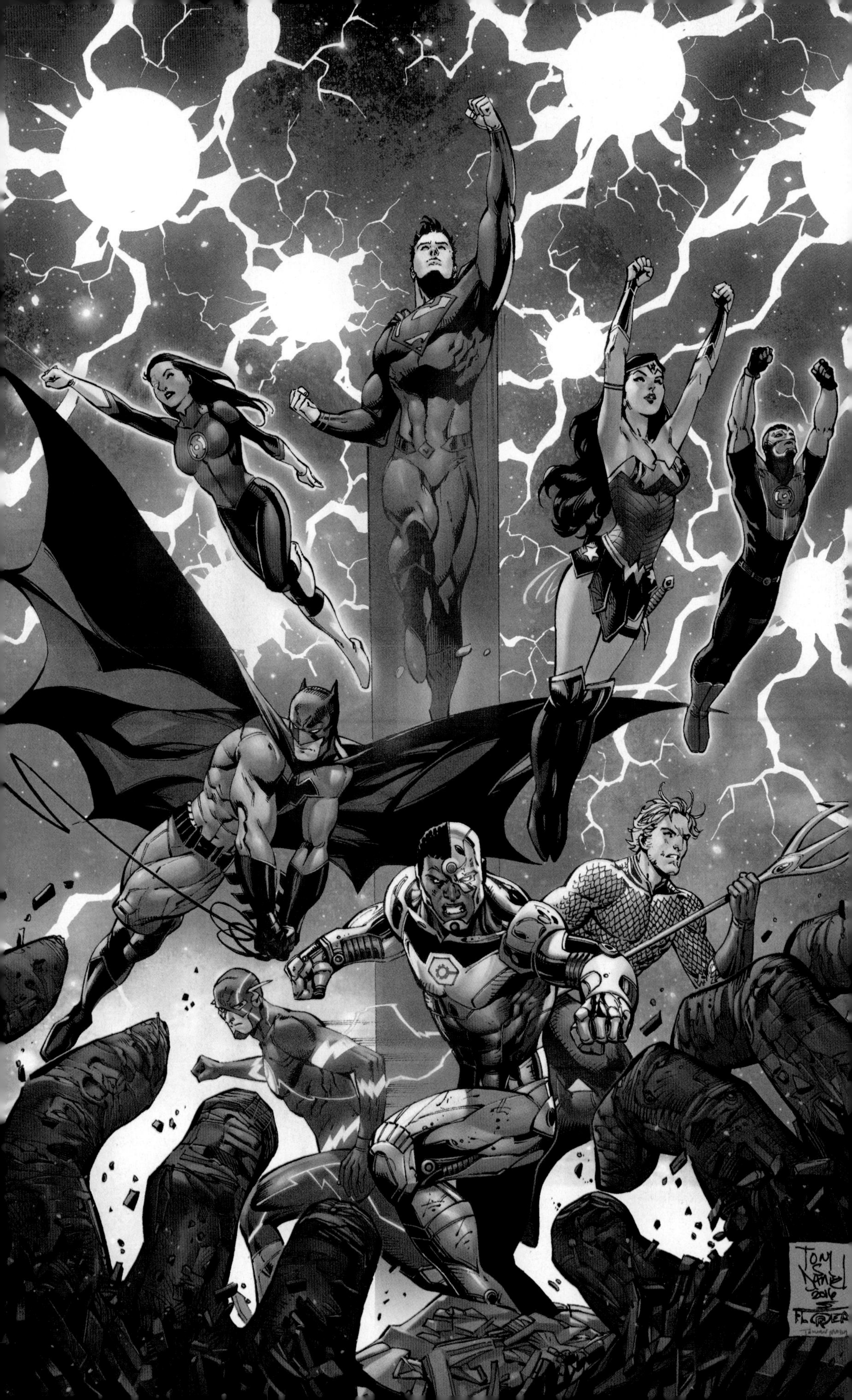
TONY S DANIEL
2016

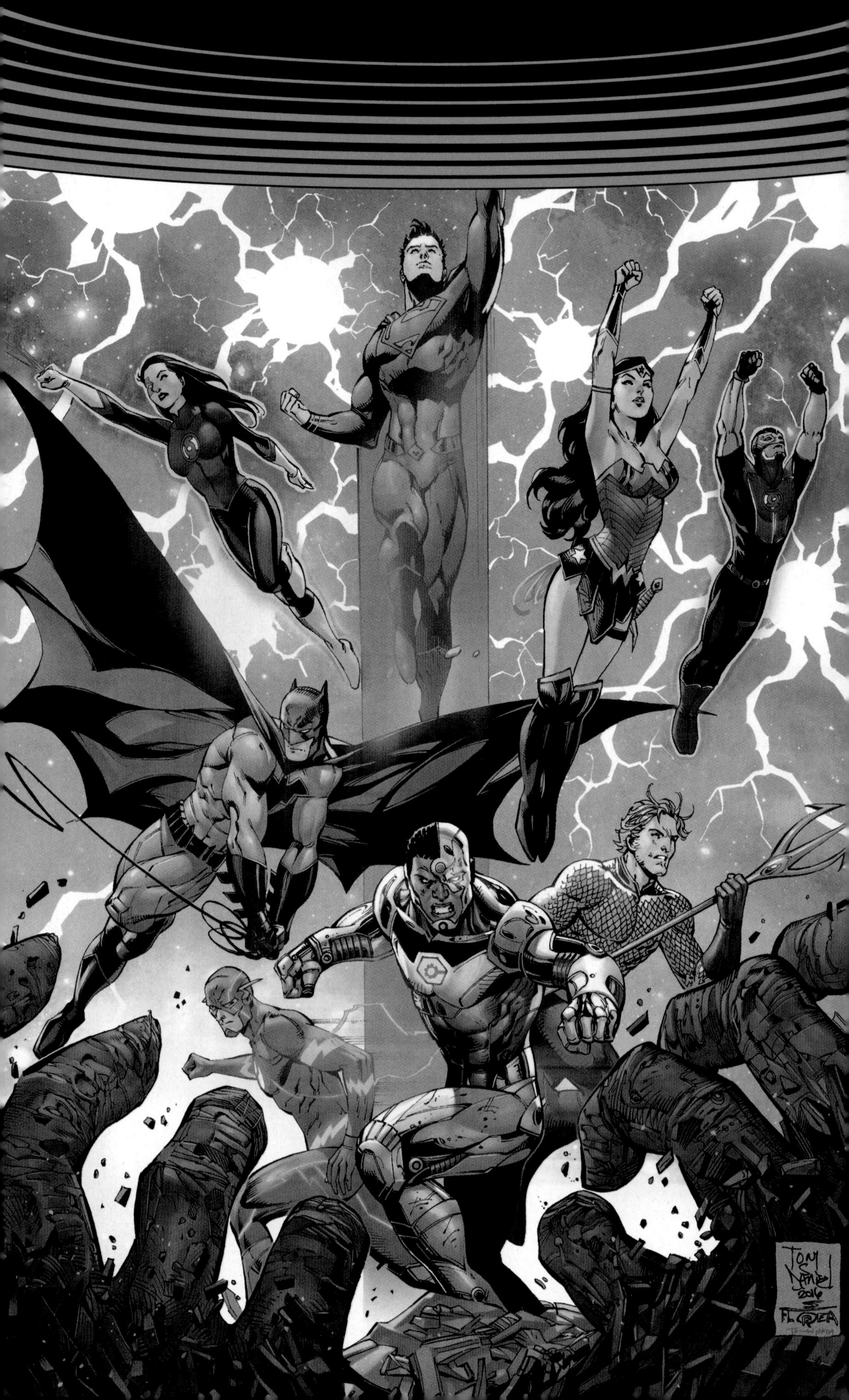

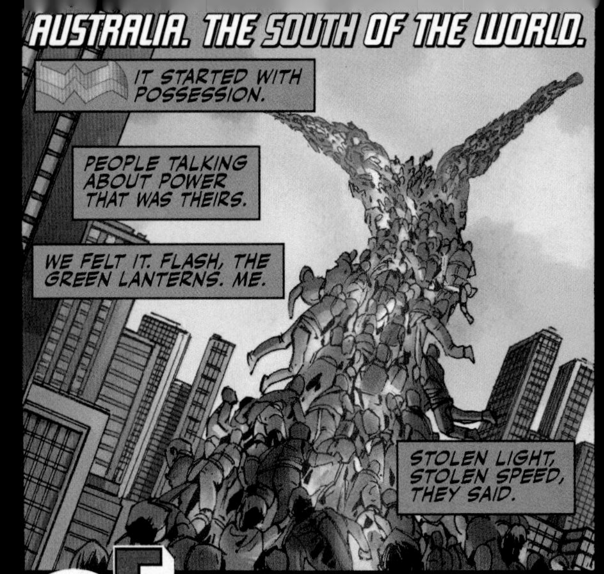
AUSTRALIA. THE SOUTH OF THE WORLD.
IT STARTED WITH POSSESSION.
PEOPLE TALKING ABOUT POWER THAT WAS THEIRS.
WE FELT IT. FLASH, THE GREEN LANTERNS. ME.
STOLEN LIGHT, STOLEN SPEED, THEY SAID.

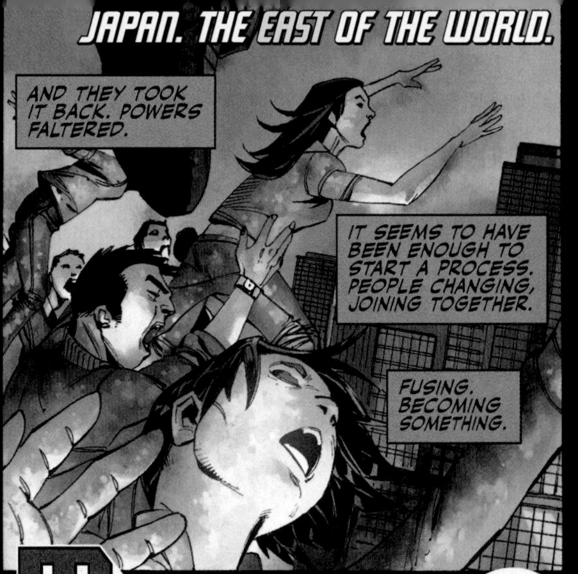
JAPAN. THE EAST OF THE WORLD.
AND THEY TOOK IT BACK. POWERS FALTERED.
IT SEEMS TO HAVE BEEN ENOUGH TO START A PROCESS. PEOPLE CHANGING, JOINING TOGETHER.
FUSING. BECOMING SOMETHING.

# THE EXTINCTION MACHINES PART THREE

WRITTEN by BRYAN HITCH PENCILLED by TONY S. DANIEL INKED by SANDU FLOREA

COLORED by TOMEU MOREY LETTERED by RICHARD STARKINGS & COMICRAFT COVER by TONY S. DANIEL & TOMEU MOREY VARIANT COVER by YANICK PAQUETTE & NATHAN FAIRBAIRN ASSISTS by AMEDEO TURTURRO EDITS by BRIAN CUNNINGHAM

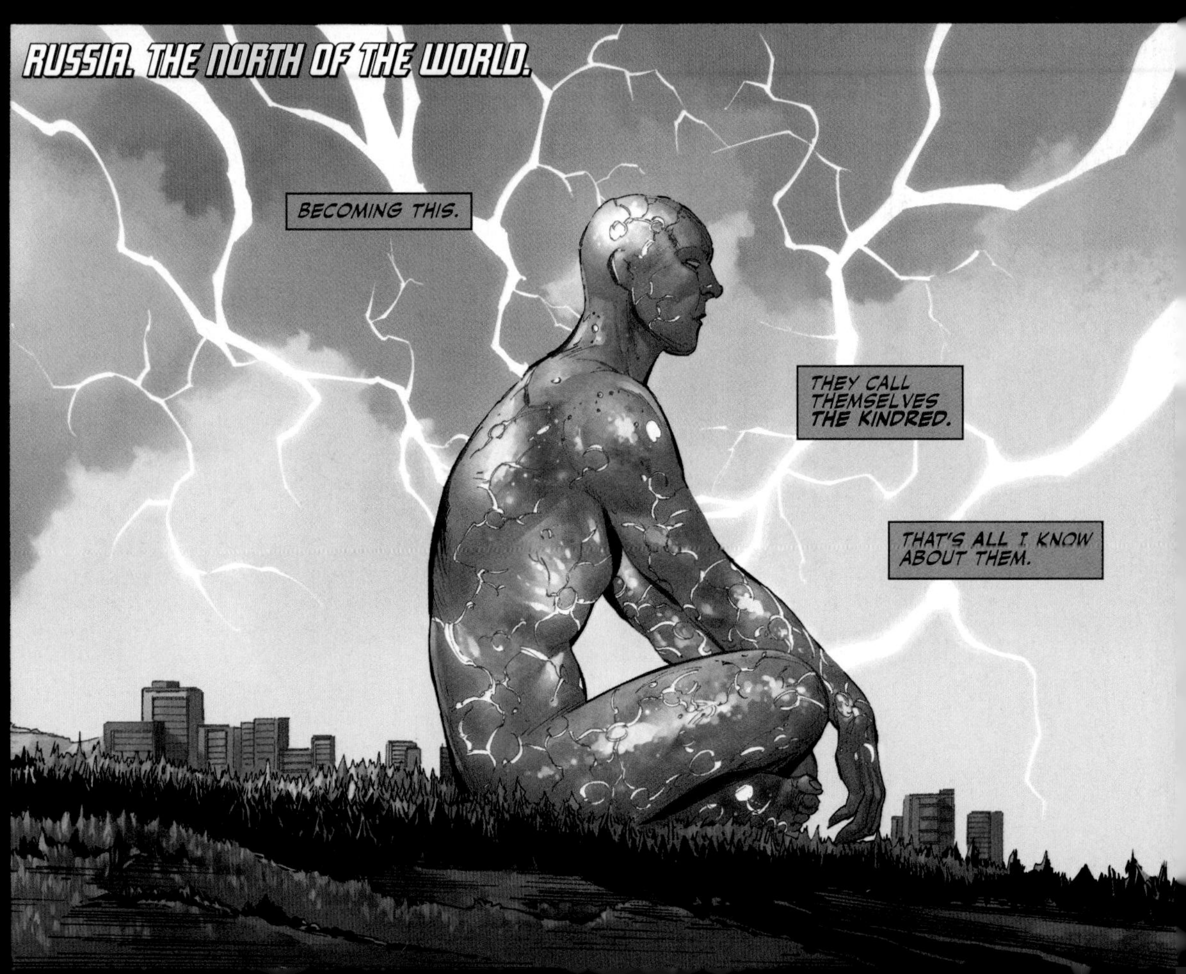
RUSSIA. THE NORTH OF THE WORLD.
BECOMING THIS.
THEY CALL THEMSELVES THE KINDRED.
THAT'S ALL I KNOW ABOUT THEM.

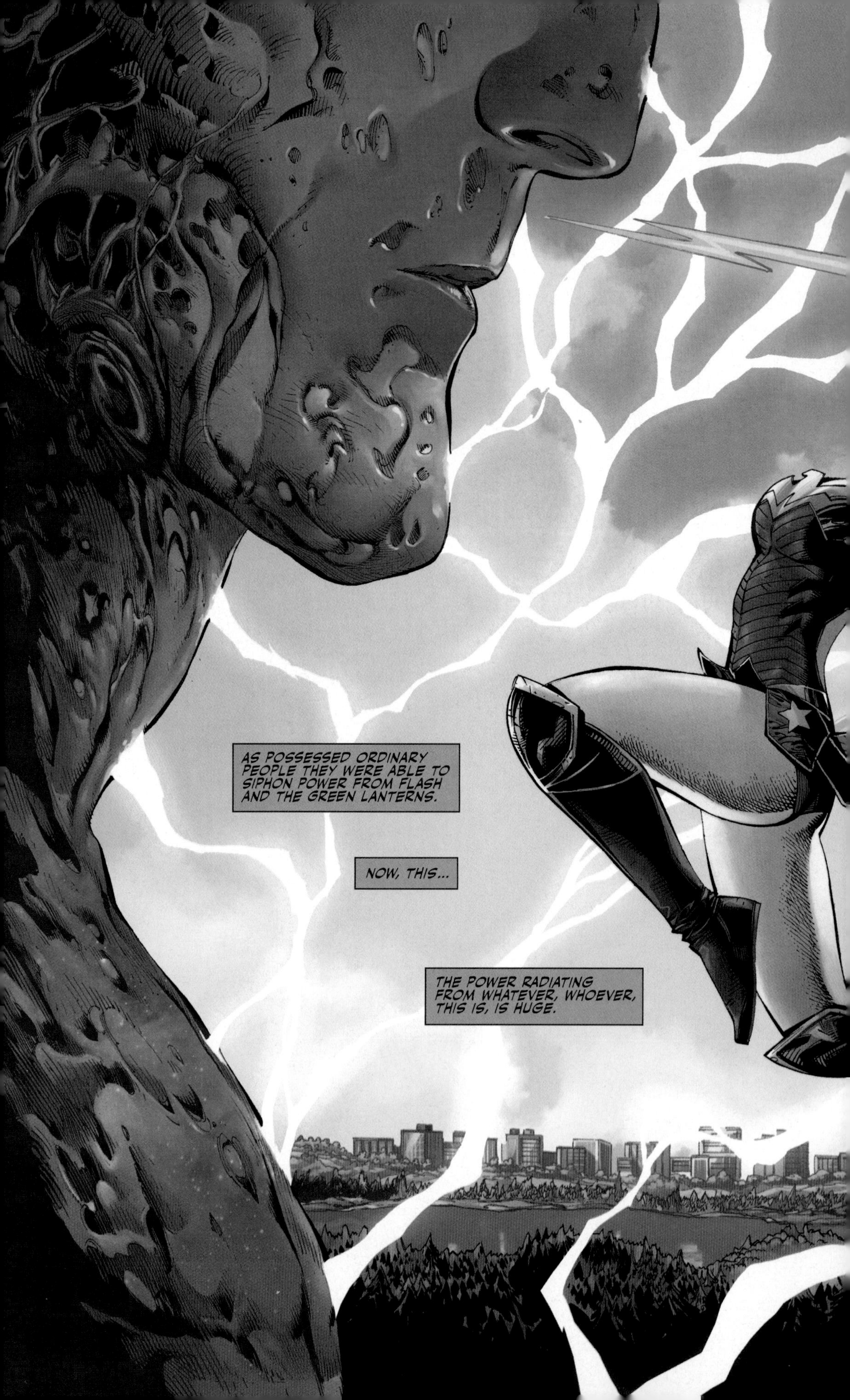
AS POSSESSED ORDINARY PEOPLE THEY WERE ABLE TO SIPHON POWER FROM FLASH AND THE GREEN LANTERNS.
NOW, THIS...
THE POWER RADIATING FROM WHATEVER, WHOEVER, THIS IS, IS HUGE.

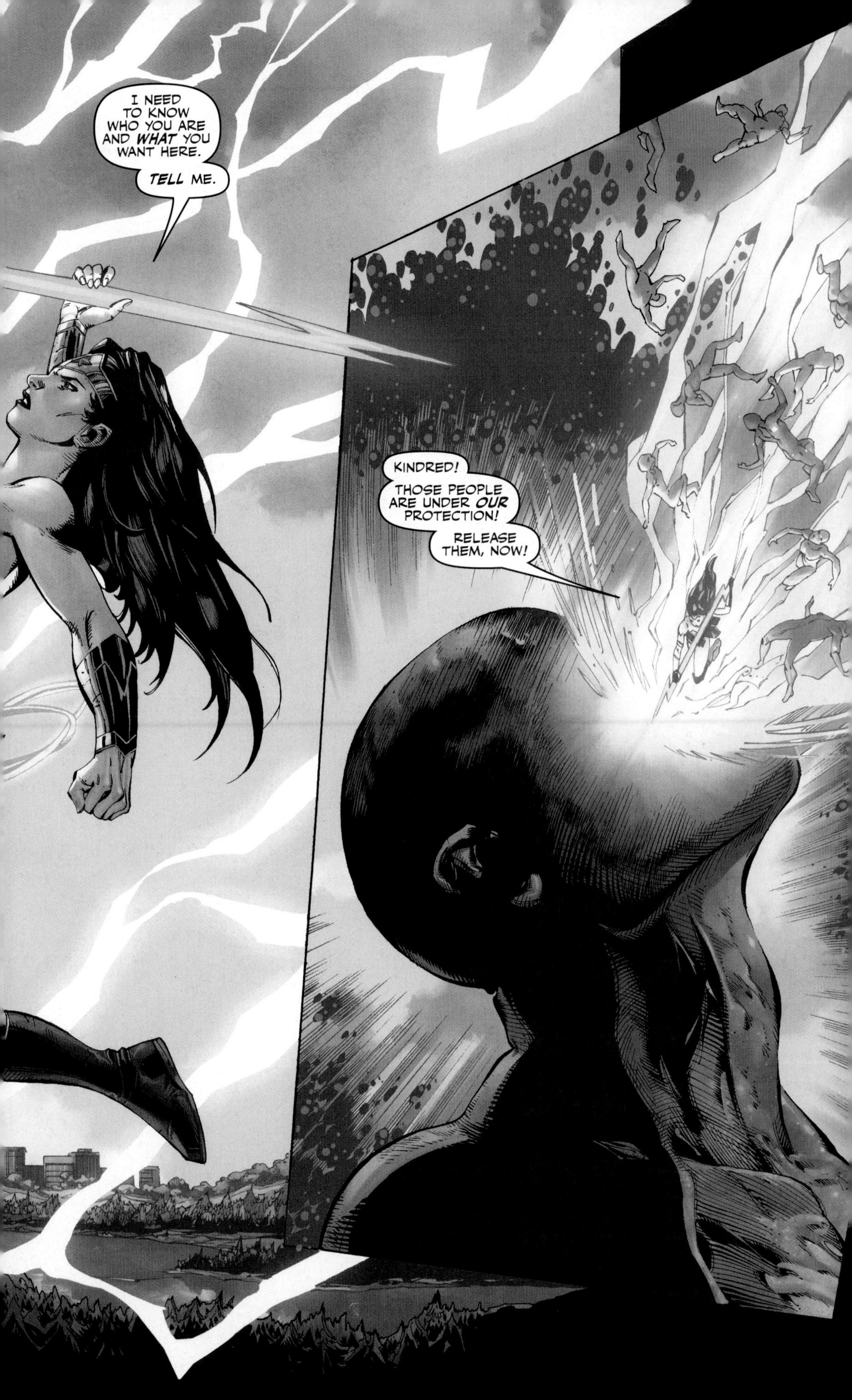
I NEED TO KNOW WHO YOU ARE AND *WHAT* YOU WANT HERE.
*TELL* ME.
KINDRED!
THOSE PEOPLE ARE UNDER *OUR* PROTECTION!
RELEASE THEM, NOW!

OUR PURPOSE WAS WITHIN ALL PEOPLE SO WE WOULD EMERGE FROM THEM WHEREVER THEY WOULD BE.

ON ANY WORLD, AT ANY TIME. WE WOULD *COME* TO END FOREVER.

IF IT'S PEOPLE THAT MAKE YOU, THEN I'LL PULL THEM OUT AND *UNMAKE* YOU.

NO.

YOU HAVE A *PURPOSE* HERE ALSO.

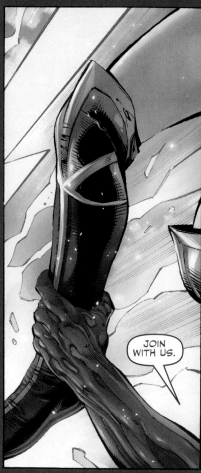

JOIN WITH US.

PURPOSE? WHAT PURPOSE?

YOU WILL RELEASE ALL OF THESE *PEOPLE*.

LET THEM GO!

JOIN US.

JOIN US. JOIN US.

JOIN US.

JOIN US. JOIN US.

JOIN US.

JOIN US. JOIN US.

JOIN US.

JOIN US.

JOIN US AND LEARN.

NO!

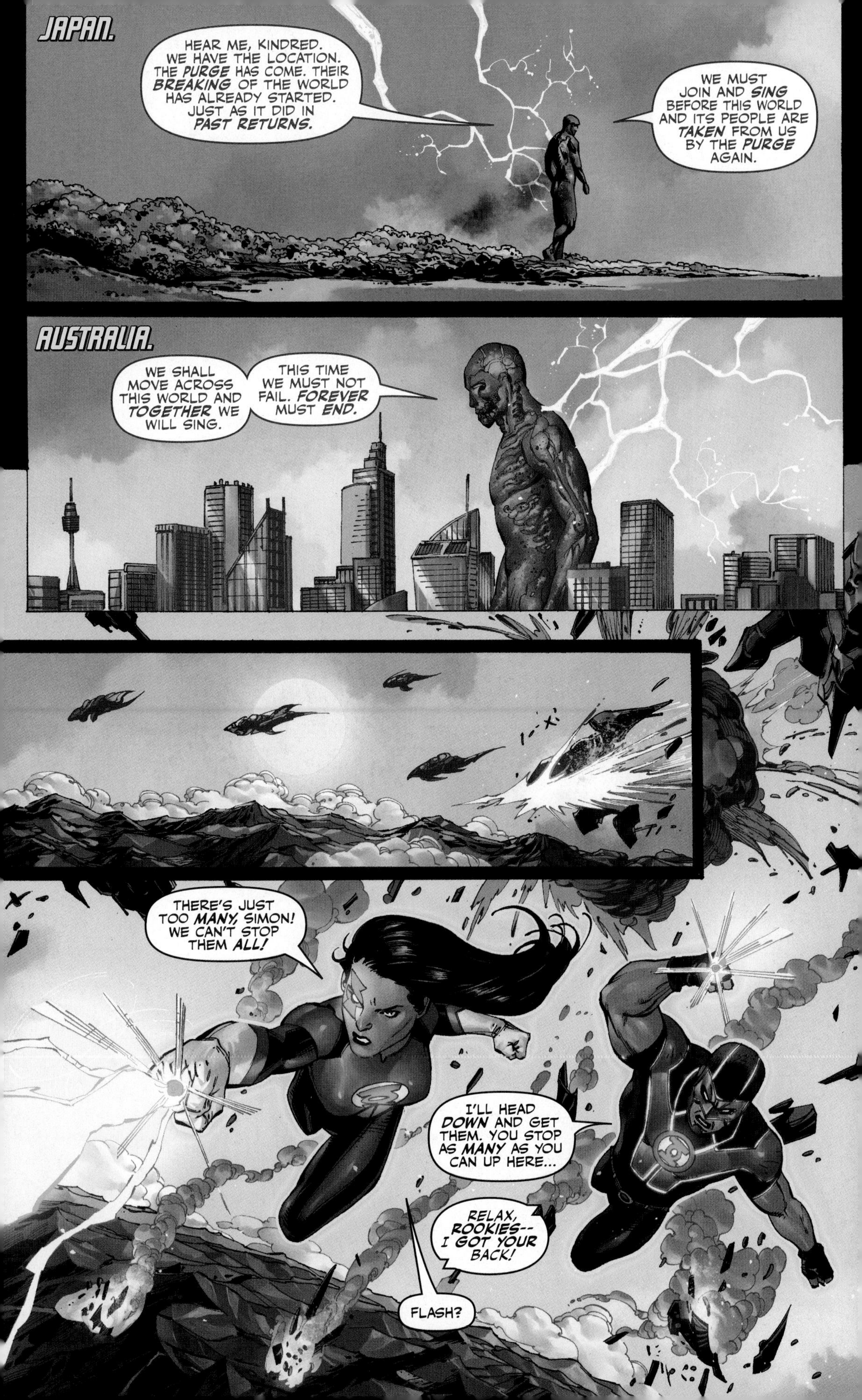
JAPAN.
HEAR ME, KINDRED. WE HAVE THE LOCATION. THE PURGE HAS COME. THEIR BREAKING OF THE WORLD HAS ALREADY STARTED. JUST AS IT DID IN PAST RETURNS.
WE MUST JOIN AND SING BEFORE THIS WORLD AND ITS PEOPLE ARE TAKEN FROM US BY THE PURGE AGAIN.
AUSTRALIA.
WE SHALL MOVE ACROSS THIS WORLD AND TOGETHER WE WILL SING.
THIS TIME WE MUST NOT FAIL. FOREVER MUST END.
THERE'S JUST TOO MANY, SIMON! WE CAN'T STOP THEM ALL!
I'LL HEAD DOWN AND GET THEM. YOU STOP AS MANY AS YOU CAN UP HERE...
RELAX, ROOKIES-- I GOT YOUR BACK!
FLASH?

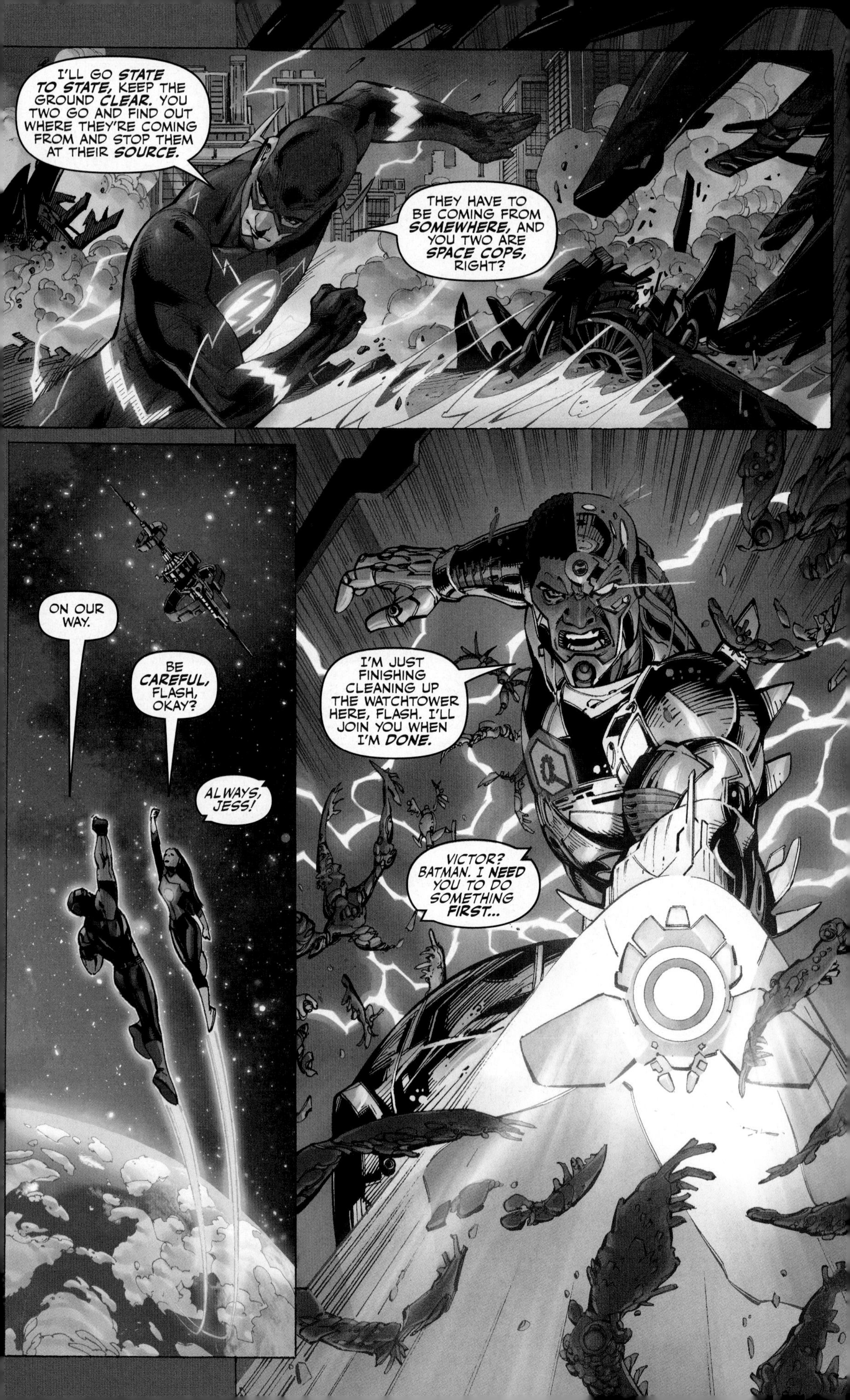
I'LL GO STATE TO STATE, KEEP THE GROUND CLEAR. YOU TWO GO AND FIND OUT WHERE THEY'RE COMING FROM AND STOP THEM AT THEIR SOURCE.
THEY HAVE TO BE COMING FROM SOMEWHERE, AND YOU TWO ARE SPACE COPS, RIGHT?
ON OUR WAY.
BE CAREFUL, FLASH, OKAY?
ALWAYS, JESS!
I'M JUST FINISHING CLEANING UP THE WATCHTOWER HERE, FLASH. I'LL JOIN YOU WHEN I'M DONE.
VICTOR? BATMAN. I NEED YOU TO DO SOMETHING FIRST...

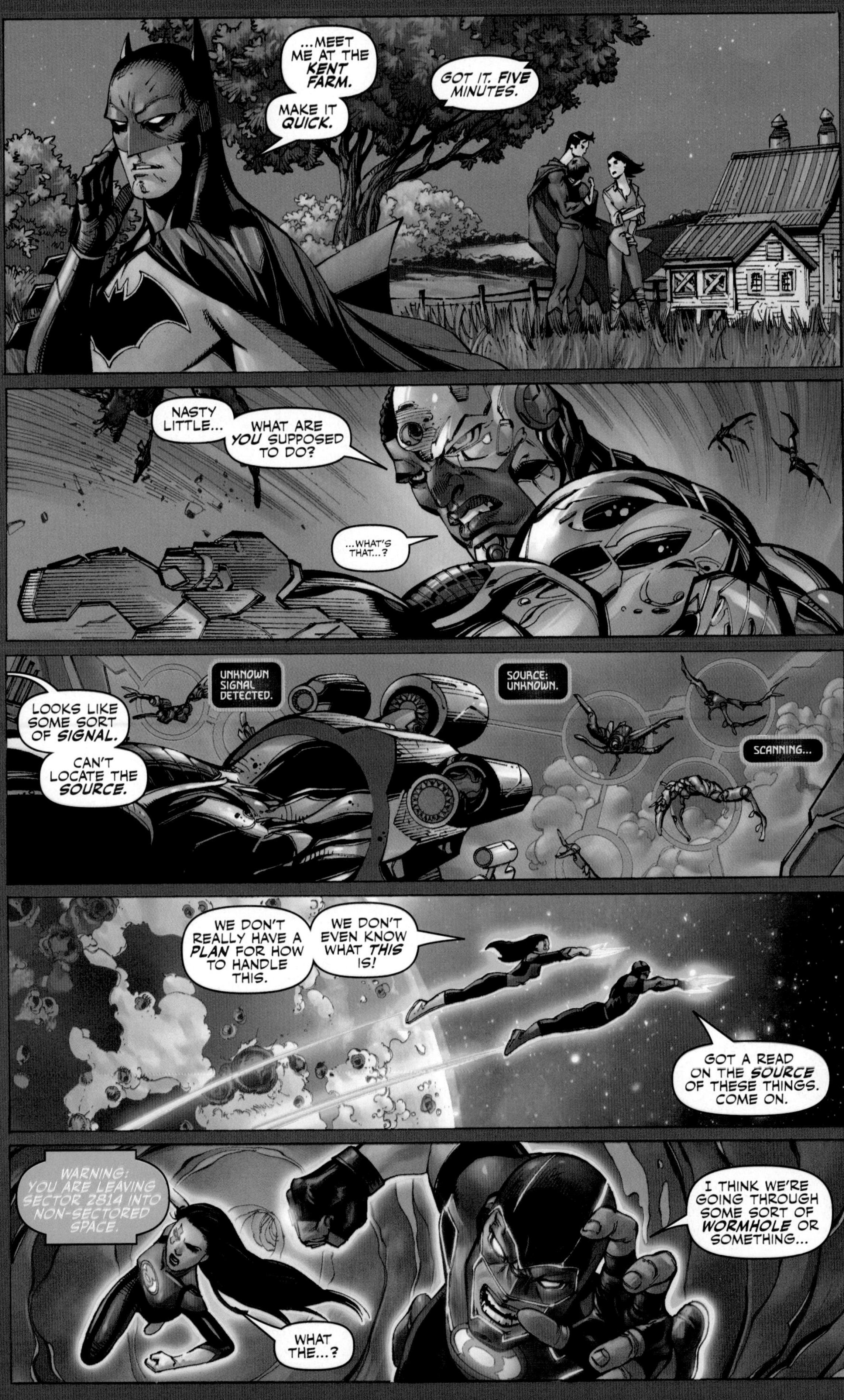
...MEET ME AT THE KENT FARM.
MAKE IT QUICK.
GOT IT. FIVE MINUTES.
NASTY LITTLE...
WHAT ARE YOU SUPPOSED TO DO?
...WHAT'S THAT...?
LOOKS LIKE SOME SORT OF SIGNAL.
CAN'T LOCATE THE SOURCE.
UNKNOWN SIGNAL DETECTED.
SOURCE: UNKNOWN.
SCANNING...
WE DON'T REALLY HAVE A PLAN FOR HOW TO HANDLE THIS.
WE DON'T EVEN KNOW WHAT THIS IS!
GOT A READ ON THE SOURCE OF THESE THINGS. COME ON.
WARNING: YOU ARE LEAVING SECTOR 2814 INTO NON-SECTORED SPACE.
I THINK WE'RE GOING THROUGH SOME SORT OF WORMHOLE OR SOMETHING...
WHAT THE...?

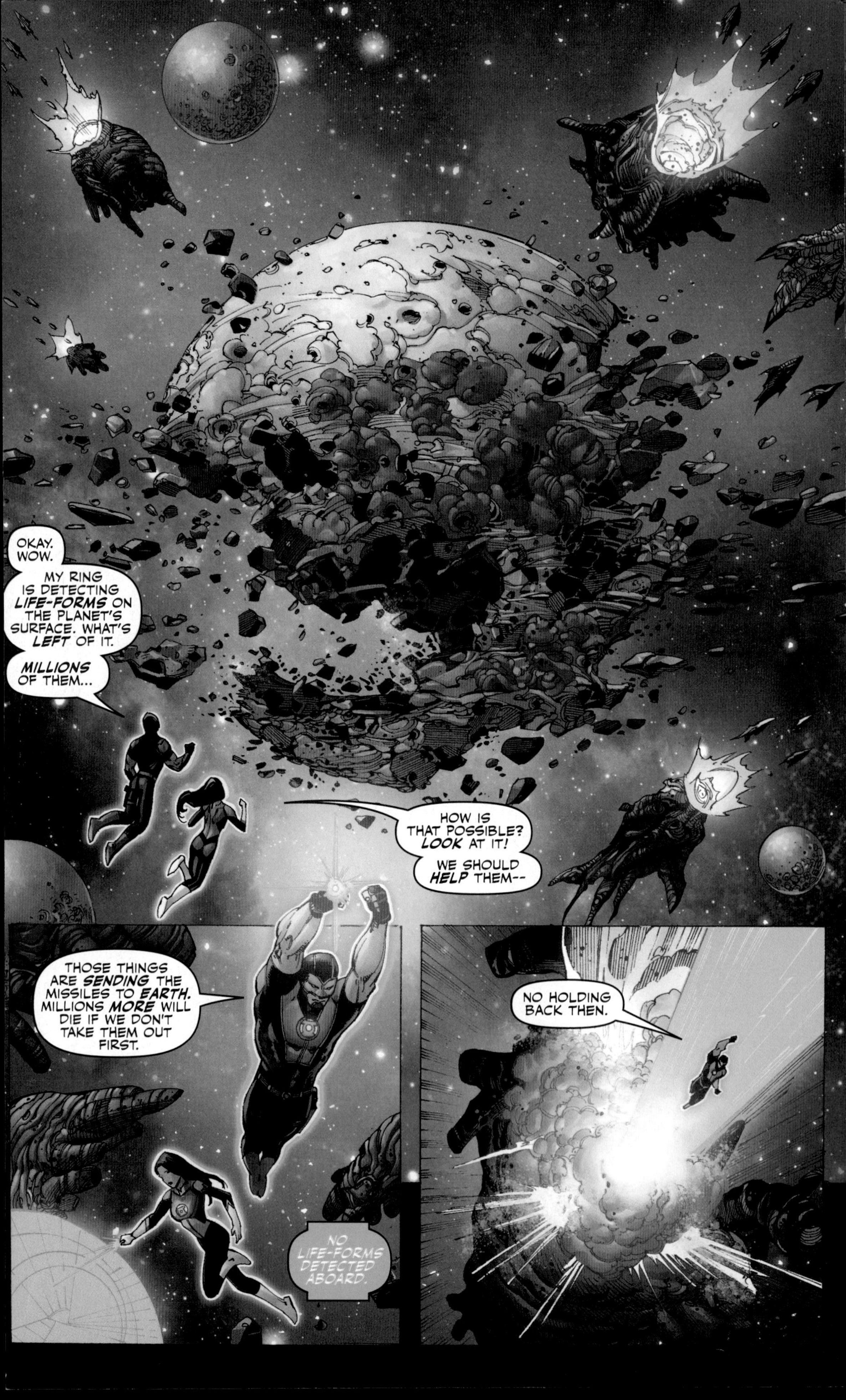
OKAY. WOW.
MY RING IS DETECTING LIFE-FORMS ON THE PLANET'S SURFACE. WHAT'S LEFT OF IT.
MILLIONS OF THEM...
HOW IS THAT POSSIBLE? LOOK AT IT!
WE SHOULD HELP THEM--
THOSE THINGS ARE SENDING THE MISSILES TO EARTH. MILLIONS MORE WILL DIE IF WE DON'T TAKE THEM OUT FIRST.
NO LIFE-FORMS DETECTED ABOARD.
NO HOLDING BACK THEN.

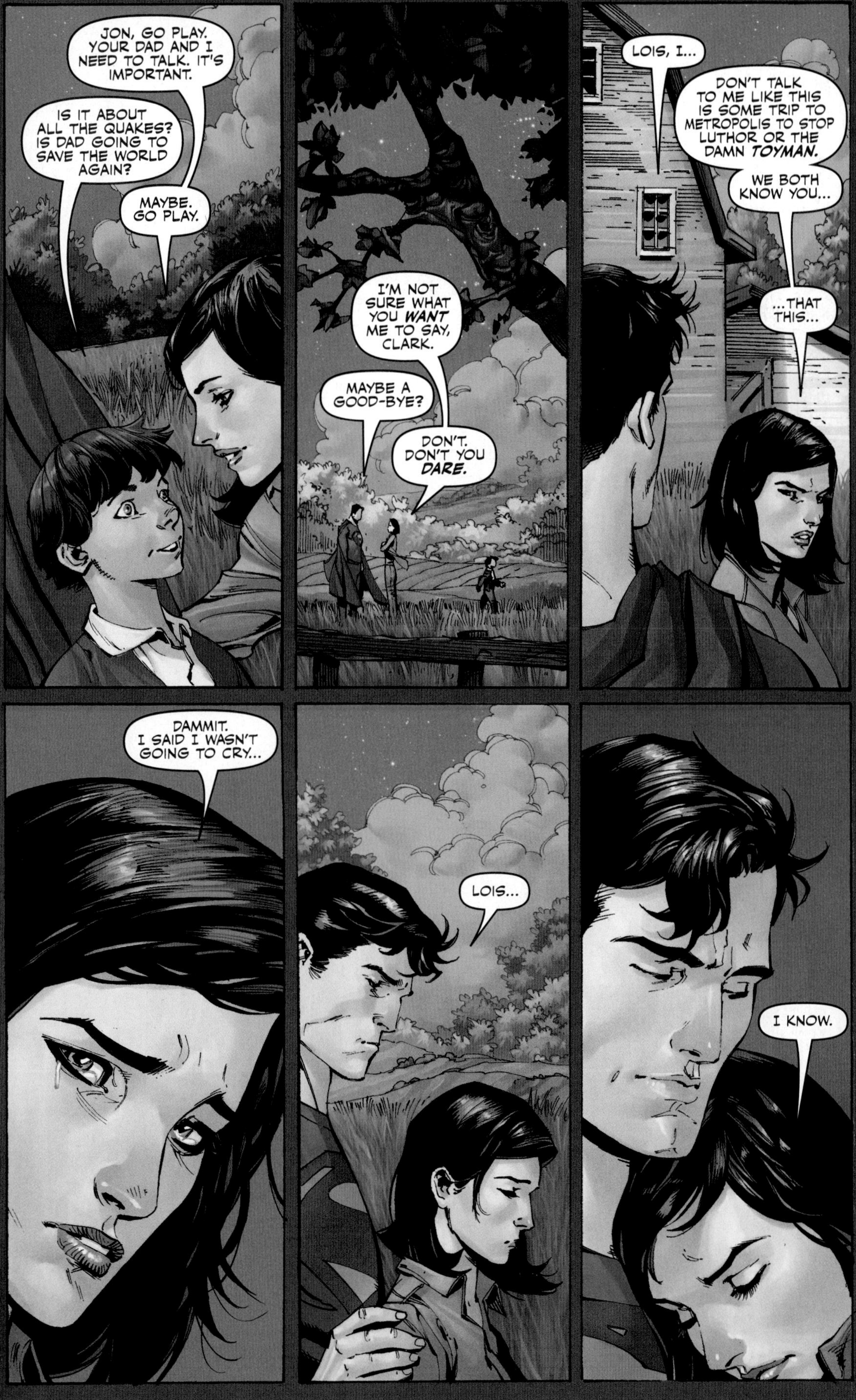
JON, GO PLAY. YOUR DAD AND I NEED TO TALK. IT'S IMPORTANT.
IS IT ABOUT ALL THE QUAKES? IS DAD GOING TO SAVE THE WORLD AGAIN?
MAYBE. GO PLAY.
I'M NOT SURE WHAT YOU WANT ME TO SAY, CLARK.
MAYBE A GOOD-BYE?
DON'T. DON'T YOU DARE.
LOIS, I...
DON'T TALK TO ME LIKE THIS IS SOME TRIP TO METROPOLIS TO STOP LUTHOR OR THE DAMN TOYMAN.
WE BOTH KNOW YOU...
...THAT THIS...
DAMMIT. I SAID I WASN'T GOING TO CRY...
LOIS...
I KNOW.

IT *IS* DANGEROUS. BUT IF I *DON'T* TRY, IT COULD MEAN THE LIFE OF *EVERY* FAMILY ON EARTH.

IF I *DON'T* DO THIS, YOU AND JON WILL DIE.

IF YOU DO THIS, *YOU* WILL.

I CAME BACK BEFORE.

NOT *HERE.* WE'VE ALREADY SEEN IT DOESN'T WORK LIKE THAT HERE.

LOIS...

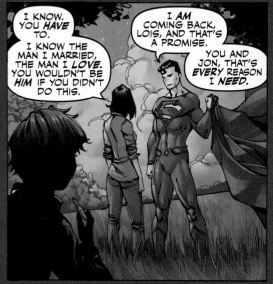

I KNOW. YOU *HAVE* TO.

I KNOW THE MAN I MARRIED, THE MAN I *LOVE.* YOU WOULDN'T BE *HIM* IF YOU DIDN'T DO THIS.

I *AM* COMING BACK, LOIS, AND THAT'S A PROMISE.

YOU AND JON, THAT'S *EVERY* REASON I *NEED.*

RIGHT. LET'S GET THIS *DONE.*

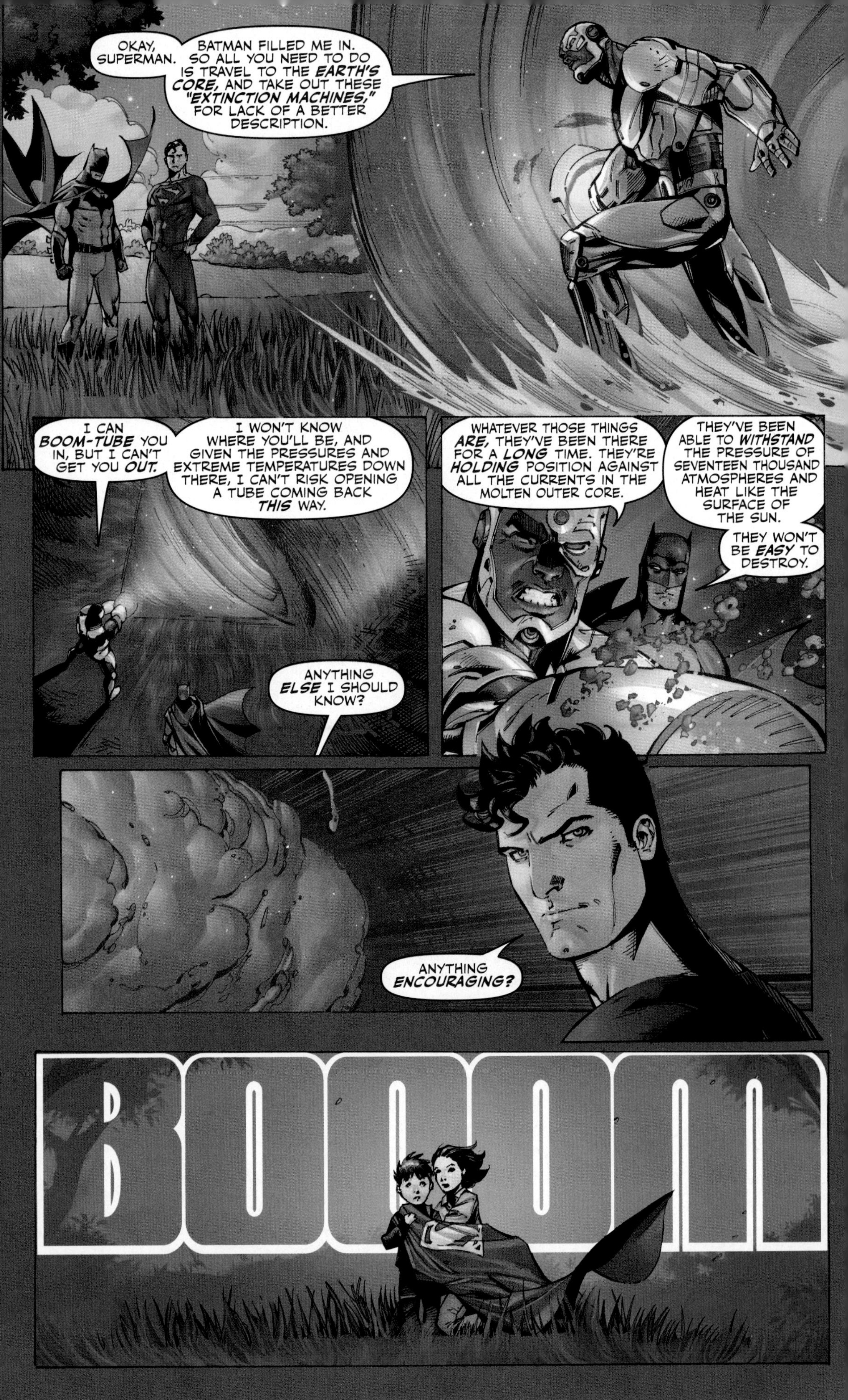
OKAY, SUPERMAN.
BATMAN FILLED ME IN. SO ALL YOU NEED TO DO IS TRAVEL TO THE EARTH'S CORE, AND TAKE OUT THESE "EXTINCTION MACHINES," FOR LACK OF A BETTER DESCRIPTION.
I CAN BOOM-TUBE YOU IN, BUT I CAN'T GET YOU OUT.
I WON'T KNOW WHERE YOU'LL BE, AND GIVEN THE PRESSURES AND EXTREME TEMPERATURES DOWN THERE, I CAN'T RISK OPENING A TUBE COMING BACK THIS WAY.
ANYTHING ELSE I SHOULD KNOW?
WHATEVER THOSE THINGS ARE, THEY'VE BEEN THERE FOR A LONG TIME. THEY'RE HOLDING POSITION AGAINST ALL THE CURRENTS IN THE MOLTEN OUTER CORE.
THEY'VE BEEN ABLE TO WITHSTAND THE PRESSURE OF SEVENTEEN THOUSAND ATMOSPHERES AND HEAT LIKE THE SURFACE OF THE SUN.
THEY WON'T BE EASY TO DESTROY.
ANYTHING ENCOURAGING?
BOOOM

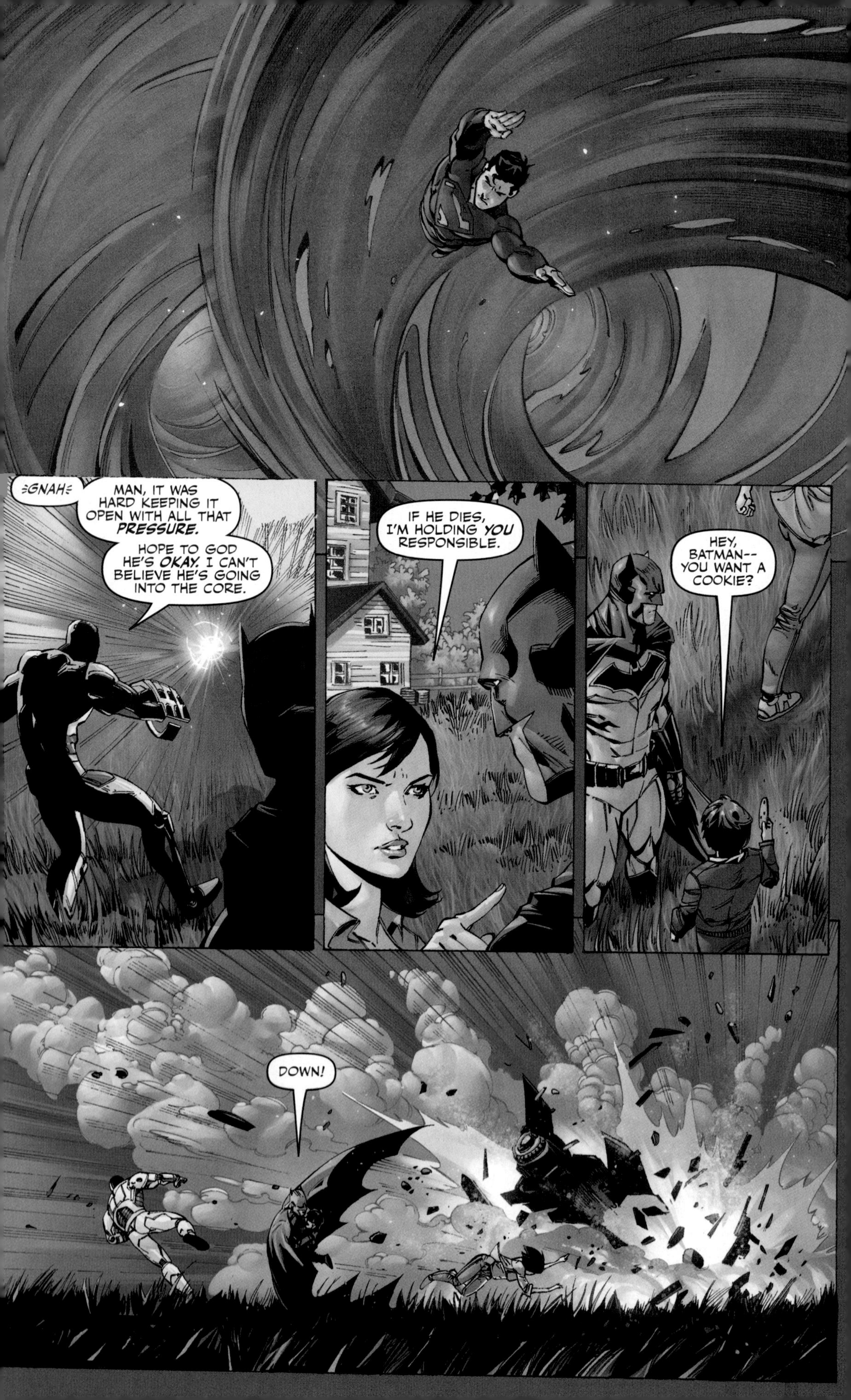
GNAH
MAN, IT WAS HARD KEEPING IT OPEN WITH ALL THAT PRESSURE.
HOPE TO GOD HE'S OKAY. I CAN'T BELIEVE HE'S GOING INTO THE CORE.
IF HE DIES, I'M HOLDING YOU RESPONSIBLE.
HEY, BATMAN-- YOU WANT A COOKIE?
DOWN!

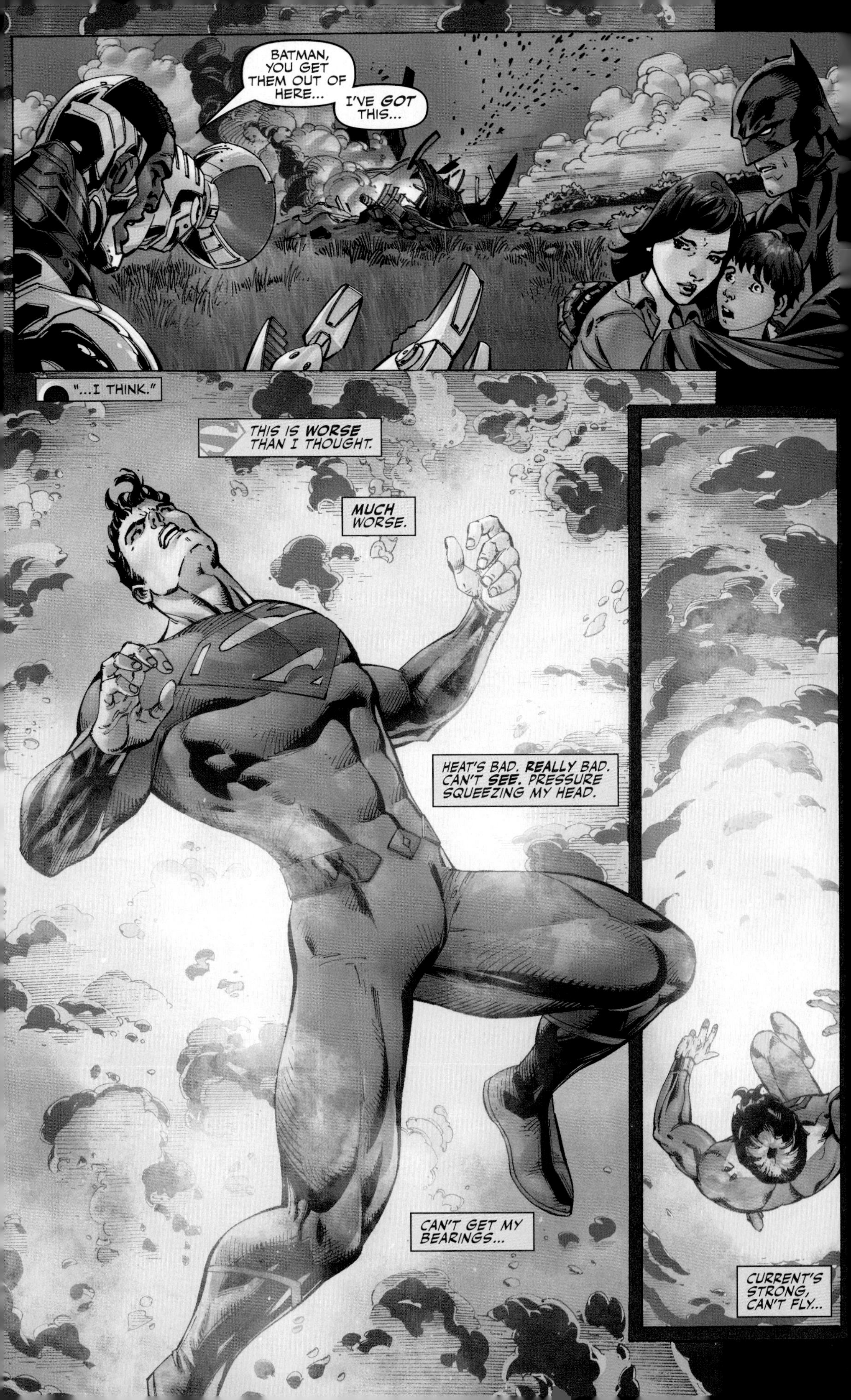
BATMAN, YOU GET THEM OUT OF HERE...
I'VE GOT THIS...
"...I THINK."
THIS IS WORSE THAN I THOUGHT.
MUCH WORSE.
HEAT'S BAD. REALLY BAD. CAN'T SEE. PRESSURE SQUEEZING MY HEAD.
CAN'T GET MY BEARINGS...
CURRENT'S STRONG, CAN'T FLY...

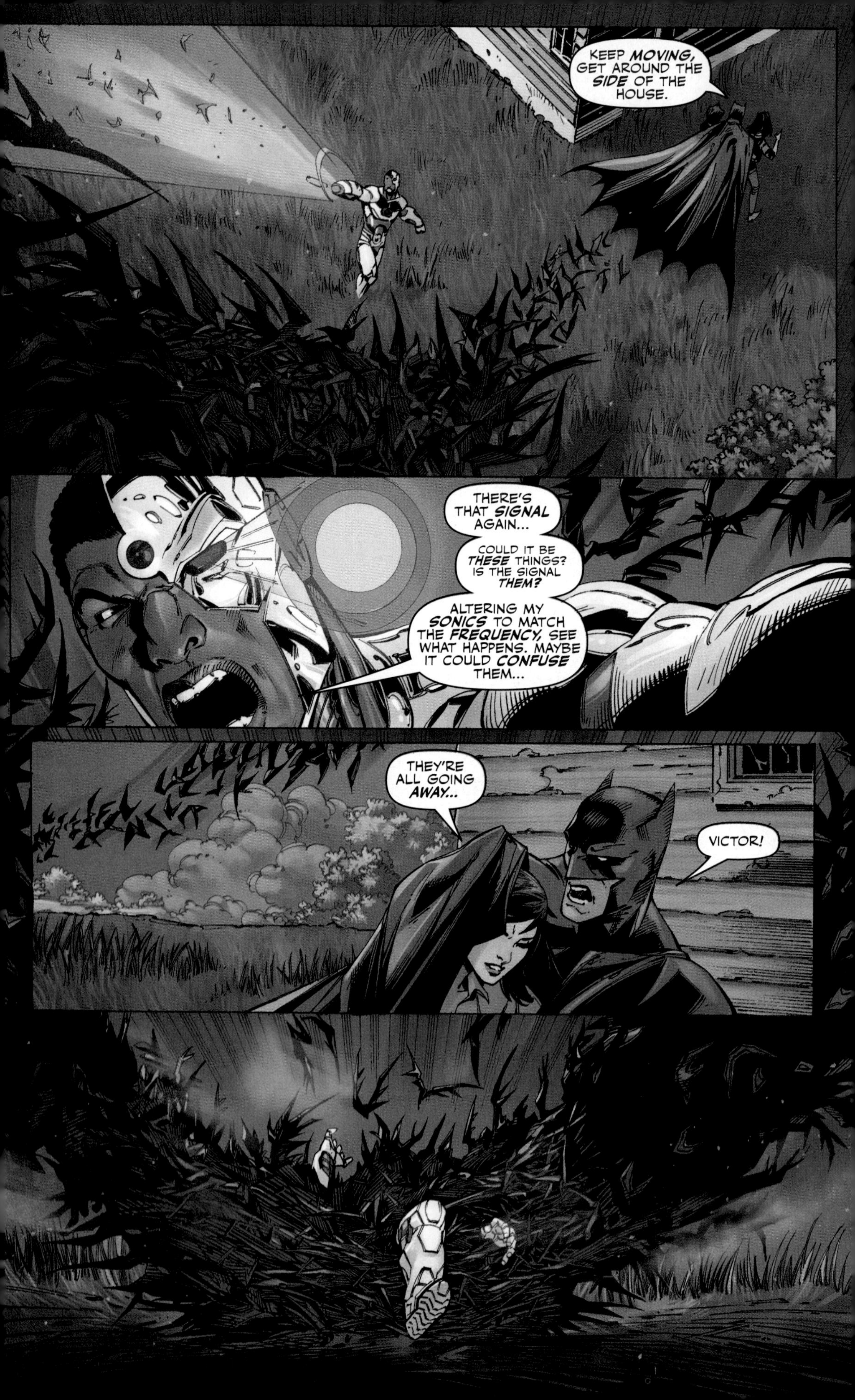
KEEP MOVING, GET AROUND THE SIDE OF THE HOUSE.
THERE'S THAT SIGNAL AGAIN...
COULD IT BE THESE THINGS? IS THE SIGNAL THEM?
ALTERING MY SONICS TO MATCH THE FREQUENCY, SEE WHAT HAPPENS. MAYBE IT COULD CONFUSE THEM...
THEY'RE ALL GOING AWAY...
VICTOR!

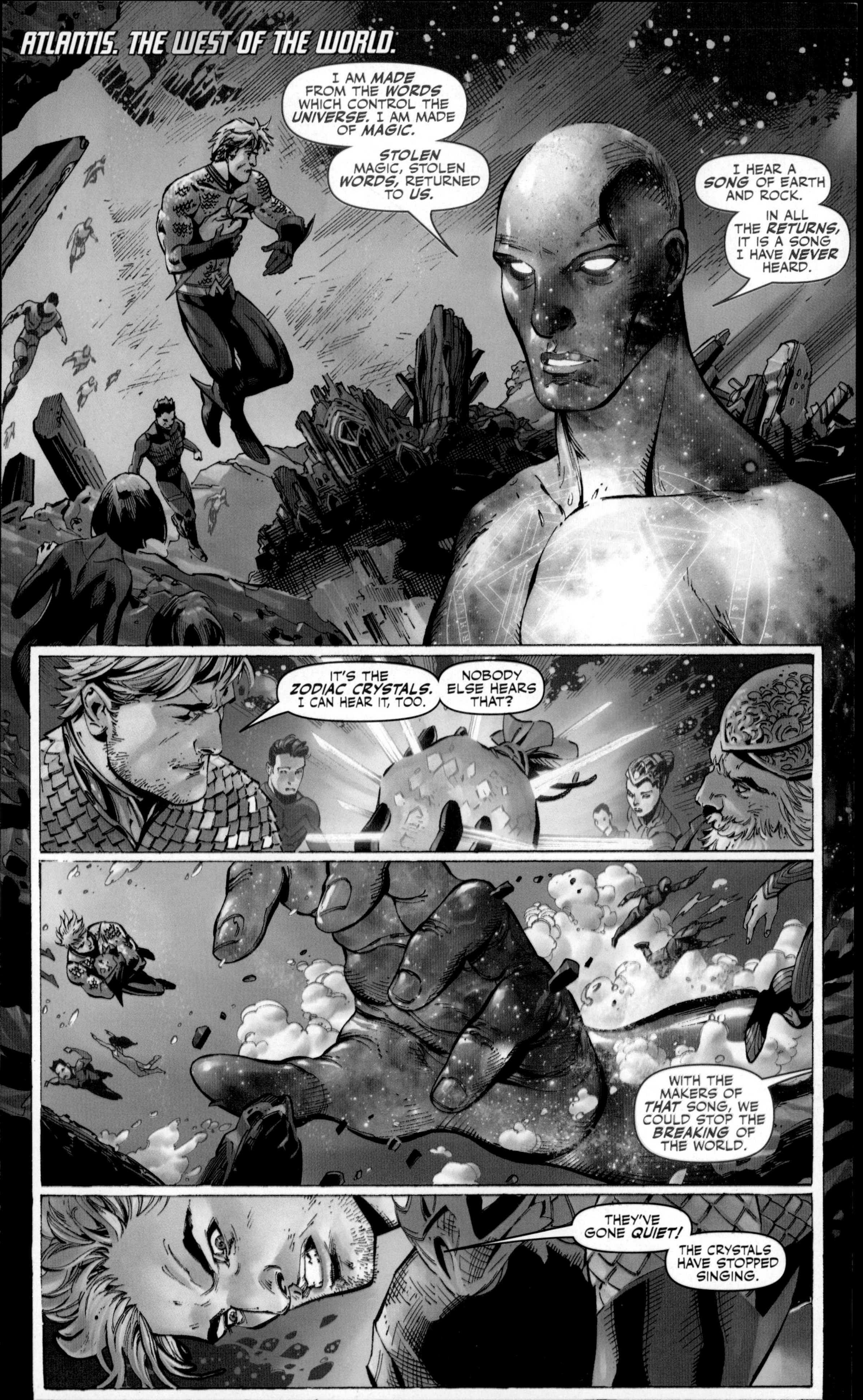
ATLANTIS. THE WEST OF THE WORLD.
I AM MADE FROM THE WORDS WHICH CONTROL THE UNIVERSE. I AM MADE OF MAGIC.
STOLEN MAGIC, STOLEN WORDS, RETURNED TO US.
I HEAR A SONG OF EARTH AND ROCK.
IN ALL THE RETURNS, IT IS A SONG I HAVE NEVER HEARD.
IT'S THE ZODIAC CRYSTALS. I CAN HEAR IT, TOO.
NOBODY ELSE HEARS THAT?
WITH THE MAKERS OF THAT SONG, WE COULD STOP THE BREAKING OF THE WORLD.
THEY'VE GONE QUIET!
THE CRYSTALS HAVE STOPPED SINGING.

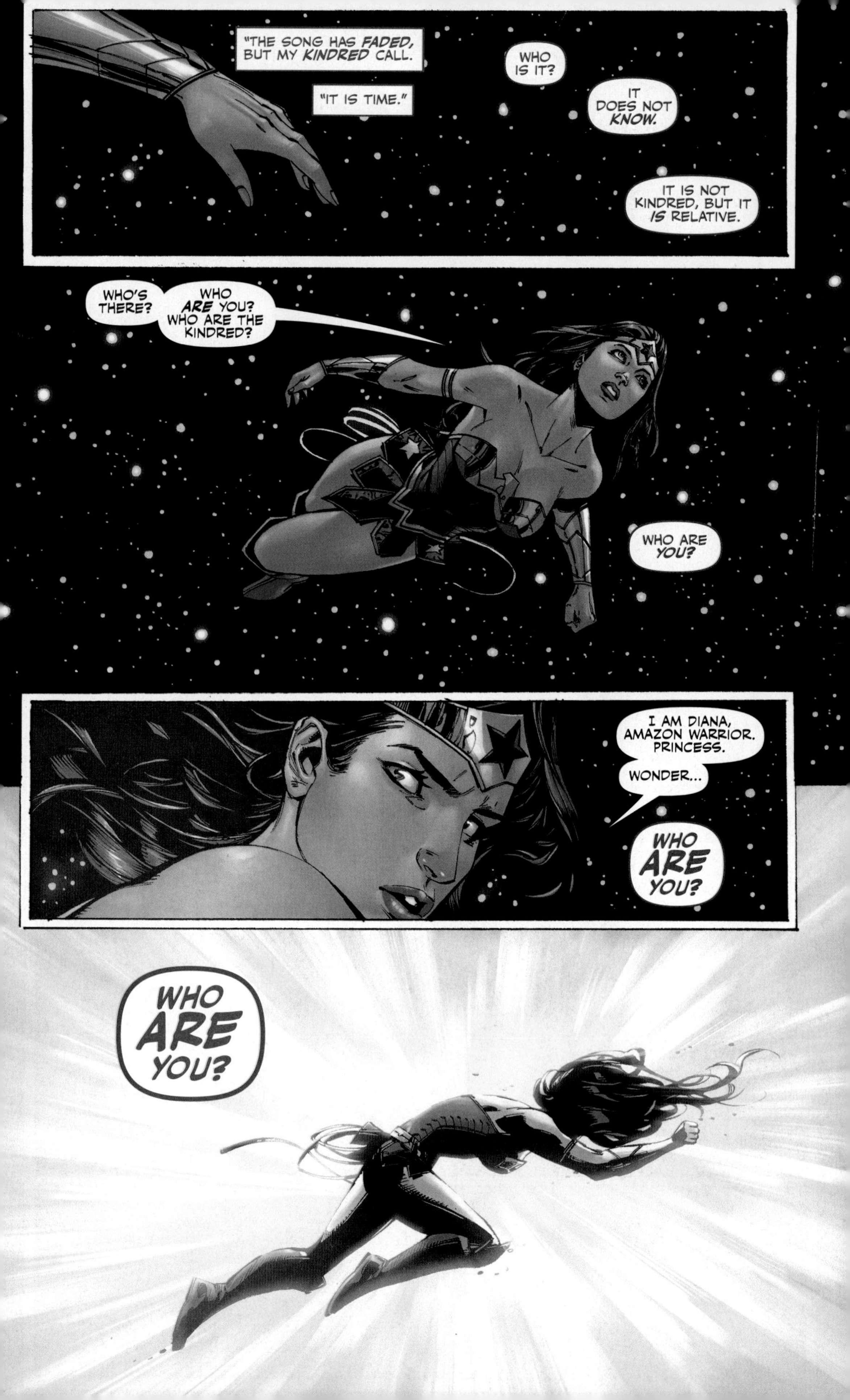
"THE SONG HAS FADED, BUT MY KINDRED CALL.
"IT IS TIME."
WHO IS IT?
IT DOES NOT KNOW.
IT IS NOT KINDRED, BUT IT IS RELATIVE.
WHO'S THERE?
WHO ARE YOU? WHO ARE THE KINDRED?
WHO ARE YOU?
I AM DIANA, AMAZON WARRIOR. PRINCESS.
WONDER...
WHO ARE YOU?
WHO ARE YOU?

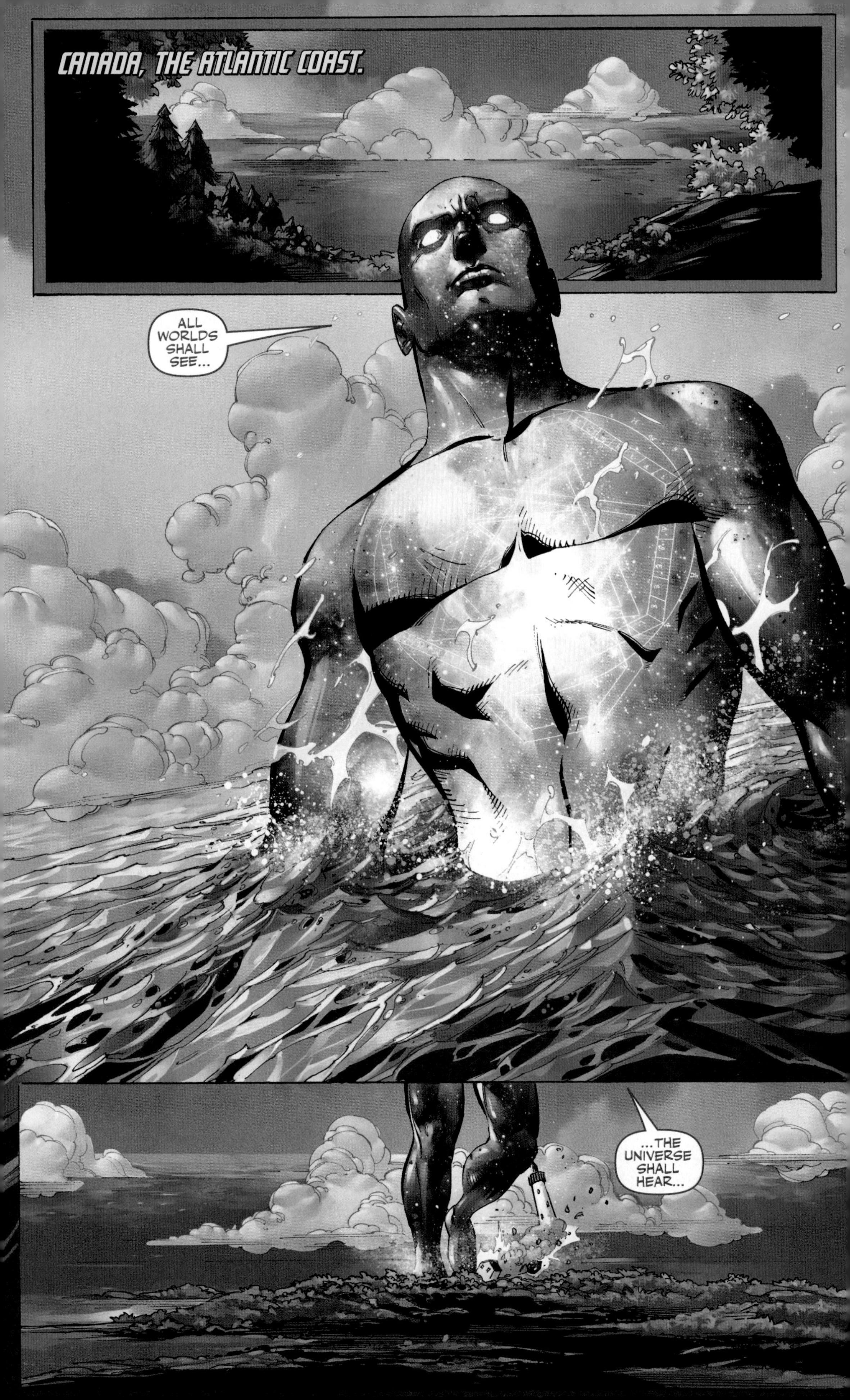
CANADA, THE ATLANTIC COAST.
ALL WORLDS SHALL SEE...
...THE UNIVERSE SHALL HEAR...

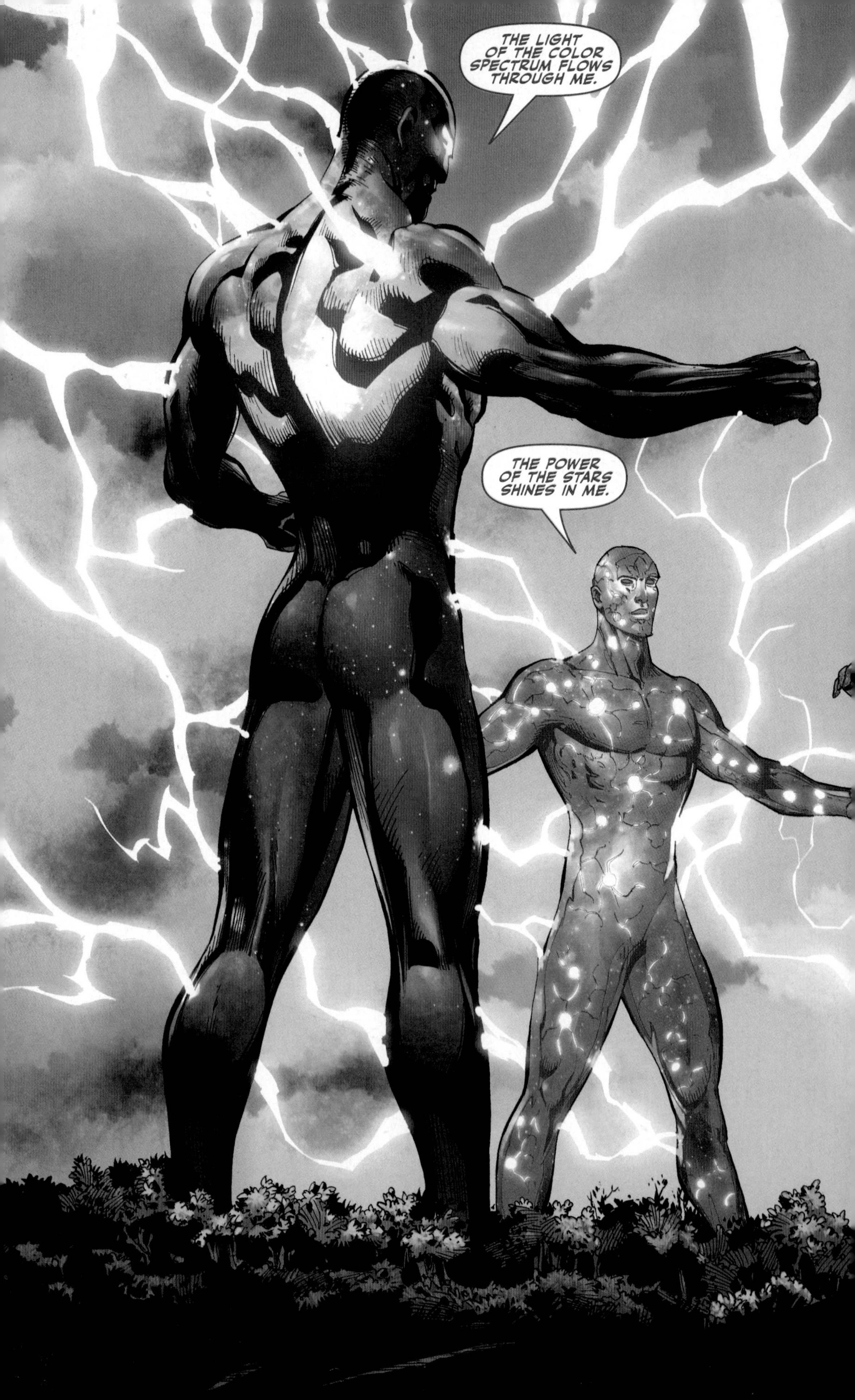
THE LIGHT OF THE COLOR SPECTRUM FLOWS THROUGH ME.
THE POWER OF THE STARS SHINES IN ME.

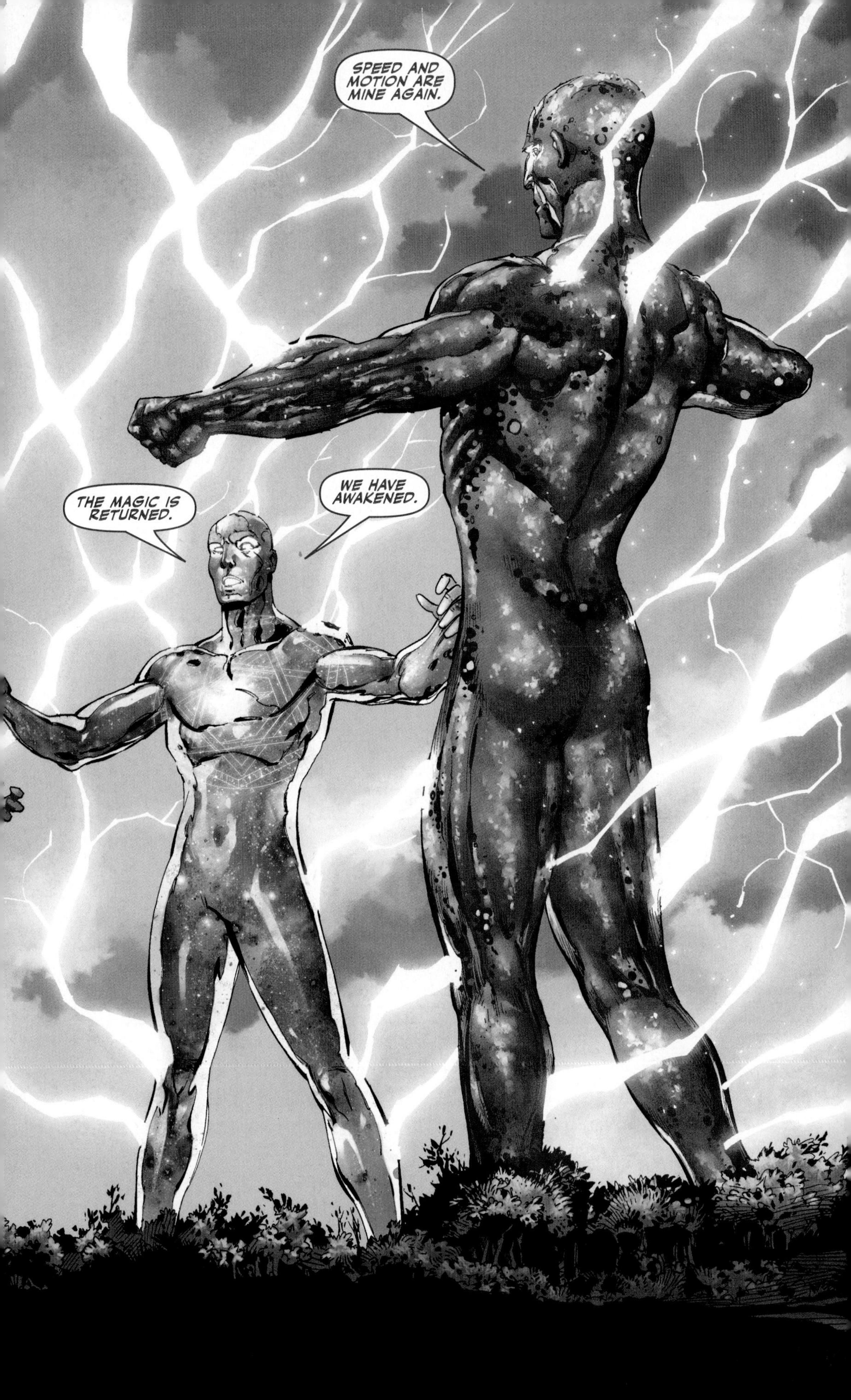
SPEED AND MOTION ARE MINE AGAIN.
THE MAGIC IS RETURNED.
WE HAVE AWAKENED.

GOT TO GET...
UNDER *CONTROL*...

HEAT AND PRESSURE
LIKE BEING COOKED.
BARELY OPEN MY EYES...

...NEED TO FIND
THESE THINGS...

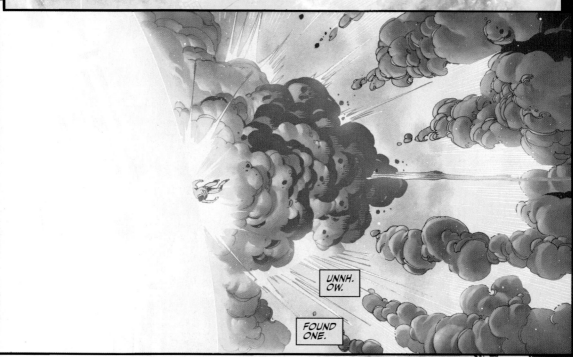

UNNH.
OW.

FOUND
ONE.

HEAT VISION.

NO. STUPID. HOTTER *HERE*
THAN I CAN MAKE IT.

I DON'T KNOW
WHAT TO DO.

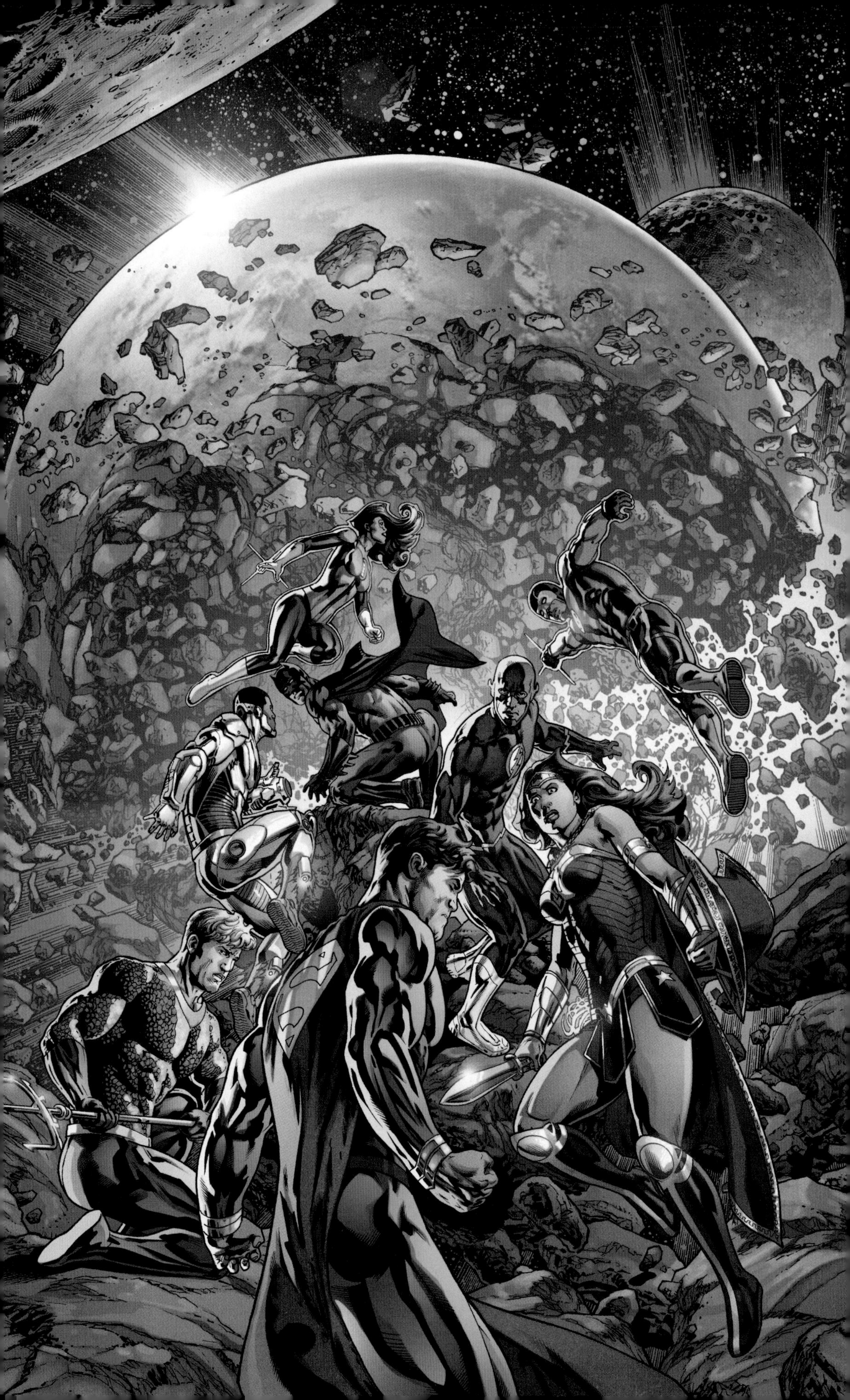

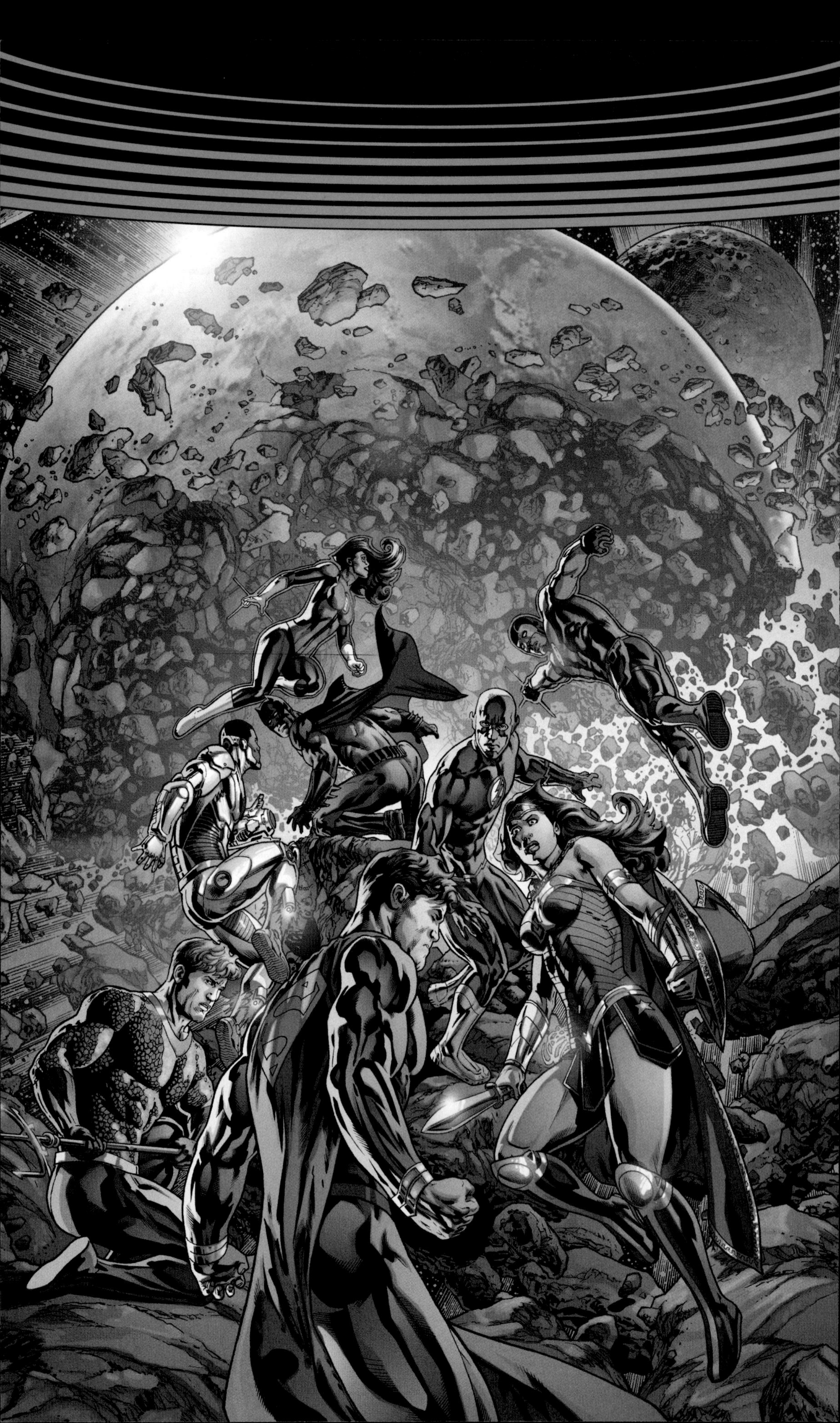

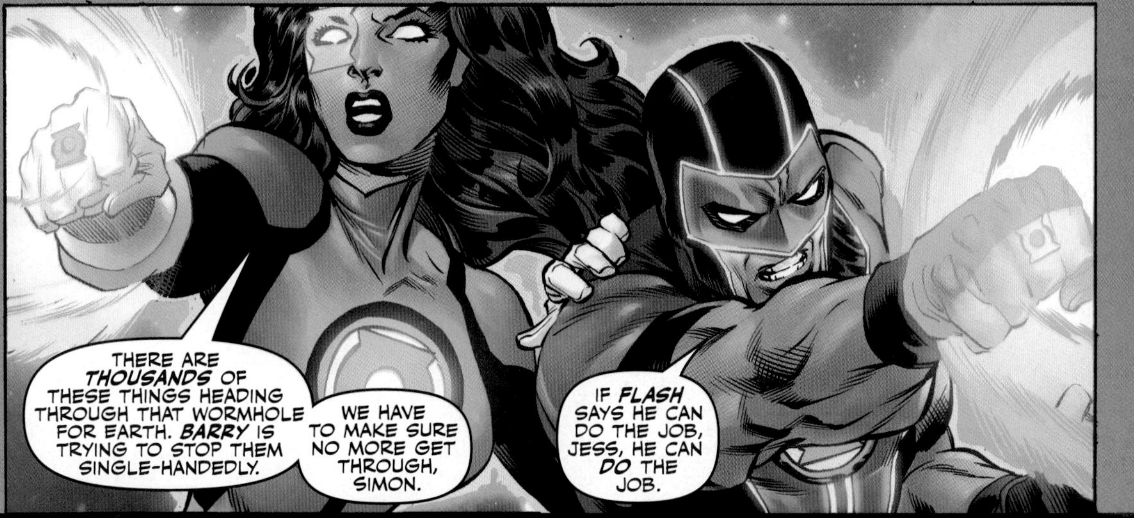
THERE ARE THOUSANDS OF THESE THINGS HEADING THROUGH THAT WORMHOLE FOR EARTH. BARRY IS TRYING TO STOP THEM SINGLE-HANDEDLY.
WE HAVE TO MAKE SURE NO MORE GET THROUGH, SIMON.
IF FLASH SAYS HE CAN DO THE JOB, JESS, HE CAN DO THE JOB.

# THE EXTINCTION MACHINES PART FOUR

WRITTEN by BRYAN HITCH PENCILLED by JESUS MERINO INKED by ANDY OWENS & JESUS MERINO

COLORED by TOMEU MOREY LETTERED by RICHARD STARKINGS & COMICRAFT COVER by FERNANDO PASARIN & BRAD ANDERSON VARIANT COVER by YANICK PAQUETTE & NATHAN FAIRBAIRN ASSISTS by AMEDEO TURTURRO & DIEGO LOPEZ EDITS by BRIAN CUNNINGHAM

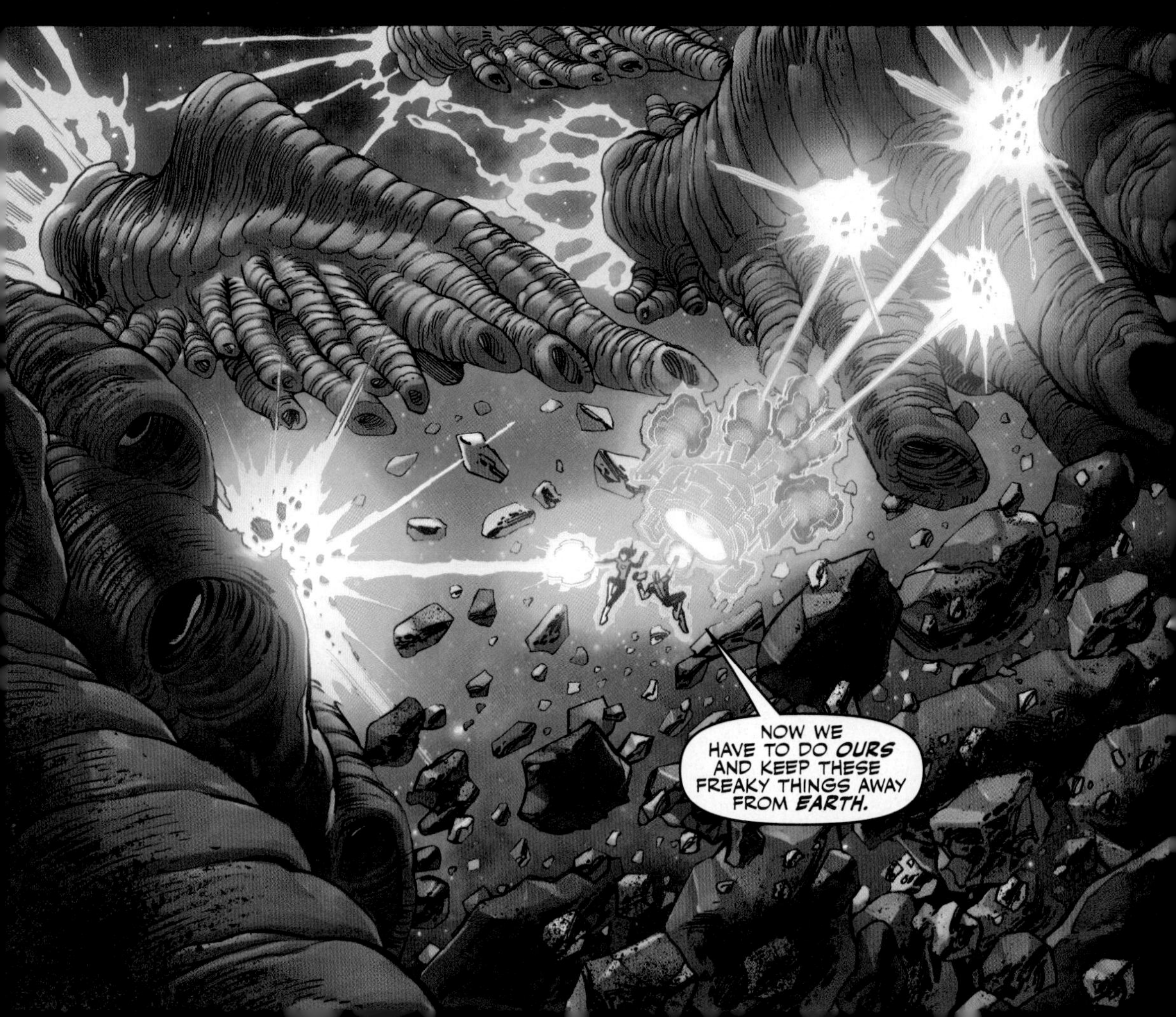
NOW WE HAVE TO DO OURS AND KEEP THESE FREAKY THINGS AWAY FROM EARTH.

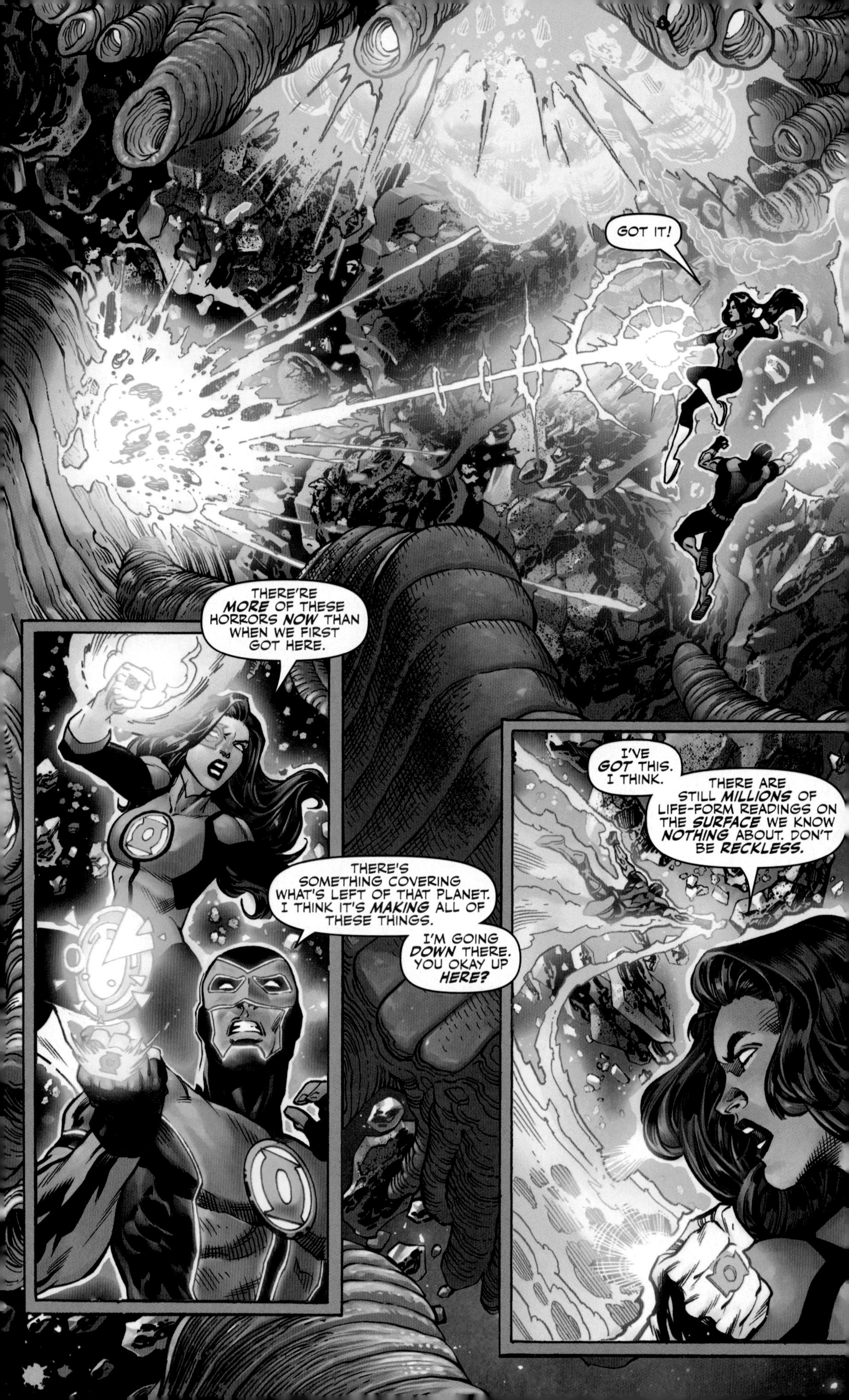
GOT IT!
THERE'RE MORE OF THESE HORRORS NOW THAN WHEN WE FIRST GOT HERE.
THERE'S SOMETHING COVERING WHAT'S LEFT OF THAT PLANET. I THINK IT'S MAKING ALL OF THESE THINGS.
I'M GOING DOWN THERE. YOU OKAY UP HERE?
I'VE GOT THIS. I THINK.
THERE ARE STILL MILLIONS OF LIFE-FORM READINGS ON THE SURFACE WE KNOW NOTHING ABOUT. DON'T BE RECKLESS.

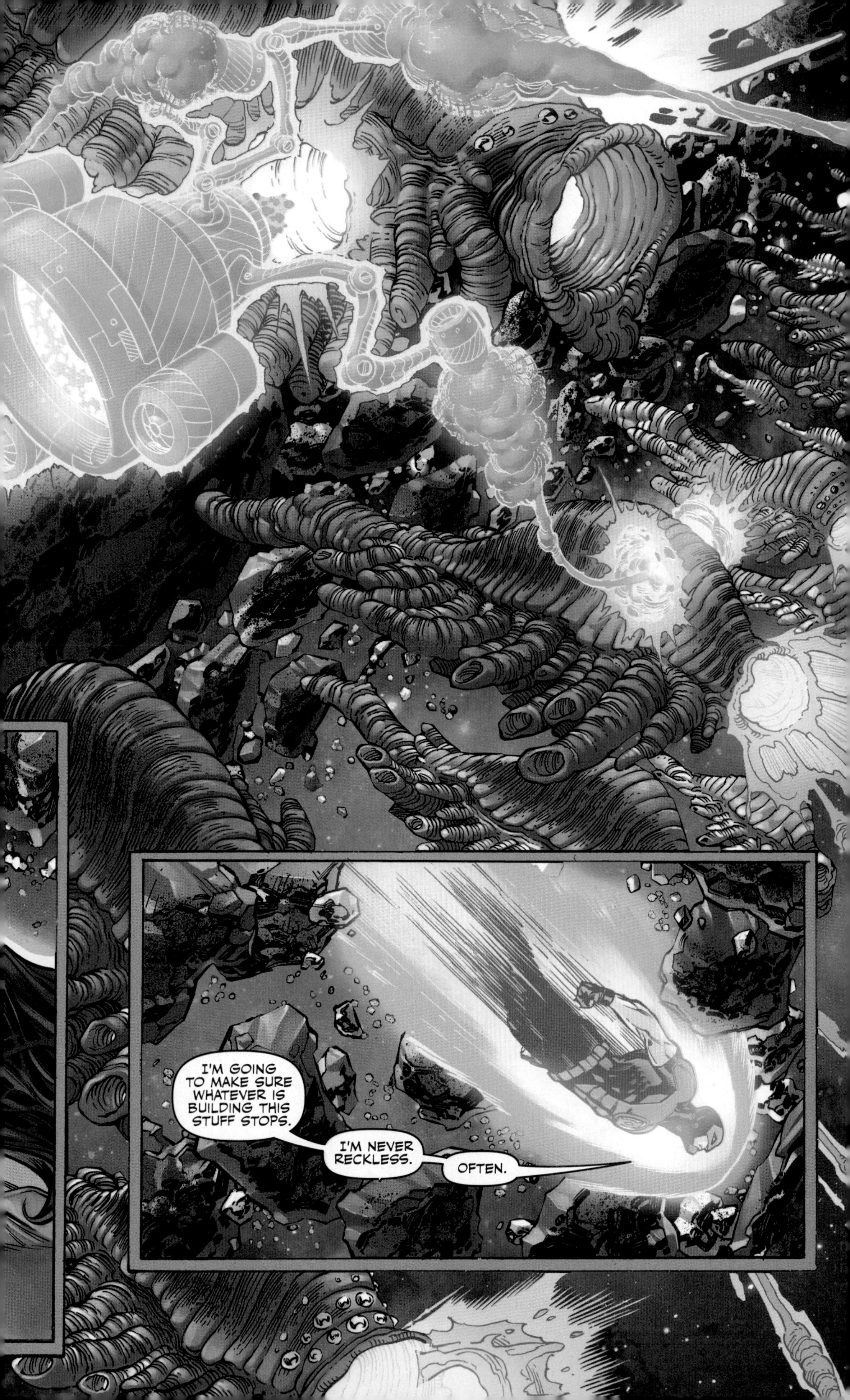
I'M GOING TO MAKE SURE WHATEVER IS BUILDING THIS STUFF STOPS.
I'M NEVER RECKLESS.
OFTEN.

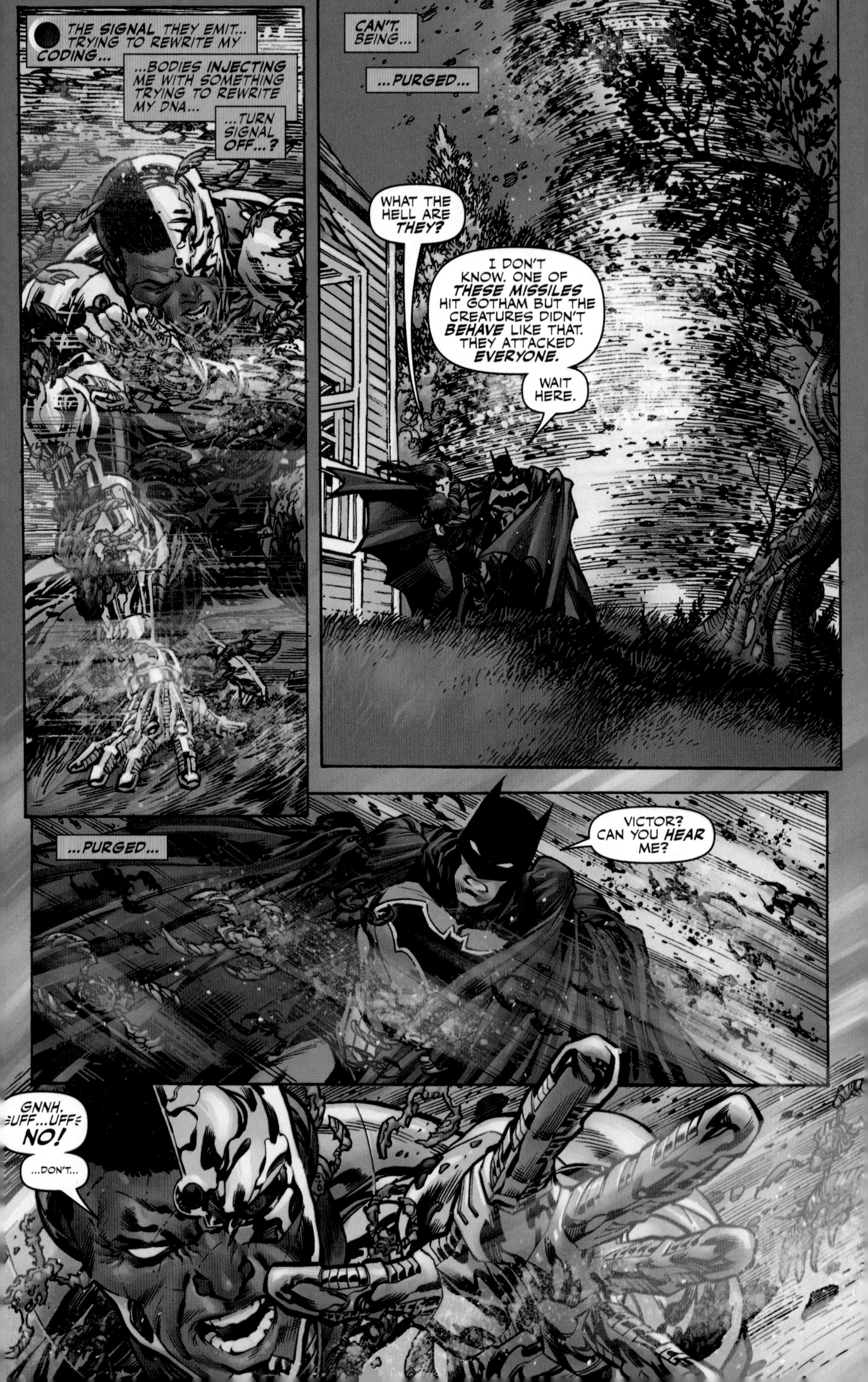
THE SIGNAL THEY EMIT... TRYING TO REWRITE MY CODING...
...BODIES INJECTING ME WITH SOMETHING TRYING TO REWRITE MY DNA...
...TURN SIGNAL OFF...?
CAN'T. BEING...
...PURGED...
WHAT THE HELL ARE THEY?
I DON'T KNOW. ONE OF THESE MISSILES HIT GOTHAM BUT THE CREATURES DIDN'T BEHAVE LIKE THAT. THEY ATTACKED EVERYONE.
WAIT HERE.
...PURGED...
VICTOR? CAN YOU HEAR ME?
GNNH. UFF...UFF NO!
...DON'T...

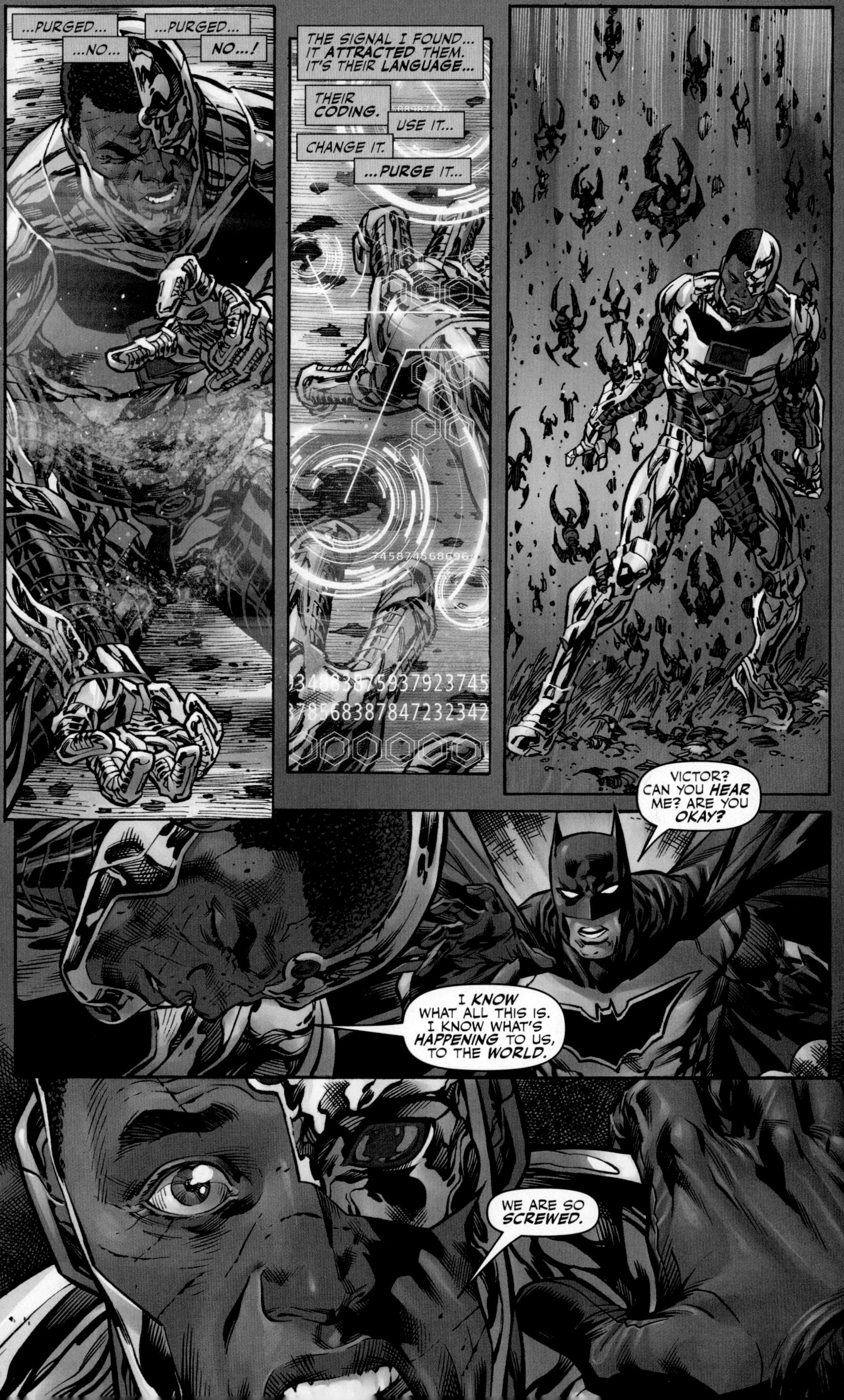
...PURGED...
...NO...
...PURGED...
NO...!
THE SIGNAL I FOUND... IT ATTRACTED THEM. IT'S THEIR LANGUAGE...
THEIR CODING.
USE IT...
CHANGE IT.
...PURGE IT...
VICTOR? CAN YOU HEAR ME? ARE YOU OKAY?
I KNOW WHAT ALL THIS IS. I KNOW WHAT'S HAPPENING TO US, TO THE WORLD.
WE ARE SO SCREWED.

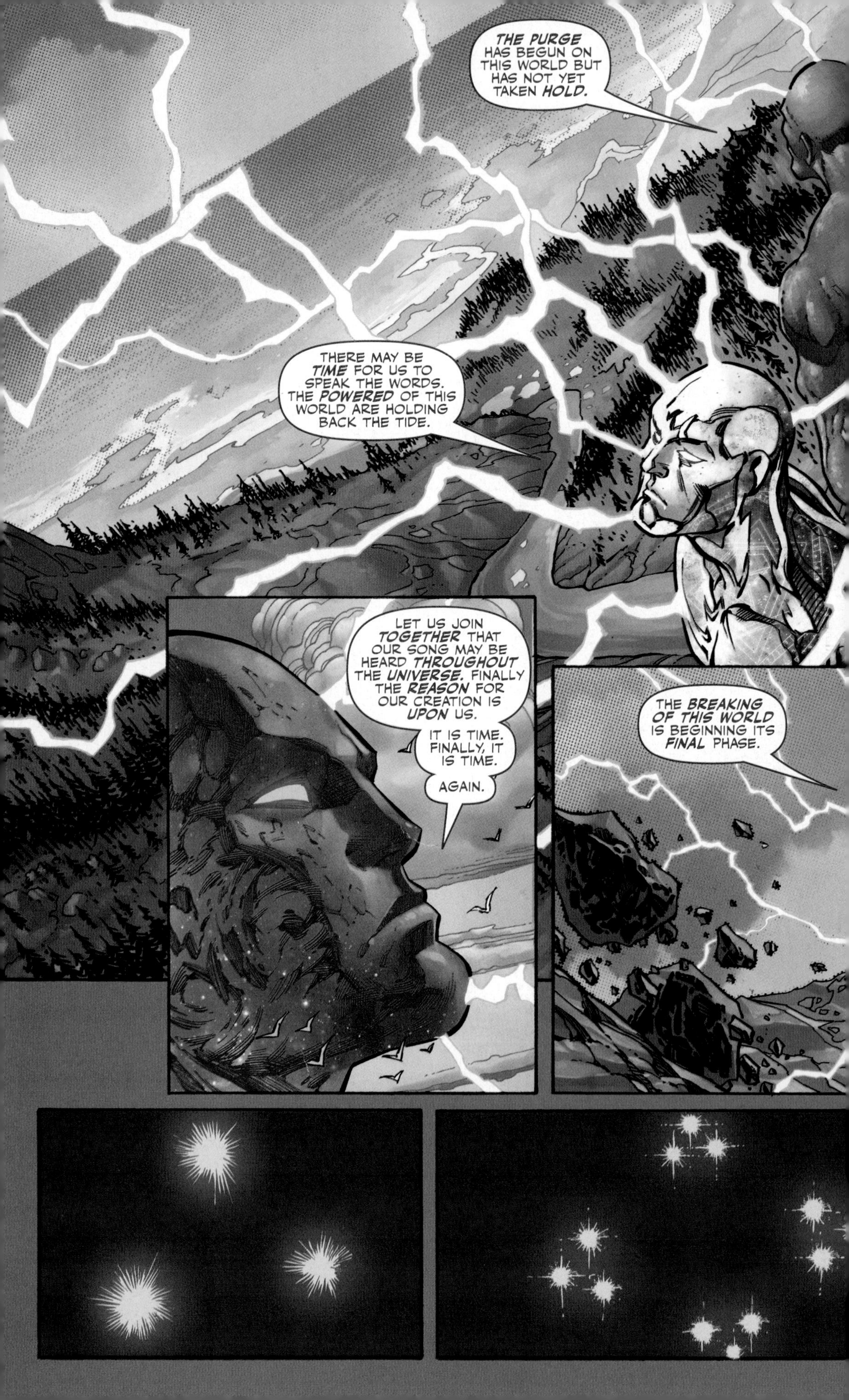
THE PURGE HAS BEGUN ON THIS WORLD BUT HAS NOT YET TAKEN HOLD.
THERE MAY BE TIME FOR US TO SPEAK THE WORDS. THE POWERED OF THIS WORLD ARE HOLDING BACK THE TIDE.
LET US JOIN TOGETHER THAT OUR SONG MAY BE HEARD THROUGHOUT THE UNIVERSE. FINALLY THE REASON FOR OUR CREATION IS UPON US.
IT IS TIME. FINALLY, IT IS TIME.
AGAIN.
THE BREAKING OF THIS WORLD IS BEGINNING ITS FINAL PHASE.

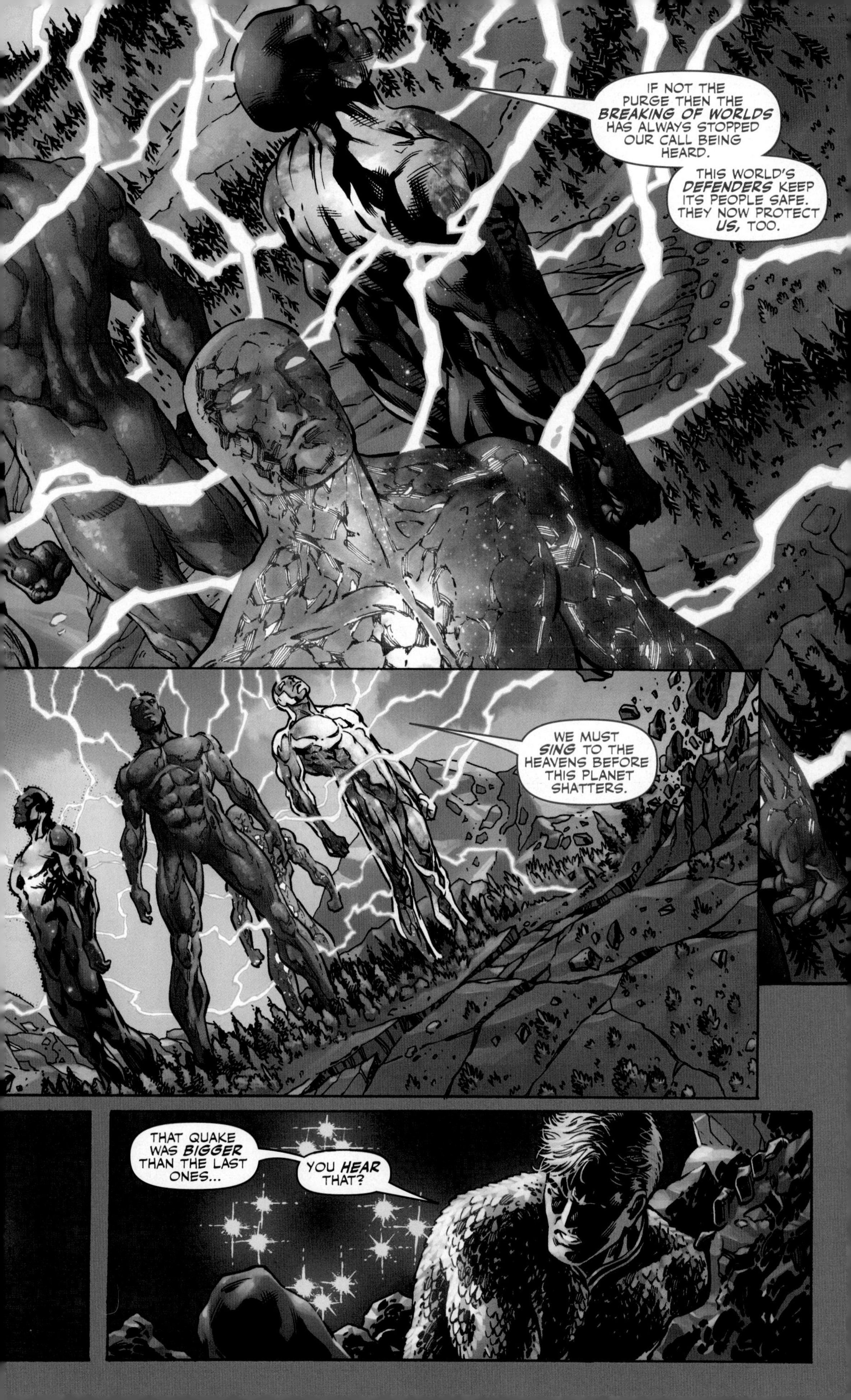
IF NOT THE PURGE THEN THE BREAKING OF WORLDS HAS ALWAYS STOPPED OUR CALL BEING HEARD.
THIS WORLD'S DEFENDERS KEEP ITS PEOPLE SAFE. THEY NOW PROTECT US, TOO.
WE MUST SING TO THE HEAVENS BEFORE THIS PLANET SHATTERS.
THAT QUAKE WAS BIGGER THAN THE LAST ONES...
YOU HEAR THAT?

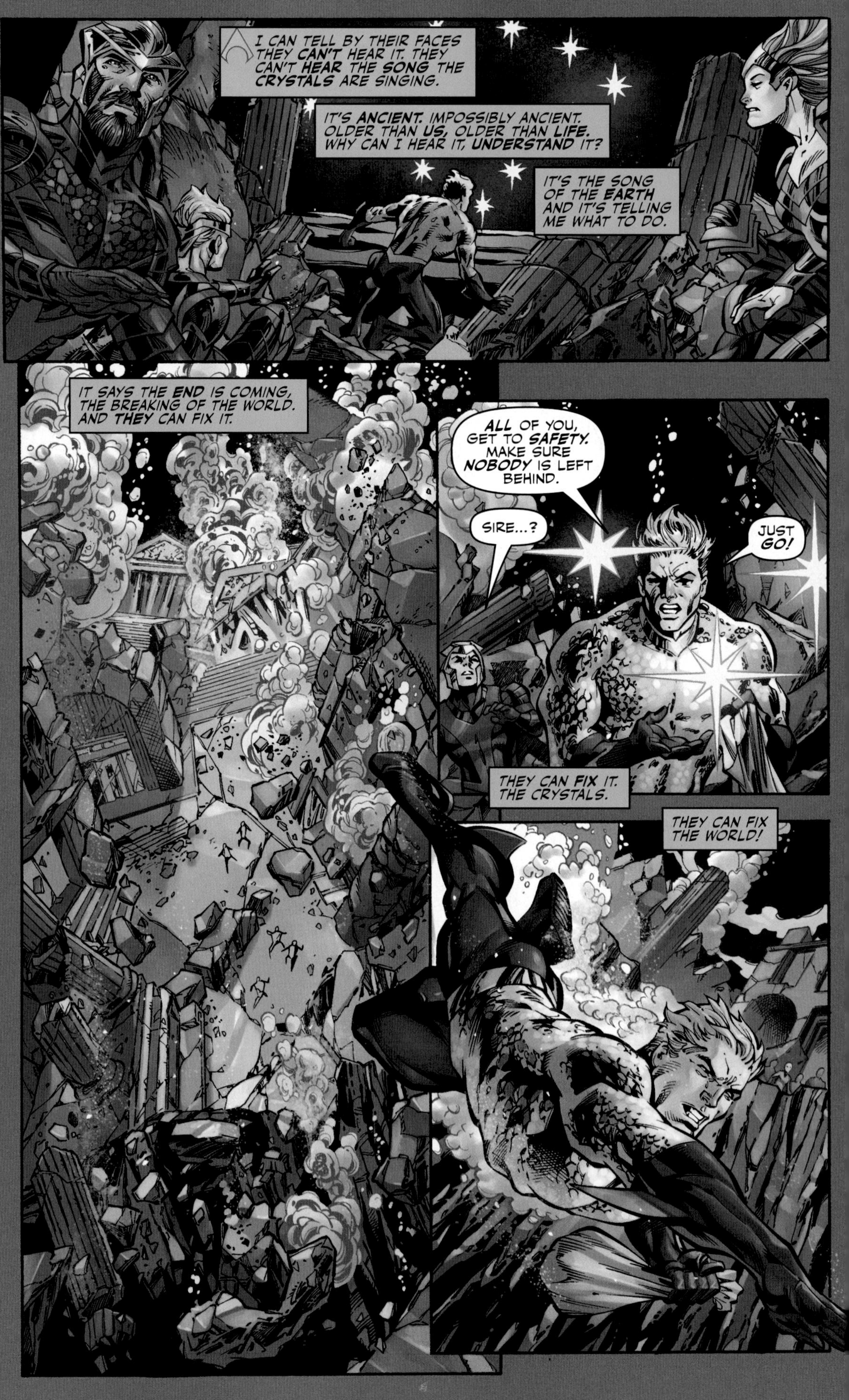
I CAN TELL BY THEIR FACES THEY CAN'T HEAR IT. THEY CAN'T HEAR THE SONG THE CRYSTALS ARE SINGING.
IT'S ANCIENT. IMPOSSIBLY ANCIENT. OLDER THAN US, OLDER THAN LIFE. WHY CAN I HEAR IT, UNDERSTAND IT?
IT'S THE SONG OF THE EARTH AND IT'S TELLING ME WHAT TO DO.
IT SAYS THE END IS COMING, THE BREAKING OF THE WORLD. AND THEY CAN FIX IT.
ALL OF YOU, GET TO SAFETY. MAKE SURE NOBODY IS LEFT BEHIND.
SIRE...?
JUST GO!
THEY CAN FIX IT. THE CRYSTALS.
THEY CAN FIX THE WORLD!

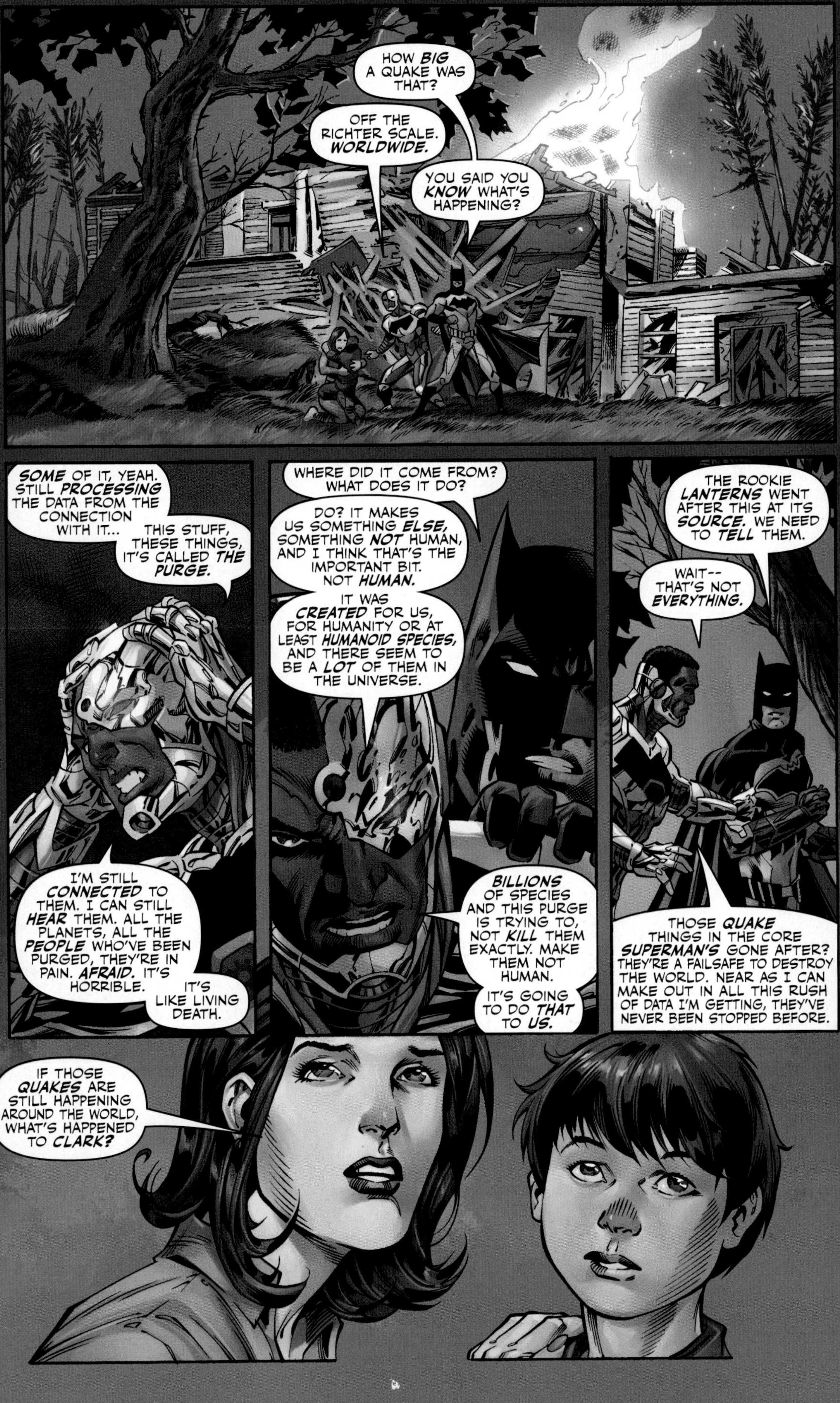
HOW BIG A QUAKE WAS THAT?
OFF THE RICHTER SCALE. WORLDWIDE.
YOU SAID YOU KNOW WHAT'S HAPPENING?
SOME OF IT, YEAH. STILL PROCESSING THE DATA FROM THE CONNECTION WITH IT...
THIS STUFF, THESE THINGS, IT'S CALLED THE PURGE.
I'M STILL CONNECTED TO THEM. I CAN STILL HEAR THEM. ALL THE PLANETS, ALL THE PEOPLE WHO'VE BEEN PURGED, THEY'RE IN PAIN. AFRAID. IT'S HORRIBLE.
IT'S LIKE LIVING DEATH.
WHERE DID IT COME FROM? WHAT DOES IT DO?
DO? IT MAKES US SOMETHING ELSE, SOMETHING NOT HUMAN, AND I THINK THAT'S THE IMPORTANT BIT. NOT HUMAN.
IT WAS CREATED FOR US, FOR HUMANITY OR AT LEAST HUMANOID SPECIES, AND THERE SEEM TO BE A LOT OF THEM IN THE UNIVERSE.
BILLIONS OF SPECIES AND THIS PURGE IS TRYING TO, NOT KILL THEM EXACTLY. MAKE THEM NOT HUMAN.
IT'S GOING TO DO THAT TO US.
THE ROOKIE LANTERNS WENT AFTER THIS AT ITS SOURCE. WE NEED TO TELL THEM.
WAIT-- THAT'S NOT EVERYTHING.
THOSE QUAKE THINGS IN THE CORE SUPERMAN'S GONE AFTER? THEY'RE A FAILSAFE TO DESTROY THE WORLD. NEAR AS I CAN MAKE OUT IN ALL THIS RUSH OF DATA I'M GETTING, THEY'VE NEVER BEEN STOPPED BEFORE.
IF THOSE QUAKES ARE STILL HAPPENING AROUND THE WORLD, WHAT'S HAPPENED TO CLARK?

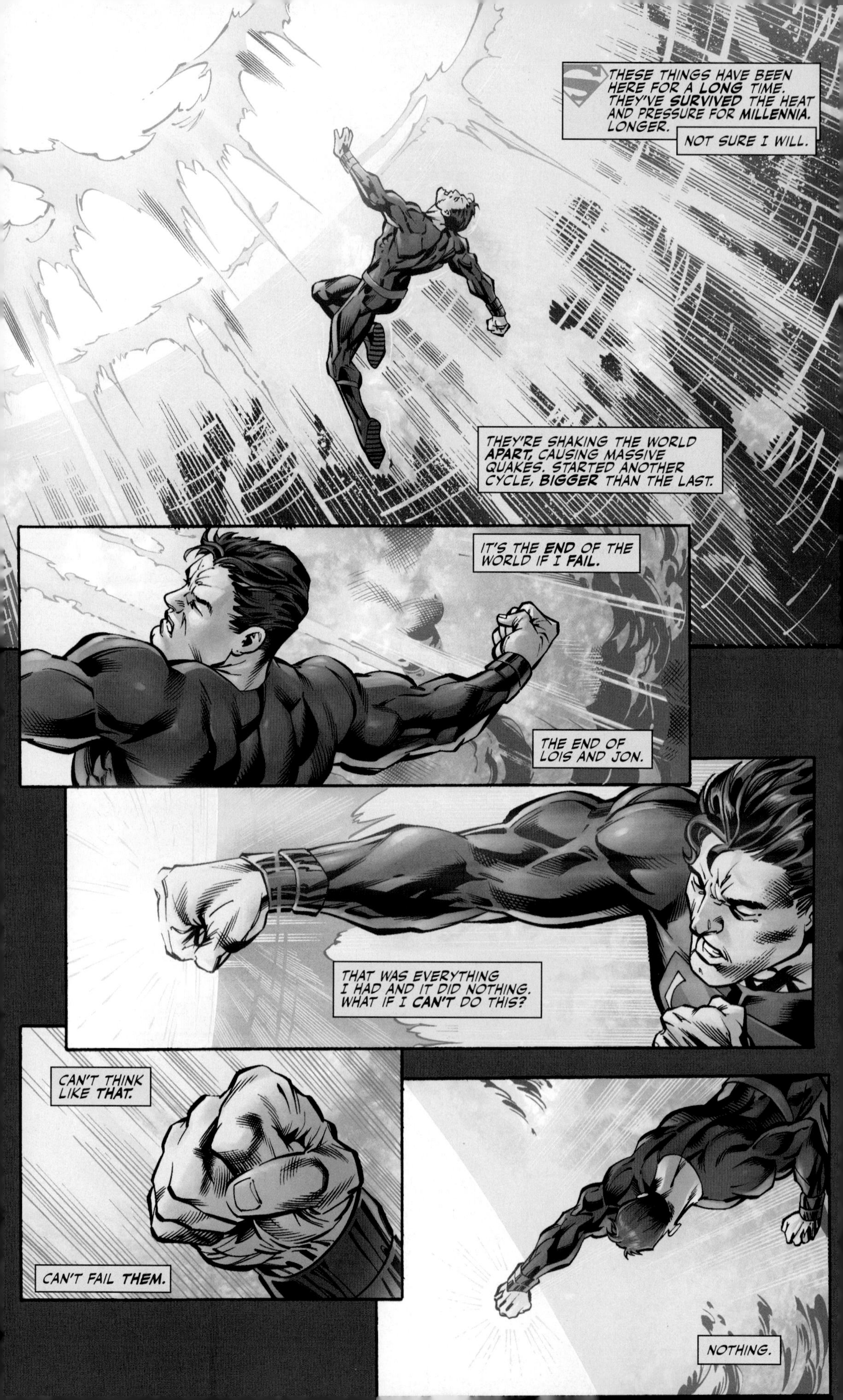
THESE THINGS HAVE BEEN HERE FOR A LONG TIME. THEY'VE SURVIVED THE HEAT AND PRESSURE FOR MILLENNIA. LONGER.
NOT SURE I WILL.
THEY'RE SHAKING THE WORLD APART, CAUSING MASSIVE QUAKES. STARTED ANOTHER CYCLE, BIGGER THAN THE LAST.
IT'S THE END OF THE WORLD IF I FAIL.
THE END OF LOIS AND JON.
THAT WAS EVERYTHING I HAD AND IT DID NOTHING. WHAT IF I CAN'T DO THIS?
CAN'T THINK LIKE THAT.
CAN'T FAIL THEM.
NOTHING.

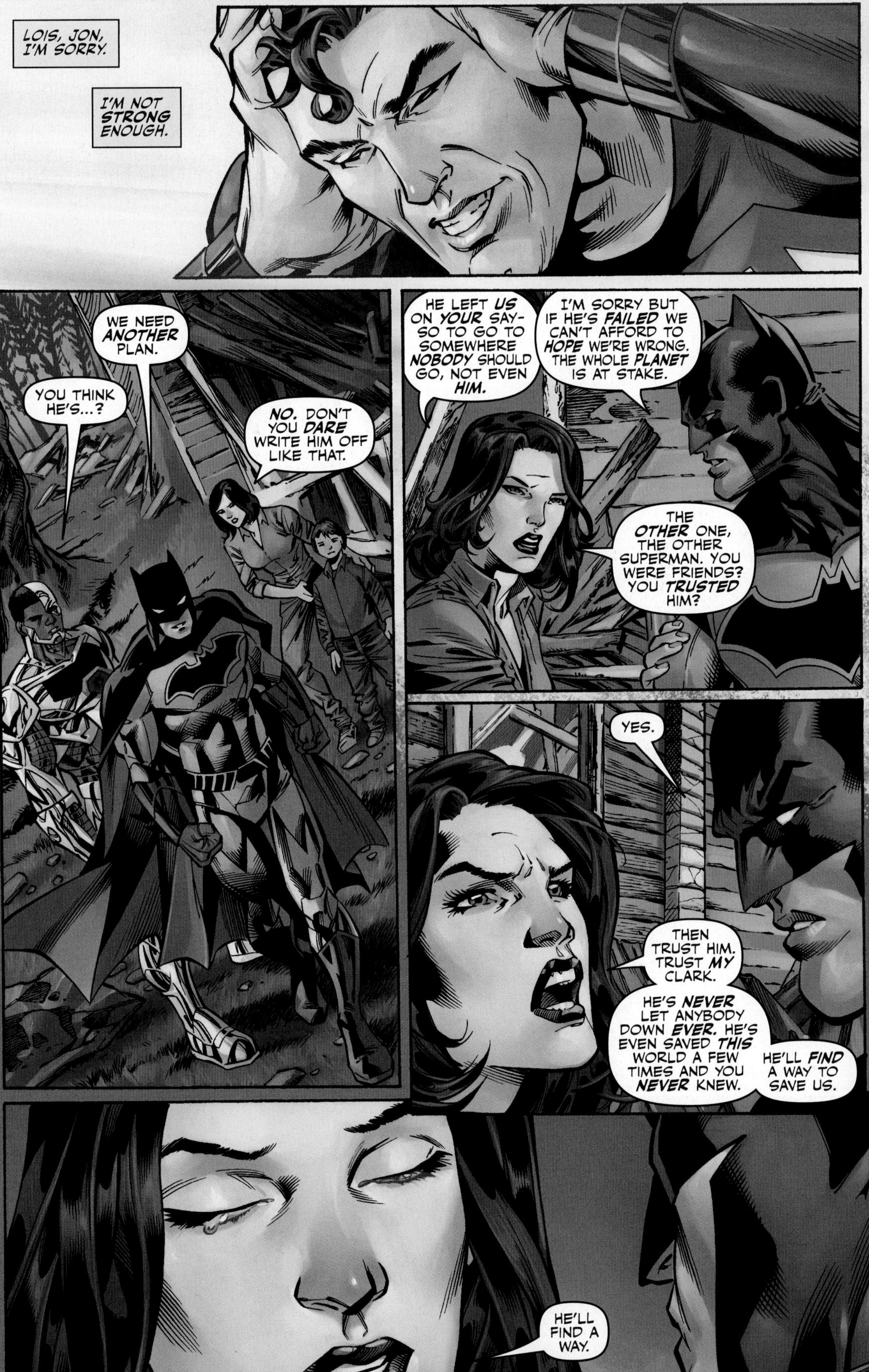

LOIS, JON, I'M SORRY.
I'M NOT STRONG ENOUGH.
YOU THINK HE'S...?
WE NEED ANOTHER PLAN.
NO. DON'T YOU DARE WRITE HIM OFF LIKE THAT.
HE LEFT US ON YOUR SAY-SO TO GO TO SOMEWHERE NOBODY SHOULD GO, NOT EVEN HIM.
I'M SORRY BUT IF HE'S FAILED WE CAN'T AFFORD TO HOPE WE'RE WRONG. THE WHOLE PLANET IS AT STAKE.
THE OTHER ONE, THE OTHER SUPERMAN. YOU WERE FRIENDS? YOU TRUSTED HIM?
YES.
THEN TRUST HIM. TRUST MY CLARK.
HE'S NEVER LET ANYBODY DOWN EVER. HE'S EVEN SAVED THIS WORLD A FEW TIMES AND YOU NEVER KNEW.
HE'LL FIND A WAY TO SAVE US.
HE'LL FIND A WAY.

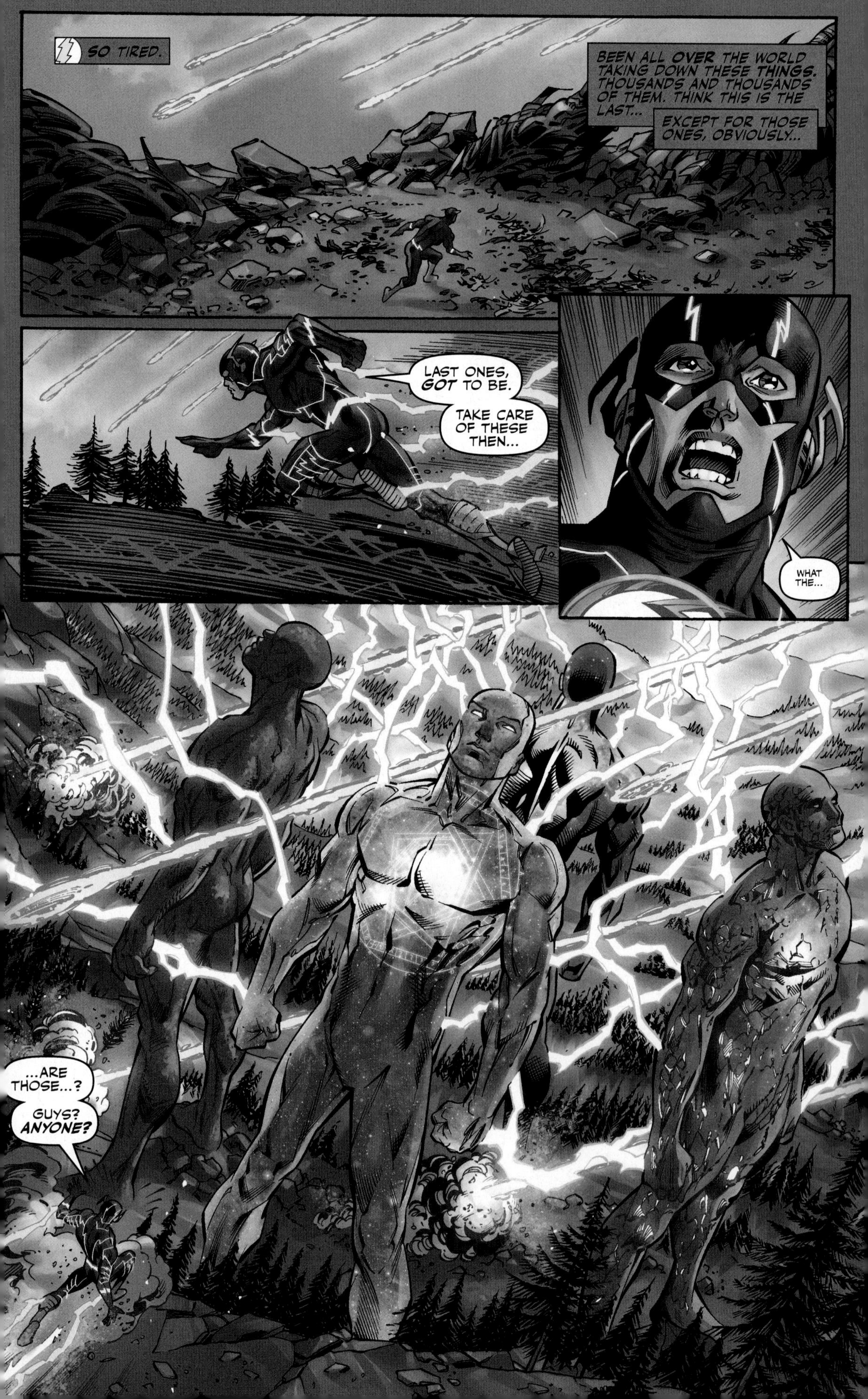
SO TIRED.
BEEN ALL OVER THE WORLD TAKING DOWN THESE THINGS. THOUSANDS AND THOUSANDS OF THEM. THINK THIS IS THE LAST...
EXCEPT FOR THOSE ONES, OBVIOUSLY...
LAST ONES, GOT TO BE.
TAKE CARE OF THESE THEN...
WHAT THE...
...ARE THOSE...?
GUYS? ANYONE?

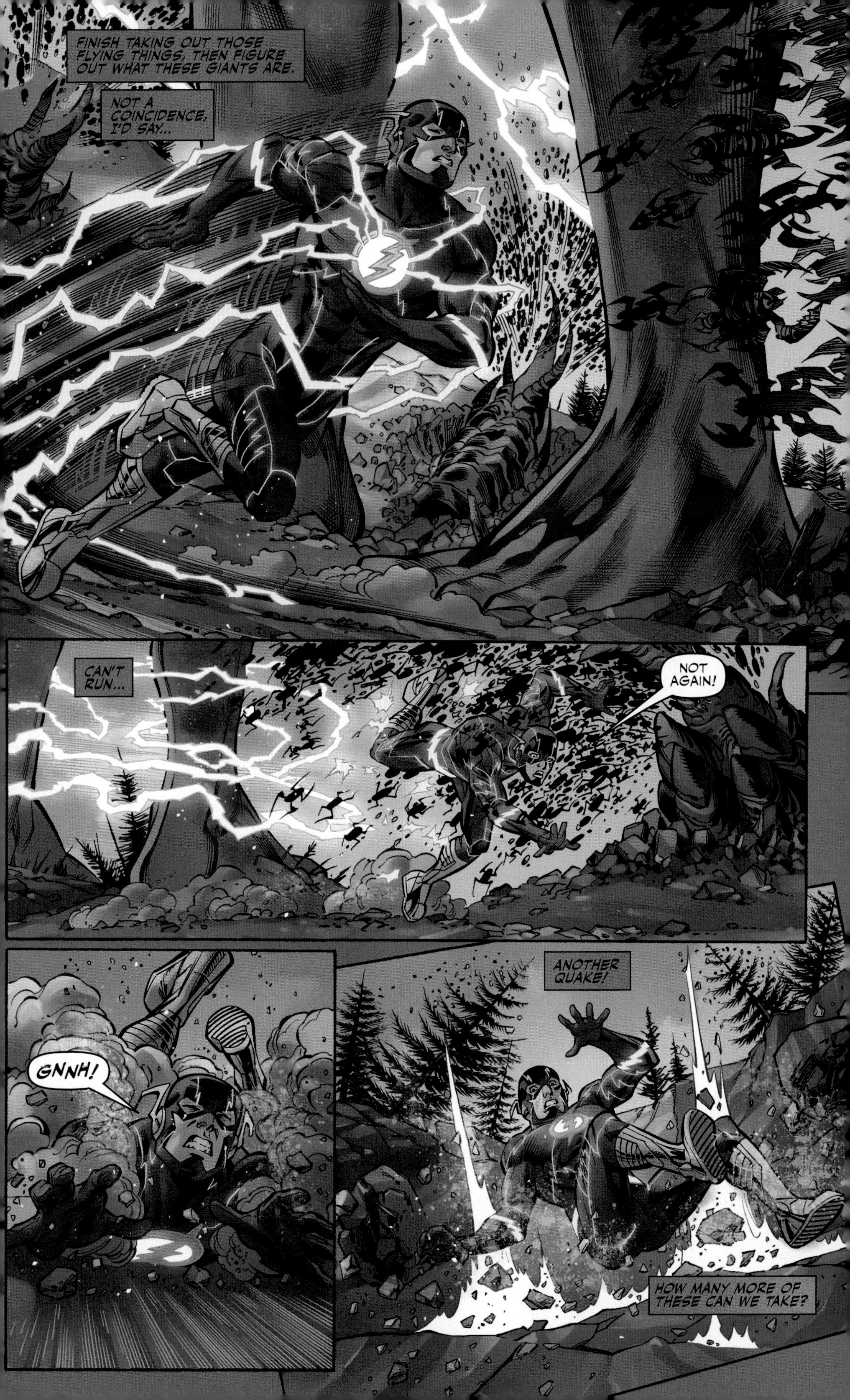
FINISH TAKING OUT THOSE FLYING THINGS, THEN FIGURE OUT WHAT THESE GIANTS ARE.
NOT A COINCIDENCE, I'D SAY...
CAN'T RUN...
NOT AGAIN!
GNNH!
ANOTHER QUAKE!
HOW MANY MORE OF THESE CAN WE TAKE?

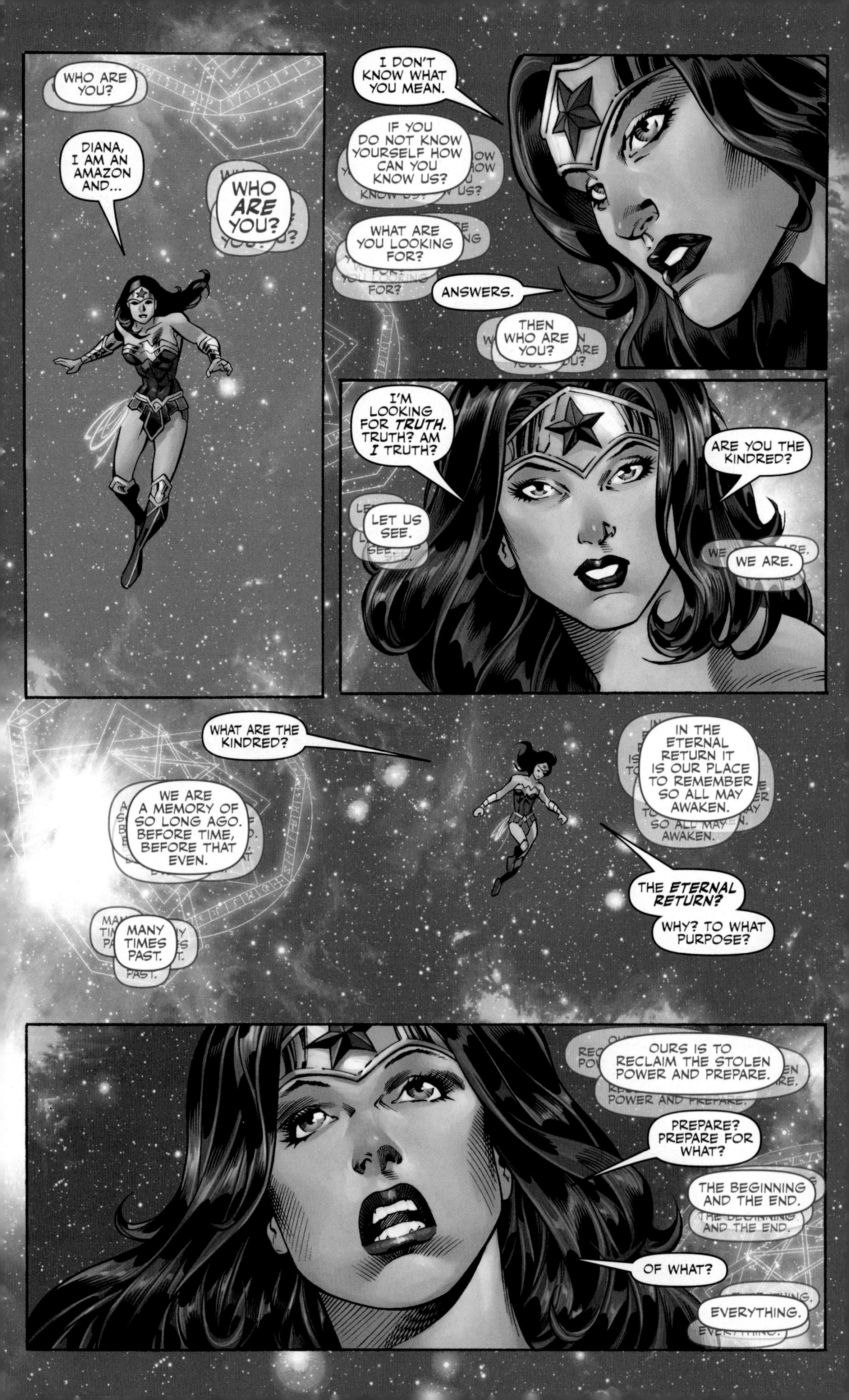
WHO ARE YOU?
DIANA, I AM AN AMAZON AND...
WHO ARE YOU?
I DON'T KNOW WHAT YOU MEAN.
IF YOU DO NOT KNOW YOURSELF HOW CAN YOU KNOW US?
WHAT ARE YOU LOOKING FOR?
ANSWERS.
THEN WHO ARE YOU?
I'M LOOKING FOR TRUTH. TRUTH? AM I TRUTH?
LET US SEE.
ARE YOU THE KINDRED?
WE ARE.
WHAT ARE THE KINDRED?
WE ARE A MEMORY OF SO LONG AGO. BEFORE TIME, BEFORE THAT EVEN.
MANY TIMES PAST.
IN THE ETERNAL RETURN IT IS OUR PLACE TO REMEMBER SO ALL MAY AWAKEN.
THE ETERNAL RETURN?
WHY? TO WHAT PURPOSE?
OURS IS TO RECLAIM THE STOLEN POWER AND PREPARE.
PREPARE? PREPARE FOR WHAT?
THE BEGINNING AND THE END.
OF WHAT?
EVERYTHING.

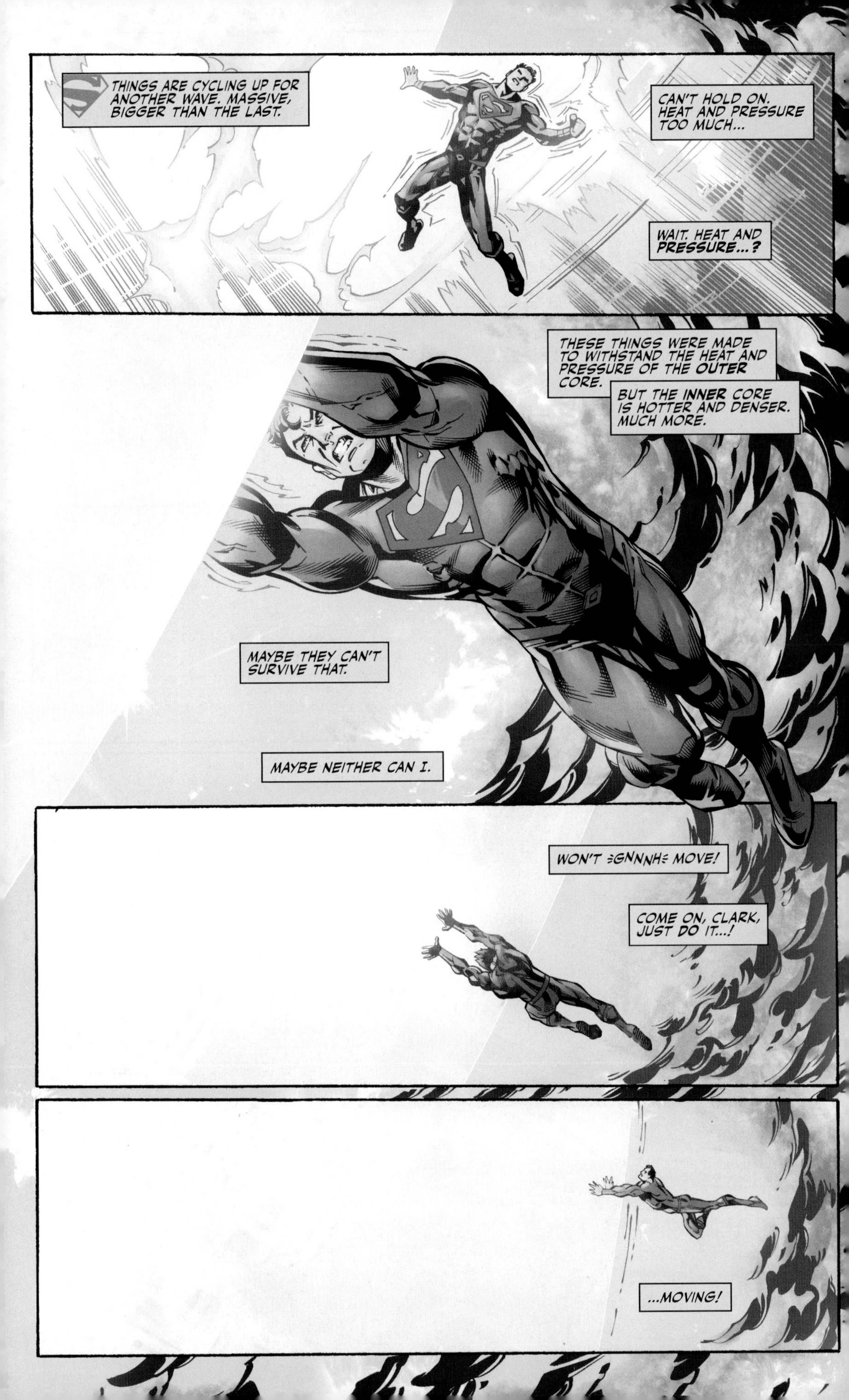
THINGS ARE CYCLING UP FOR ANOTHER WAVE. MASSIVE, BIGGER THAN THE LAST.
CAN'T HOLD ON. HEAT AND PRESSURE TOO MUCH...
WAIT. HEAT AND PRESSURE...?
THESE THINGS WERE MADE TO WITHSTAND THE HEAT AND PRESSURE OF THE OUTER CORE.
BUT THE INNER CORE IS HOTTER AND DENSER. MUCH MORE.
MAYBE THEY CAN'T SURVIVE THAT.
MAYBE NEITHER CAN I.
WON'T =GNNNH= MOVE!
COME ON, CLARK, JUST DO IT...!
...MOVING!

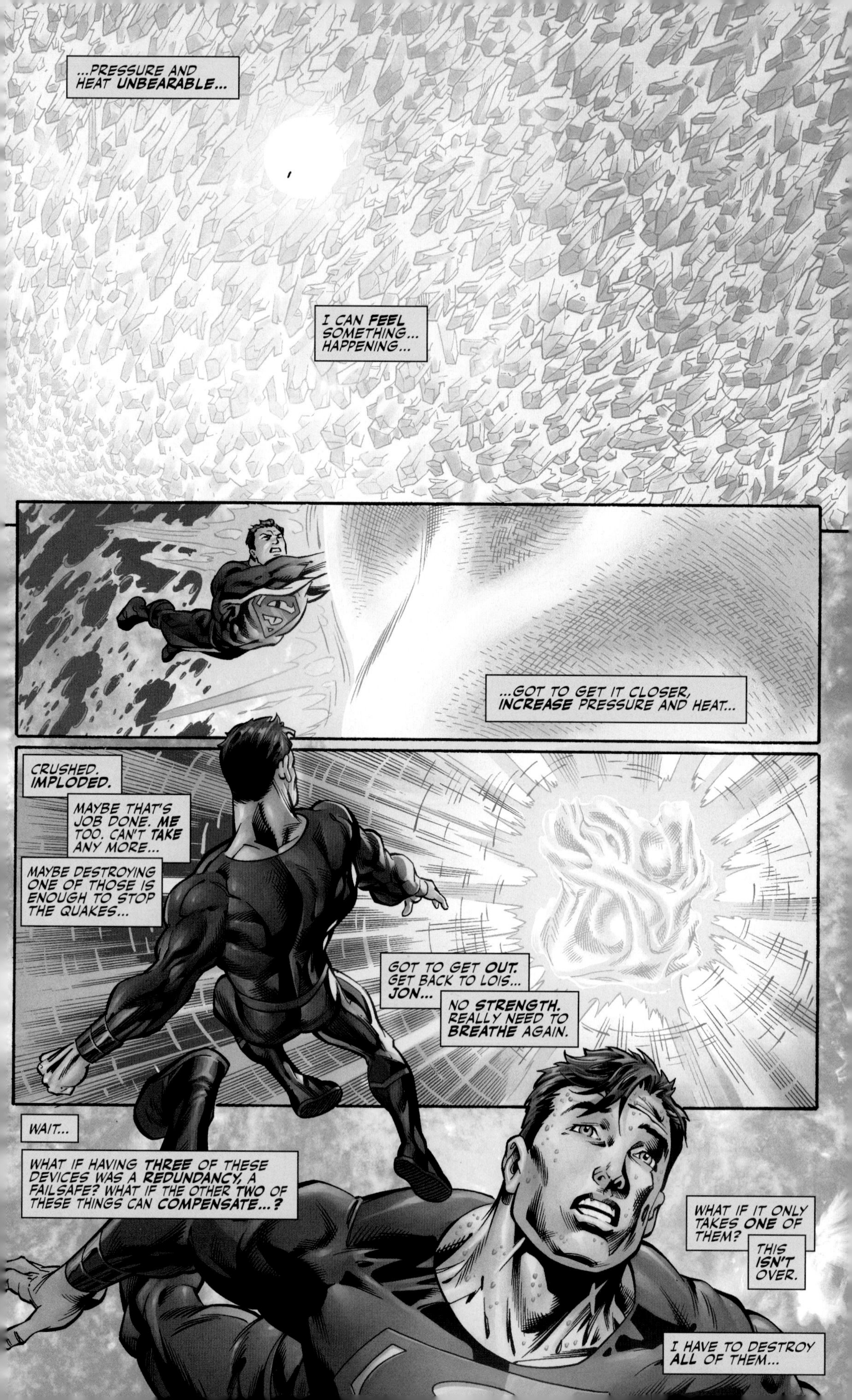

...PRESSURE AND HEAT UNBEARABLE...
I CAN FEEL SOMETHING... HAPPENING...
...GOT TO GET IT CLOSER, INCREASE PRESSURE AND HEAT...
CRUSHED. IMPLODED.
MAYBE THAT'S JOB DONE. ME TOO. CAN'T TAKE ANY MORE...
MAYBE DESTROYING ONE OF THOSE IS ENOUGH TO STOP THE QUAKES...
GOT TO GET OUT. GET BACK TO LOIS... JON...
NO STRENGTH. REALLY NEED TO BREATHE AGAIN.
WAIT...
WHAT IF HAVING THREE OF THESE DEVICES WAS A REDUNDANCY, A FAILSAFE? WHAT IF THE OTHER TWO OF THESE THINGS CAN COMPENSATE...?
WHAT IF IT ONLY TAKES ONE OF THEM?
THIS ISN'T OVER.
I HAVE TO DESTROY ALL OF THEM...

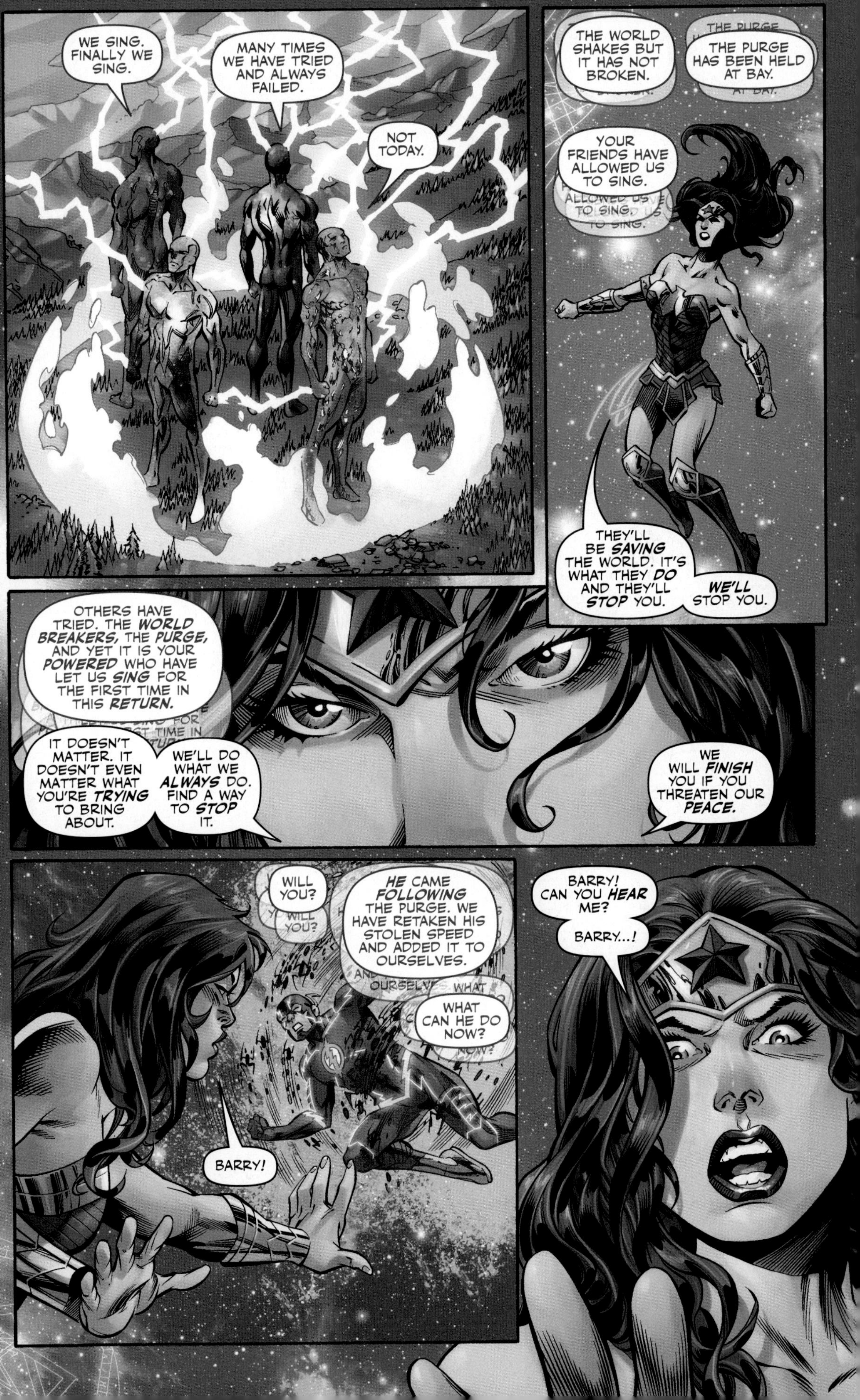
WE SING. FINALLY WE SING.
MANY TIMES WE HAVE TRIED AND ALWAYS FAILED.
NOT TODAY.
THE WORLD SHAKES BUT IT HAS NOT BROKEN.
THE PURGE HAS BEEN HELD AT BAY.
YOUR FRIENDS HAVE ALLOWED US TO SING.
THEY'LL BE SAVING THE WORLD. IT'S WHAT THEY DO AND THEY'LL STOP YOU.
WE'LL STOP YOU.
OTHERS HAVE TRIED. THE WORLD BREAKERS, THE PURGE, AND YET IT IS YOUR POWERED WHO HAVE LET US SING FOR THE FIRST TIME IN THIS RETURN.
IT DOESN'T MATTER. IT DOESN'T EVEN MATTER WHAT YOU'RE TRYING TO BRING ABOUT.
WE'LL DO WHAT WE ALWAYS DO. FIND A WAY TO STOP IT.
WE WILL FINISH YOU IF YOU THREATEN OUR PEACE.
WILL YOU?
HE CAME FOLLOWING THE PURGE. WE HAVE RETAKEN HIS STOLEN SPEED AND ADDED IT TO OURSELVES.
WHAT CAN HE DO NOW?
BARRY!
BARRY! CAN YOU HEAR ME?
BARRY...!

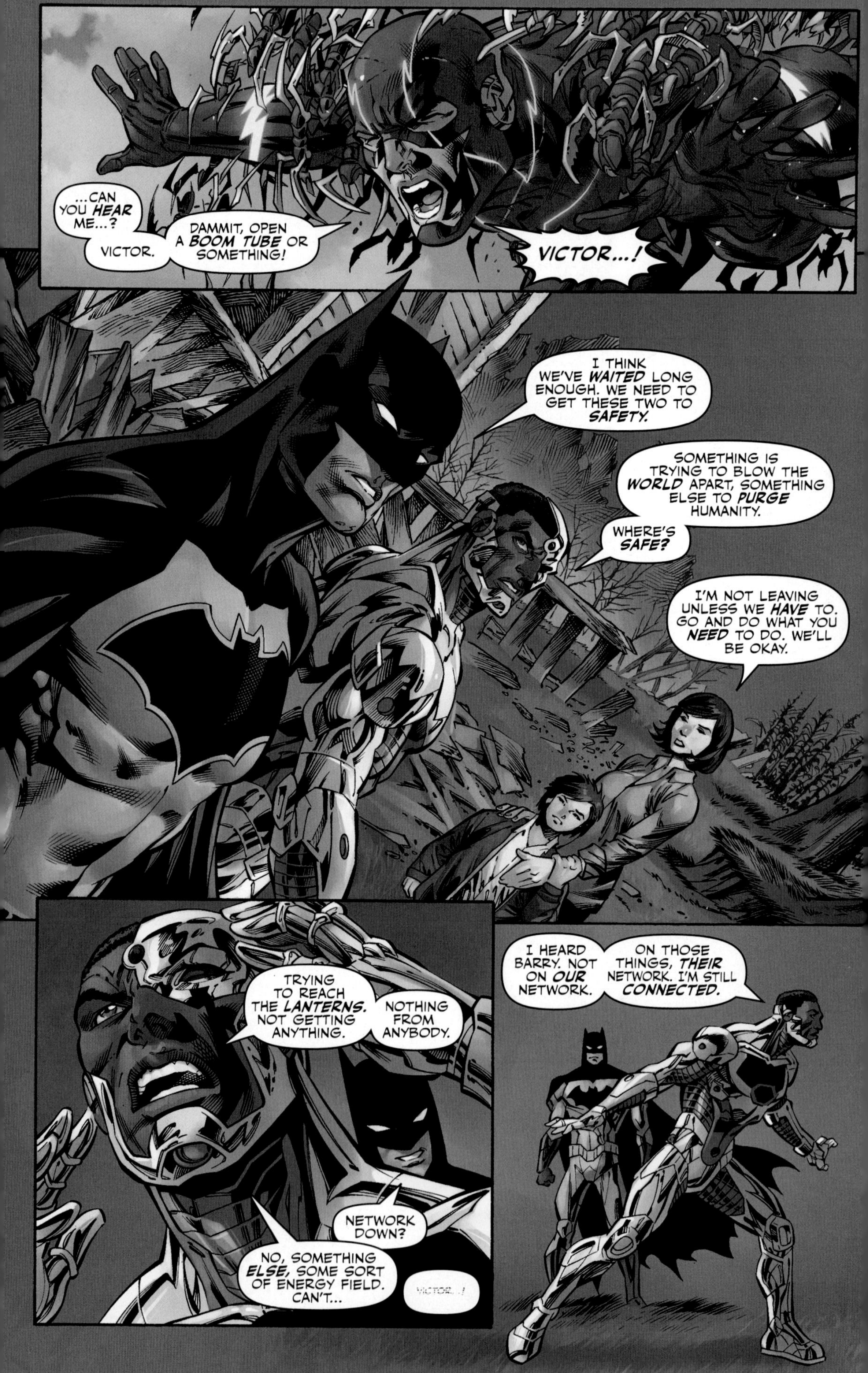
...CAN YOU HEAR ME...? VICTOR.
DAMMIT, OPEN A BOOM TUBE OR SOMETHING!
VICTOR...!
I THINK WE'VE WAITED LONG ENOUGH. WE NEED TO GET THESE TWO TO SAFETY.
SOMETHING IS TRYING TO BLOW THE WORLD APART, SOMETHING ELSE TO PURGE HUMANITY.
WHERE'S SAFE?
I'M NOT LEAVING UNLESS WE HAVE TO. GO AND DO WHAT YOU NEED TO DO. WE'LL BE OKAY.
TRYING TO REACH THE LANTERNS. NOT GETTING ANYTHING.
NOTHING FROM ANYBODY.
NETWORK DOWN?
NO, SOMETHING ELSE, SOME SORT OF ENERGY FIELD. CAN'T...
VICTOR...!
I HEARD BARRY. NOT ON OUR NETWORK.
ON THOSE THINGS, THEIR NETWORK. I'M STILL CONNECTED.

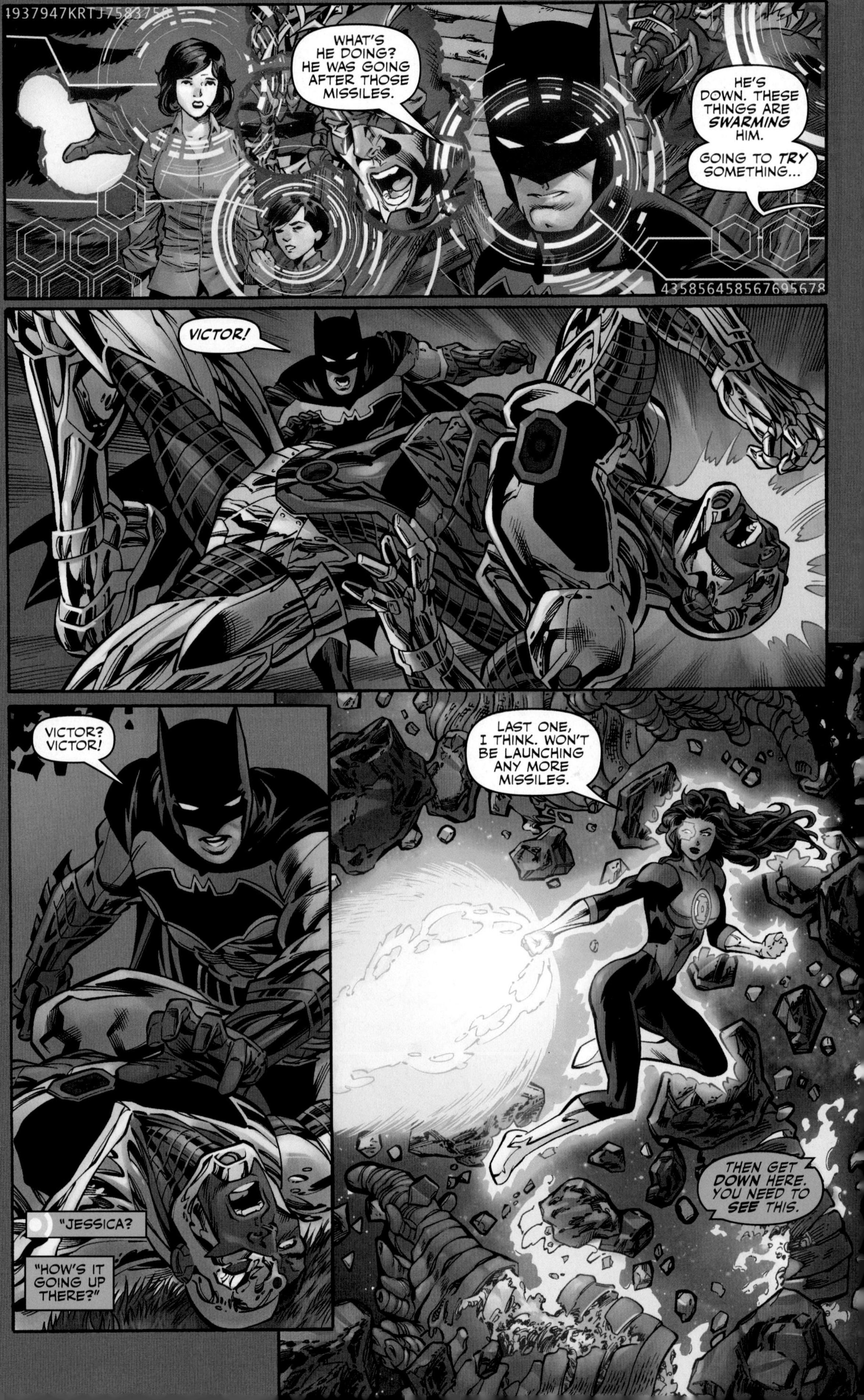
4937947KRTJ758375
WHAT'S HE DOING? HE WAS GOING AFTER THOSE MISSILES.
HE'S DOWN. THESE THINGS ARE SWARMING HIM.
GOING TO TRY SOMETHING...
435856458567695678
VICTOR!
VICTOR? VICTOR!
"JESSICA?
"HOW'S IT GOING UP THERE?"
LAST ONE, I THINK. WON'T BE LAUNCHING ANY MORE MISSILES.
THEN GET DOWN HERE. YOU NEED TO SEE THIS.

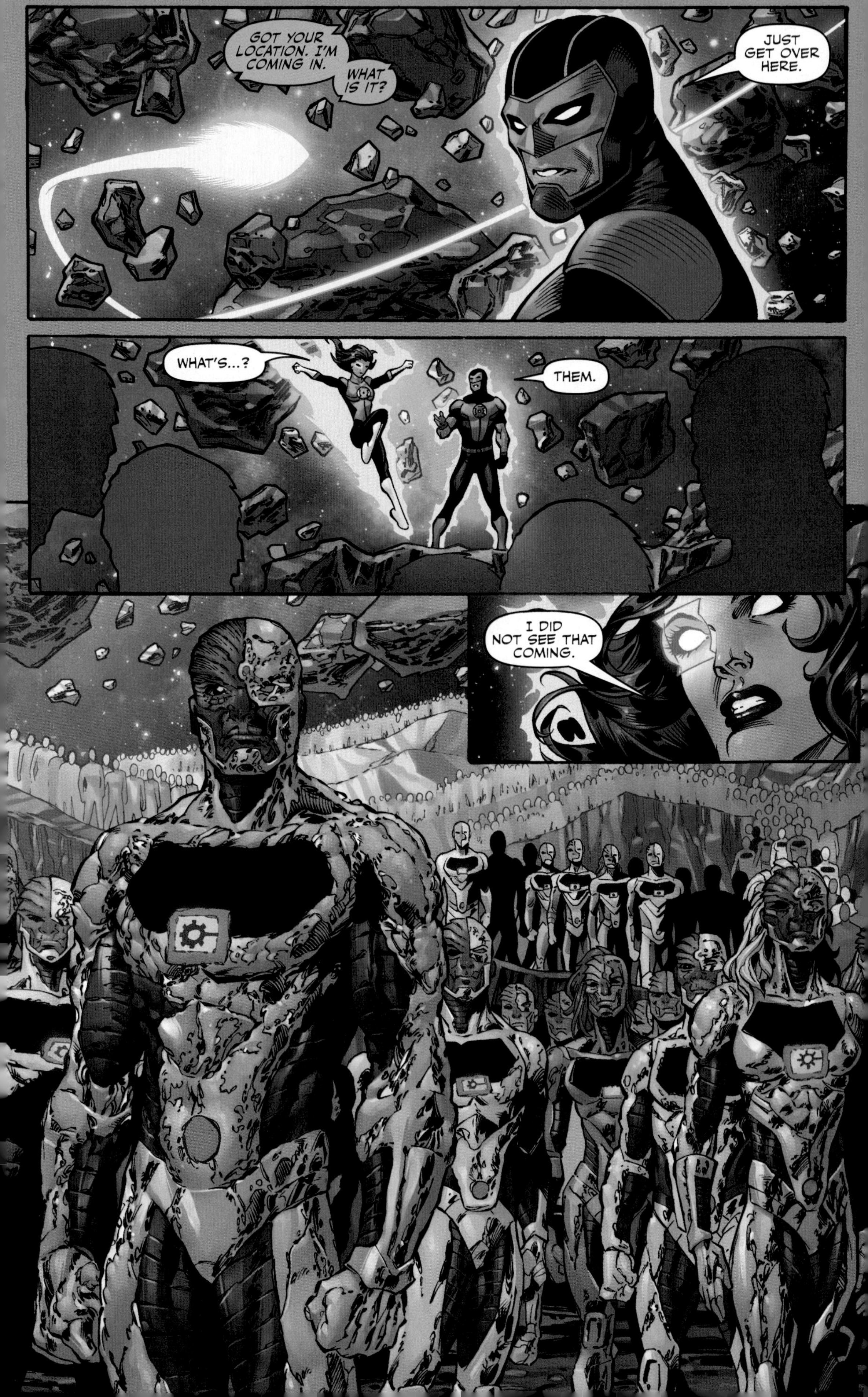
GOT YOUR LOCATION. I'M COMING IN.
WHAT IS IT?
JUST GET OVER HERE.
WHAT'S...?
THEM.
I DID NOT SEE THAT COMING.

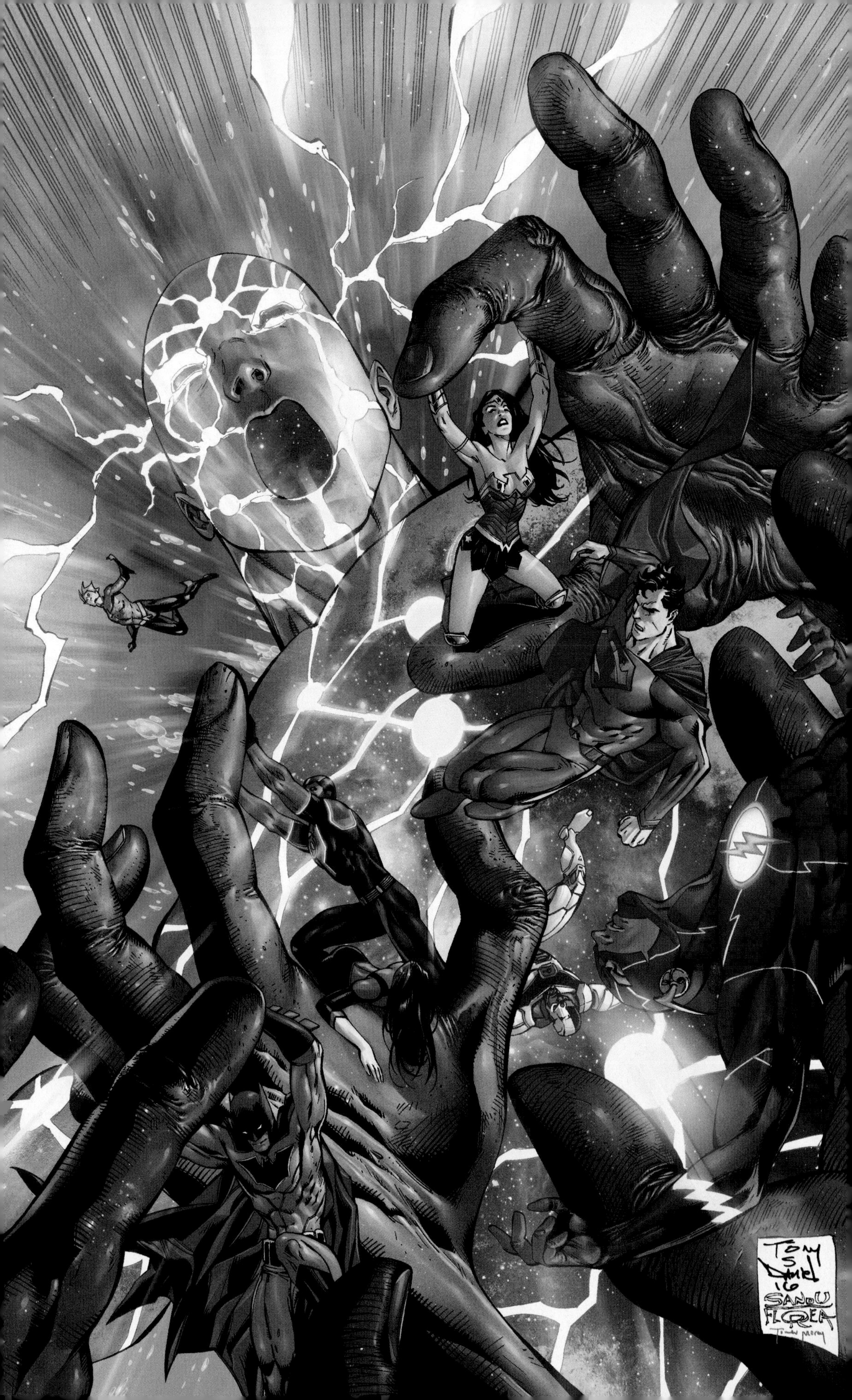
TONY S DANIEL '16
SANDU FLOREA

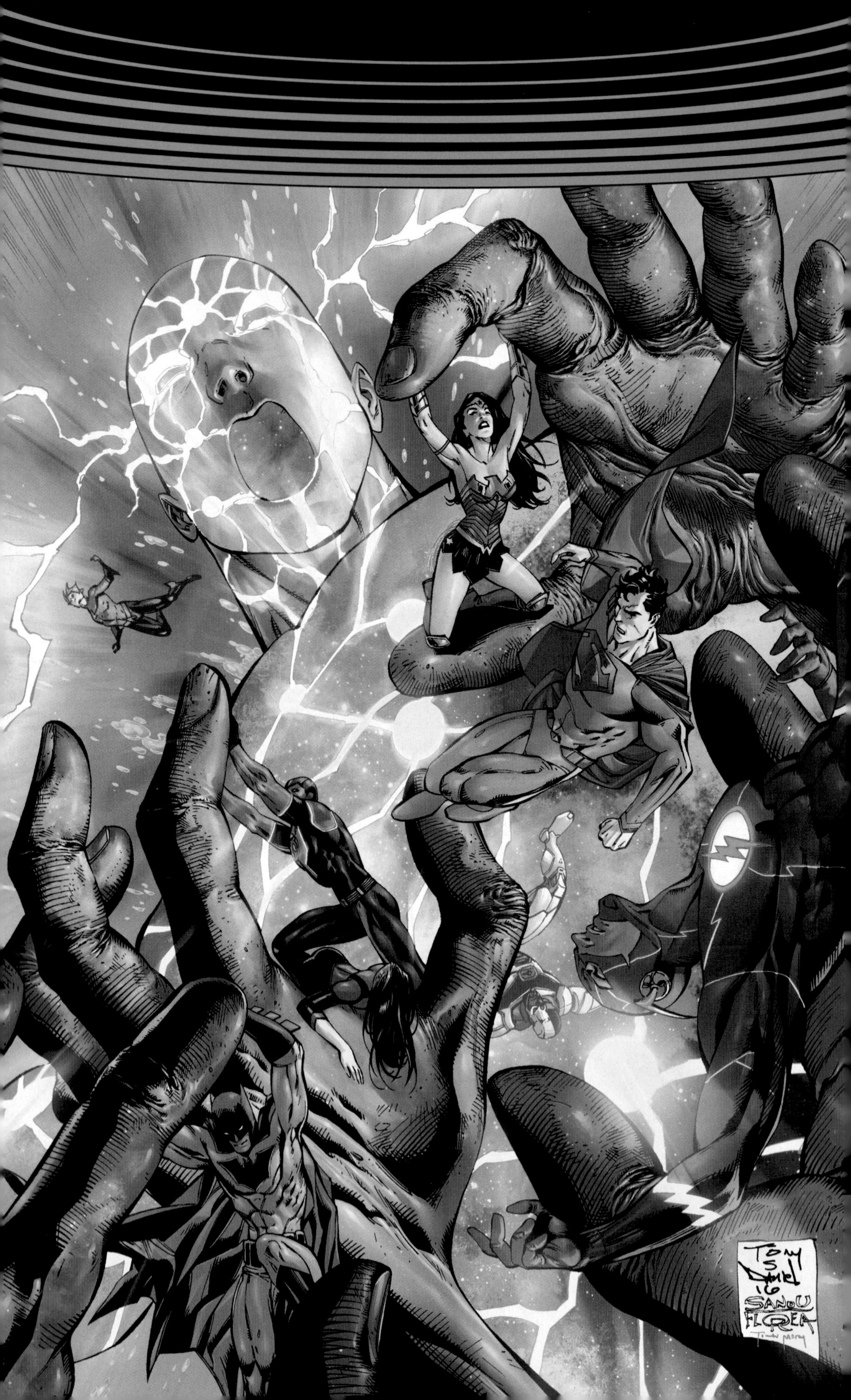
TONY S DANIEL '16
SANDU FLOREA

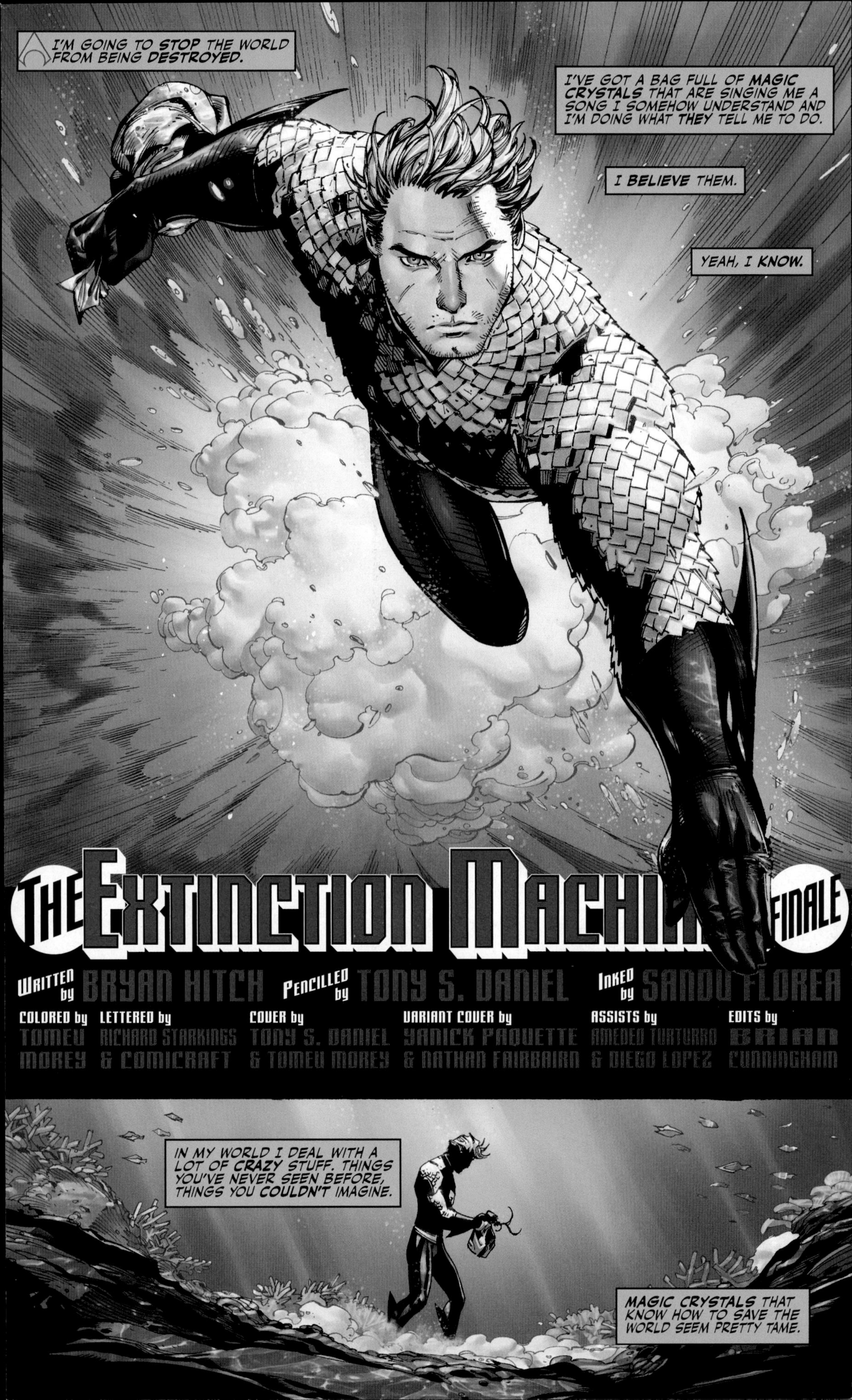
I'M GOING TO STOP THE WORLD FROM BEING DESTROYED.
I'VE GOT A BAG FULL OF MAGIC CRYSTALS THAT ARE SINGING ME A SONG I SOMEHOW UNDERSTAND AND I'M DOING WHAT THEY TELL ME TO DO.
I BELIEVE THEM.
YEAH, I KNOW.
THE EXTINCTION MACHI
FINALE
Written by BRYAN HITCH Pencilled by TONY S. DANIEL Inked by SANDU FLOREA
COLORED by TOMEU MOREY
LETTERED by RICHARD STARKINGS & COMICRAFT
COVER by TONY S. DANIEL & TOMEU MOREY
VARIANT COVER by YANICK PAQUETTE & NATHAN FAIRBAIRN
ASSISTS by AMEDEO TURTURRO & DIEGO LOPEZ
EDITS by BRIAN CUNNINGHAM
IN MY WORLD I DEAL WITH A LOT OF CRAZY STUFF. THINGS YOU'VE NEVER SEEN BEFORE, THINGS YOU COULDN'T IMAGINE.
MAGIC CRYSTALS THAT KNOW HOW TO SAVE THE WORLD SEEM PRETTY TAME.

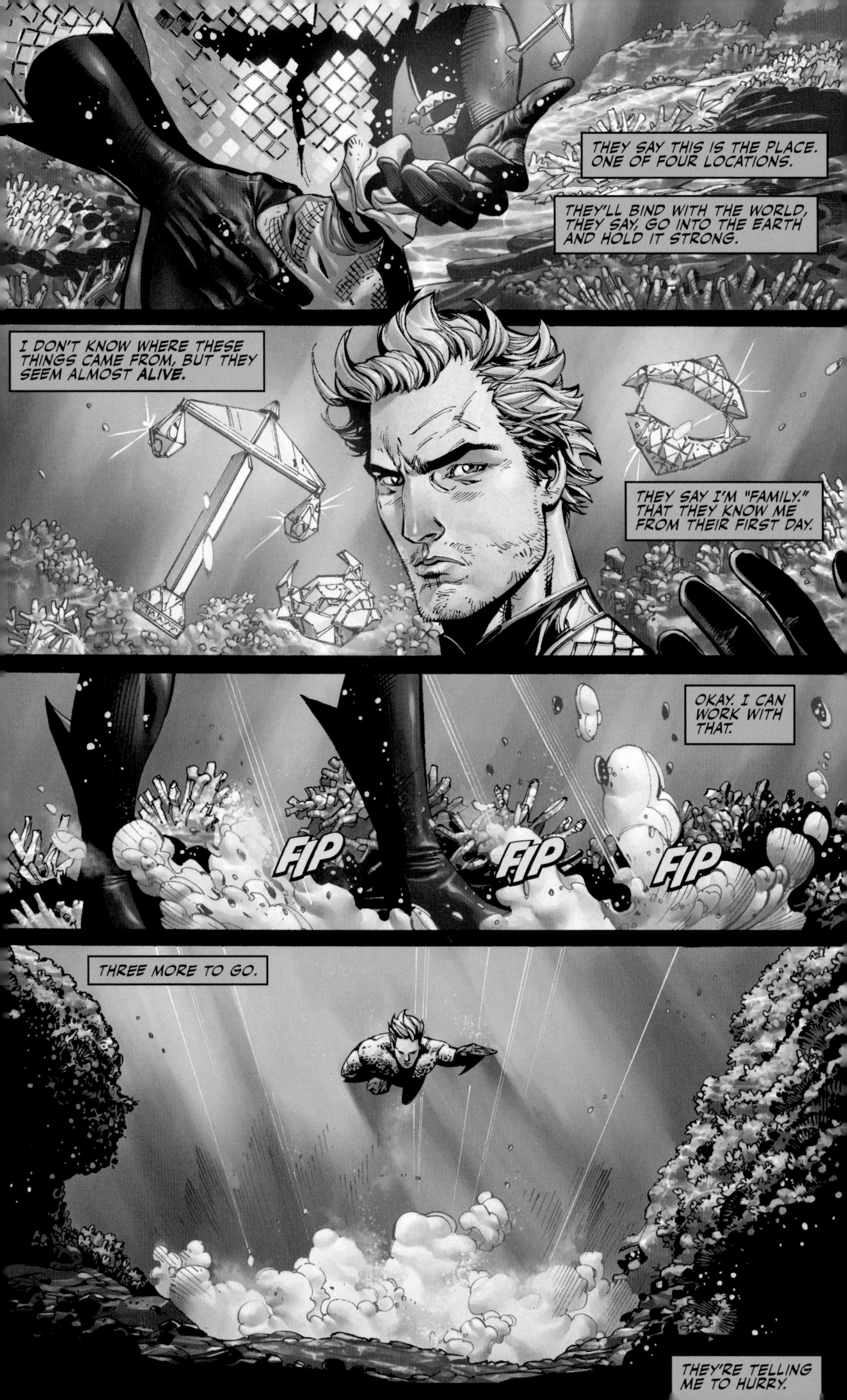
THEY SAY THIS IS THE PLACE. ONE OF FOUR LOCATIONS.
THEY'LL BIND WITH THE WORLD, THEY SAY, GO INTO THE EARTH AND HOLD IT STRONG.
I DON'T KNOW WHERE THESE THINGS CAME FROM, BUT THEY SEEM ALMOST ALIVE.
THEY SAY I'M "FAMILY." THAT THEY KNOW ME FROM THEIR FIRST DAY.
OKAY. I CAN WORK WITH THAT.
FIP
FIP
FIP
THREE MORE TO GO.
THEY'RE TELLING ME TO HURRY.

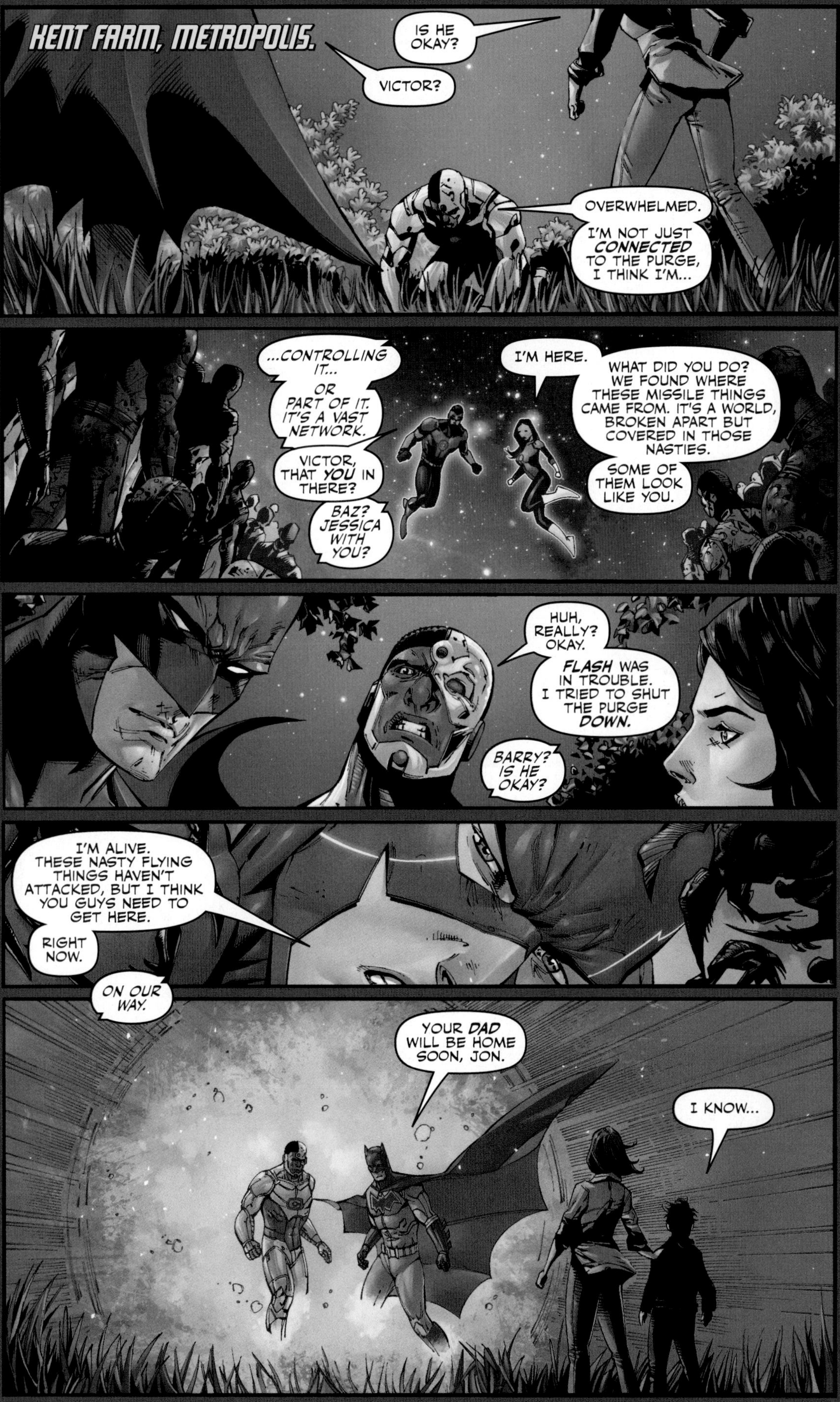
KENT FARM, METROPOLIS.
IS HE OKAY?
VICTOR?
OVERWHELMED.
I'M NOT JUST *CONNECTED* TO THE PURGE, I THINK I'M...
...CONTROLLING IT...
OR PART OF IT. IT'S A VAST NETWORK.
VICTOR, THAT *YOU* IN THERE?
BAZ? JESSICA WITH YOU?
I'M HERE.
WHAT DID YOU DO? WE FOUND WHERE THESE MISSILE THINGS CAME FROM. IT'S A WORLD, BROKEN APART BUT COVERED IN THOSE NASTIES.
SOME OF THEM LOOK LIKE YOU.
HUH, REALLY? OKAY.
*FLASH* WAS IN TROUBLE. I TRIED TO SHUT THE PURGE *DOWN.*
BARRY? IS HE OKAY?
I'M ALIVE. THESE NASTY FLYING THINGS HAVEN'T ATTACKED, BUT I THINK YOU GUYS NEED TO GET HERE.
RIGHT NOW.
ON OUR WAY.
YOUR *DAD* WILL BE HOME SOON, JON.
I KNOW...

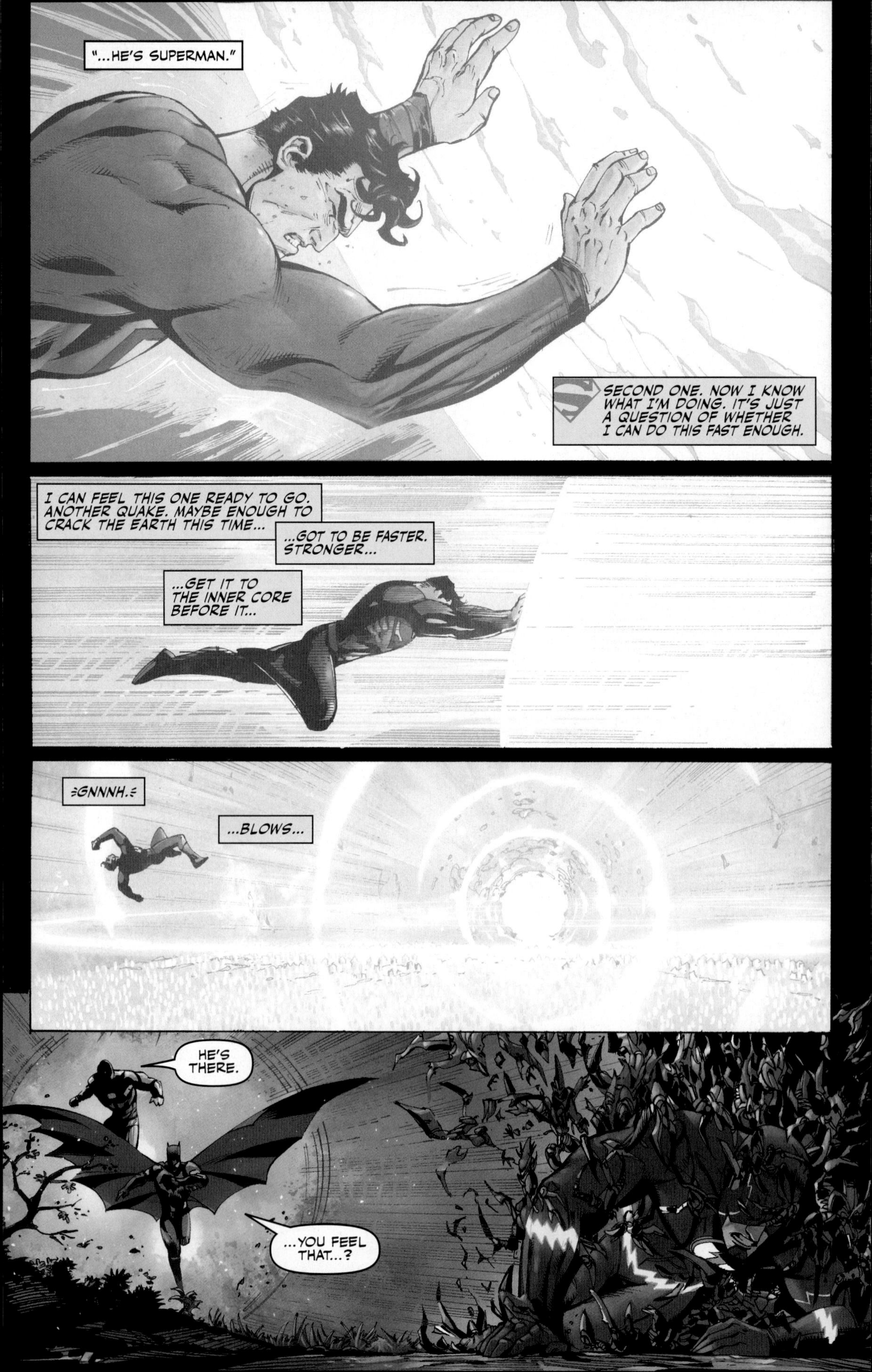
"...HE'S SUPERMAN."
SECOND ONE. NOW I KNOW WHAT I'M DOING. IT'S JUST A QUESTION OF WHETHER I CAN DO THIS FAST ENOUGH.
I CAN FEEL THIS ONE READY TO GO. ANOTHER QUAKE. MAYBE ENOUGH TO CRACK THE EARTH THIS TIME...
...GOT TO BE FASTER. STRONGER...
...GET IT TO THE INNER CORE BEFORE IT...
GNNNH.
...BLOWS...
HE'S THERE.
...YOU FEEL THAT...?

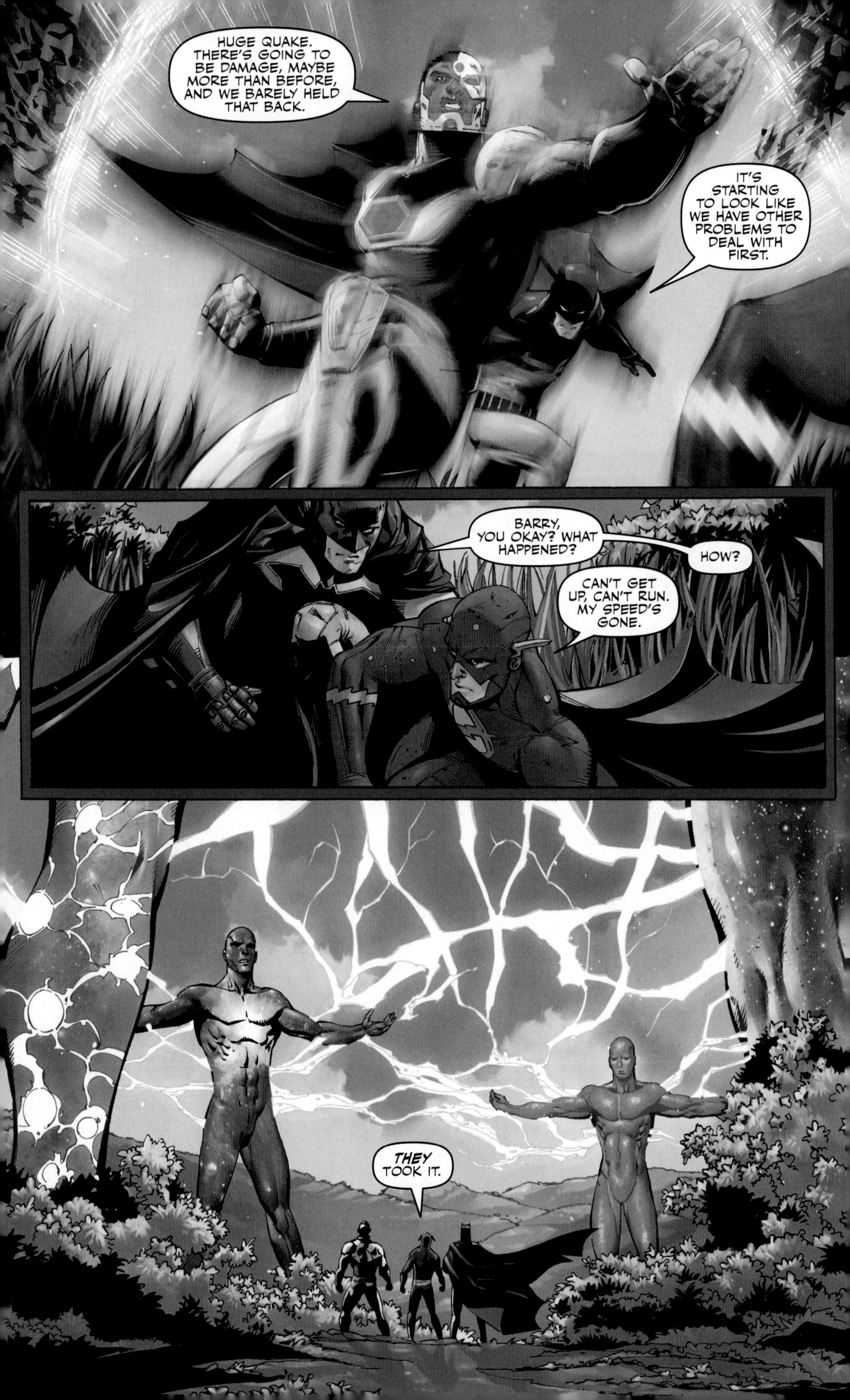
HUGE QUAKE. THERE'S GOING TO BE DAMAGE, MAYBE MORE THAN BEFORE, AND WE BARELY HELD THAT BACK.
IT'S STARTING TO LOOK LIKE WE HAVE OTHER PROBLEMS TO DEAL WITH FIRST.
BARRY, YOU OKAY? WHAT HAPPENED?
CAN'T GET UP, CAN'T RUN. MY SPEED'S GONE.
HOW?
THEY TOOK IT.

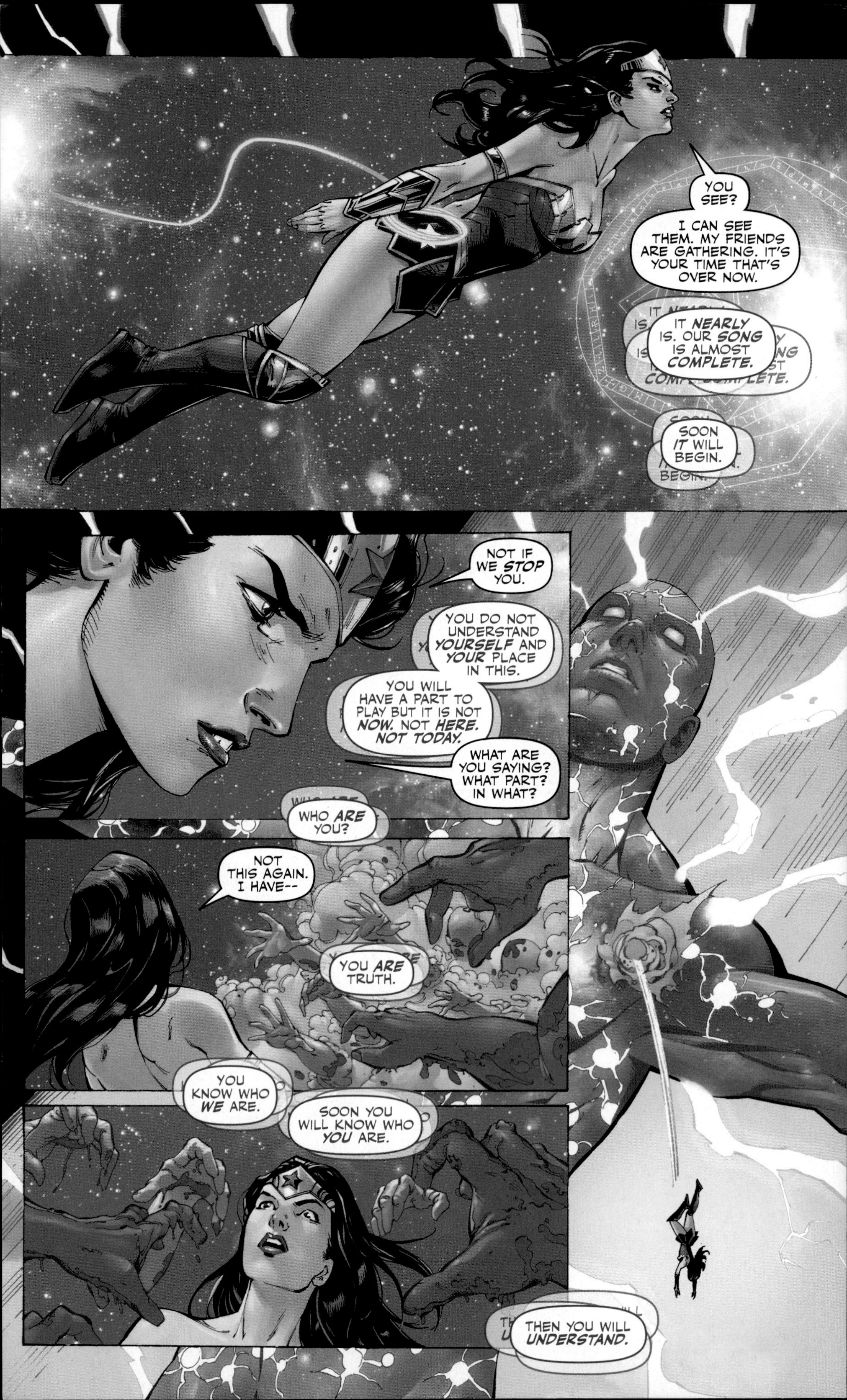
YOU SEE?
I CAN SEE THEM. MY FRIENDS ARE GATHERING. IT'S YOUR TIME THAT'S OVER NOW.
IT NEARLY IS. OUR SONG IS ALMOST COMPLETE.
SOON IT WILL BEGIN.
NOT IF WE STOP YOU.
YOU DO NOT UNDERSTAND YOURSELF AND YOUR PLACE IN THIS.
YOU WILL HAVE A PART TO PLAY BUT IT IS NOT NOW. NOT HERE. NOT TODAY.
WHAT ARE YOU SAYING? WHAT PART? IN WHAT?
WHO ARE YOU?
NOT THIS AGAIN. I HAVE--
YOU ARE TRUTH.
YOU KNOW WHO WE ARE.
SOON YOU WILL KNOW WHO YOU ARE.
THEN YOU WILL UNDERSTAND.

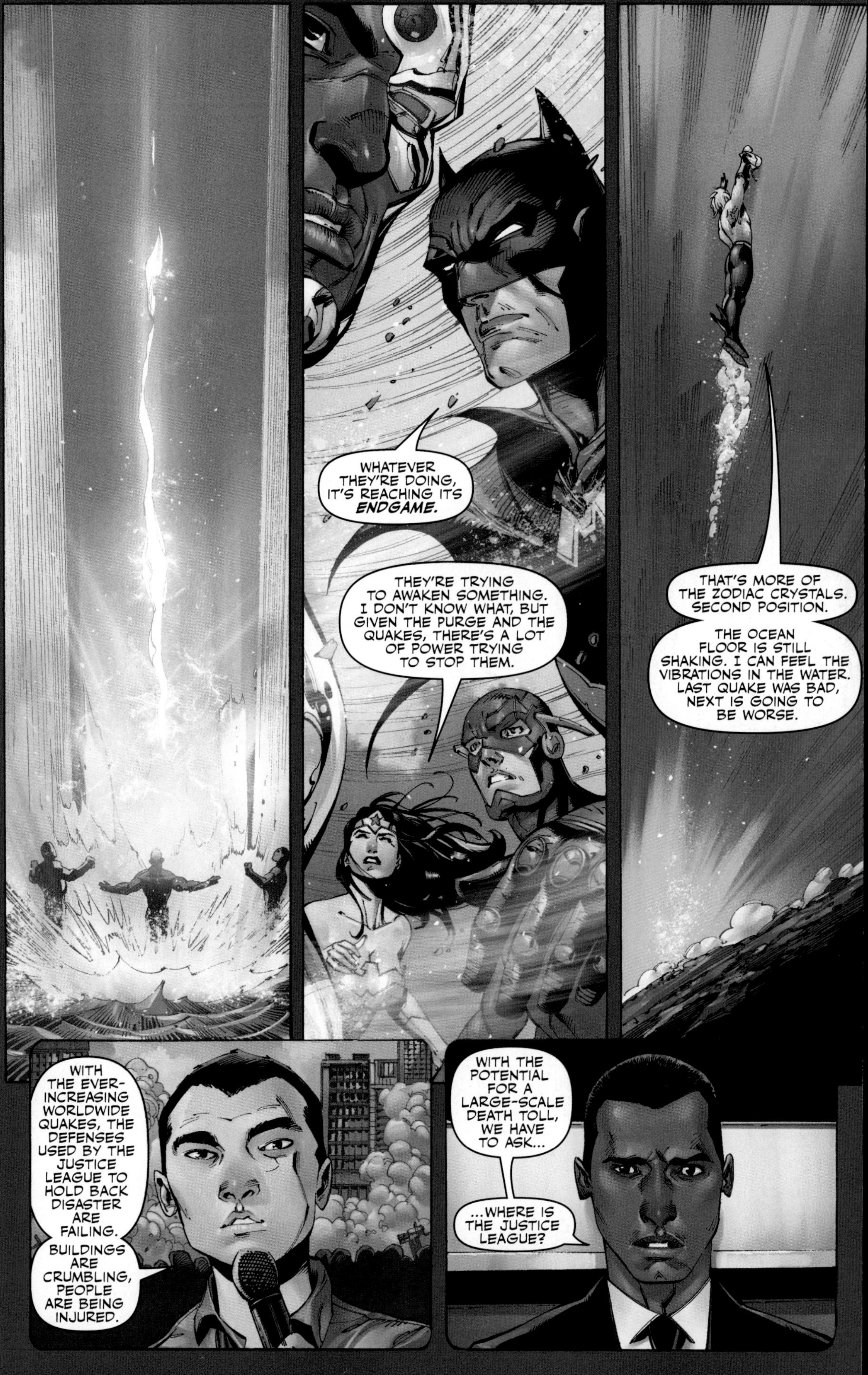
WHATEVER THEY'RE DOING, IT'S REACHING ITS ENDGAME.
THEY'RE TRYING TO AWAKEN SOMETHING. I DON'T KNOW WHAT, BUT GIVEN THE PURGE AND THE QUAKES, THERE'S A LOT OF POWER TRYING TO STOP THEM.
THAT'S MORE OF THE ZODIAC CRYSTALS. SECOND POSITION.
THE OCEAN FLOOR IS STILL SHAKING. I CAN FEEL THE VIBRATIONS IN THE WATER. LAST QUAKE WAS BAD, NEXT IS GOING TO BE WORSE.
WITH THE EVER-INCREASING WORLDWIDE QUAKES, THE DEFENSES USED BY THE JUSTICE LEAGUE TO HOLD BACK DISASTER ARE FAILING.
BUILDINGS ARE CRUMBLING, PEOPLE ARE BEING INJURED.
WITH THE POTENTIAL FOR A LARGE-SCALE DEATH TOLL, WE HAVE TO ASK...
...WHERE IS THE JUSTICE LEAGUE?

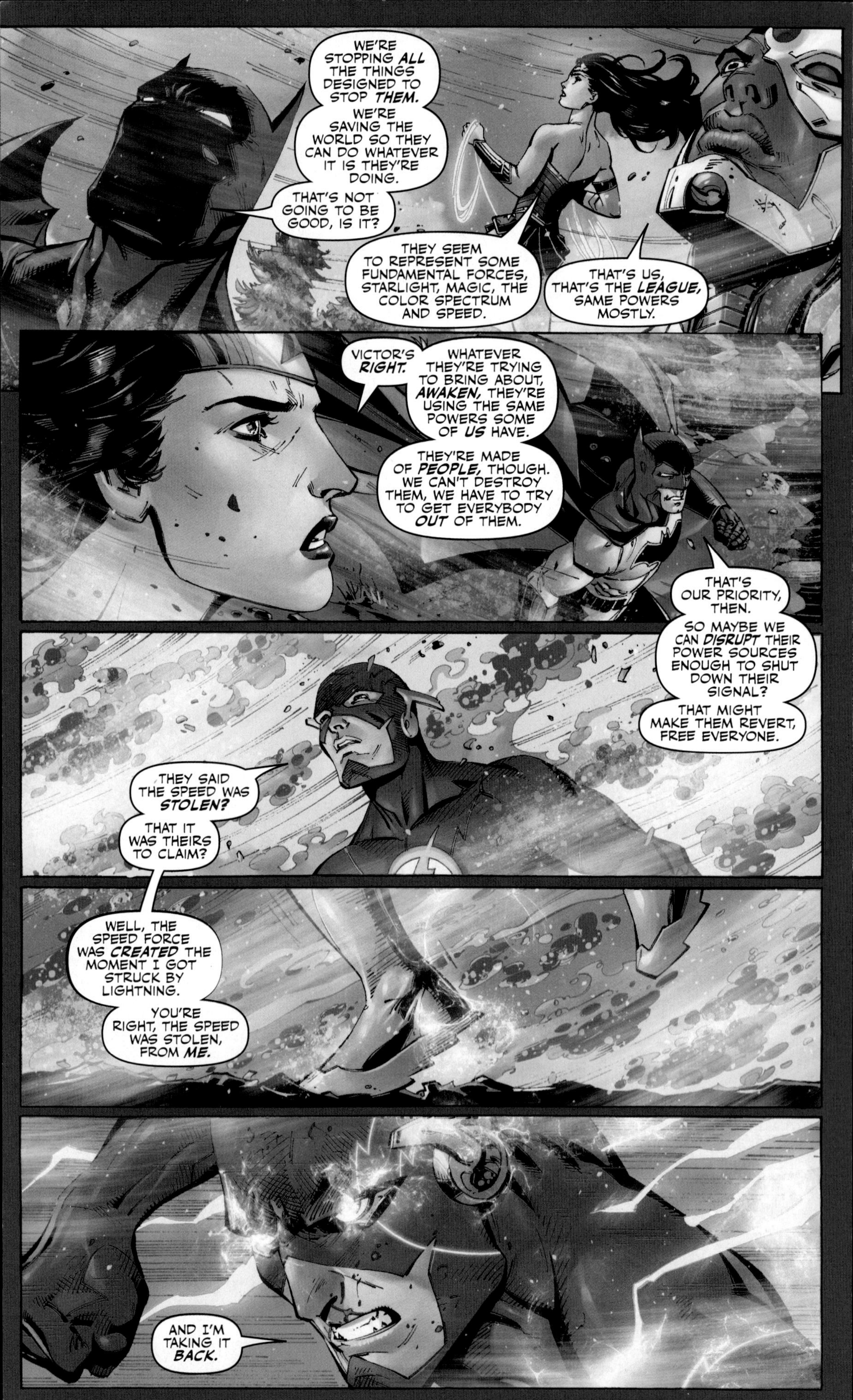
WE'RE STOPPING ALL THE THINGS DESIGNED TO STOP THEM.
WE'RE SAVING THE WORLD SO THEY CAN DO WHATEVER IT IS THEY'RE DOING.
THAT'S NOT GOING TO BE GOOD, IS IT?
THEY SEEM TO REPRESENT SOME FUNDAMENTAL FORCES, STARLIGHT, MAGIC, THE COLOR SPECTRUM AND SPEED.
THAT'S US, THAT'S THE LEAGUE, SAME POWERS MOSTLY.
VICTOR'S RIGHT.
WHATEVER THEY'RE TRYING TO BRING ABOUT, AWAKEN, THEY'RE USING THE SAME POWERS SOME OF US HAVE.
THEY'RE MADE OF PEOPLE, THOUGH. WE CAN'T DESTROY THEM, WE HAVE TO TRY TO GET EVERYBODY OUT OF THEM.
THAT'S OUR PRIORITY, THEN.
SO MAYBE WE CAN DISRUPT THEIR POWER SOURCES ENOUGH TO SHUT DOWN THEIR SIGNAL?
THAT MIGHT MAKE THEM REVERT, FREE EVERYONE.
THEY SAID THE SPEED WAS STOLEN?
THAT IT WAS THEIRS TO CLAIM?
WELL, THE SPEED FORCE WAS CREATED THE MOMENT I GOT STRUCK BY LIGHTNING.
YOU'RE RIGHT, THE SPEED WAS STOLEN, FROM ME.
AND I'M TAKING IT BACK.

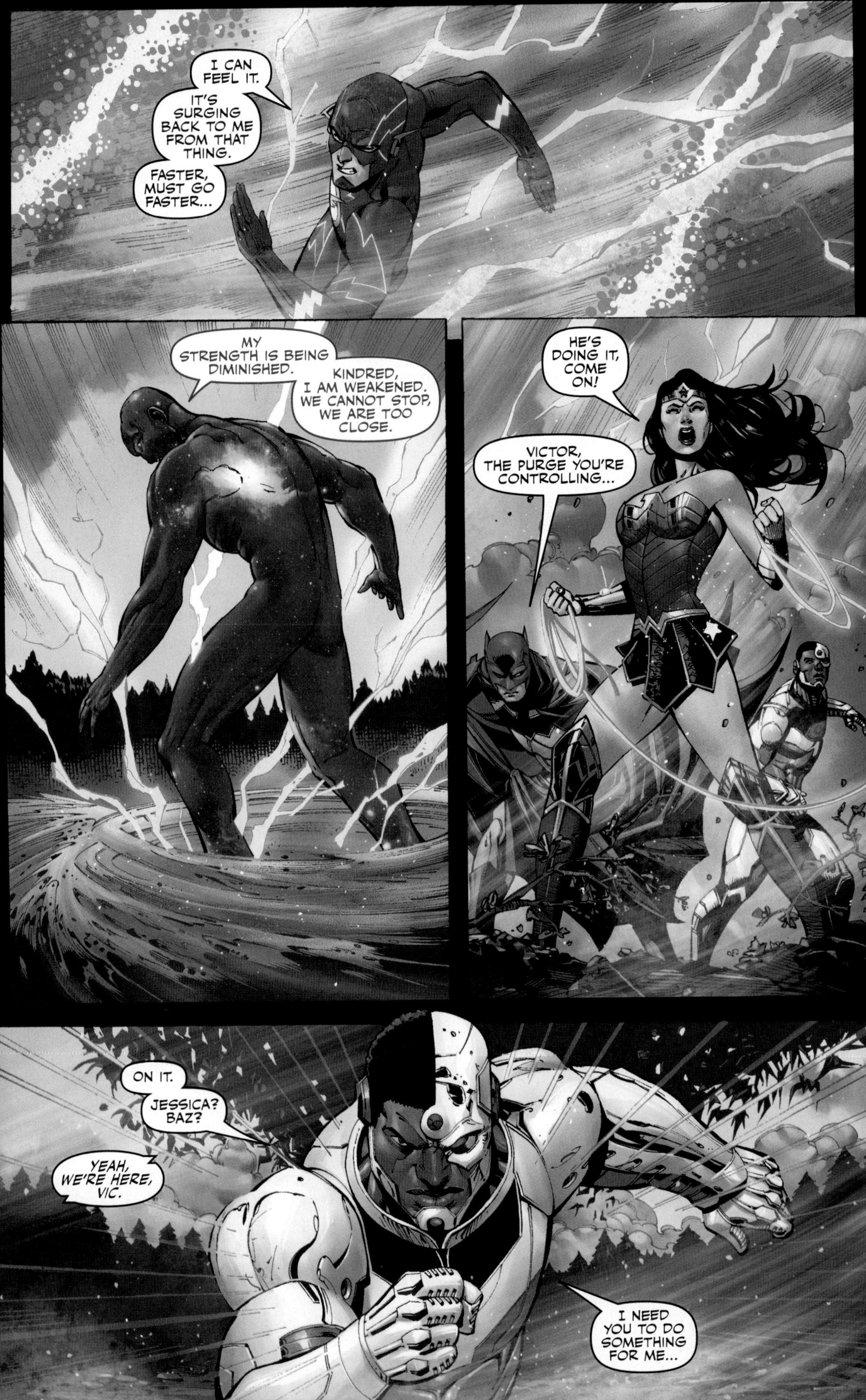
I CAN FEEL IT.
IT'S SURGING BACK TO ME FROM THAT THING.
FASTER, MUST GO FASTER...
MY STRENGTH IS BEING DIMINISHED.
KINDRED, I AM WEAKENED. WE CANNOT STOP, WE ARE TOO CLOSE.
HE'S DOING IT, COME ON!
VICTOR, THE PURGE YOU'RE CONTROLLING...
ON IT.
JESSICA? BAZ?
YEAH, WE'RE HERE, VIC.
I NEED YOU TO DO SOMETHING FOR ME...

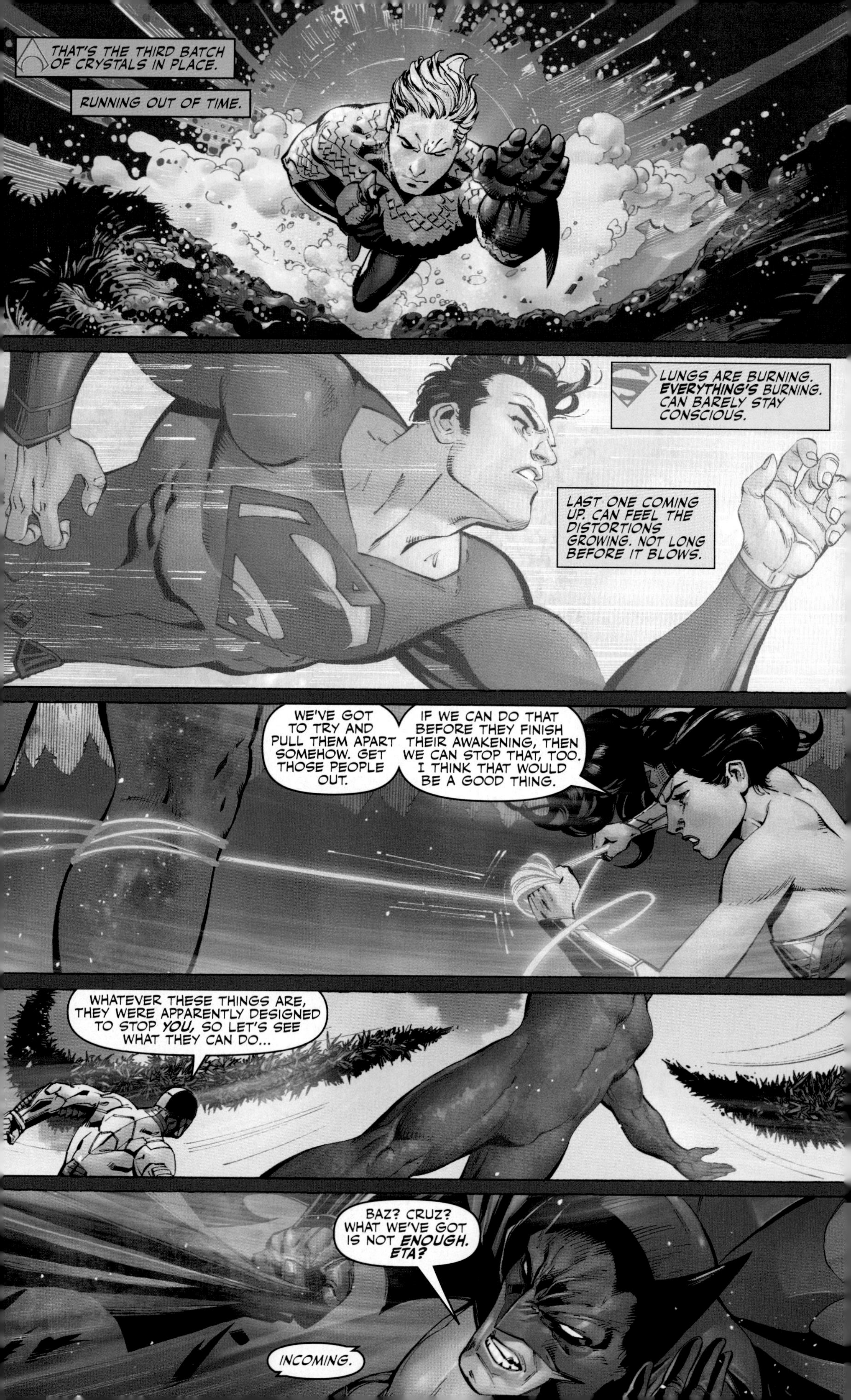
THAT'S THE THIRD BATCH OF CRYSTALS IN PLACE.
RUNNING OUT OF TIME.
LUNGS ARE BURNING. EVERYTHING'S BURNING. CAN BARELY STAY CONSCIOUS.
LAST ONE COMING UP. CAN FEEL THE DISTORTIONS GROWING. NOT LONG BEFORE IT BLOWS.
WE'VE GOT TO TRY AND PULL THEM APART SOMEHOW. GET THOSE PEOPLE OUT.
IF WE CAN DO THAT BEFORE THEY FINISH THEIR AWAKENING, THEN WE CAN STOP THAT, TOO. I THINK THAT WOULD BE A GOOD THING.
WHATEVER THESE THINGS ARE, THEY WERE APPARENTLY DESIGNED TO STOP YOU, SO LET'S SEE WHAT THEY CAN DO...
BAZ? CRUZ? WHAT WE'VE GOT IS NOT ENOUGH. ETA?
INCOMING.

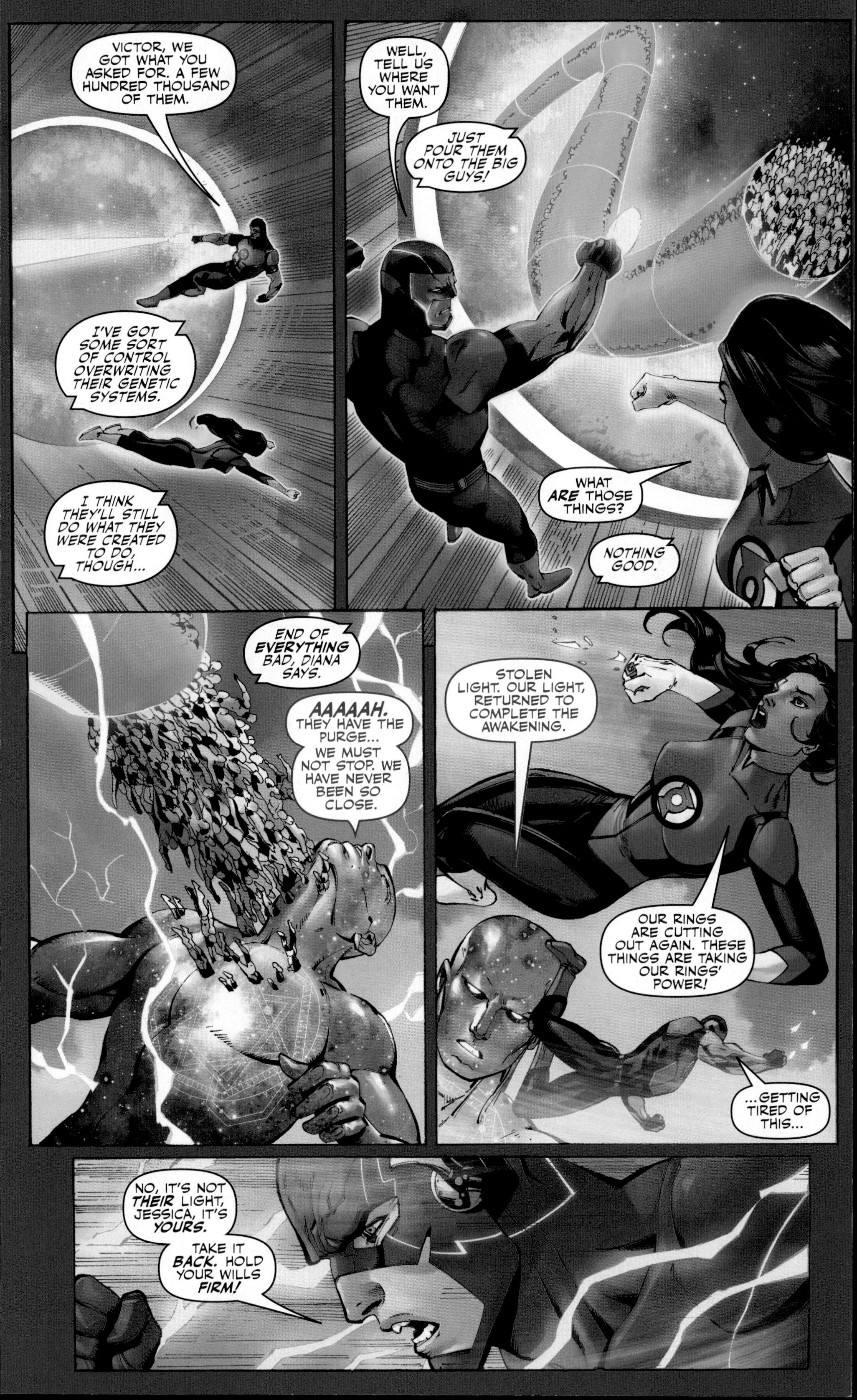
VICTOR, WE GOT WHAT YOU ASKED FOR. A FEW HUNDRED THOUSAND OF THEM.
I'VE GOT SOME SORT OF CONTROL OVERWRITING THEIR GENETIC SYSTEMS.
I THINK THEY'LL STILL DO WHAT THEY WERE CREATED TO DO, THOUGH...
WELL, TELL US WHERE YOU WANT THEM.
JUST POUR THEM ONTO THE BIG GUYS!
WHAT ARE THOSE THINGS?
NOTHING GOOD.
END OF EVERYTHING BAD, DIANA SAYS.
AAAAAH. THEY HAVE THE PURGE... WE MUST NOT STOP. WE HAVE NEVER BEEN SO CLOSE.
STOLEN LIGHT. OUR LIGHT, RETURNED TO COMPLETE THE AWAKENING.
OUR RINGS ARE CUTTING OUT AGAIN. THESE THINGS ARE TAKING OUR RINGS' POWER!
...GETTING TIRED OF THIS...
NO, IT'S NOT THEIR LIGHT, JESSICA, IT'S YOURS.
TAKE IT BACK. HOLD YOUR WILLS FIRM!

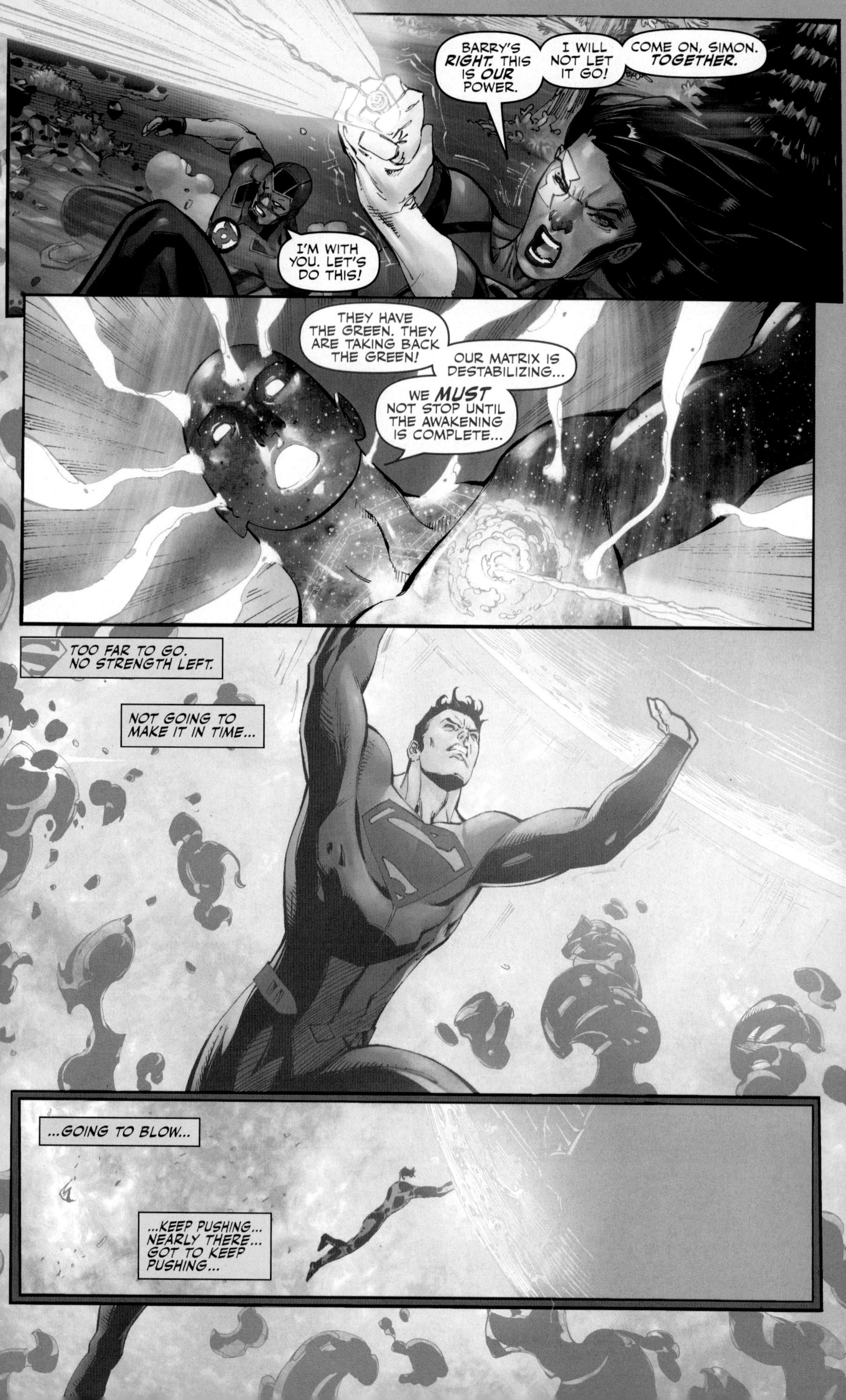

BARRY'S RIGHT. THIS IS OUR POWER.
I WILL NOT LET IT GO!
COME ON, SIMON. TOGETHER.
I'M WITH YOU. LET'S DO THIS!
THEY HAVE THE GREEN. THEY ARE TAKING BACK THE GREEN!
OUR MATRIX IS DESTABILIZING...
WE MUST NOT STOP UNTIL THE AWAKENING IS COMPLETE...
TOO FAR TO GO. NO STRENGTH LEFT.
NOT GOING TO MAKE IT IN TIME...
...GOING TO BLOW...
...KEEP PUSHING... NEARLY THERE... GOT TO KEEP PUSHING...

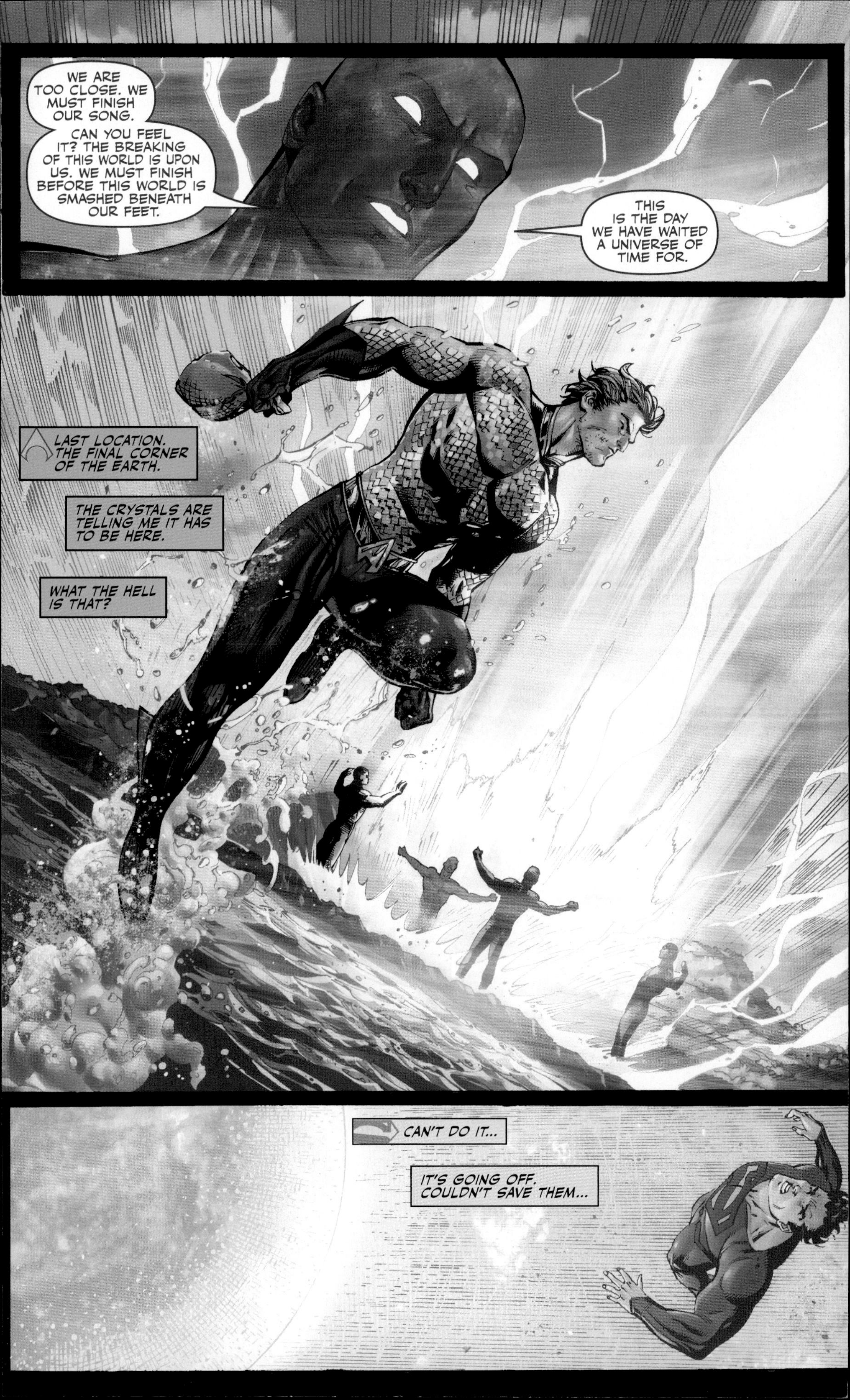
WE ARE TOO CLOSE. WE MUST FINISH OUR SONG.
CAN YOU FEEL IT? THE BREAKING OF THIS WORLD IS UPON US. WE MUST FINISH BEFORE THIS WORLD IS SMASHED BENEATH OUR FEET.
THIS IS THE DAY WE HAVE WAITED A UNIVERSE OF TIME FOR.
LAST LOCATION. THE FINAL CORNER OF THE EARTH.
THE CRYSTALS ARE TELLING ME IT HAS TO BE HERE.
WHAT THE HELL IS THAT?
CAN'T DO IT...
IT'S GOING OFF. COULDN'T SAVE THEM...

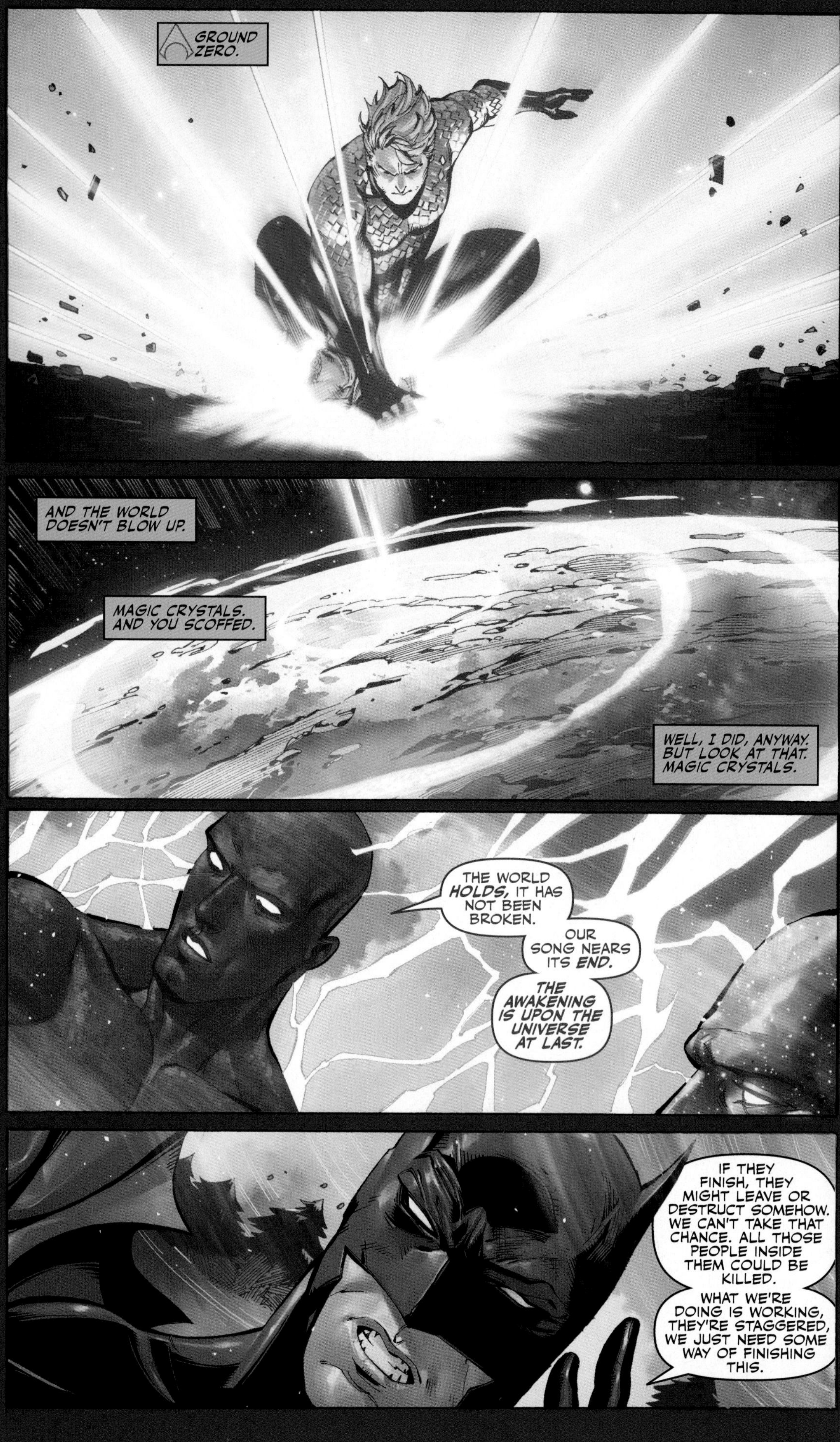
GROUND ZERO.
AND THE WORLD DOESN'T BLOW UP.
MAGIC CRYSTALS. AND YOU SCOFFED.
WELL, I DID, ANYWAY. BUT LOOK AT THAT. MAGIC CRYSTALS.
THE WORLD HOLDS, IT HAS NOT BEEN BROKEN.
OUR SONG NEARS ITS END.
THE AWAKENING IS UPON THE UNIVERSE AT LAST.
IF THEY FINISH, THEY MIGHT LEAVE OR DESTRUCT SOMEHOW. WE CAN'T TAKE THAT CHANCE. ALL THOSE PEOPLE INSIDE THEM COULD BE KILLED.
WHAT WE'RE DOING IS WORKING, THEY'RE STAGGERED, WE JUST NEED SOME WAY OF FINISHING THIS.

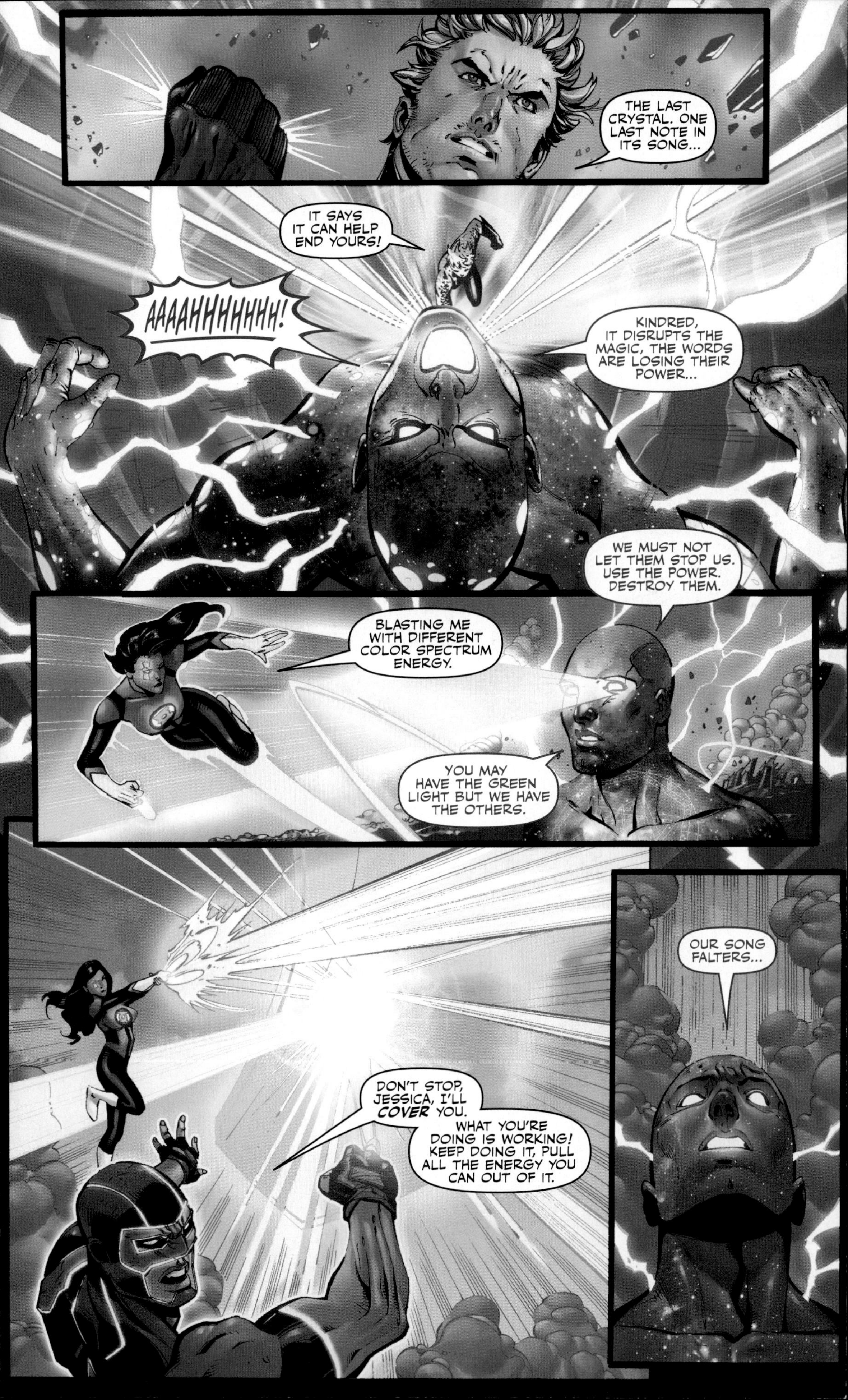
THE LAST CRYSTAL. ONE LAST NOTE IN ITS SONG...
IT SAYS IT CAN HELP END YOURS!
AAAAHHHHHHH!
KINDRED, IT DISRUPTS THE MAGIC, THE WORDS ARE LOSING THEIR POWER...
WE MUST NOT LET THEM STOP US. USE THE POWER. DESTROY THEM.
BLASTING ME WITH DIFFERENT COLOR SPECTRUM ENERGY.
YOU MAY HAVE THE GREEN LIGHT BUT WE HAVE THE OTHERS.
DON'T STOP, JESSICA, I'LL COVER YOU.
WHAT YOU'RE DOING IS WORKING! KEEP DOING IT, PULL ALL THE ENERGY YOU CAN OUT OF IT.
OUR SONG FALTERS...

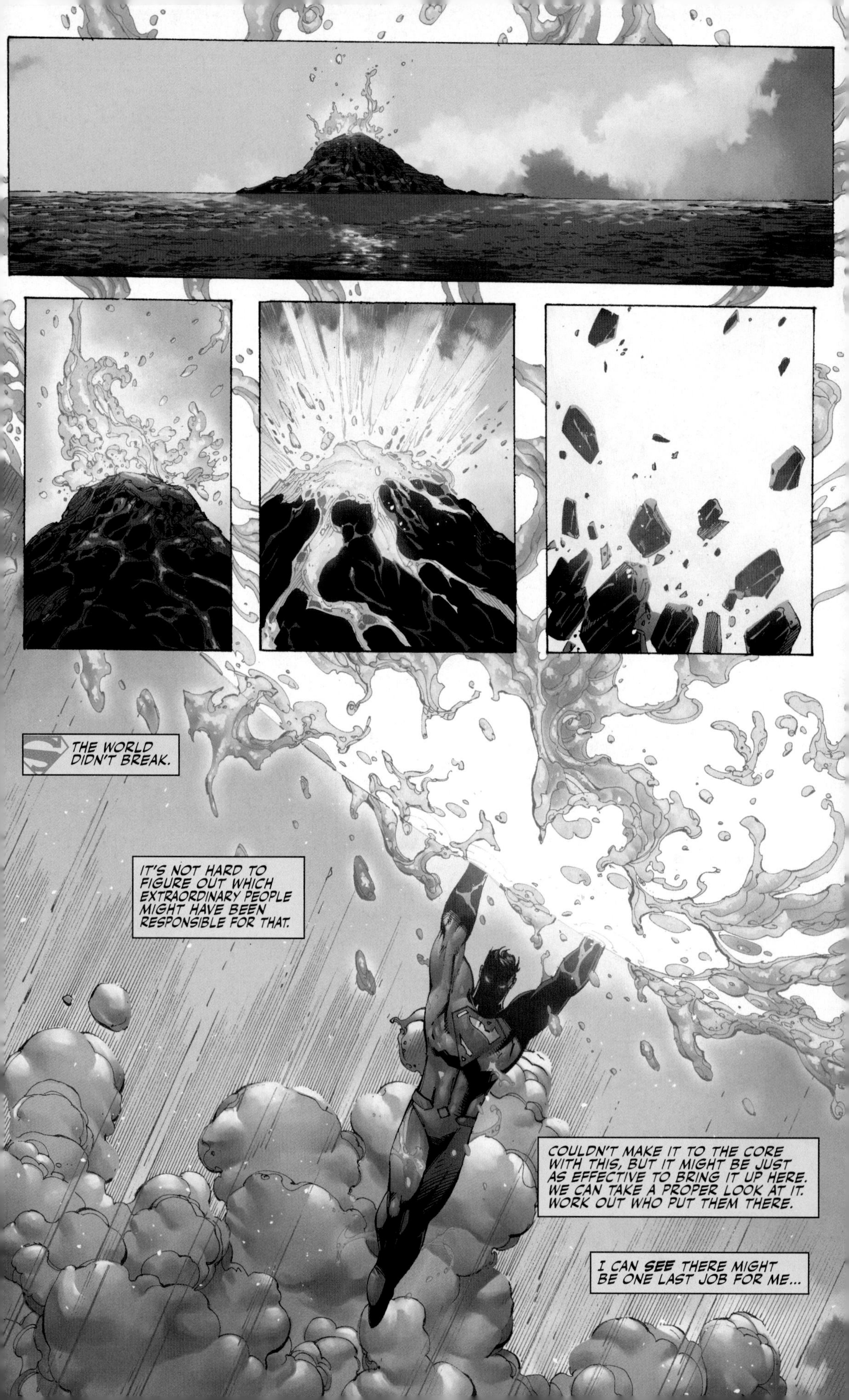
THE WORLD DIDN'T BREAK.
IT'S NOT HARD TO FIGURE OUT WHICH EXTRAORDINARY PEOPLE MIGHT HAVE BEEN RESPONSIBLE FOR THAT.
COULDN'T MAKE IT TO THE CORE WITH THIS, BUT IT MIGHT BE JUST AS EFFECTIVE TO BRING IT UP HERE. WE CAN TAKE A PROPER LOOK AT IT. WORK OUT WHO PUT THEM THERE.
I CAN SEE THERE MIGHT BE ONE LAST JOB FOR ME...

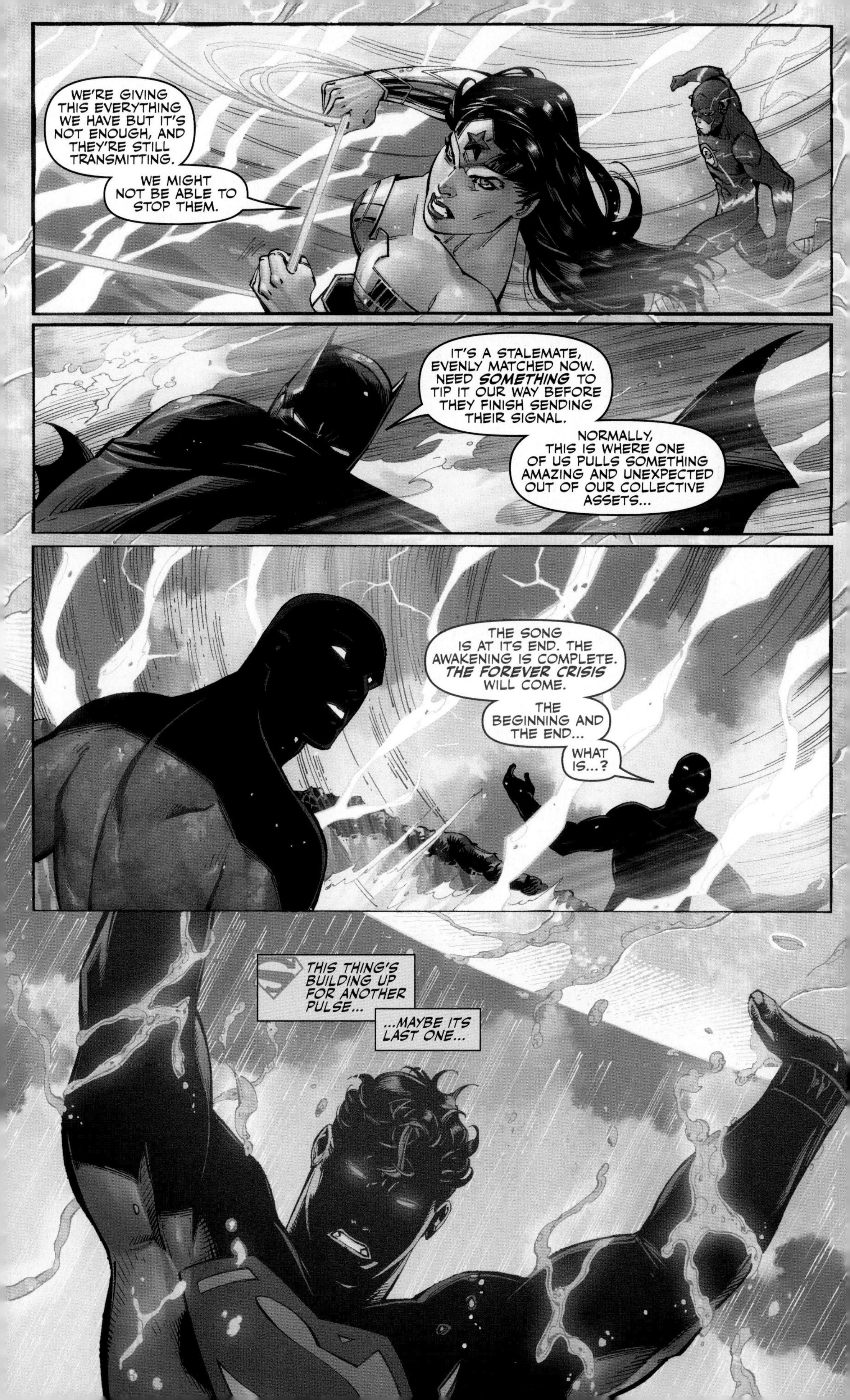
WE'RE GIVING THIS EVERYTHING WE HAVE BUT IT'S NOT ENOUGH, AND THEY'RE STILL TRANSMITTING.
WE MIGHT NOT BE ABLE TO STOP THEM.
IT'S A STALEMATE, EVENLY MATCHED NOW. NEED SOMETHING TO TIP IT OUR WAY BEFORE THEY FINISH SENDING THEIR SIGNAL.
NORMALLY, THIS IS WHERE ONE OF US PULLS SOMETHING AMAZING AND UNEXPECTED OUT OF OUR COLLECTIVE ASSETS...
THE SONG IS AT ITS END. THE AWAKENING IS COMPLETE. THE FOREVER CRISIS WILL COME.
THE BEGINNING AND THE END...
WHAT IS...?
THIS THING'S BUILDING UP FOR ANOTHER PULSE...
...MAYBE ITS LAST ONE...

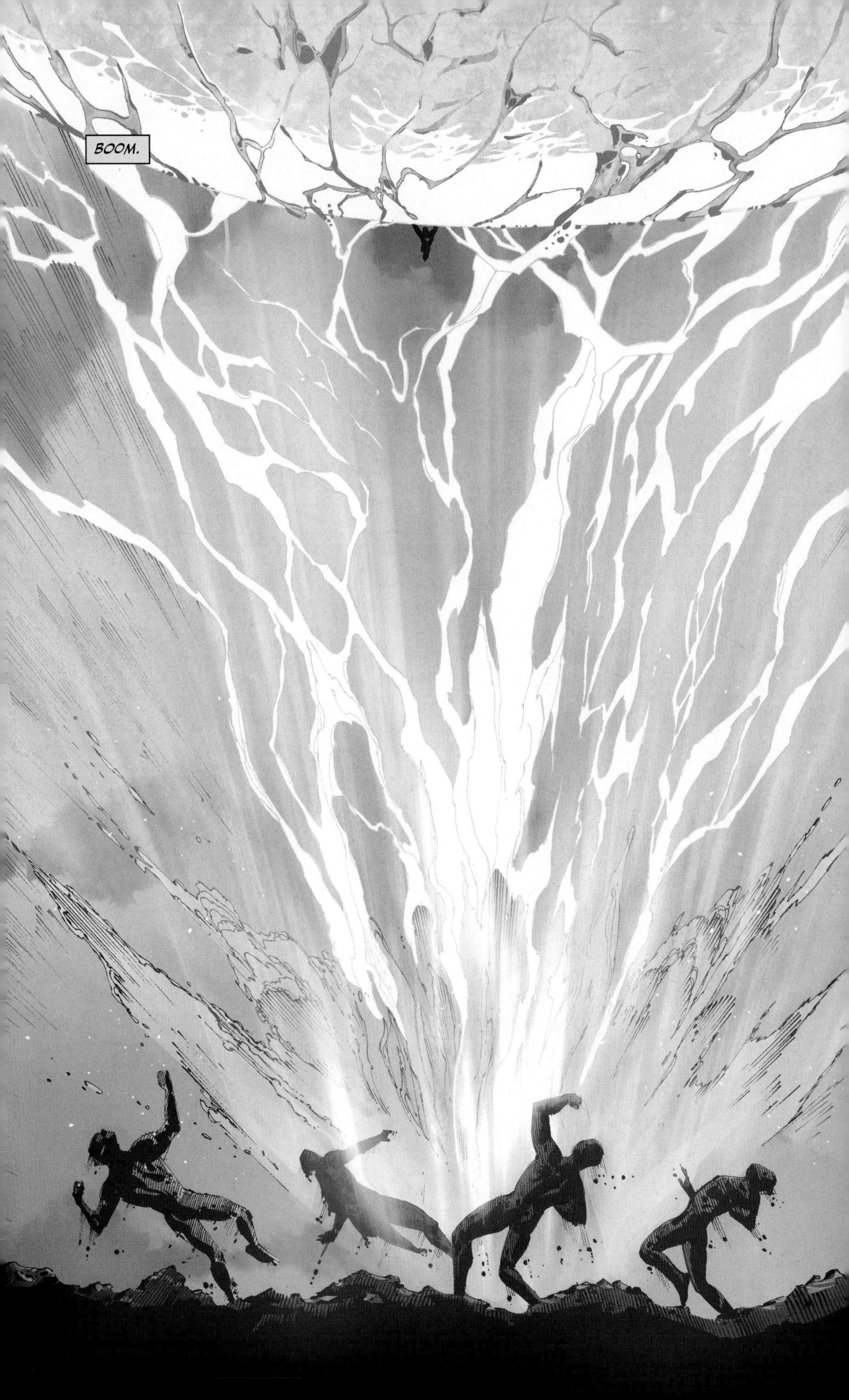
BOOM.

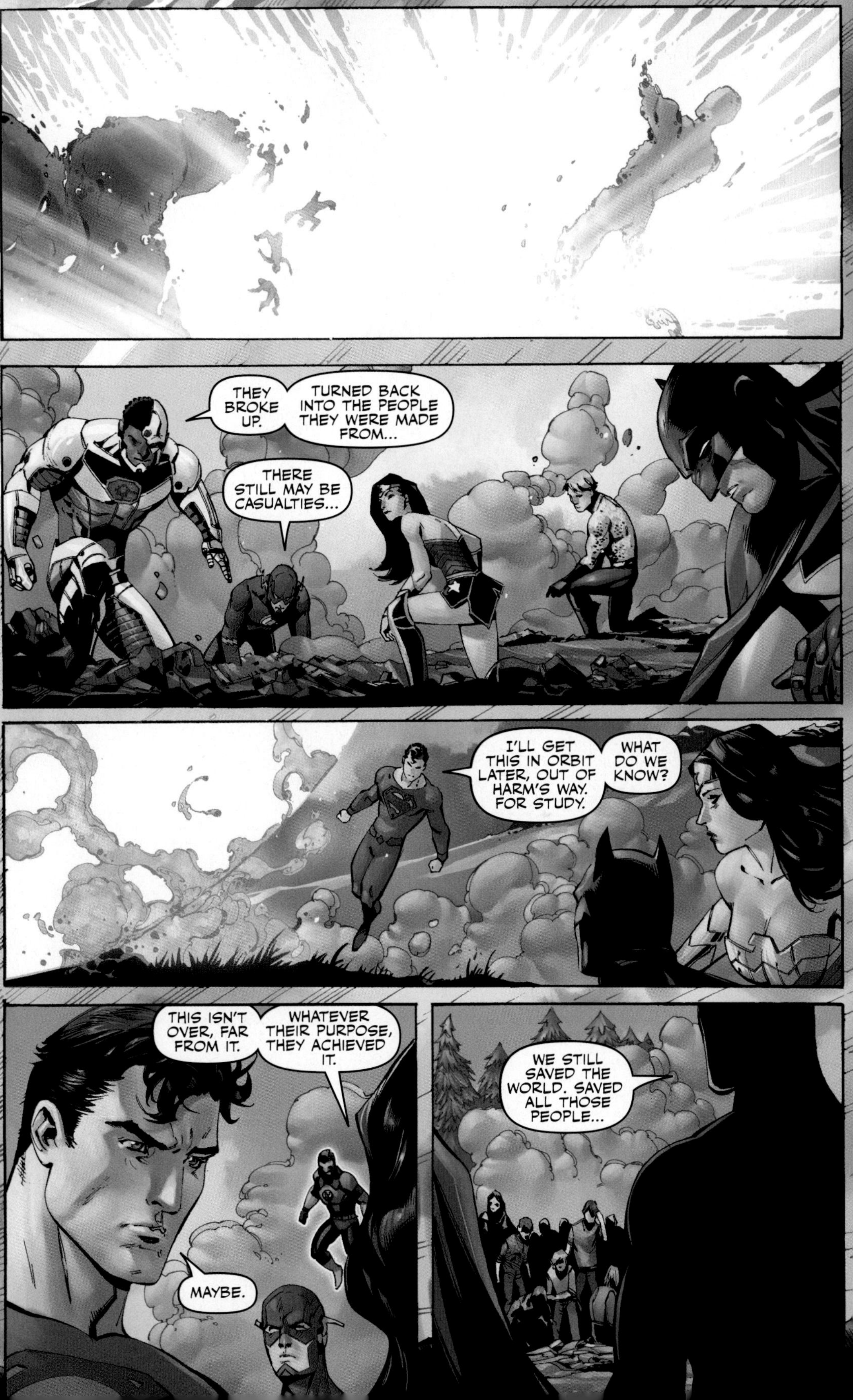
THEY BROKE UP.
TURNED BACK INTO THE PEOPLE THEY WERE MADE FROM...
THERE STILL MAY BE CASUALTIES...
I'LL GET THIS IN ORBIT LATER, OUT OF HARM'S WAY. FOR STUDY.
WHAT DO WE KNOW?
THIS ISN'T OVER, FAR FROM IT.
WHATEVER THEIR PURPOSE, THEY ACHIEVED IT.
MAYBE.
WE STILL SAVED THE WORLD. SAVED ALL THOSE PEOPLE...

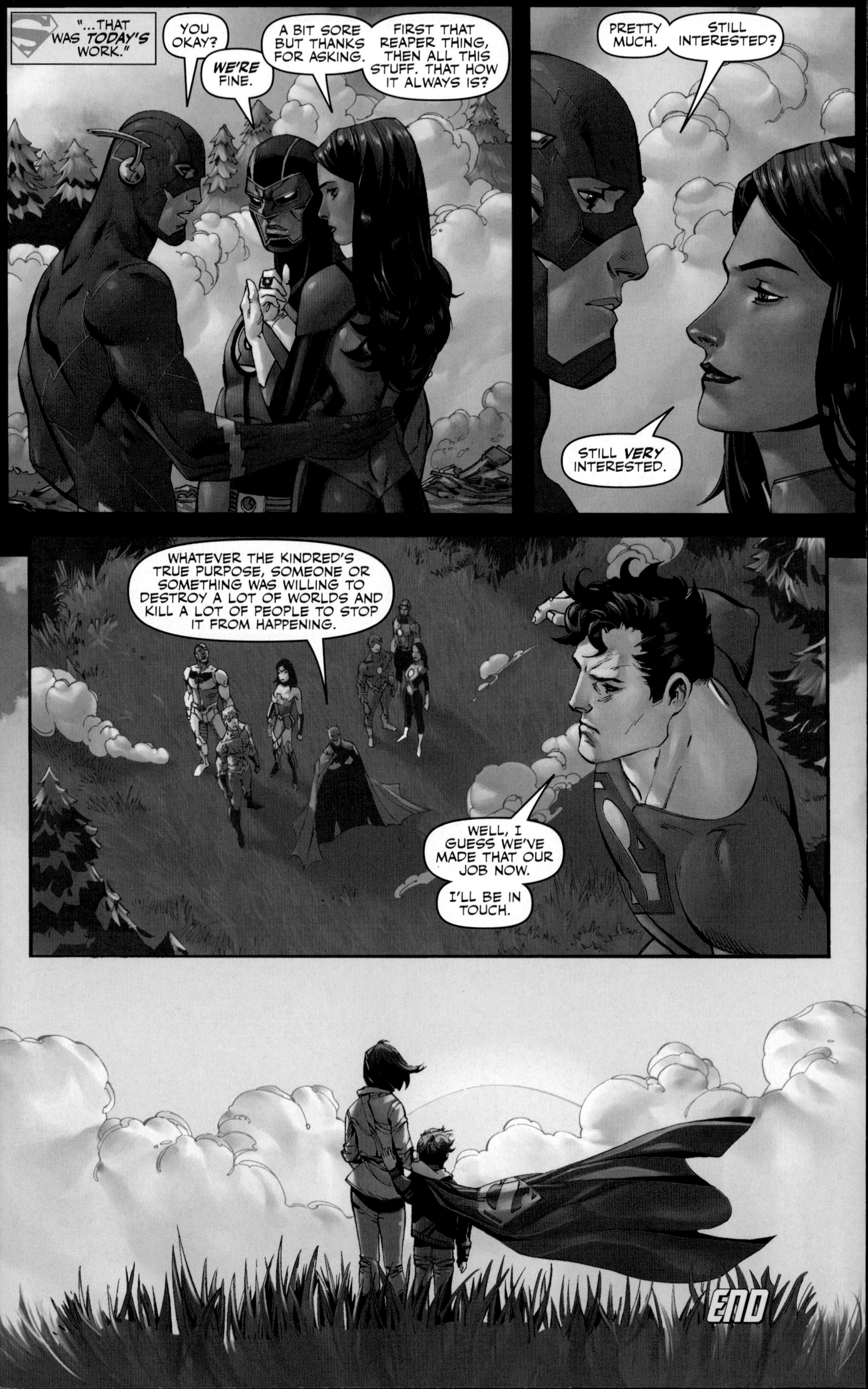
"...THAT WAS TODAY'S WORK."
YOU OKAY?
WE'RE FINE.
A BIT SORE BUT THANKS FOR ASKING.
FIRST THAT REAPER THING, THEN ALL THIS STUFF. THAT HOW IT ALWAYS IS?
PRETTY MUCH.
STILL INTERESTED?
STILL VERY INTERESTED.
WHATEVER THE KINDRED'S TRUE PURPOSE, SOMEONE OR SOMETHING WAS WILLING TO DESTROY A LOT OF WORLDS AND KILL A LOT OF PEOPLE TO STOP IT FROM HAPPENING.
WELL, I GUESS WE'VE MADE THAT OUR JOB NOW.
I'LL BE IN TOUCH.
END

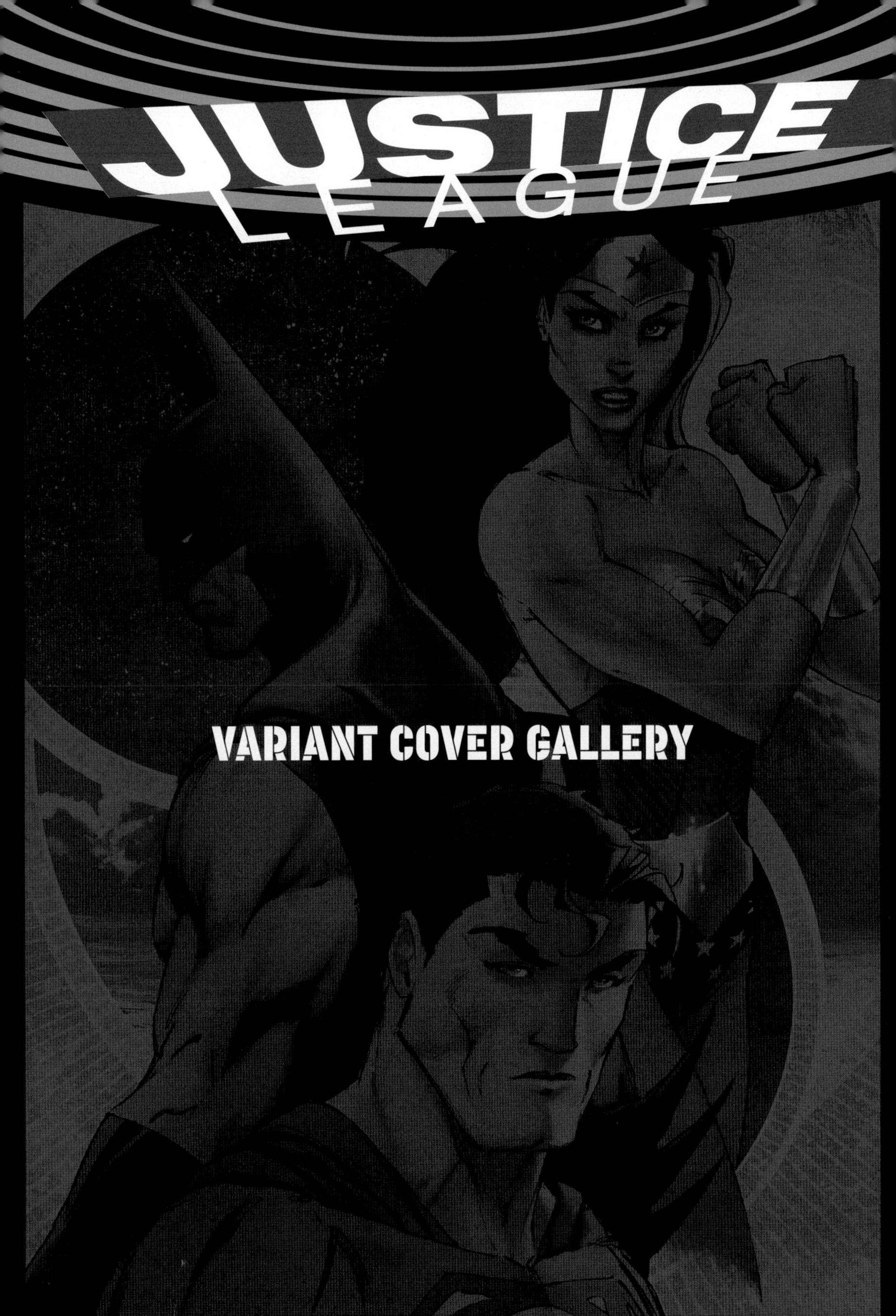
JUSTICE LEAGUE

# VARIANT COVER GALLERY

JUSTICE LEAGUE: REBIRTH #1 variant cover by Joe Madureira and Alex Sinclair

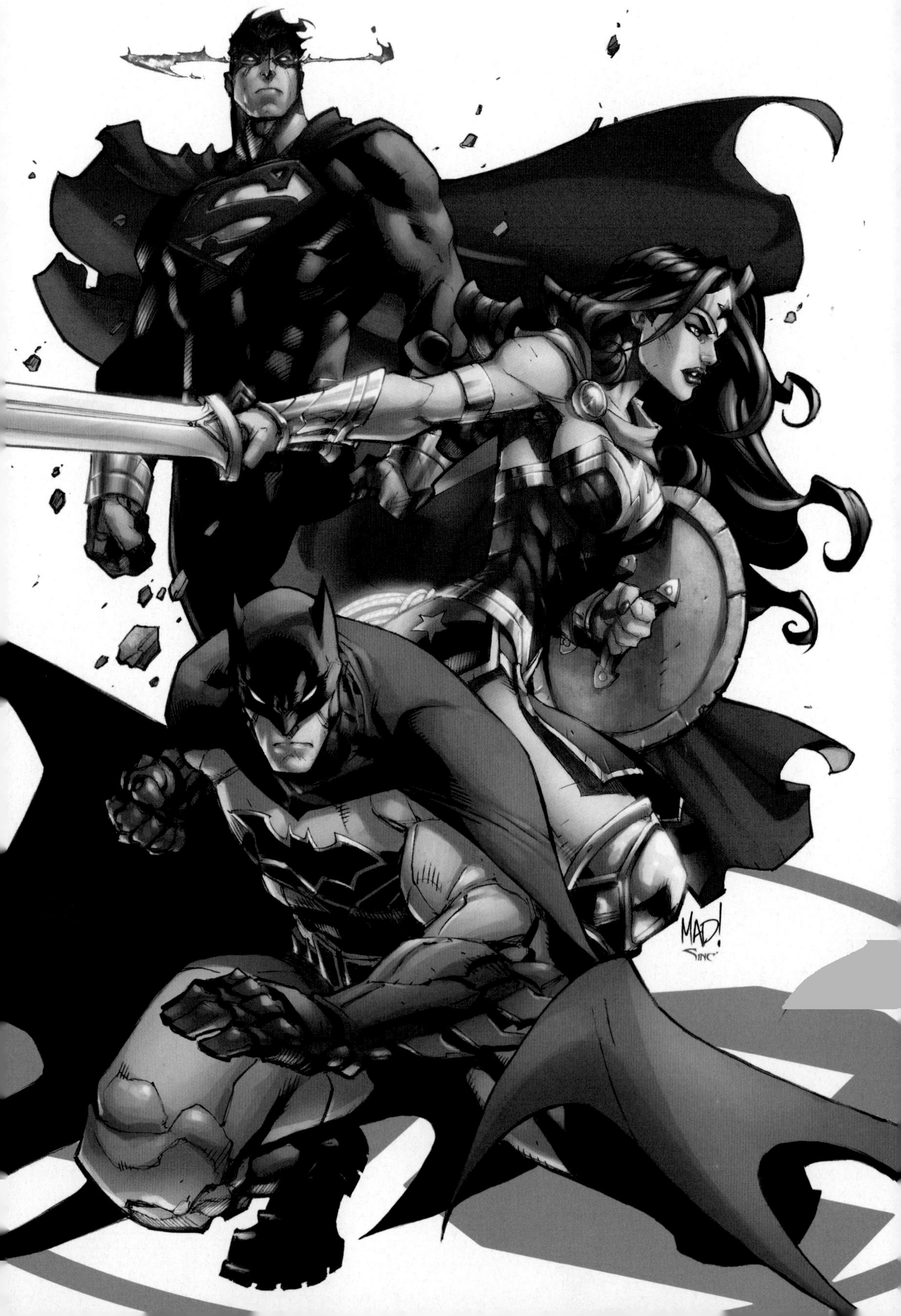
MAD!

JUSTICE LEAGUE #1 variant by Eric Basaldua and Nei Ruffino

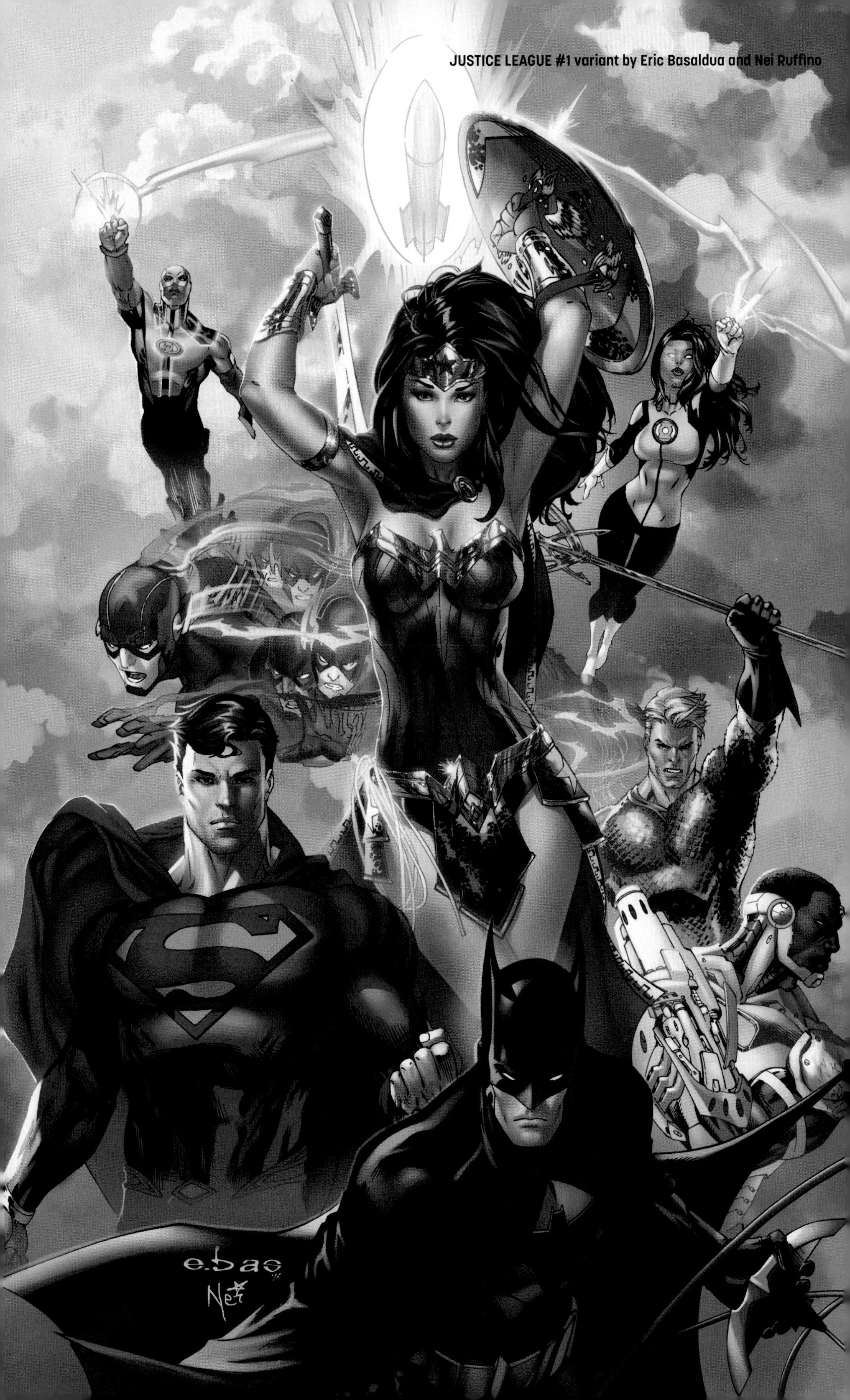

JUSTICE LEAGUE #1 variant by Ed Benes and FCO Plascencia

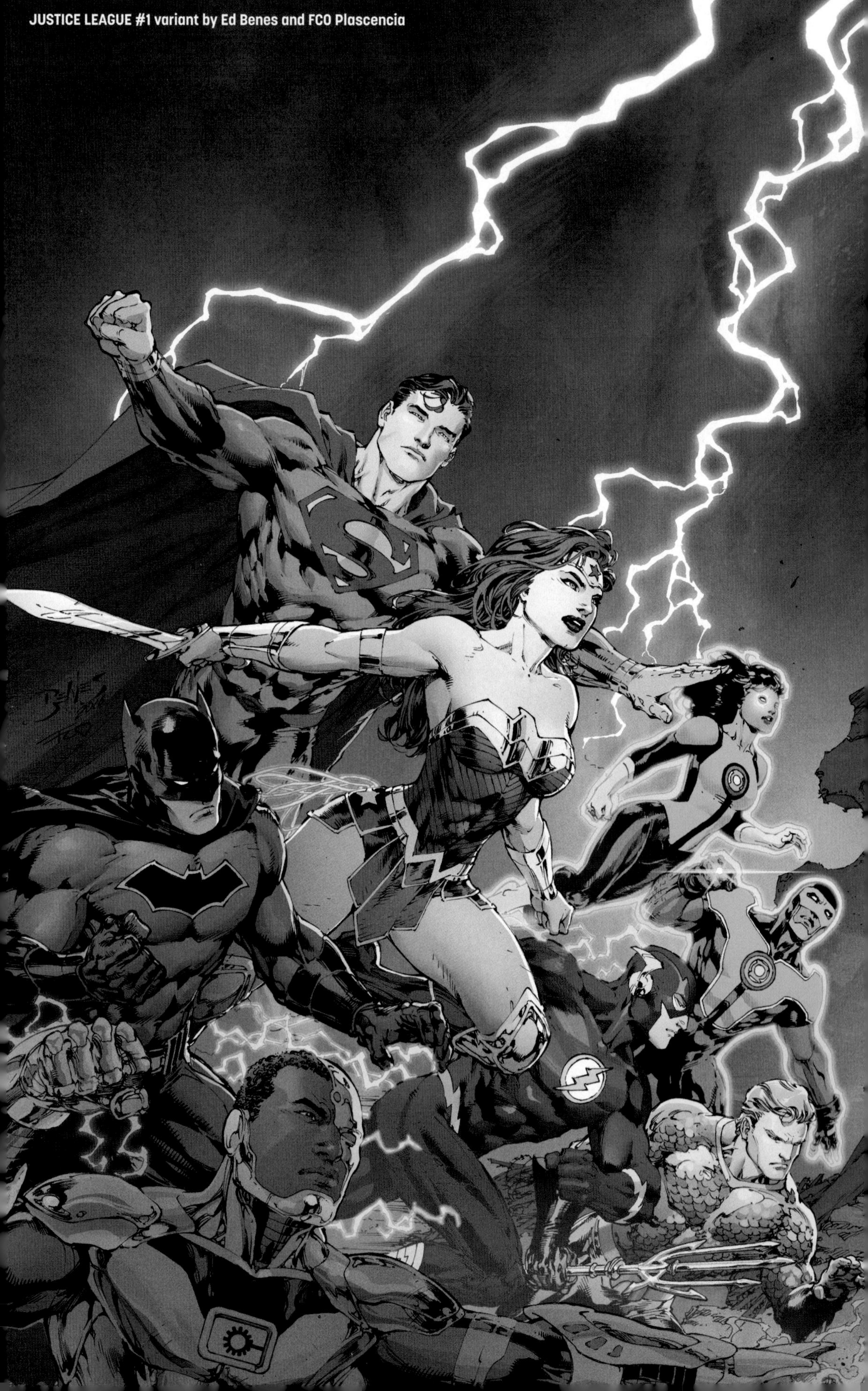

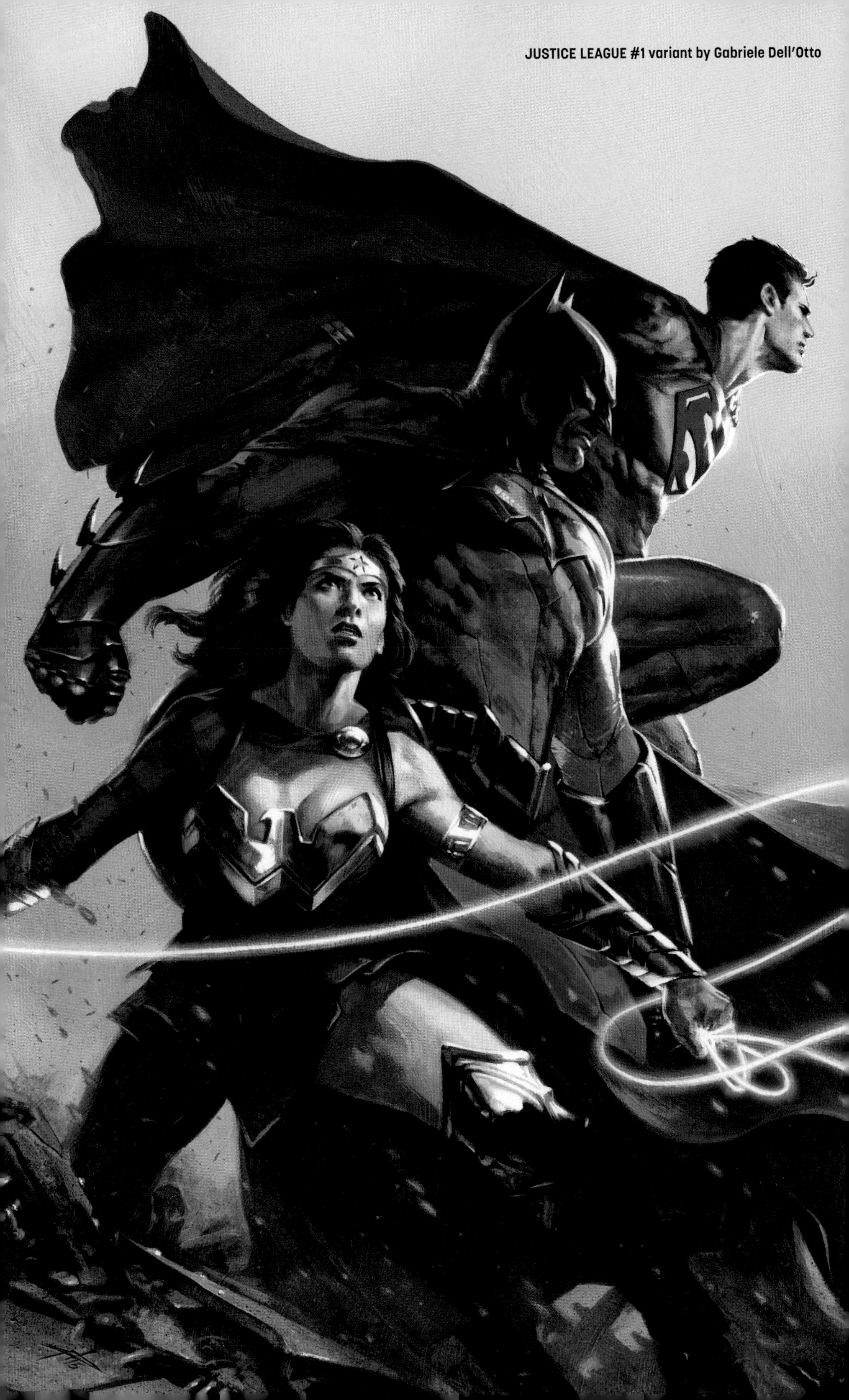

JUSTICE LEAGUE #1 variant by Gabriele Dell'Otto

JUSTICE LEAGUE #1 variant by Terry and Rachel Dodson

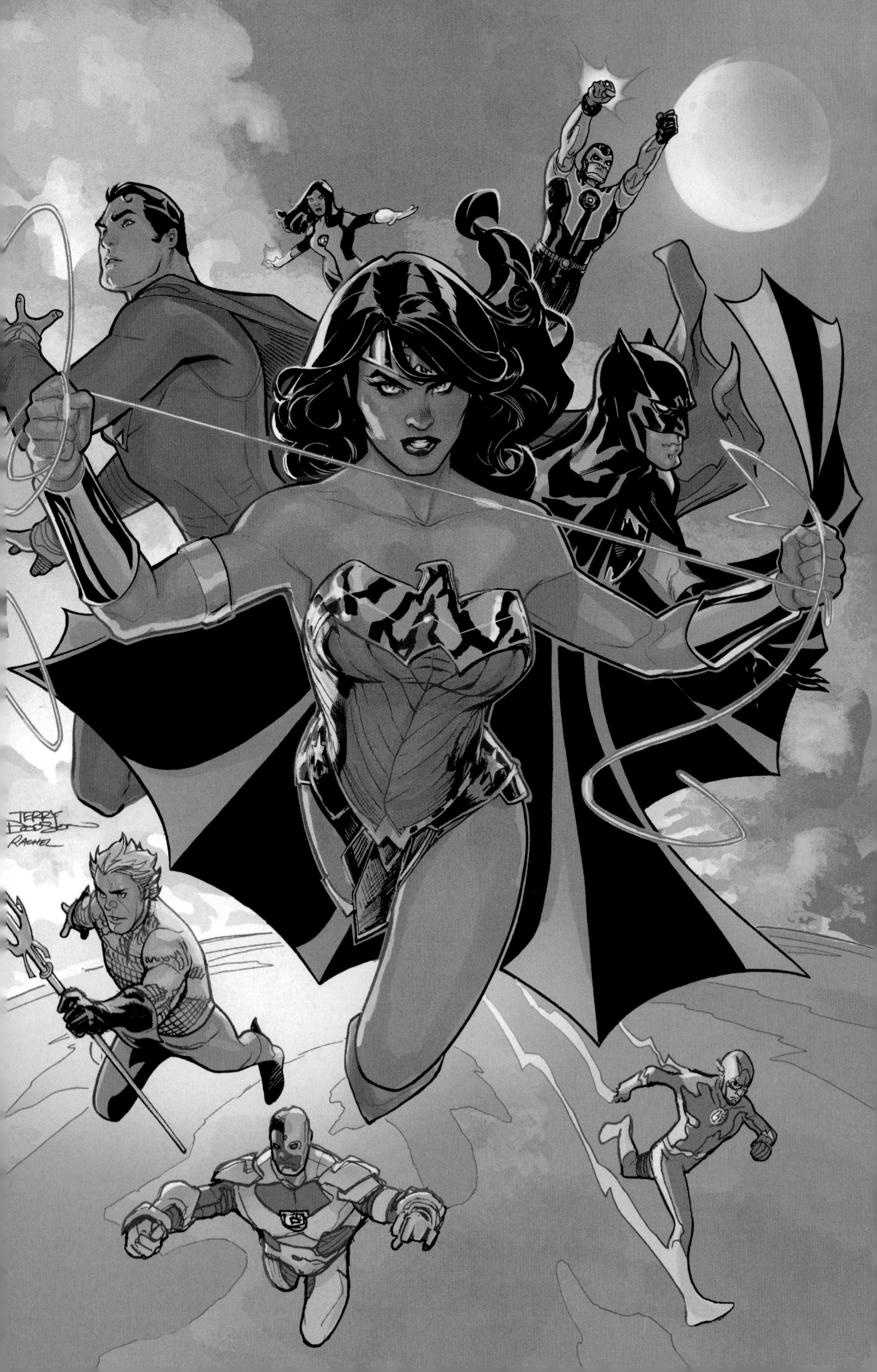

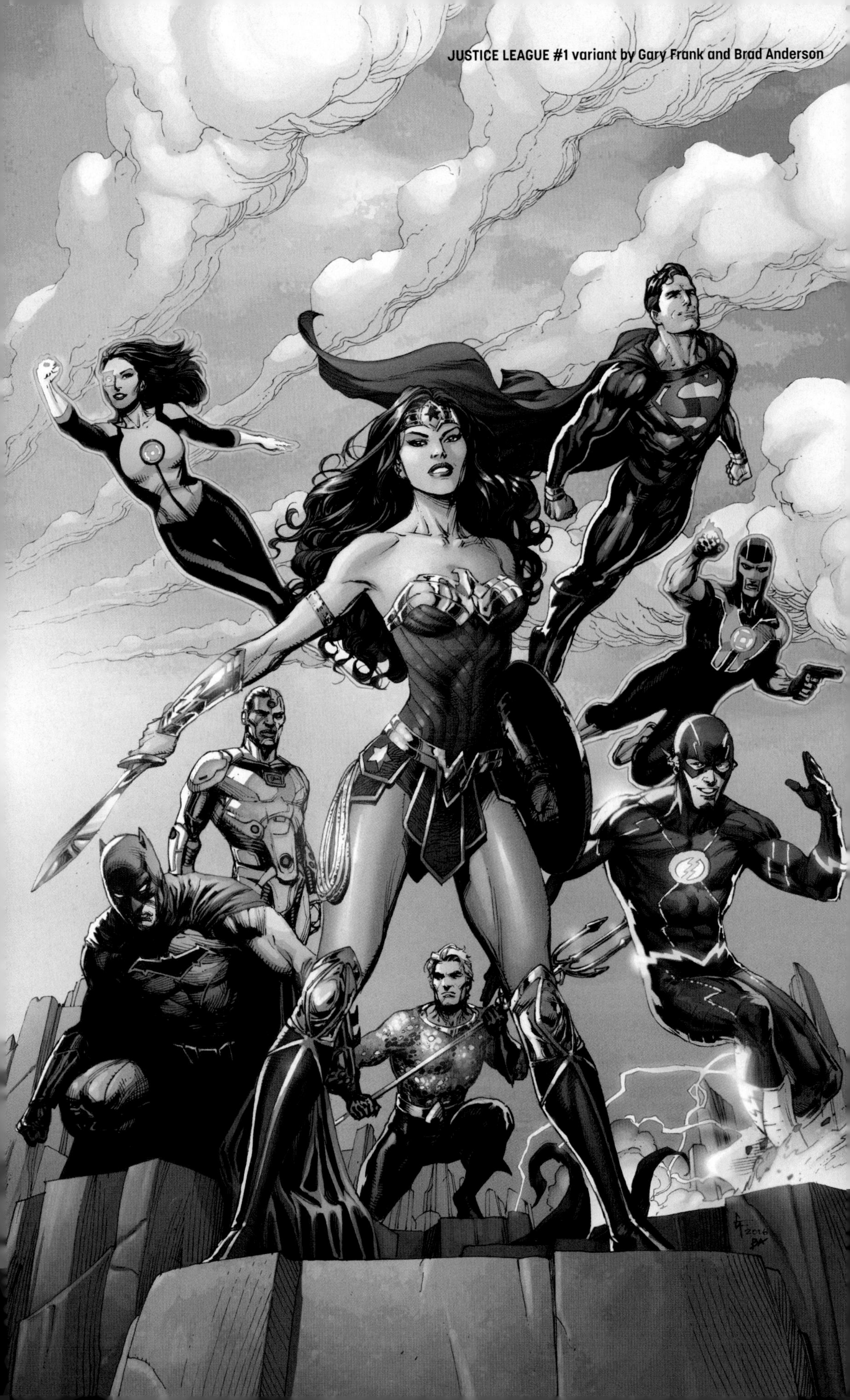

JUSTICE LEAGUE #1 variant by Gary Frank and Brad Anderson

JUSTICE LEAGUE #1 variant by Tyler Kirkham and Tomeu Morey

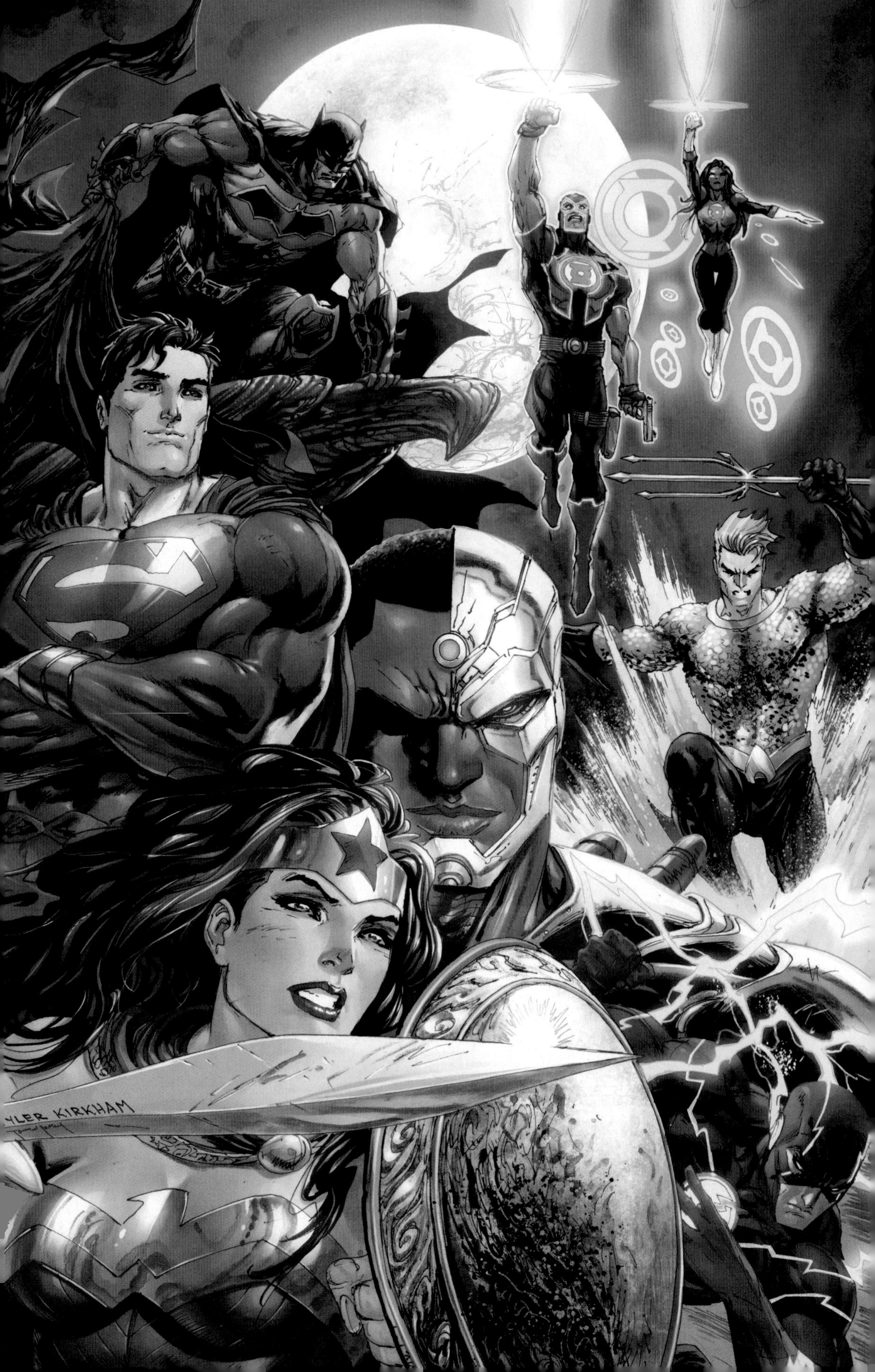

JUSTICE LEAGUE #1 variant by José Luis García-López

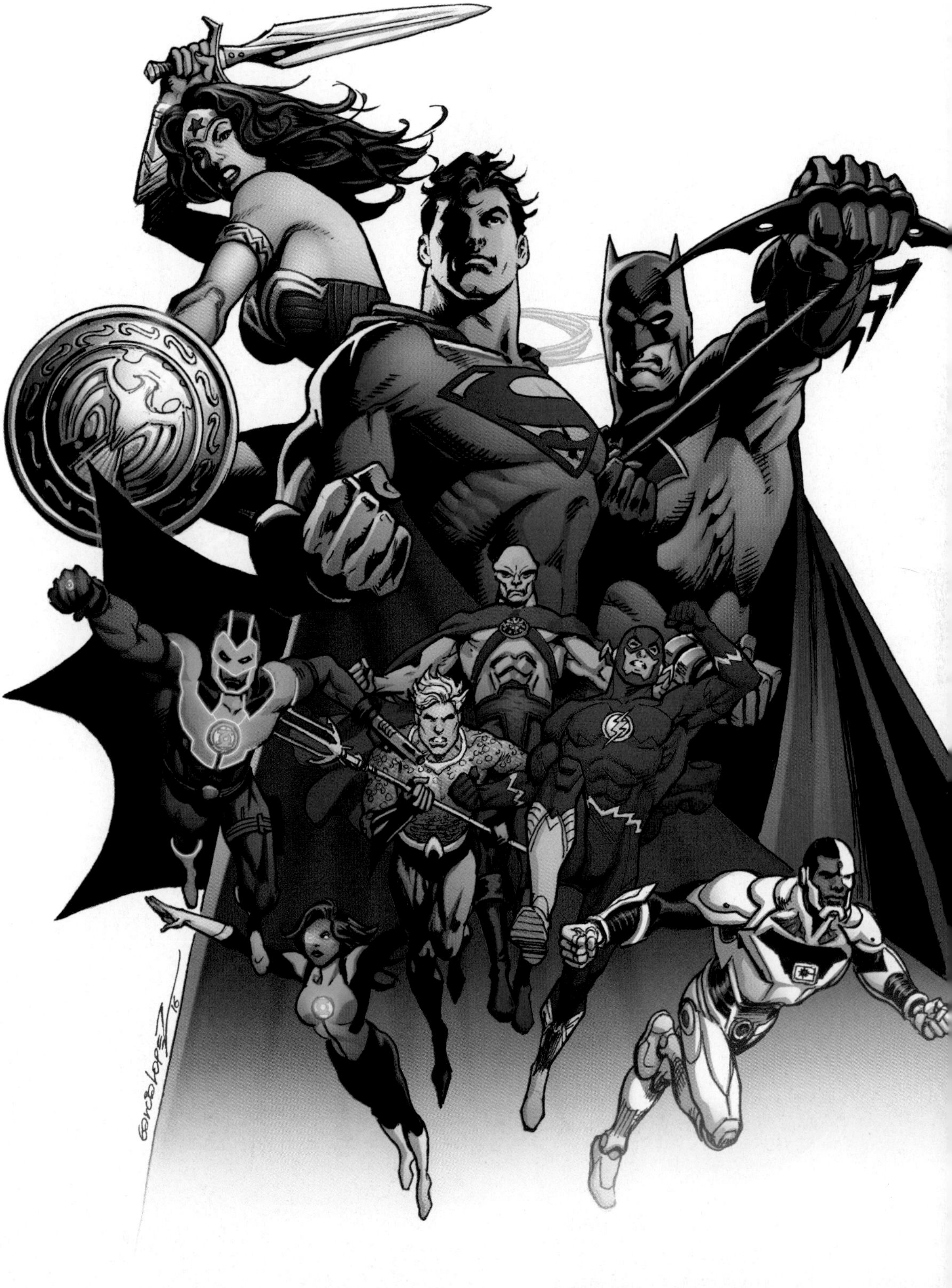

JUSTICE LEAGUE #1 variant by Kevin Maguire

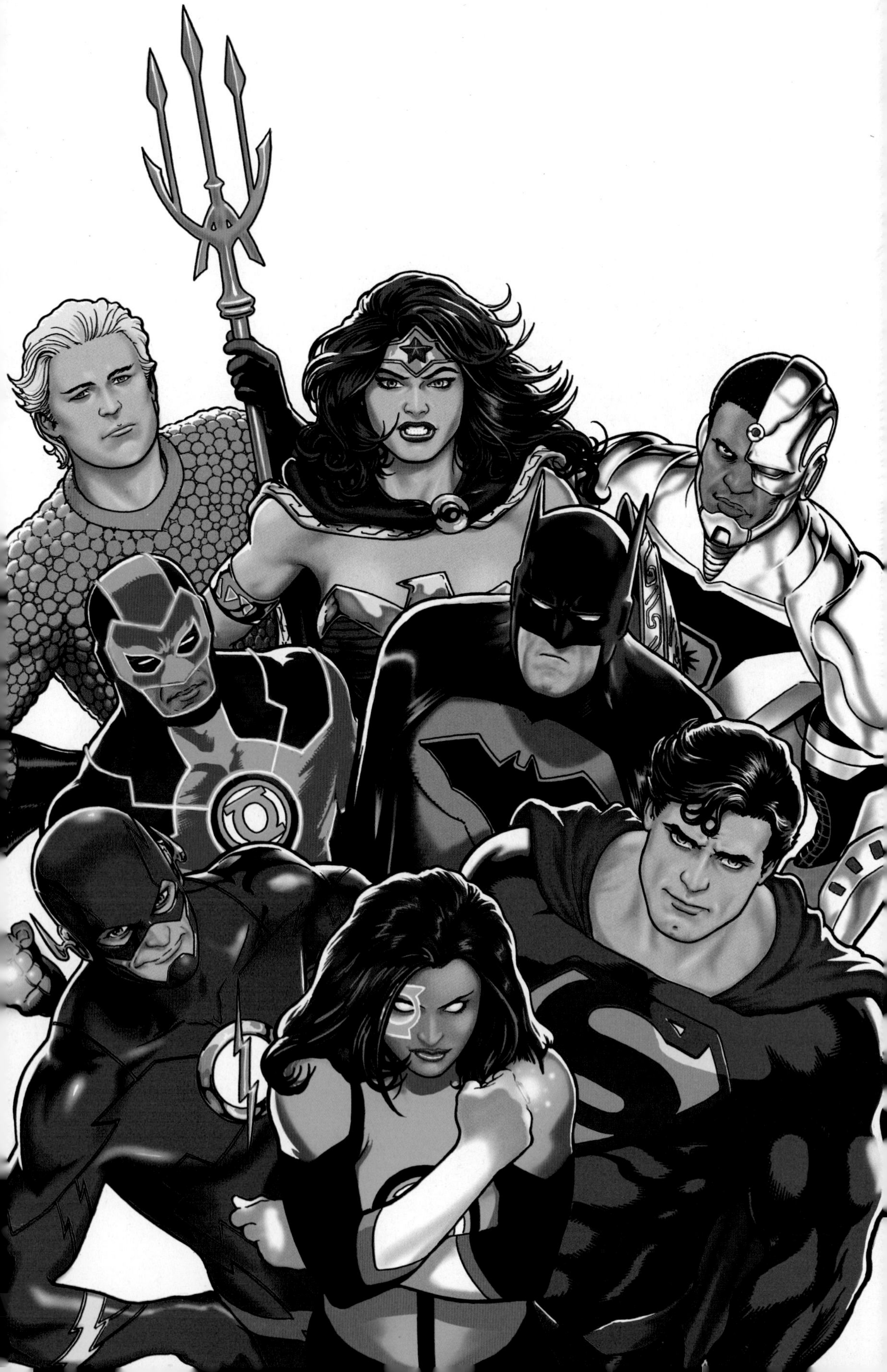

JUSTICE LEAGUE #1 variant by Darick Robertson and Diego Rodriguez

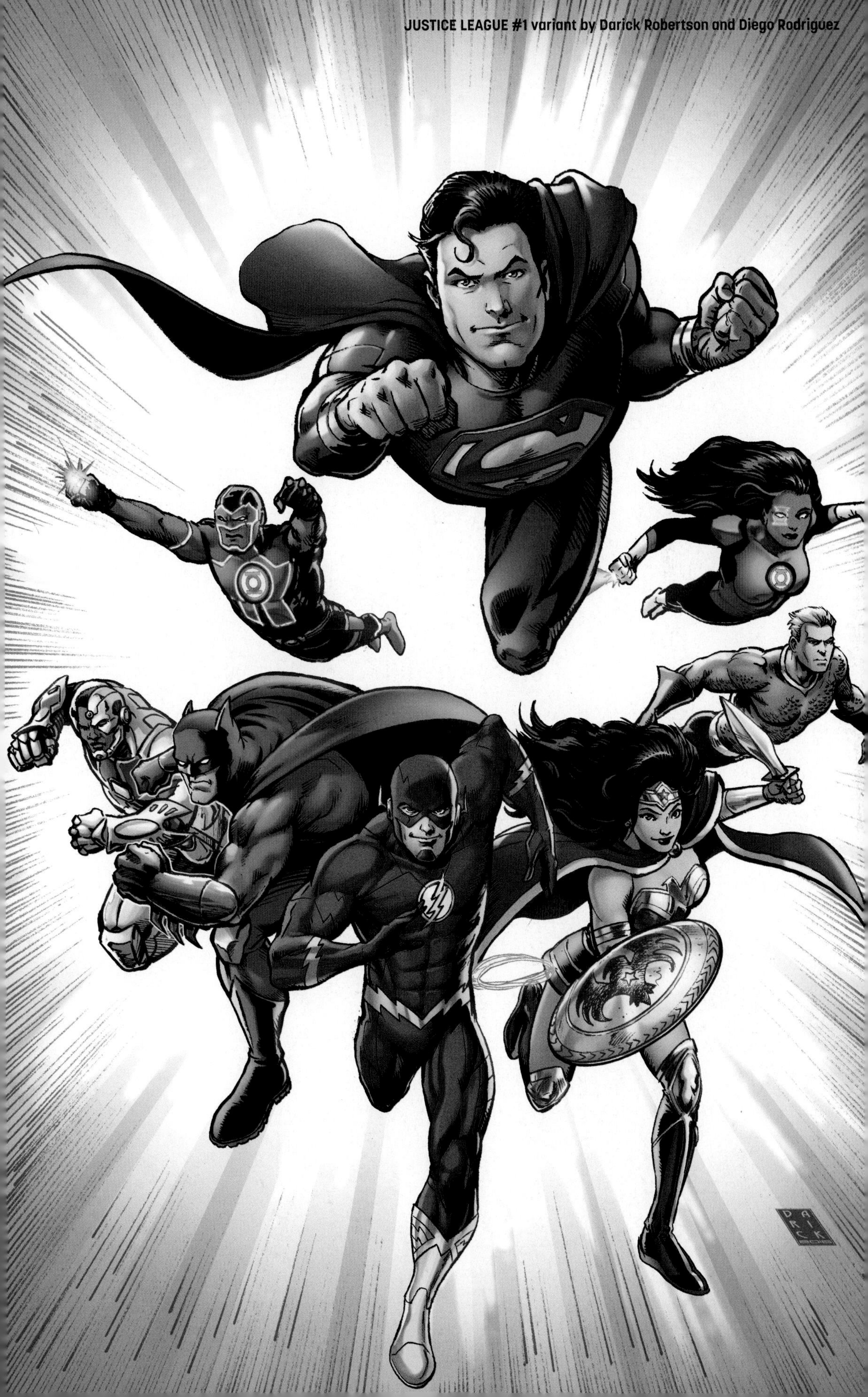

JUSTICE LEAGUE #1 variant by Michael Turner and Peter Steigerwald

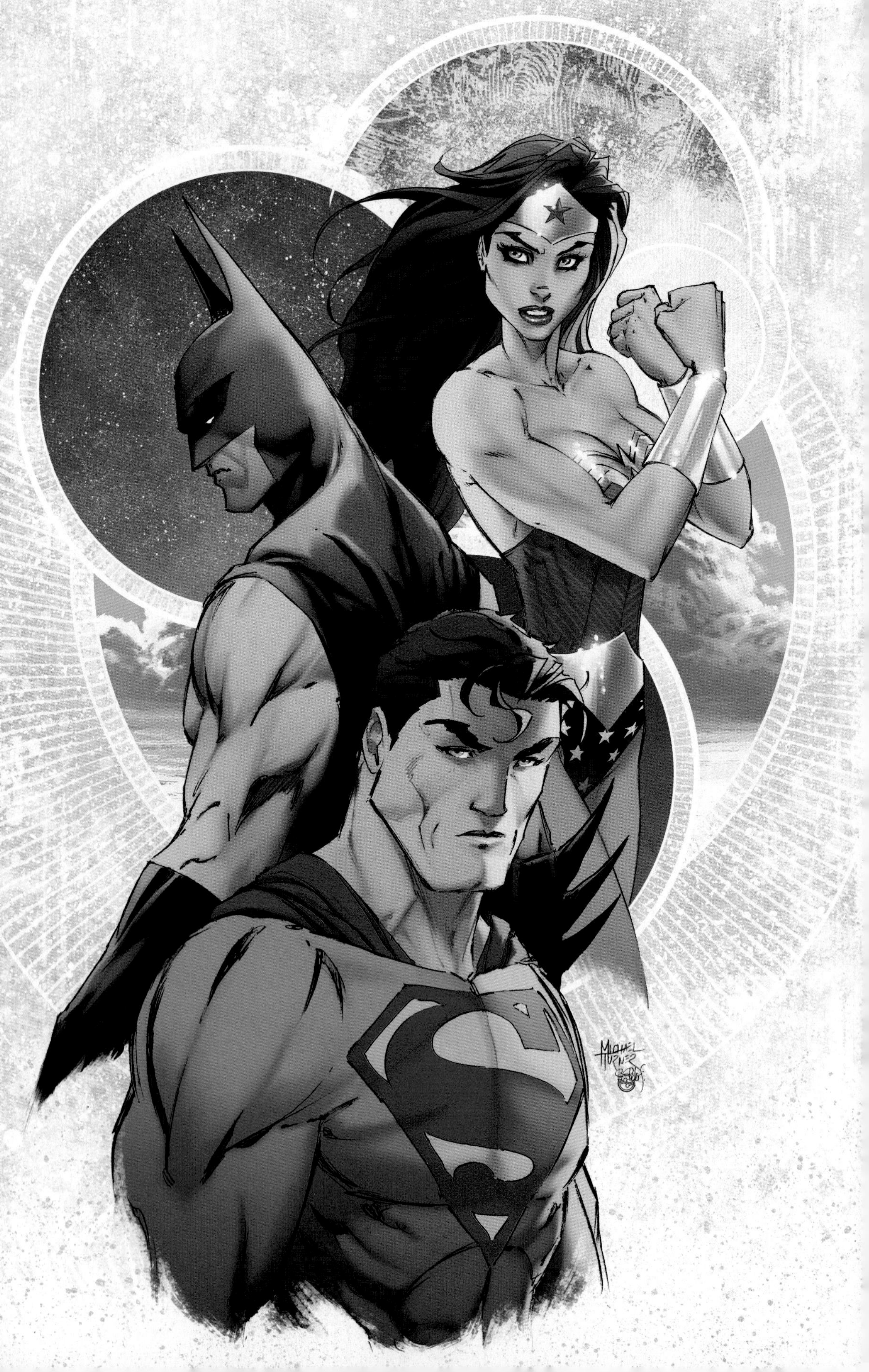

JUSTICE LEAGUE #1 variant by
Yanick Paquette and Nathan Fairbairn

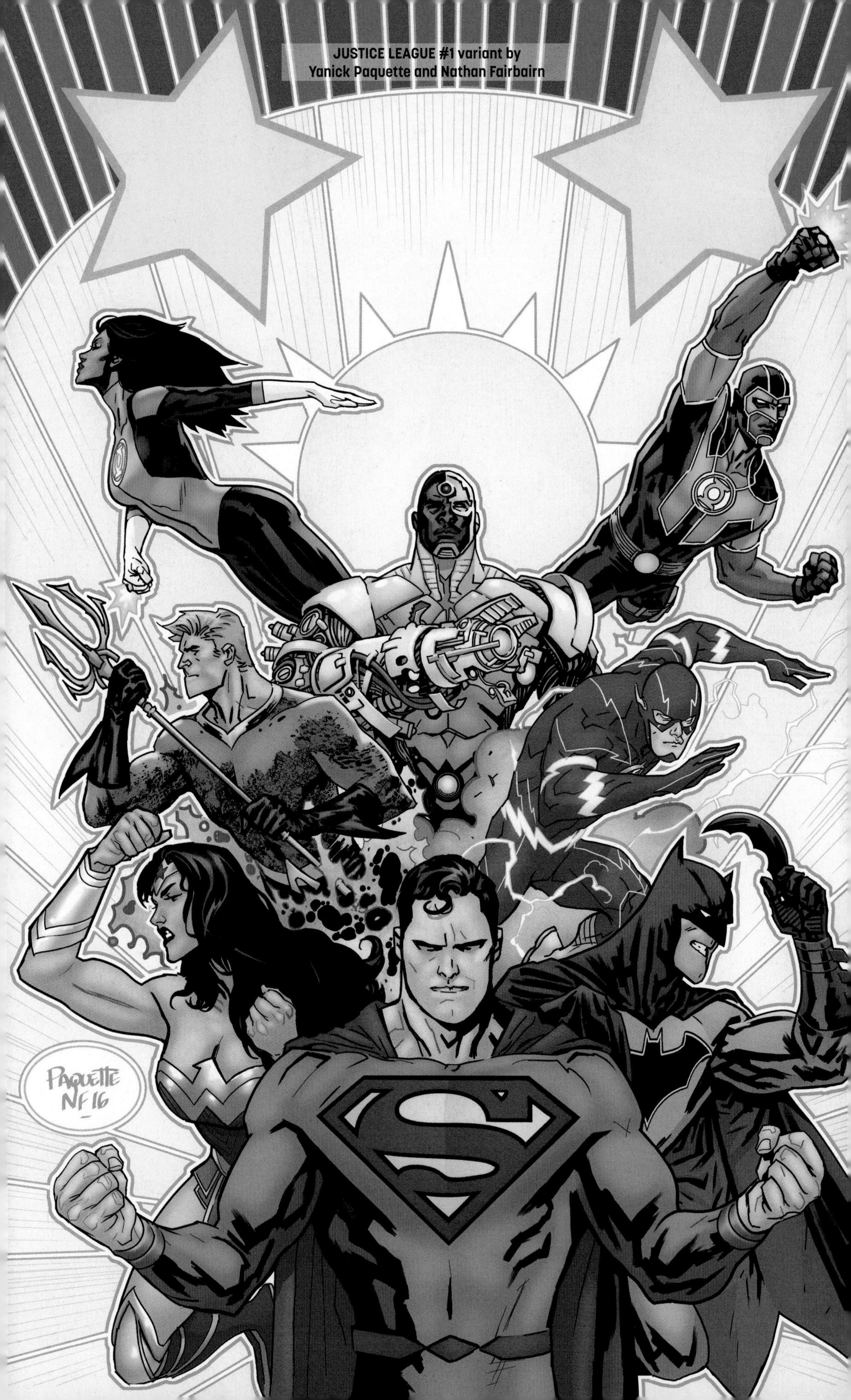
PAQUETTE
NF 16

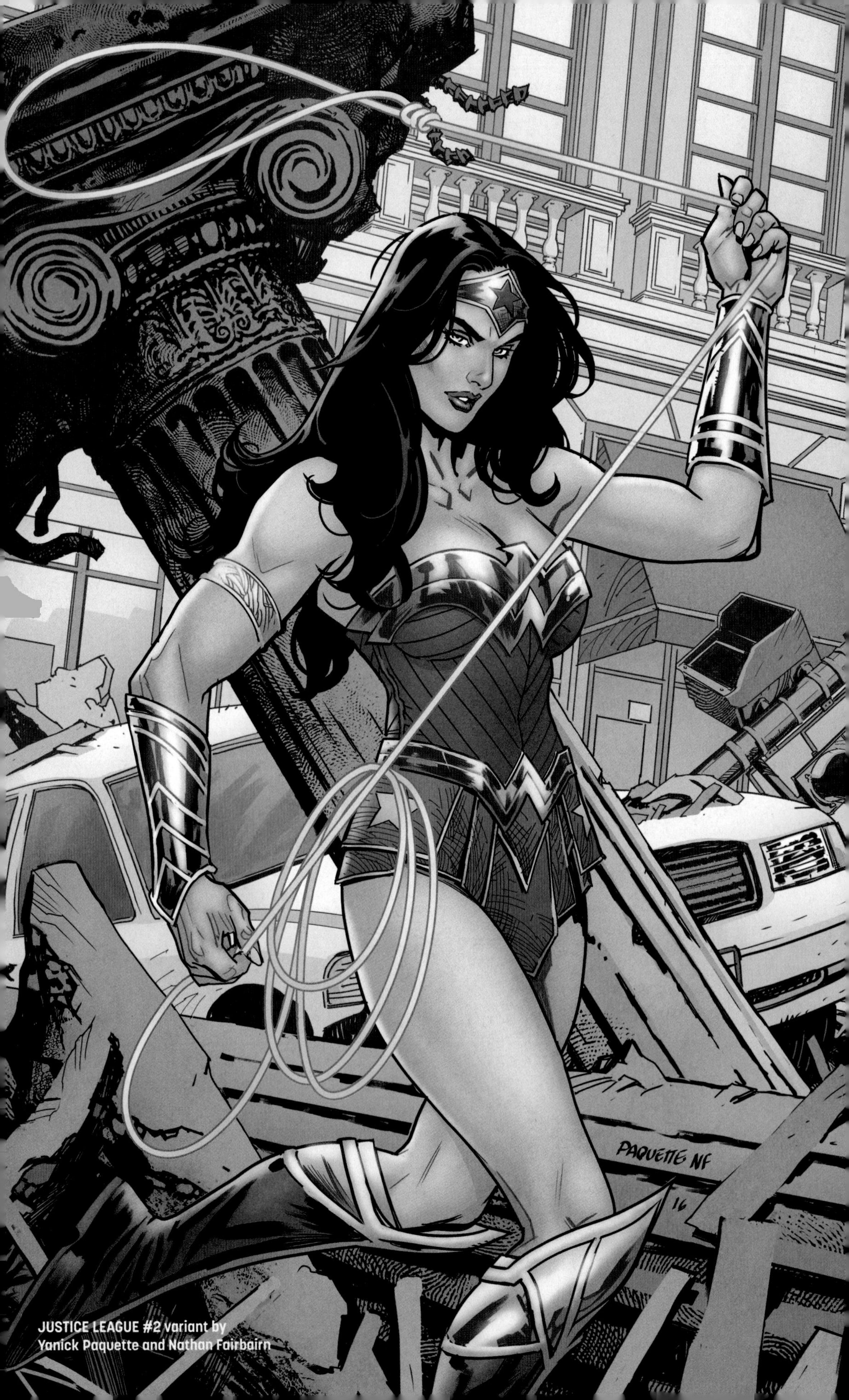
PAQUETTE NF
16

JUSTICE LEAGUE #2 variant by
Yanick Paquette and Nathan Fairbairn

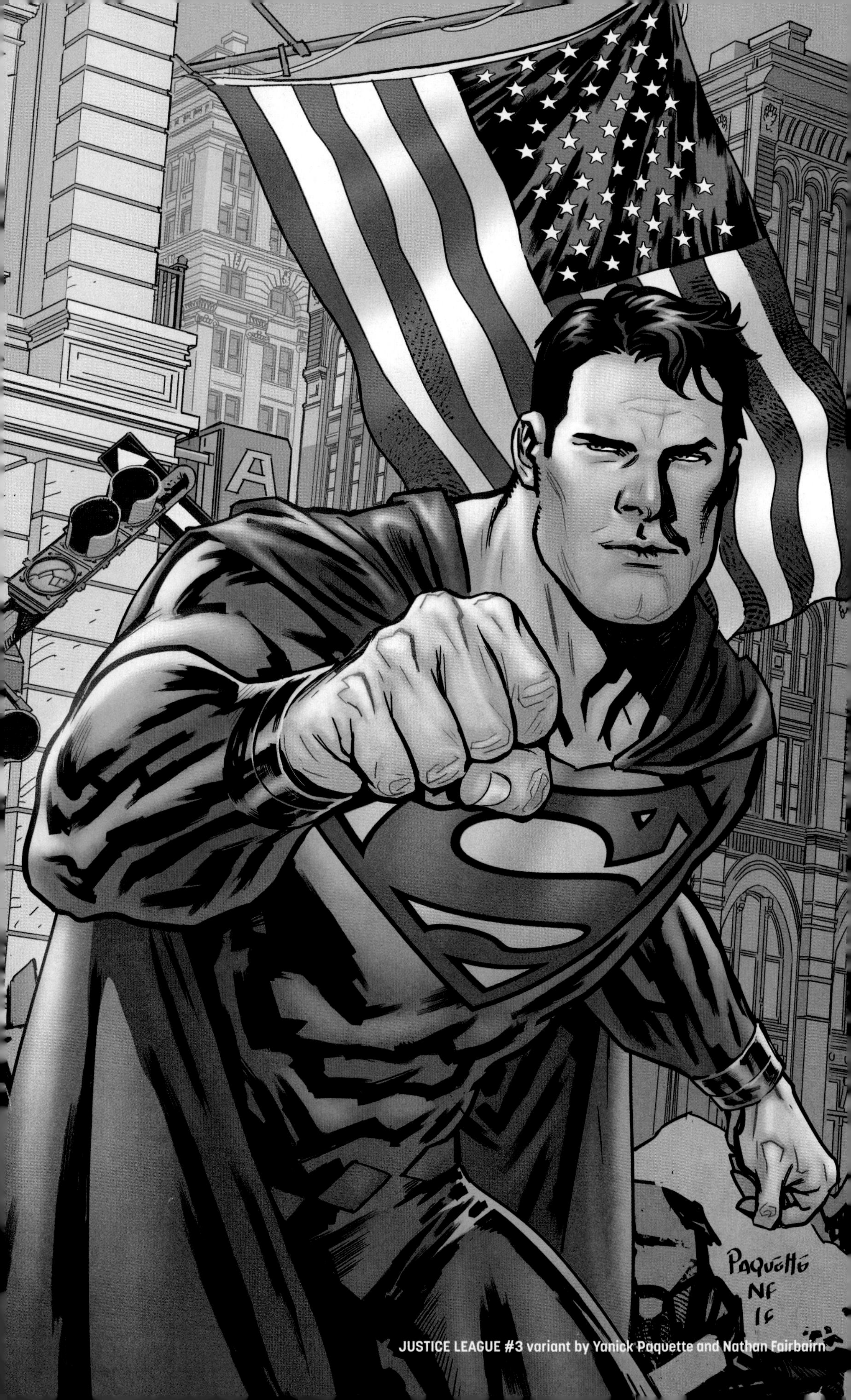
JUSTICE LEAGUE #3 variant by Yanick Paquette and Nathan Fairbairn

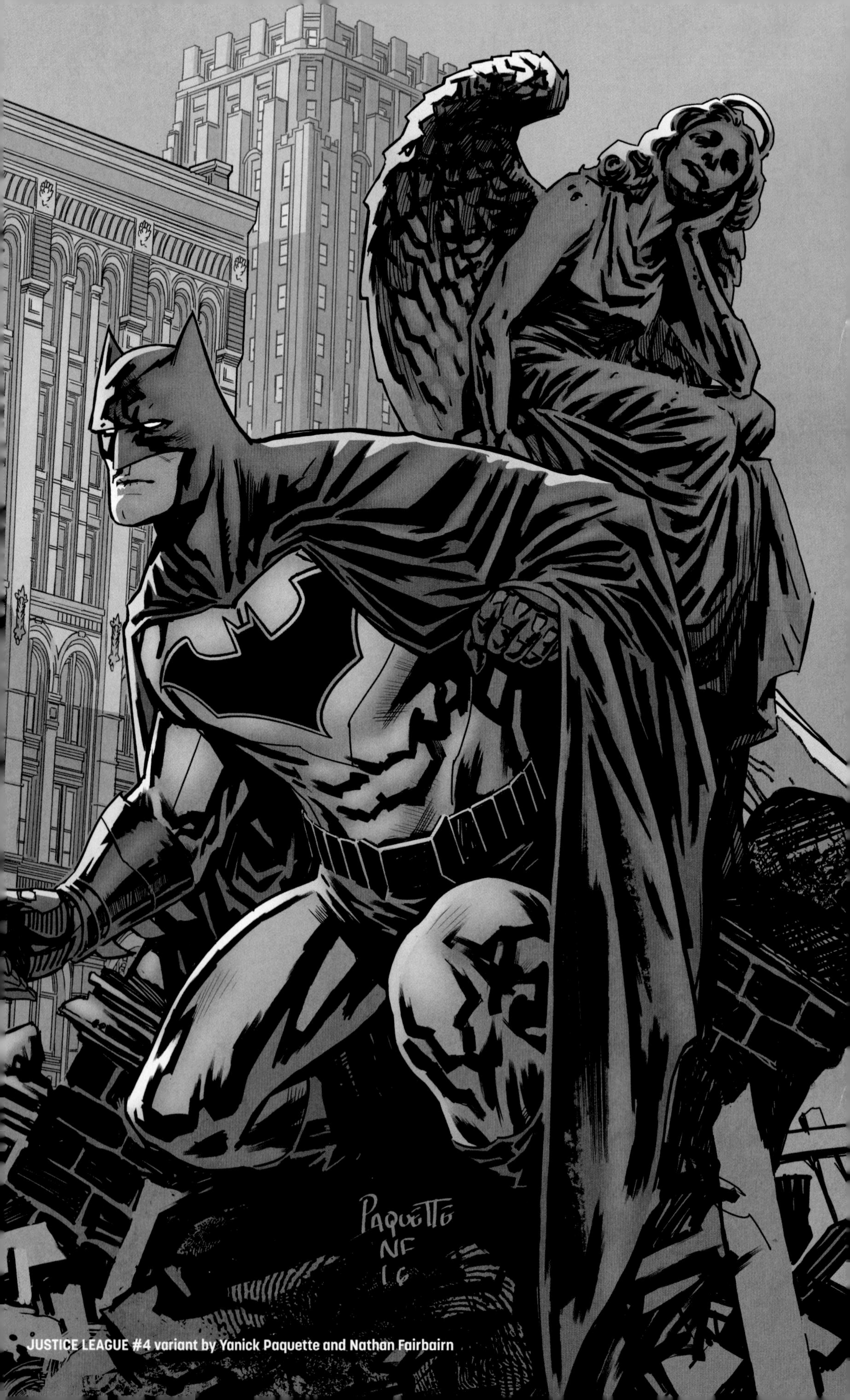
PAQUETTE
NF
16

JUSTICE LEAGUE #4 variant by Yanick Paquette and Nathan Fairbairn

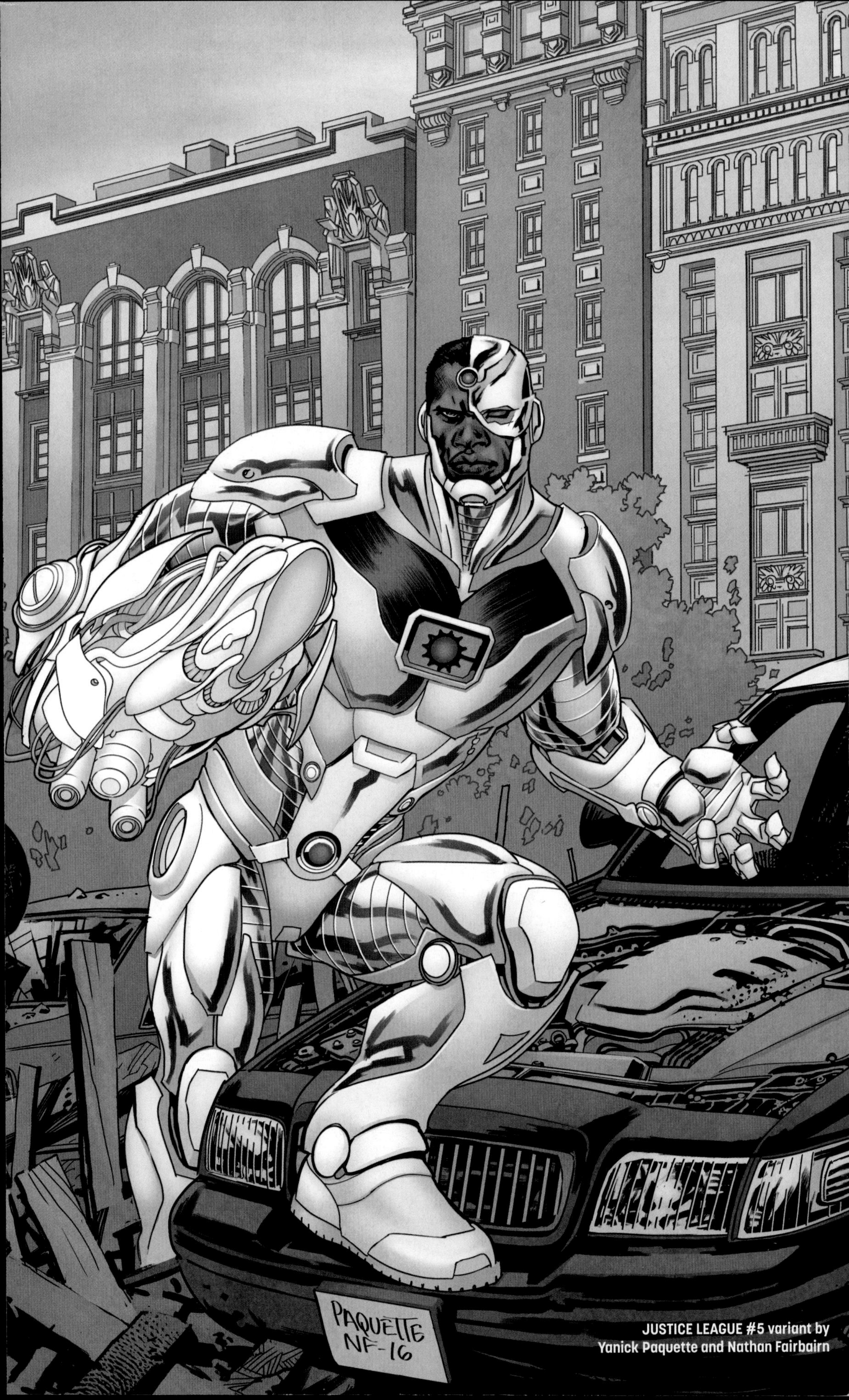
PAQUETTE
NF-16

**JUSTICE LEAGUE #5 variant by**
**Yanick Paquette and Nathan Fairbairn**

AQUAMAN
Design by Brad Walker

**VERSION 1.2**

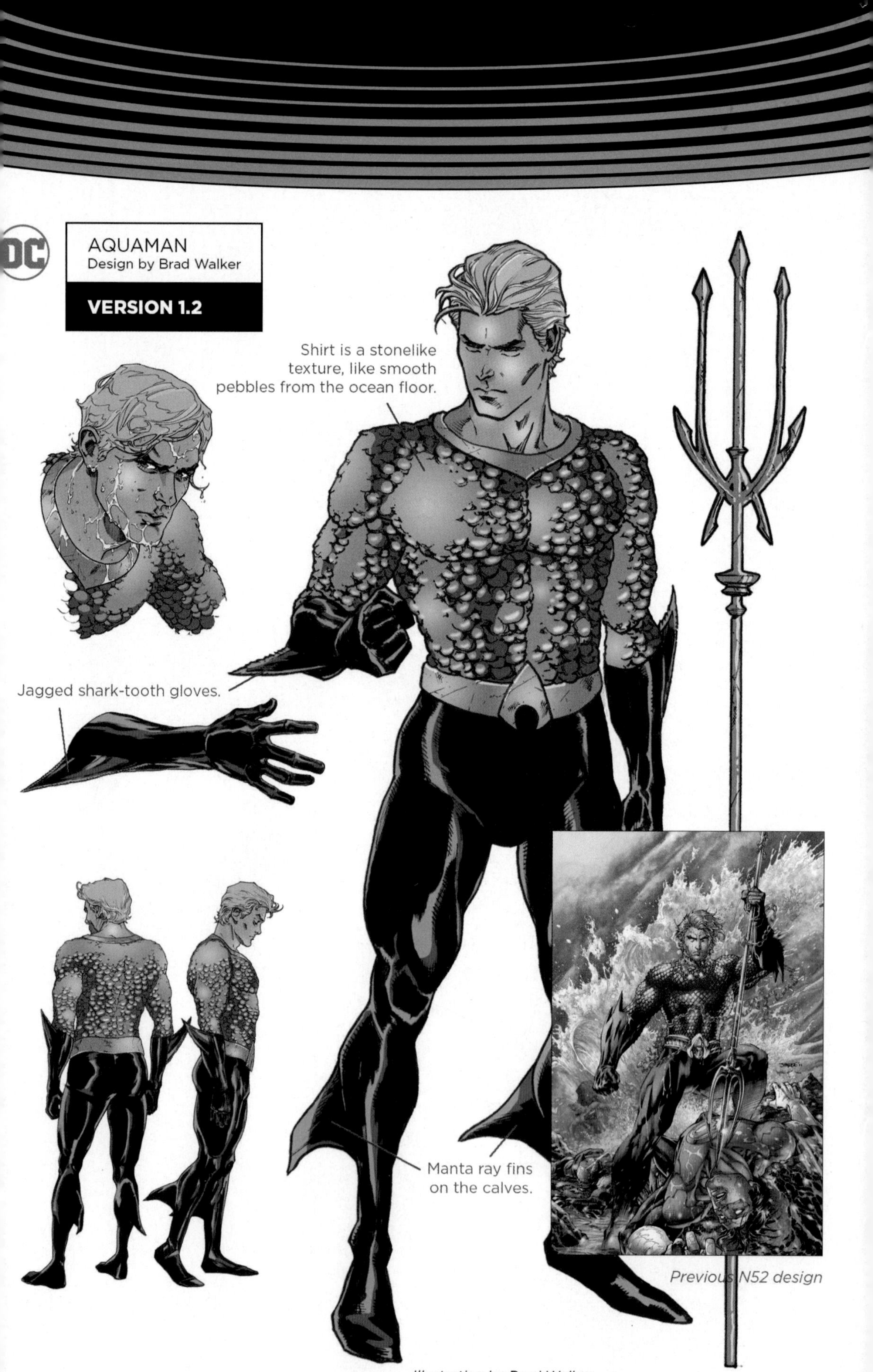
Shirt is a stonelike texture, like smooth pebbles from the ocean floor.
Jagged shark-tooth gloves.
Manta ray fins on the calves.

*Previous N52 design*

*Illustration by Brad Walker*

**BATMAN**
Design by Greg Capullo

**VERSION 1.2**

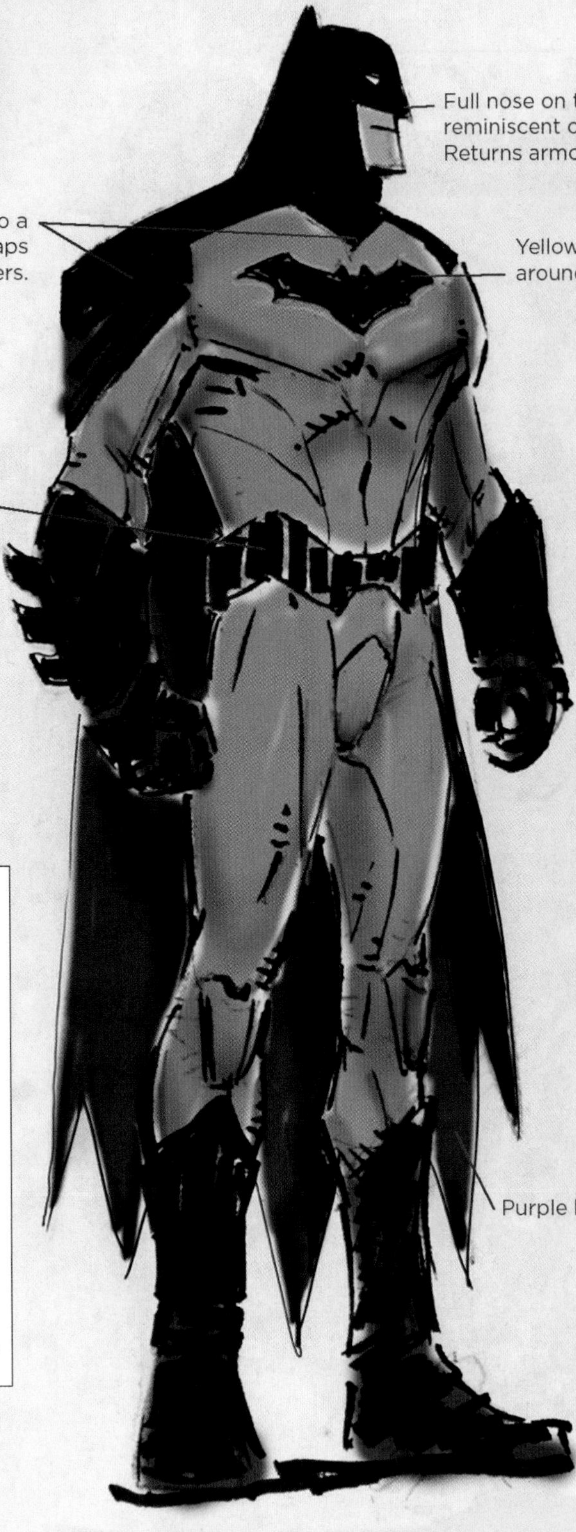

Full nose on the cowl reminiscent of the Dark Knight Returns armor and 1943 serial.
Black cape comes to a black point and wraps around shoulders.
Yellow outline around Bat symbol.
Bat-like belt: fangs on front, wings on obliques. Black with yellow piping.
Purple lining inside cape.


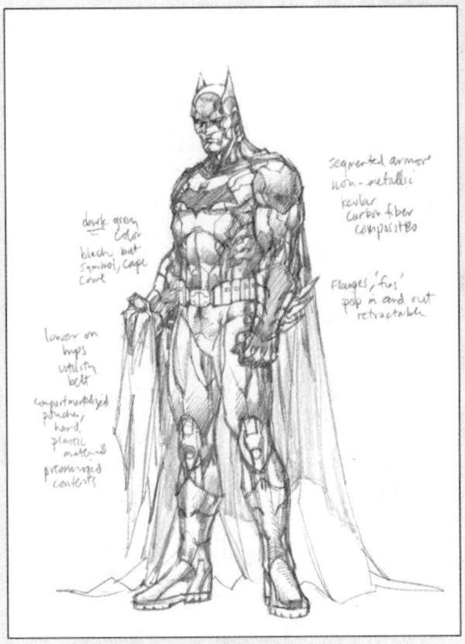

segmented armor
non-metallic
kevlar
carbon fiber
composites
dark grey color
black bat symbol, cape cowl
Flanges, 'fins' pop in and out retractable
lower on hips utility belt
compartmentalized pouches, hard plastic material
preorganized contents


*Previous N52 design*

*Illustration by Greg Capullo*

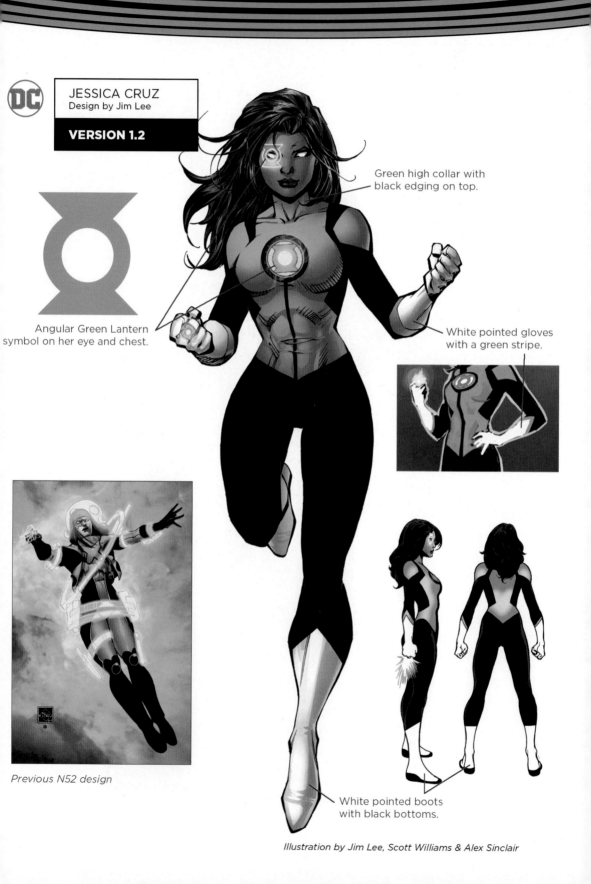

JESSICA CRUZ
Design by Jim Lee

**VERSION 1.2**

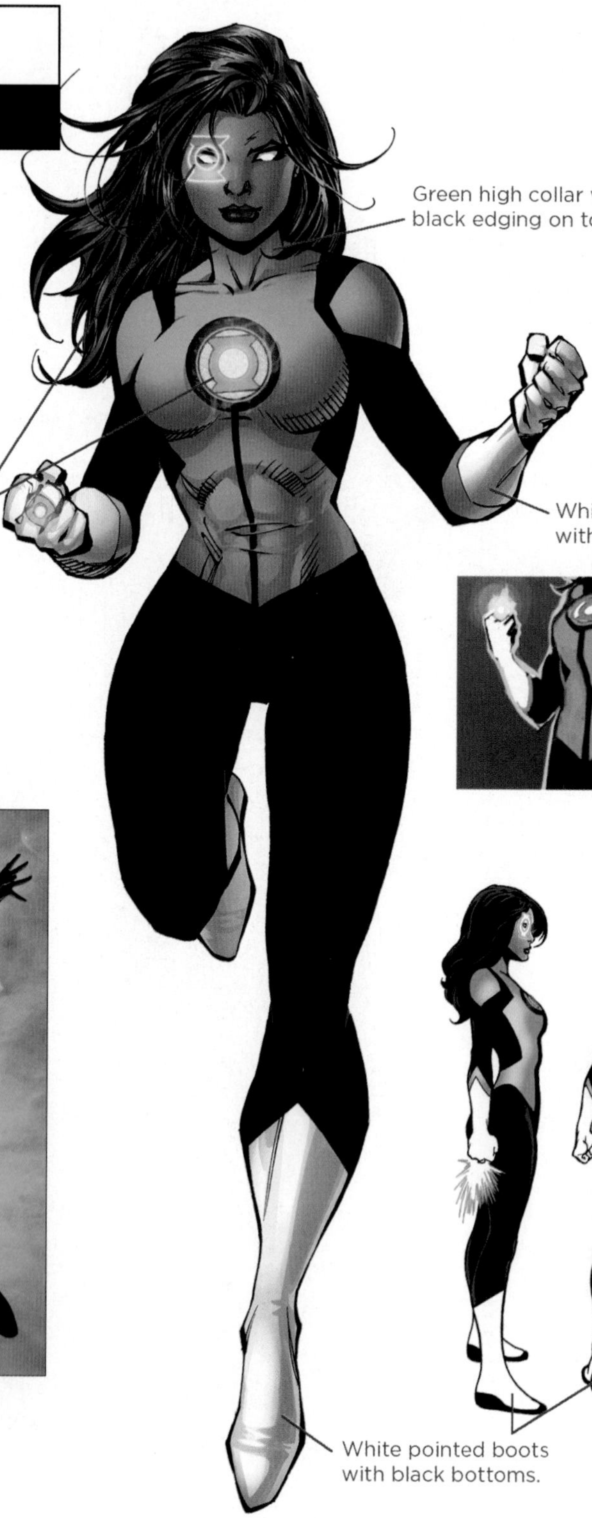

Green high collar with black edging on top.

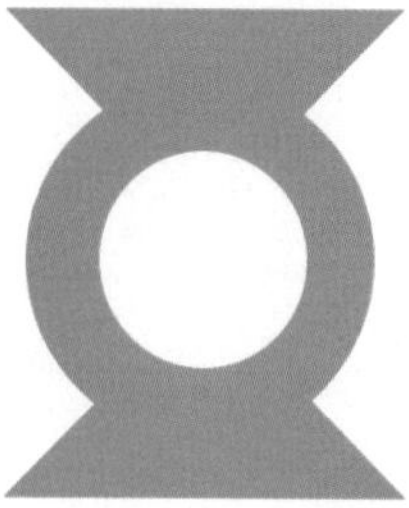

Angular Green Lantern symbol on her eye and chest.

White pointed gloves with a green stripe.

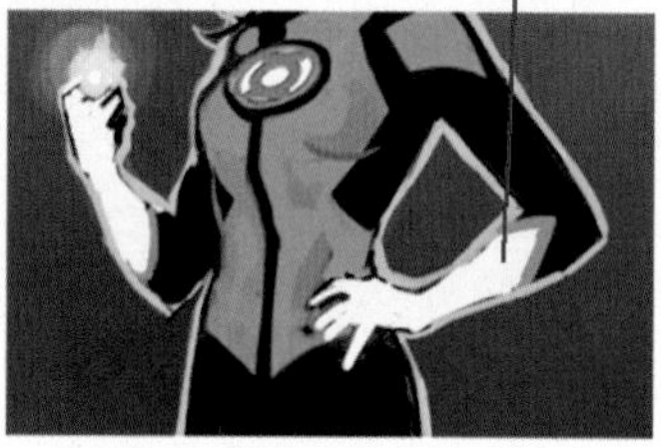

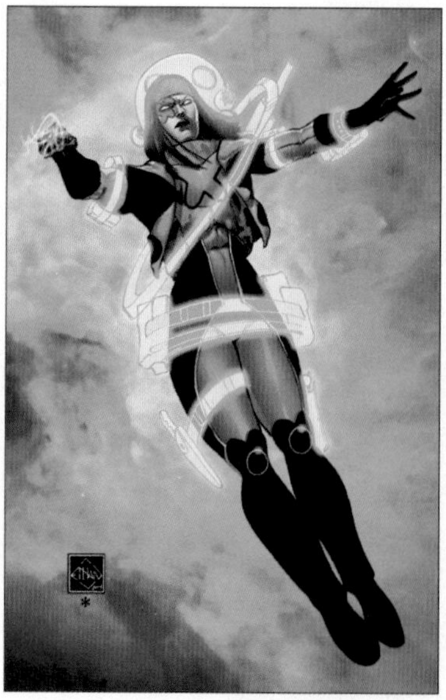

*Previous N52 design*

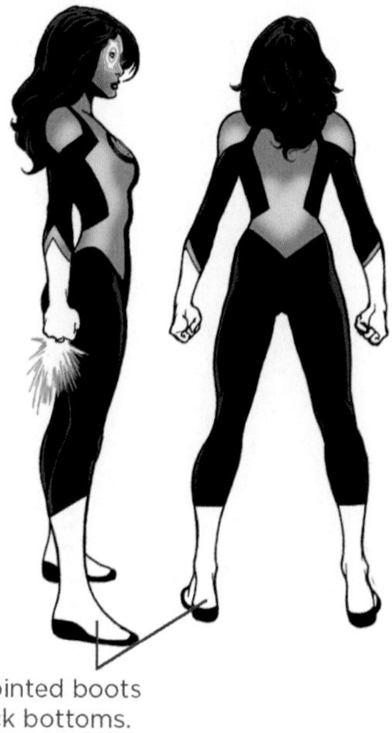

White pointed boots with black bottoms.

*Illustration by Jim Lee, Scott Williams & Alex Sinclair*

**SIMON BAZ**
Design by Doug Mahnke

**VERSION 1.2**

*Illustration by Jim Lee, Scott Williams & Alex Sinclair*

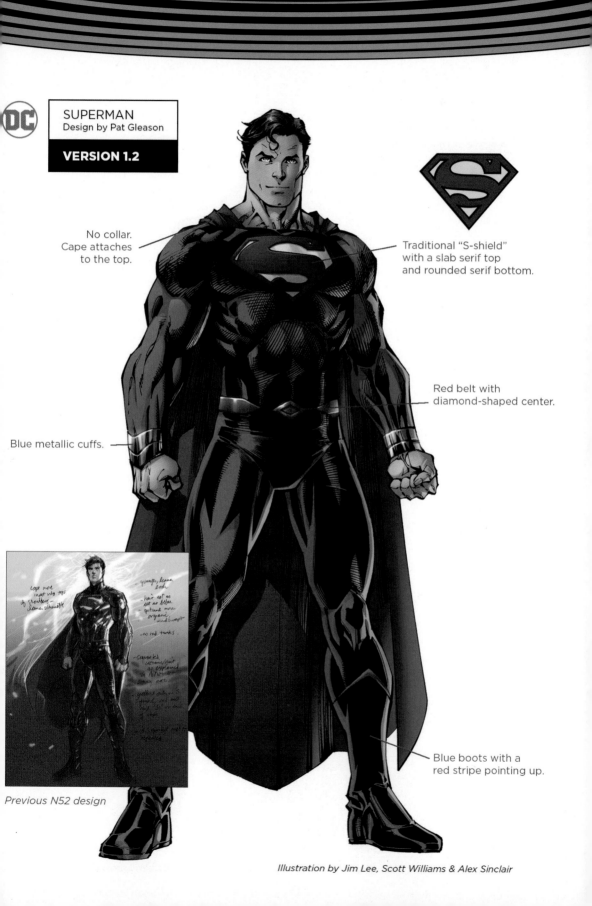

SUPERMAN
Design by Pat Gleason

**VERSION 1.2**

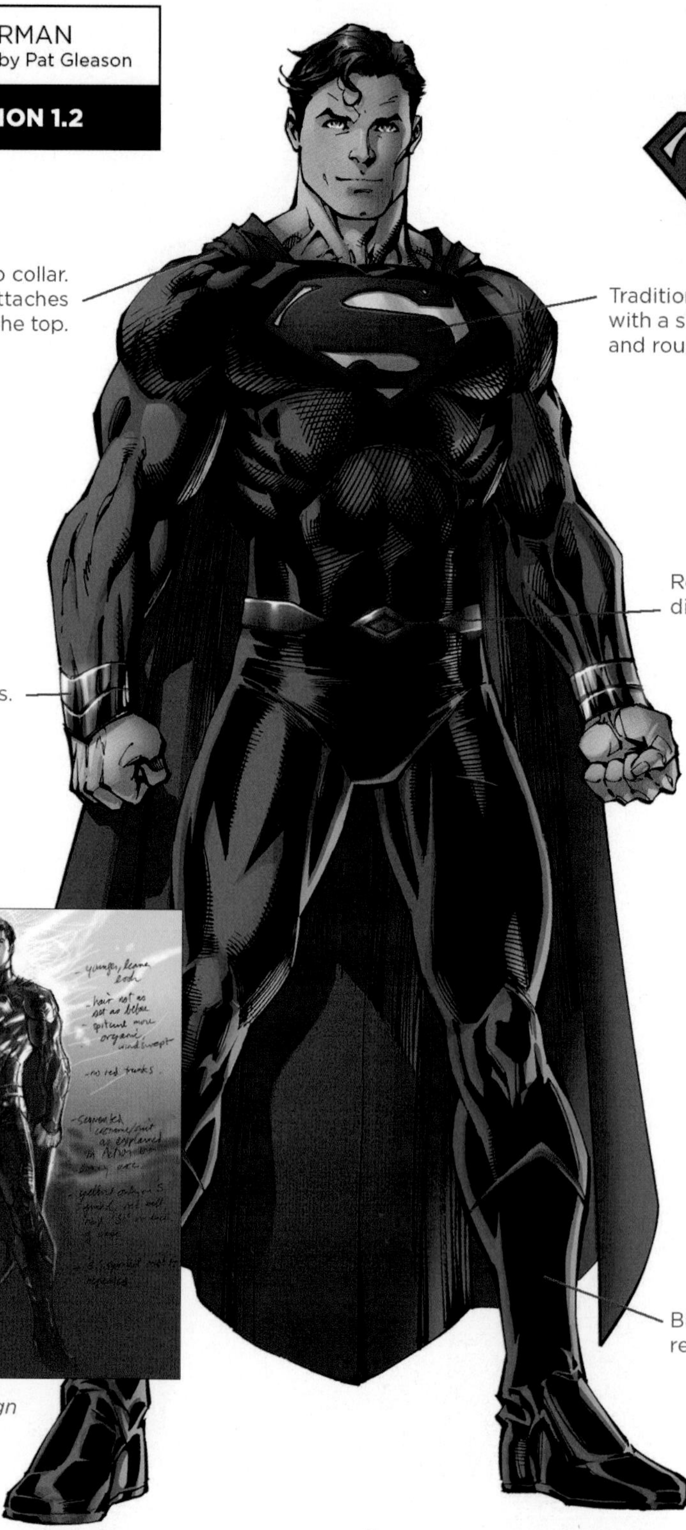

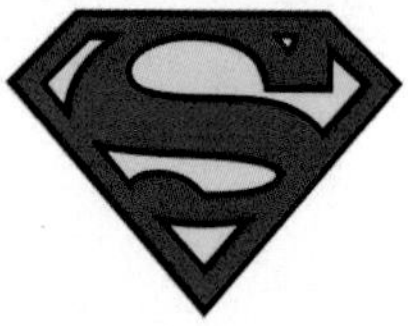

No collar. Cape attaches to the top.

Traditional "S-shield" with a slab serif top and rounded serif bottom.

Red belt with diamond-shaped center.

Blue metallic cuffs.

Blue boots with a red stripe pointing up.

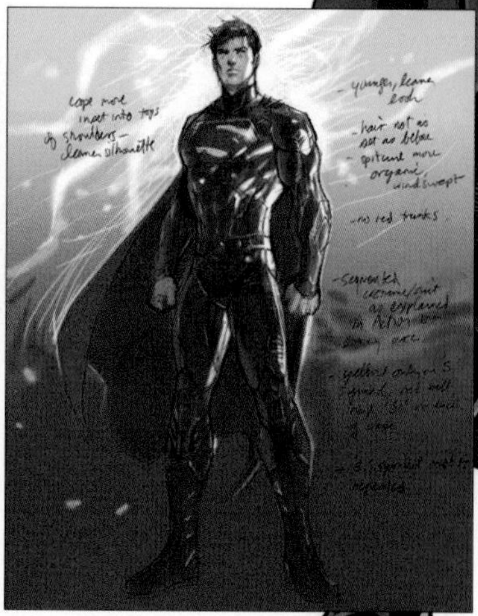

*Previous N52 design*

*Illustration by Jim Lee, Scott Williams & Alex Sinclair*

WONDER WOMAN
Design by Tony Daniel

**VERSION 1.2**

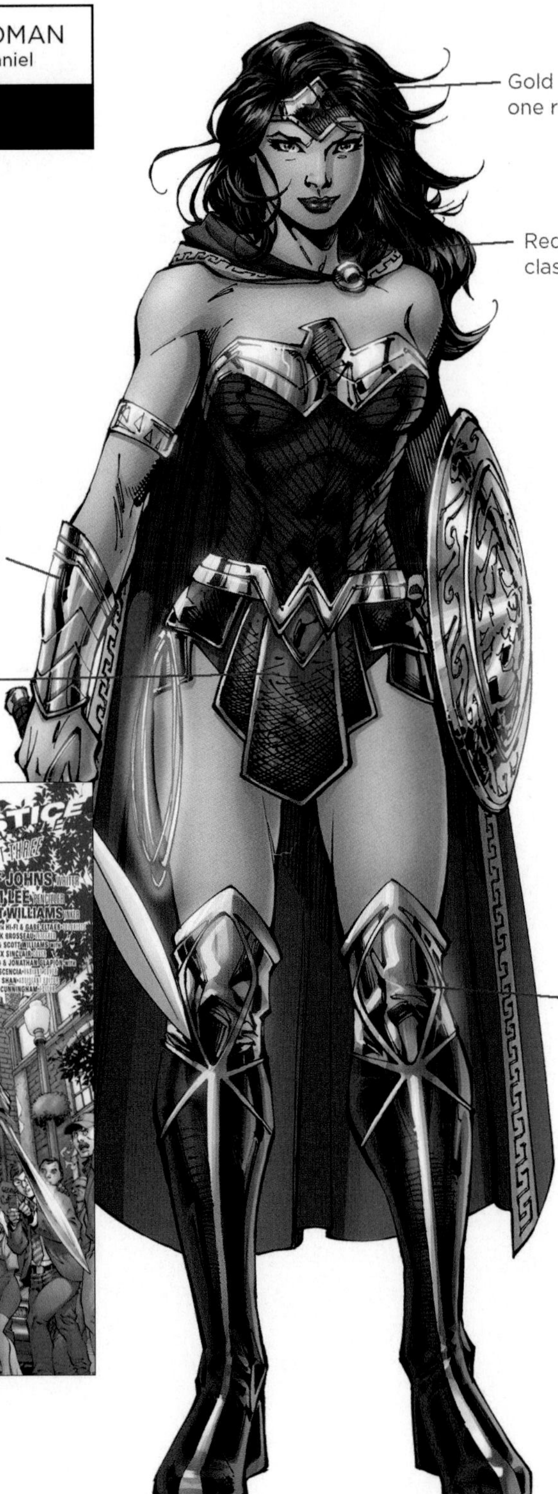

Gold tiara with one red star.
Red cape with gold clasp and edge.
Silver forearm guards with recessed detailing.
Blue leather skirt with gold edges and two stars.
Red knee-high boots with gold knee guard and accents.


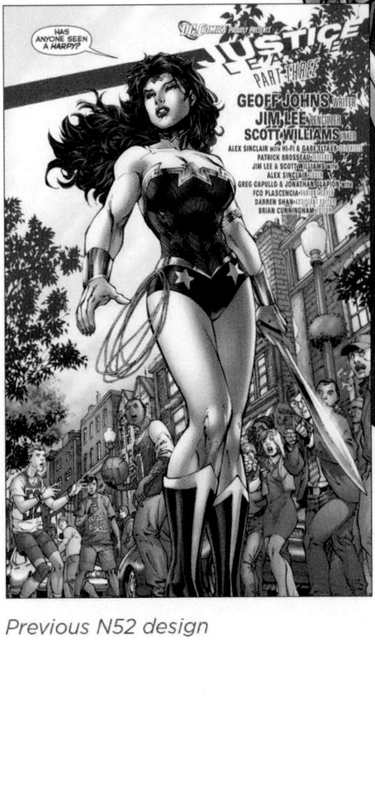

HAS ANYONE SEEN A HARPY?
JUSTICE LEAGUE
PART THREE
GEOFF JOHNS
JIM LEE
SCOTT WILLIAMS


*Previous N52 design*

*Illustration by Jim Lee, Scott Williams & Alex Sinclair*

**Pencil art from JUSTICE LEAGUE #1 by Tony S. Daniel**

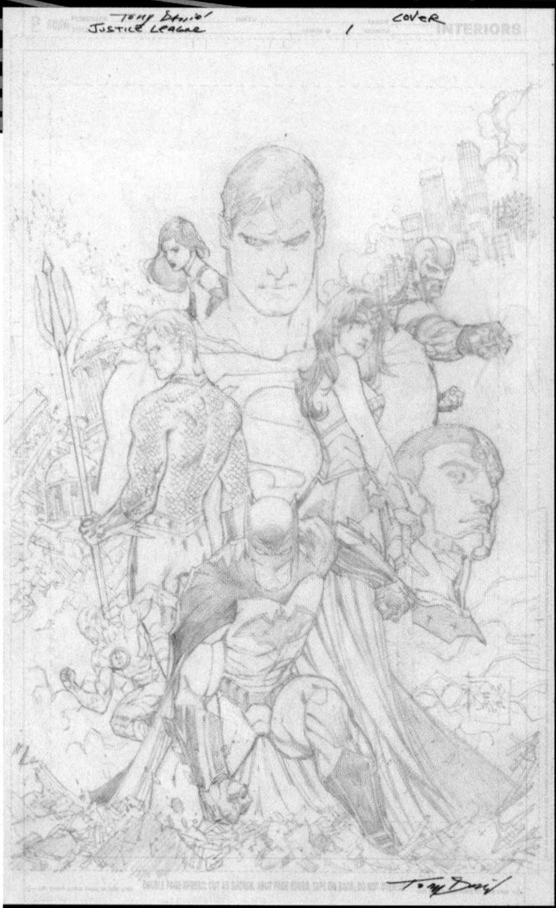
Tony Daniel
JUSTICE LEAGUE
1
COVER
INTERIORS

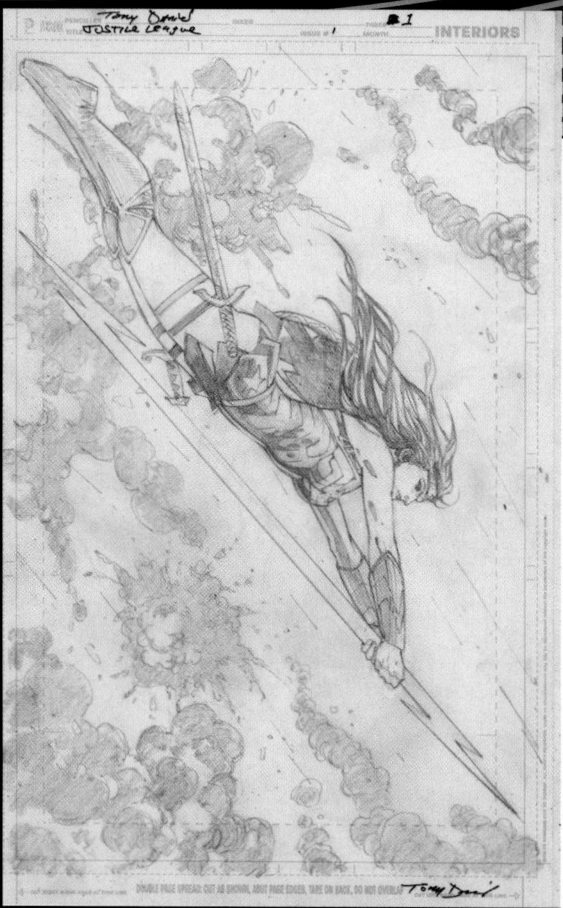
Tony Daniel
JUSTICE LEAGUE
INTERIORS

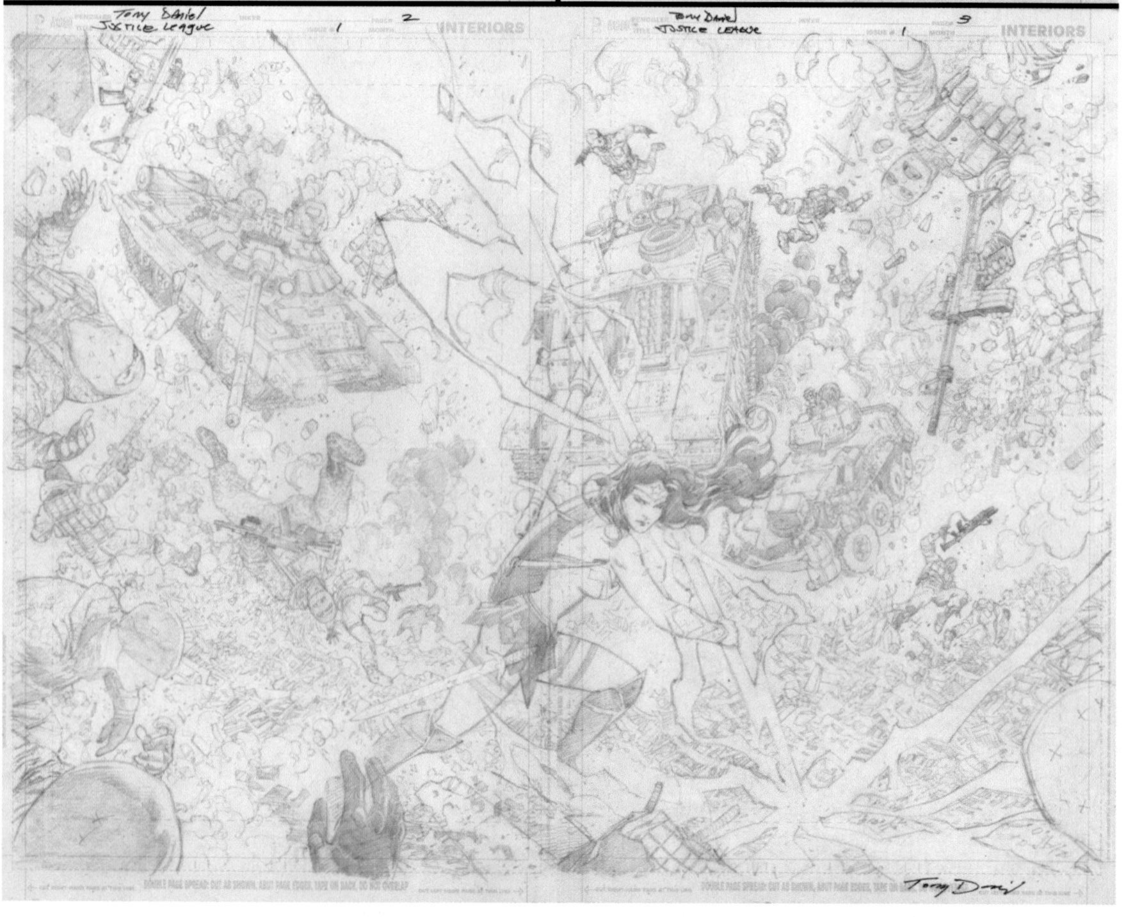
Tony Daniel
JUSTICE LEAGUE
1
2
INTERIORS
Tony Daniel
JUSTICE LEAGUE
1
3
INTERIORS

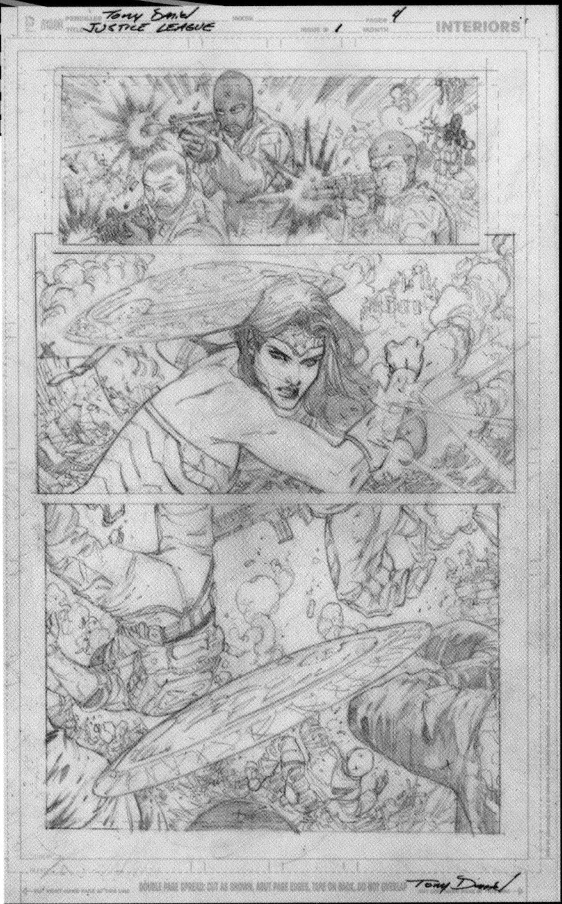
Tony Daniel
JUSTICE LEAGUE
1
4
INTERIORS
DOUBLE PAGE SPREAD: CUT AS SHOWN, ABUT PAGE EDGES, TAPE ON BACK, DO NOT OVERLAP
Tony Daniel

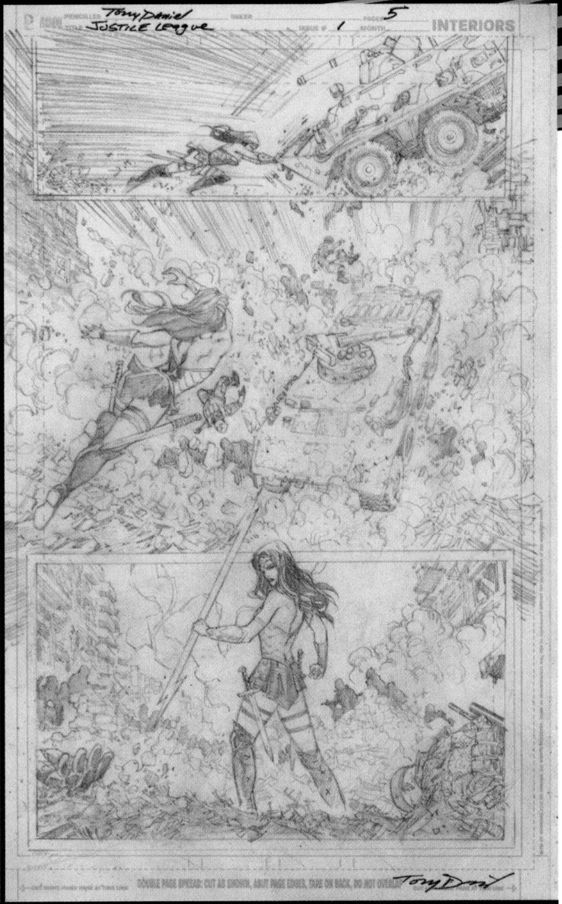
Tony Daniel
JUSTICE LEAGUE
1
5
INTERIORS
DOUBLE PAGE SPREAD: CUT AS SHOWN, ABUT PAGE EDGES, TAPE ON BACK, DO NOT OVERLAP
Tony Daniel

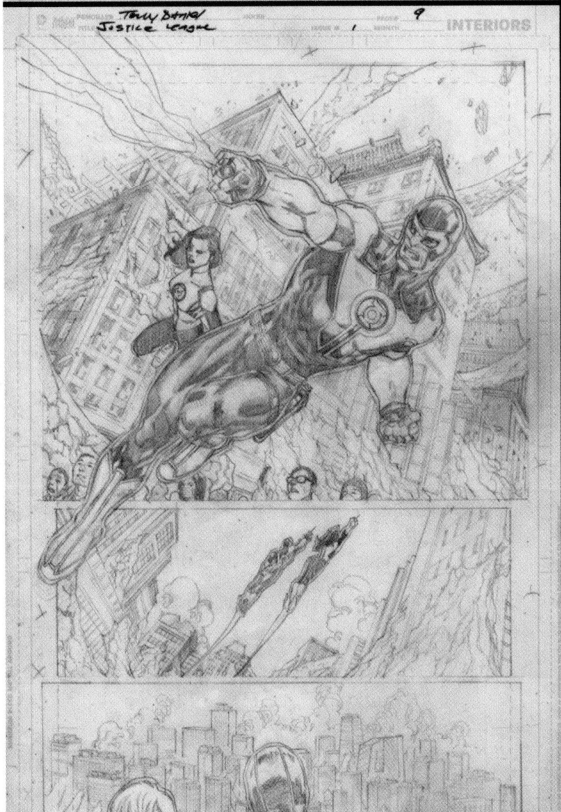
Tony Daniel
JUSTICE LEAGUE
1
9
INTERIORS
DOUBLE PAGE SPREAD: CUT AS SHOWN, ABUT PAGE EDGES, TAPE ON BACK, DO NOT OVERLAP
Tony Daniel

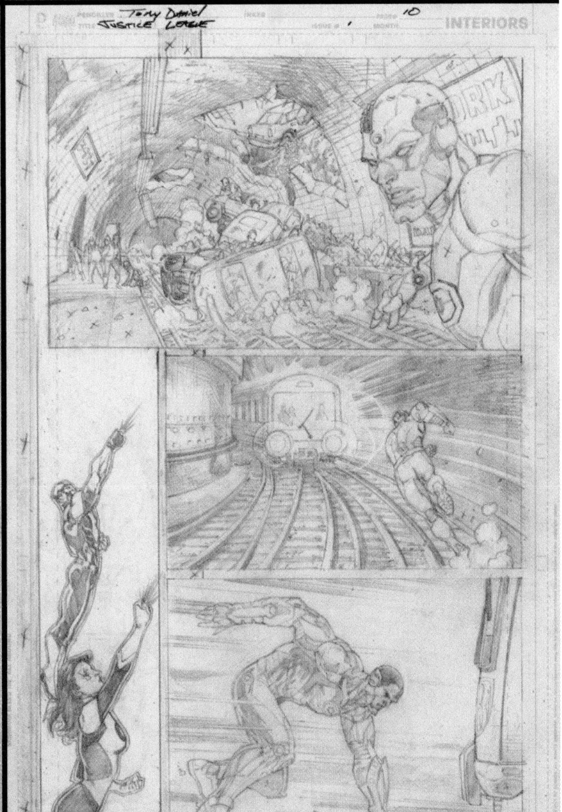
Tony Daniel
JUSTICE LEAGUE
1
10
INTERIORS
DOUBLE PAGE SPREAD: CUT AS SHOWN, ABUT PAGE EDGES, TAPE ON BACK, DO NOT OVERLAP
Tony Daniel

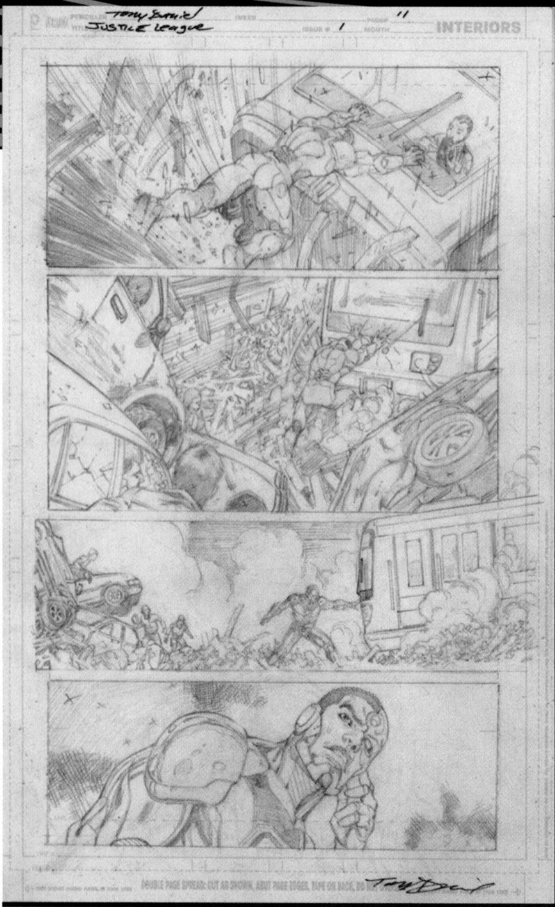
Tony Daniel
JUSTICE LEAGUE
1
11
INTERIORS
Tony Daniel

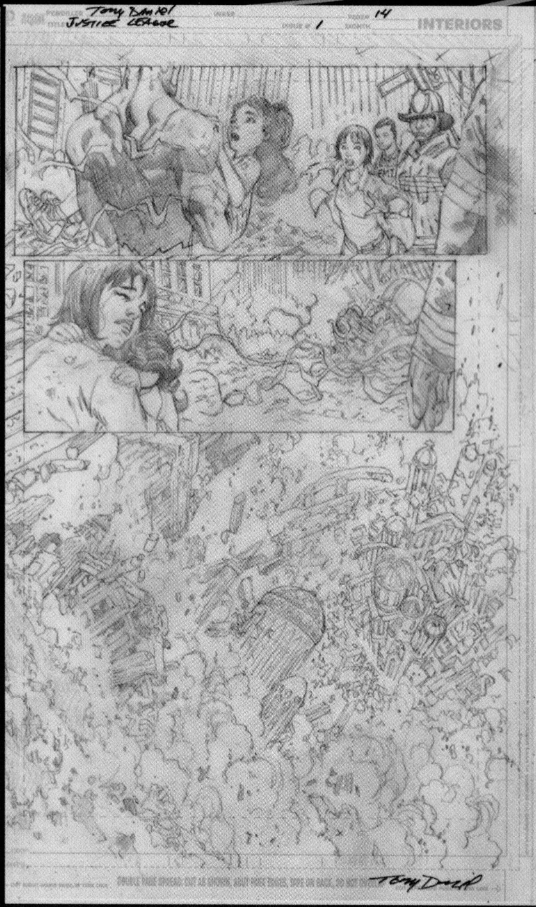
Tony Daniel
JUSTICE LEAGUE
1
14
INTERIORS
Tony Daniel

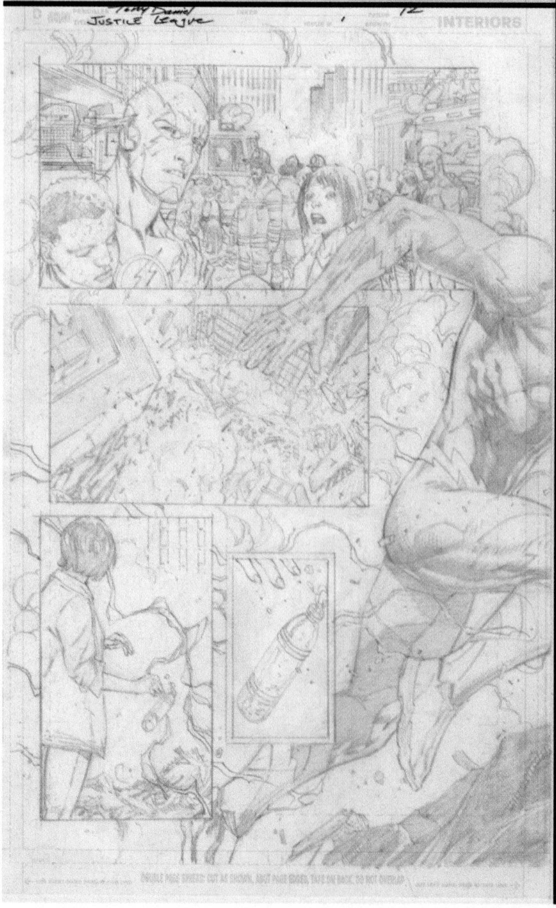
Tony Daniel
JUSTICE LEAGUE
1
12
INTERIORS

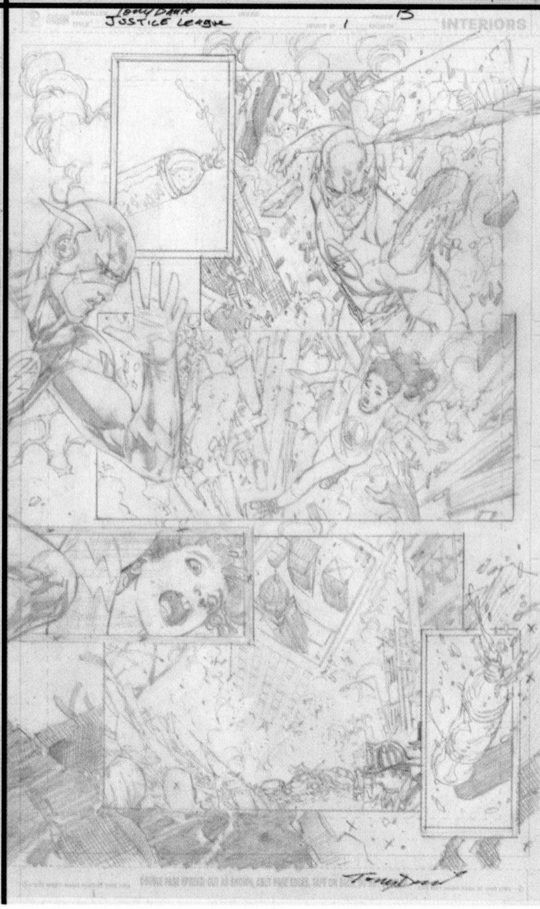
Tony Daniel
JUSTICE LEAGUE
1
13
INTERIORS
Tony Daniel

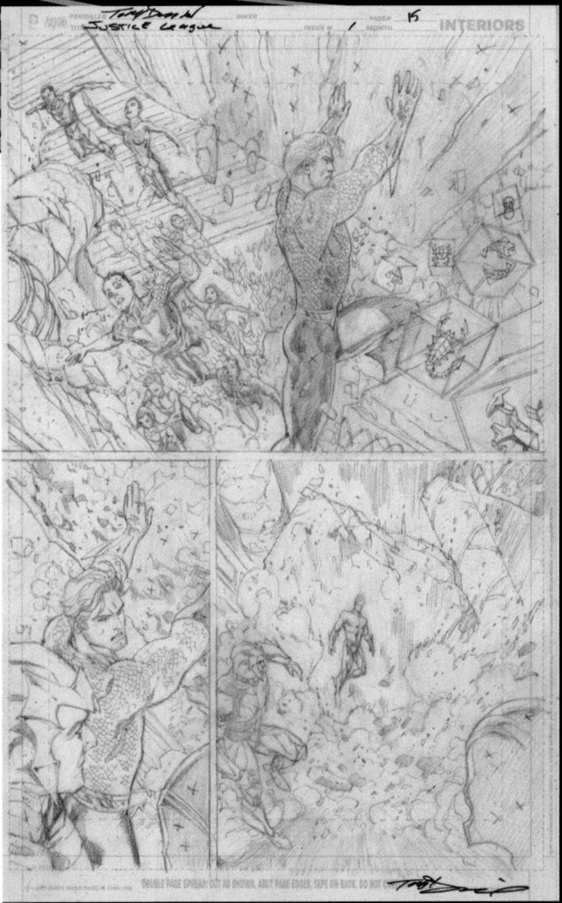
Tony Daniel
JUSTICE LEAGUE
1
15
INTERIORS

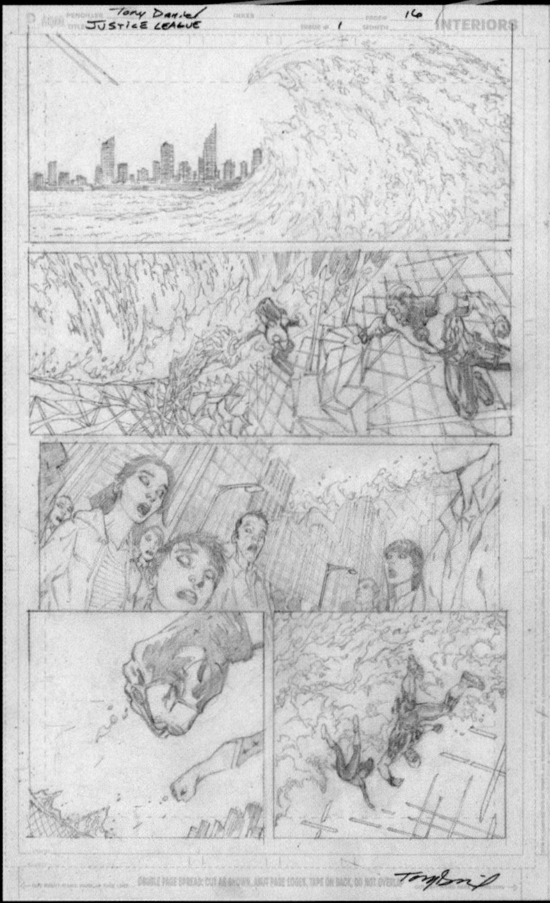
Tony Daniel
JUSTICE LEAGUE
1
16
INTERIORS

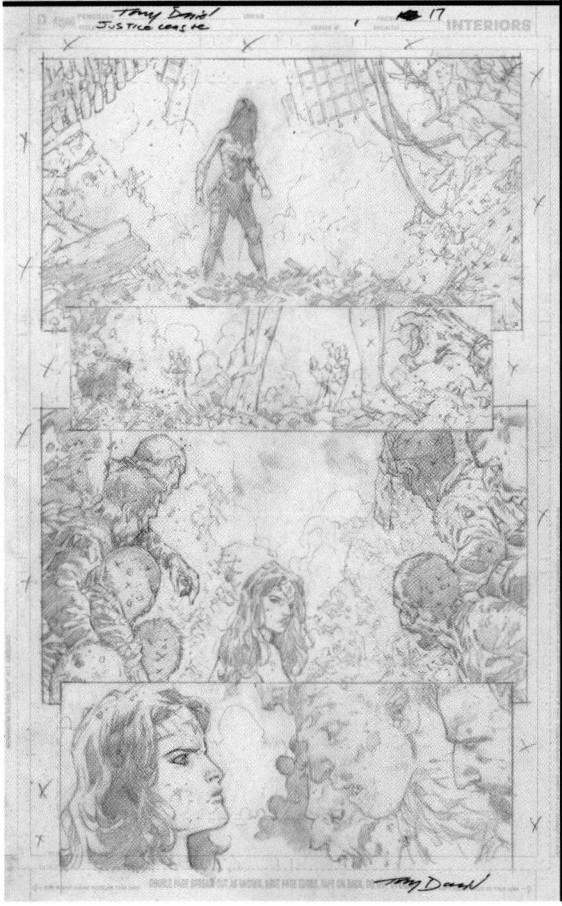
Tony Daniel
JUSTICE LEAGUE
1
17
INTERIORS

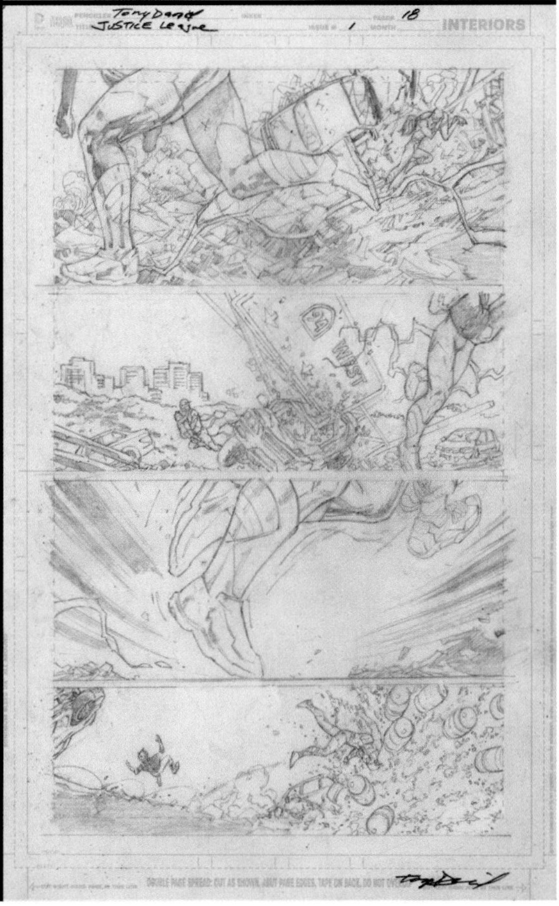
Tony Daniel
JUSTICE LEAGUE
1
18
INTERIORS

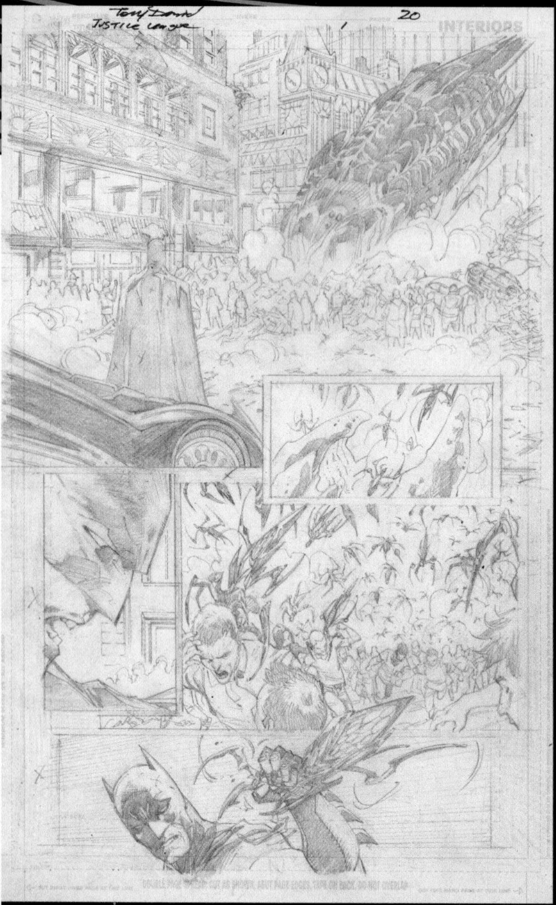
Tony Daniel
Justice League
1
20
INTERIORS

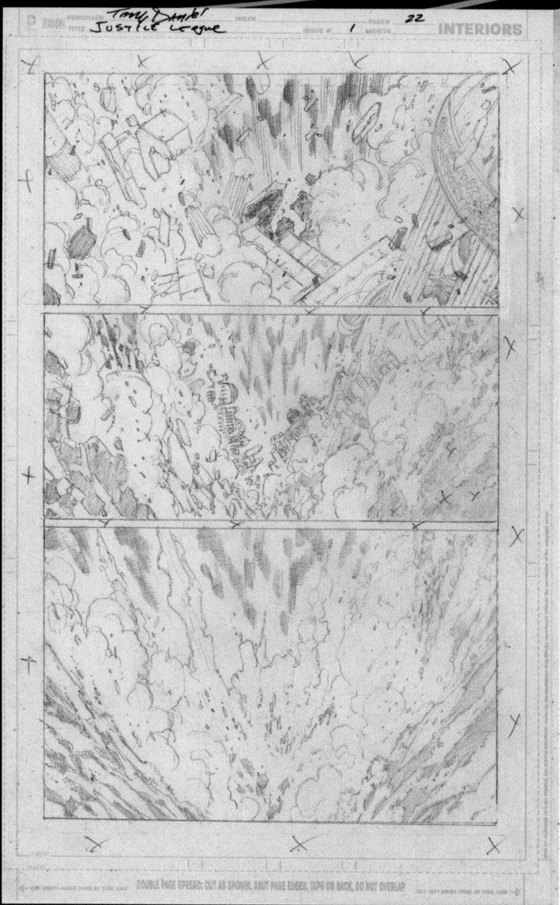
Tony Daniel
Justice League
1
22
INTERIORS
DOUBLE PAGE SPREAD: CUT AS SHOWN, ABUT PAGE EDGES, TAPE ON BACK, DO NOT OVERLAP

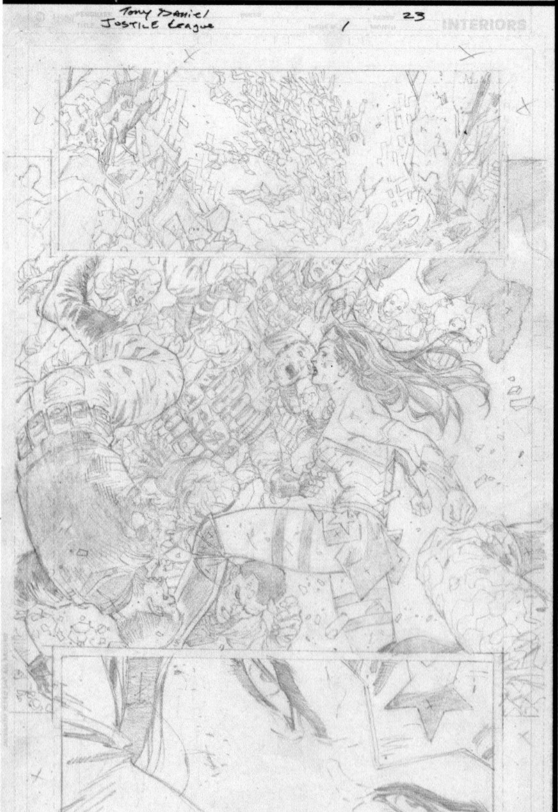
Tony Daniel
Justice League
1
23
INTERIORS

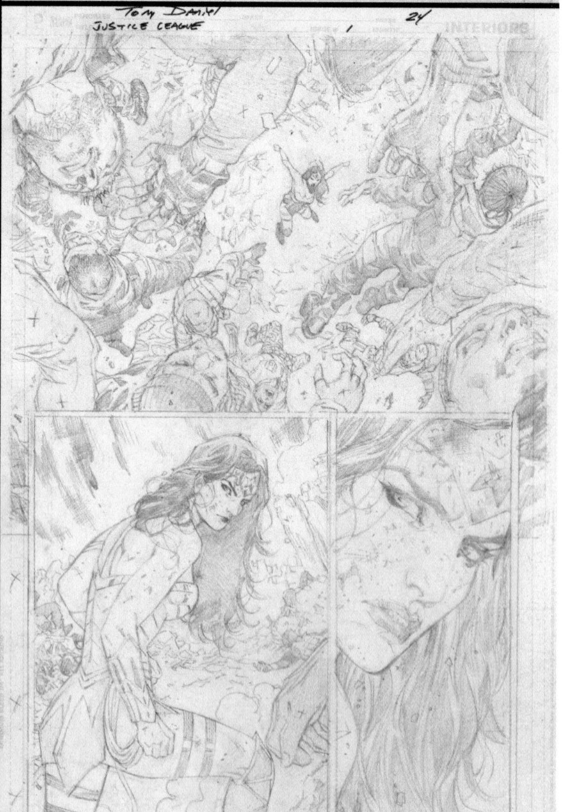
Tony Daniel
Justice League
1
24
INTERIORS